Grid Computing

IBM Press Series—Information Management

On Demand Computing Books

On Demand Computing
Fellenstein

Grid Computing
Joseph and Fellenstein

Autonomic Computing
Murch

Business Intelligence for the Enterprise
Biere

DB2 Books

DB2 Universal Database v8.1 Certification Exam 700 Study Guide
Sanders

DB2 Universal Database v8.1 Certification Exams 701 and 706 Study Guide
Sanders

DB2 for Solaris: The Official Guide
Bauch and Wilding

DB2 Universal Database v8 for Linux, UNIX, and Windows Database Administration Certification Guide, Fifth Edition
Baklarz and Wong

Advanced DBA Certification Guide and Reference for DB2 Universal Database v8 for Linux, UNIX, and Windows
Snow and Phan

DB2 Universal Database v8 Application Development Certification Guide, Second Edition
Martineau, Sanyal, Gashyna, and Kyprianou

DB2 Version 8: The Official Guide
Zikopoulos, Baklarz, deRoos, and Melnyk

Teach Yourself DB2 Universal Database in 21 Days
Visser and Wong

DB2 UDB for OS/390 v7.1 Application Certification Guide
Lawson

DB2 SQL Procedural Language for Linux, UNIX, and Windows
Yip, Bradstock, Curtis, Gao, Janmohamed, Liu, and McArthur

DB2 Universal Database v8 Handbook for Windows, UNIX, and Linux
Gunning

Integrated Solutions with DB2
Cutlip and Medicke

DB2 Universal Database for OS/390 Version 7.1 Certification Guide
Lawson and Yevich

DB2 Universal Database v7.1 for UNIX, Linux, Windows and OS/2—Database Administration Certification Guide, Fourth Edition
Baklarz and Wong

DB2 Universal Database v7.1 Application Development Certification Guide
Sanyal, Martineau, Gashyna, and Kyprianou

DB2 UDB for OS/390: An Introduction to DB2 OS/390
Sloan and Hernandez

More Books from IBM Press

Enterprise Java Programming with IBM WebSphere, Second Edition
Brown, Craig, Hester, Stinehour, Pitt, Weitzel, Amsden, Jakab, and Berg

Grid Computing

On Demand Series

Joshy Joseph
Craig Fellenstein

PRENTICE HALL
Professional Technical Reference
Upper Saddle River, New Jersey 07458
www.phptr.com

Editorial/production supervision: *MetroVoice Publishing Services*
Cover design director: *Jerry Votta*
Cover design: *IBM Corporation*
Manufacturing manager: *Alexis Heydt-Long*
Publisher: *Jeffrey Pepper*
Editorial assistant: *Linda Ramagnano*
Marketing manager: *Robin O'Brien*
IBM Consulting Editor: *Susan Visser*

Published by Pearson Education, Inc.
Publishing as Prentice Hall Professional Technical Reference
Upper Saddle River, NJ 07458

Prentice Hall PTR offers excellent discounts on this book when ordered in quantity for bulk purchases or special sales. For more information, please contact: U.S. Corporate and Government Sales, 1-800-382-3419, corpsales@pearsontechgroup.com. For sales outside of the U.S., please contact: International Sales, 1-317-581-3793, international@pearsontechgroup.com.

Printed in the United States of America

First Printing

ISBN   0-13-145660-1

Pearson Education LTD.
Pearson Education Australia PTY, Limited
Pearson Education Singapore, Pte. Ltd.
Pearson Education North Asia Ltd.
Pearson Education Canada, Ltd.
Pearson Educación de Mexico, S.A. de C.V.
Pearson Education — Japan
Pearson Education Malaysia, Pte. Ltd.

Contents

Part 2   Grid Computing Worldwide Initiatives   25

CHAPTER 2   Grid Computing Organizations and
            Their Roles   27

CHAPTER 3   The Grid Computing Anatomy   47

Part 4   The Grid Computing Technological Viewpoints 115

CHAPTER 6   Open Grid Services Architecture (OGSA)   117

CHAPTER 7   Some Sample Use Cases that Drive
       the OGSA   121

Part 5   **The Grid Computing Toolkits**   **215**

CHAPTER 12   **GLOBUS GT3 Toolkit:**
             Programming Model   **229**

Preface

T he Grid Computing discipline involves the actual networking services and connections of a potentially unlimited number of ubiquitous computing devices within a "grid." This new innovative approach to computing can be most simply thought of as a massively large power "utility" grid, such as the one that provides power to our homes and businesses every day. This delivery of utility-based power has become second nature to many of us, worldwide. We know that by simply walking into a room and turning on the lights, the power will be directed to the proper devices of our choice at that moment in time (on demand). In this same utility fashion, Grid Computing openly seeks, and is capable of, adding an infinite number of computing devices into any grid environment, adding to the computing capability and problem resolution tasks within the operational grid environment, and at the exact time it is needed (on demand).

WHAT IS THE IMPORTANCE OF THIS BOOK?

The last few years we have witnessed the emergence of Grid Computing as an innovative extension to distributed computing technology, for computing resource sharing among participants in a *virtualized* collection of organizations. This technology leverages a combination of hardware/ software virtualization, and the distributed sharing of those virtualized resources. These resources can include all elements of computing, including: Hardware, software, applications, networking services, pervasive devices, and complex footprints of computing power. Grid Computing is one technology enabler for some of the most innovative and powerful emerging industrial solution approaches, including the IBM On Demand strategies,[1] HP utility computing,[2] and Sun N1 technologies.[3]

The emergence of open standards has a great influence on this computing technology, especially in providing seamless Grid interoperability and Grid integration facilities. We could find that technologies of Grid Computing are still evolving; however, the alignment with industry-wide open standards, and the commercial interests, quickly placed this technology into a forerunning state for infrastructure and technology development. The most notable standard we have seen in this area of Grid is the Global Grid Forum's[4] Open Grid Services Architecture (OGSA) initiative.

Until today, most of the work in Grid Computing has been concentrated at the academic, and standards level discussion and building custom solutions. However, the emergence of commercial utility services and the requirement for alignment with the rest of the organizational computing infrastructures hasten the development of open standards and interoperable commercial Grid solutions. This book is a detailed discussion on all aspects of Grid Computing, technology, applications, disciplines, and infrastructures. In this book we provide full treatment to covering the evolution of Grid Computing, existing Grid infrastructure components, emerging Grid service standards, and Grid architectures. In addition, we will explore detailed discussions on many prominent Grid middleware solutions.

WHAT YOU CAN EXPECT FROM THIS BOOK

We, the authors of this book, hope that you will find reading this book, an interesting and thought-provoking experience. In this book, we are introducing you to the basic Grid Computing principles, and to the emerging technology standards for Grid Computing. Readers will find this discussion interesting with a progressive evolution of technologies, discussed in this book in a concise, hard-hitting, and to-the-point fashion. We believe this will help the readers clearly understand the basic Grid Computing principles, the existing/emerging Grid standards, and their various usages models. We must be aware that the Grid standards are complex with a number of interrelations among themselves and other emerging standards such as XML and Web services. As we will see, this is a fast moving target and we should try to focus on this fact, early, so that we won't miss the opportunity to create Grid services and infrastructures suitable for each of our respective organizations or Grid initiatives.

In general, this book will explore:

- *The basic concepts of Grid Computing*: Grid Computing discipline has been evolving over the past few years as a means of immense computing power and distributed data sharing facilities. We will discuss the many core aspects of these infrastructure components, and the high-level services built upon the Grid infrastructure as networking services.
- *How the Grid Computing is evolving as an open standard for resource sharing*: The Grid Computing discipline is evolving. The focus is now on seamless interoperability and integration among participants of the Grid for better resources sharing. This is exceptionally challenging and a number of organizations are working collectively to provide an open and extensible standard and test beds for the Grid.
- *The influence of emerging technology standards on Grid infrastructure*: Computing is always involving some process and form of evolution. New software standards and architectures are continually evolving to meet the requirements of global industries. The most notable and latest in this row are the Service Oriented Architecture (SOA) and the

XML/Web services standards. These architectures and standards, as the reader will soon see, have tremendous influence in the emerging open Grid Computing standards.

- *The new Grid architecture and infrastructure*: Based on the experience drawn form earlier Grid infrastructures, implementations, and the influence of the emerging open standards and technologies, the Grid computing standards organizations are designing an Open Grid Service Architecture (OGSA), and Open Grid Service Infrastructure (OGSI) for Grid computing. These important contributions will soon become the core platform for all the next generation Grid Computing technologies.
- *The most prominent toolkits and middleware solutions that will impact the Grid adoption*: These open standards and technologies are not enough; we need real middleware solutions and high-level services using these standards and technologies. The most prominent middleware technology that exists today is Globus Toolkit.[5] We will explore the details on this toolkit's robust architecture, and programming model capabilities to enable the latest Grid standards on the OGSI. In addition, we will explore some architectural concepts of the OGSI.NET[6] toolkit, another notable implementation of the OGSI standard.

HOW THIS BOOK IS ORGANIZED

This book contains 15 chapters, which are organized into five parts.

Part I—Grid Computing

Part 1 consists of Chapter 1. Chapter 1 provides a detailed but high-level introduction to the Grid Computing evolution, the applications, and the infrastructure requirements for any Grid environment. In addition, this chapter discusses Grid Computing disciplines, and the factors developers and service providers must consider during the implementation phases.

Part 2—Grid Computing Worldwide Initiatives

Part 2 consists of Chapter 2, Chapter 3, and Chapter 4. This part is more on defining Grid Computing, its evolution, the factors that are affecting these evolutions and the organizations that are influencing/deciding the adoption of this new technology. In addition, we will see a general-purpose architecture solution for the emerging Grid Computing infrastructure and a road map for Grid Computing technology initiatives.

Chapter 2: "Grid Computing Organizations and Their Roles." There are a number of organizations from various industry sectors including scientific research, commercial, and standards organizations that are affecting the Grid Computing adoptions, infrastructure development, testing, standardization, and guideline developments. This chapter introduces us to the major plays in the Grid world.

Chapter 3: "The Grid Computing Anatomy." This chapter defines the problems of coordinated resource sharing, the concepts of virtual organization formation, and a protocol architecture solution for the Grid problems. In addition, this chapter examines the Grid in relation with other distributed technologies such as Web, object-oriented, distributed technologies, service provider's frameworks, clusters, and peer-to-peer computing.

Chapter 4: "The Grid Computing Road Map" is a brief. Here we will be discussing the current and prominent technology initiatives that are affecting the recent Grid Computing revolution. Some of the prominent technology initiatives that are acting as catalysts to the evolution are Business On Demand environments, autonomic computing, service oriented architectures and semantic Grid.

Part 3—The New Generation of Grid Computing Applications

Part 3 consists of Chapter 5. In this part we will explore the technology constructs of the Service Oriented Architecture (SOA) that will set the stage for the new generation of Grid Computing applications.

Chapter 5: "Merging the Grid Service Architecture with the Web Service Architecture." This is an extensive chapter, which defines the Service Oriented Architecture (SOA) and it's respective implementations, Web and Web services. Our discussion on Web services covers the details on extensible Markup Language (XML), Simple Object Access Protocol (SOAP), and Web Service Description Language (WSDL 1.1/1.2). In addition, we will explore the details of Global XML Architecture (GXA) and some emerging standards (WS-Security, WS-Policy, WS-Addressing). Another notable area covered in the chapter is the Web service interoperability (WS-I) basic profile and the tools to assert the interoperability validations. We will end the chapter with a detailed discussion on Web service state management, the concepts around stateful interactions/applications, and how Grid networking services relate to stateful Web services.

Part 4—The Grid Computing Technological Viewpoints

Part 4 consists of Chapter 6, Chapter 7, Chapter 8, Chapter 9, and Chapter 10. This part introduces the concept of Open Grid Service Architecture and the motivations that drive OGSA standardization. In addition to this, we will describe the OGSA architecture and the core infrastructure components for this architecture. This discussion will align Grid Computing with the other emerging technologies. In addition, we will define some of the core base services defined by the OGSA platform.

Chapter 6: "Open Grid Services Architecture (OGSA)." This chapter will introduce the new OGSA architecture defined for Grid Computing. This is based on open standards and a Global Grid Forum initiative. This discussion introduces us to the architectural layers as defined by OGSA. This chapter will then set the stage for the forthcoming discussions on OGSA.

Chapter 7: "Some Sample Use Cases that Drive the OGSA." Any well thought-out architecture is driven from a set of use cases, which captures the scenarios, involved parties, and the solution requirements for the architecture. This chapter will introduce some representative sample use cases from various industry sectors to illustrate this process of requirements gathering.

Chapter 8: "The OGSA Platform Components." This is a simple chapter with an illustration on IBM vision for OGSA. This chapter enhances the OGSA architecture with more detailed layering and relationship with the other existing application and system components.

Chapter 9: "Open Grid Services Infrastructure (OGSI)." This chapter discusses one of the most important aspects of the OGSA, the core infrastructure foundation for all Grid services. In this chapter we will cover the details on this infrastructure that will define the behaviors for all Grid services created for OGSA, including state management, instance naming, life cycle management, and fault handling. This chapter covers the core interfaces defined by the specification and their significance and usage patterns. In addition to this, we will define the relationship between Web services and Grid services, the similarities and differences of their description mechanisms, and the significance of the Grid Web Service Description Language (GWSDL). In this chapter, one will realize a tremendous amount of valuable information on the core infrastructure software.

Chapter 10: "OGSA Basic Services." Based on the OGSI specification and the architecture requirements, a number of core services were developed in the Grid area. These services emerged from the requirements gathered from the use cases collected from various industry sectors. This chapter will introduce the readers to some of these prominent base services. This discussion covers the details on Grid services for resource management modeling, policy enforcement, service grouping, security, metering/accounting, logging, and distributed data management.

Part 5—The Grid Computing Toolkits

Part 5 consists of Chapter 11, Chapter 12, Chapter 13, Chapter 14, and Chapter 15. In this part, we will learn about some of the prominent and emerging middleware solutions implemented using the Open Grid Service Infrastructure (OGSI) standard. The most prominent in this group is the Globus Toolkit. This part will cover the final release's software framework, entitled "Globus Toolkit 3" or GT3. Our discussion includes the GT3 architecture, programming model, sample Grid service development, and high-level services. In addition to Globus GT3, we will see another most notable software framework called OGSI.NET, which is also a realization of the OGSI specification.

Chapter 11: "GLOBUS GT3 Toolkit: Architecture." This chapter is dedicated to the Globus GT3 architecture model. We will discuss this layered architecture model provided by GT3. This software is built on Java, and enables a container model for the Grid service life cycle and instance management. This chapter introduces the reader to the architecture plug-ability of GT3 with Web service engines, and hosting capabilities in J2EE/J2SE containers. In addition, this chapter explains the GT3 security mechanisms and client side architecture details.

Chapter 12: "GLOBUS GT3 Toolkit: Programming Model." This chapter provides a detailed and in-depth analysis of the programming model supported by the GT3 software. This discussion will introduce the reader to the core service programming concepts, service data management, notification, and query processing. In addition we will discuss the service configurations, tools, and tracing options. The discussion on the client side-programming model in this chapter is also worth mentioning. Other aspects that will be discussed include security, and various message exchange models.

Chapter 13: "GLOBUS GT3 Toolkit: A Sample Implementation." In this chapter we will explore a sample Grid service implementation using a top-down approach, starting with GWSDL for a sample search service. Our discussion will provide a detailed look into each step of this service implementation, with the tools involved and the respective codes generated. In addition, the development is done in a phased manner with added complexities in each layer. Another most valuable discussion provided includes the traces of the SOAP messages exchanged during this service invocation. This helps the reader to understand the OGSI standards, and the GT3 in particular, and will provide better interoperability. In short, our sample will provide service data management, and notification. Finally we end with an EJB delegation model support provided in GT3.

Chapter 14: "GLOBUS GT3 Toolkit: High-Level Services." These high-level services are for resource discovery and monitoring, including resource allocation and data management. The prominent services introduced in this chapter are Index services, Resource Information provider (RIP) services, Grid Resource Allocation and Management (GRAM) services, and data management services. In addition, this chapter introduces the component model for information services. This discussion includes provider components, service data aggregation components, and registry components.

Chapter 15: "OGSI.NET Middleware Solutions." This chapter provides information on another OGSI specification implementation in the Microsoft .NET environment. The reader will find a detailed discussion on the architecture and programming model for developing Grid services for .NET.

NOTES

1. For information on the IBM On Demand operating environment, go to *http://www-3.ibm.com/software/info/openenvironment/*.

2. For information on HP Utility services, go to *www.hp.com/products1/promos/adaptive_enterprise/us/utility.html*.

3. For information on SUN N1 solutions, go to *wwws.sun.com/software/solutions/n1/*.

4. For information on the Global Grid Forum, go to *www.ggf.org*.

5. For information on Globus Toolkit, go to *http://www-unix.globus.org/toolkit/*.

6. For information on OGSI.NET Toolkit, go to *www.cs.virginia.edu/~gsw2c/ogsi.net.html*.

Acknowledgments _____

We would like to take this opportunity to thank several of our colleagues for their support, professional guidance, advice, and counsel in bringing together some of the complex topics addressed in this book.

We would like to thank Jaclyn Vassallo, Susan Visser, and Bill Wong at IBM, and George Joseph from Rutgers University for their outstanding and professional editorial support throughout the entire composition of this book. We would also like to thank all of the creative men and women, who contributed to the disciplines of Grid Computing, from all around the world: Without these brilliant contributions, and their commitment and hard work, the Grid successes would not be as noteworthy as they are today. Without all of these individuals, this book would not have been produced in the time frame or the quality that it has been delivered.

We would like to acknowledge a very special thank you to Jeffrey Pepper, our publisher, and the entire Prentice Hall PTR publishing staff members (and extended team). These individuals provided excellent team leadership and professional support in all of the activities throughout the entire development and production of this book. They are truly a world-class team of professionals.

From Joshy Joseph...

I would like to thank my family, my wife Lincy and my two-year-old daughter Ponnu, who continually stood behind me throughout the challenging task of creating this book. I am also very thankful to my parents and all of their help in supporting and encouraging me in my professional career aspirations. Craig, I thank you for introducing me to the world of authorship, and for helping me sort out the complexities of technical and educational book composition. Last but certainly not least, I wish to thank everyone in my family and all of my friends for their support in helping me to develop this book.

From Craig Fellenstein...

I would like to extend a very sincere thank you to my family, who is absolutely more important than Business On Demand. It was my family—Lindsey, Jimmy, and Elizabeth—who supported me in the many late night hours required to develop this book. I would also like to thank my father, Jim, my sister, Nancy, and my wife's mother, Dorothy, for their unconditional encouragement and love in helping me find the energy to complete not only this book, but a second book in parallel, entitled *Business On Demand: Technologies and Strategy Perspectives.* Joshy, I thank you for your many late night hours and outstanding leadership in the creation of this book: You are, indeed, a world-class professional role model, and expert practitioner in the discipline of Grid Computing. Thanks also to my contributing editor, Elizabeth Fellenstein. Please accept my warmest and most sincere thank you to each of you.

Grid Computing

In today's incredibly complex world of computational power, very high speed machine processing capabilities, complex data storage methods, next-generation telecommunications, new-generation operating systems and services, and extremely advanced networking services capabilities— we are entering a new era of computing. At the same time, industry, businesses, and home users alike are placing more complex and challenging demands on the networks.

In this book we explore all of these aspects in simple to understand terms as we unveil a new era of computing, simply referred to as "Grid Computing." The worldwide Grid Computing discipline involves the actual connections of a potentially unlimited number of machines within a grid, and can be most simply thought of as a massively large power "utility" grid, such as what provides power to our homes and businesses each and every day.

This part of the book unveils many of these powerful approaches to this new era of computing, and explores why so many are considering a Grid Computing environment as a single, incredibly powerful, and effective computing solution.

Introduction

In today's pervasive world of needing information anytime and anywhere, the explosive Grid Computing environments have now proven to be so significant that they are often referred to as being the world's single and most powerful computer solutions. It has been realized that with the many benefits of Grid Computing, we have consequently introduced both a complicated and complex global environment, which leverages a multitude of open standards and technologies in a wide variety of implementation schemes. As a matter of fact the complexity and dynamic nature of industrial problems in today's world are much more intensive to satisfy by the more traditional, single computational platform approaches.

GRID COMPUTING EQUATES TO THE WORLD'S LARGEST COMPUTER ...

The Grid Computing discipline involves the actual networking services and connections of a potentially unlimited number of ubiquitous computing devices within a "grid." This new innovative approach to computing can be most simply thought of as a massively large power "utility" grid, such as what provides power to our homes and businesses each and every day. This delivery of utility-based power has become second nature to many of us, worldwide. We know that by simply walking into a room and turning on the lights, the power will be directed to the proper devices of our choice for that moment in time. In this same utility fashion, Grid Computing openly seeks and is capable of adding an infinite number of computing devices into any grid environment, adding to the computing capability and problem resolution tasks within the operational grid environment.

The incredible problem resolution capabilities of Grid Computing remain yet unknown, as we continue to forge ahead and enter this new era of massively powerful grid-based problem-solving solutions.

This "Introduction" section of the book will begin to present many of the Grid Computing topics, which are discussed throughout this book. These discussions in Chapter 1 are intended only to provide a rather high-level examination of Grid Computing. Later sections of the book provide a full treatment of the topics addressed by many worldwide communities utilizing and continuing to develop Grid Computing.

The worldwide business demand requiring intense problem-solving capabilities for incredibly complex problems has driven in all global industry segments the need for dynamic collaboration of many ubiquitous computing resources to be able to work together. These difficult computational problem-solving needs have now fostered many complexities in virtually all computing technologies, while driving up costs and operational aspects of the technology environments. However, this advanced computing collaboration capability is indeed required in almost all areas of industrial and business problem solving, ranging from scientific studies to commercial solutions to academic endeavors. It is a difficult challenge across all the technical communities to achieve this level of resource collaboration needed for solving these complex and dynamic problems, within the bounds of the necessary quality requirements of the end user.

To further illustrate this environment and oftentimes very complex set of technology challenges, let us consider some common *use case* scenarios one might have already encountered, which will begin to examine the many values of a Grid Computing solution environment. These simple use cases, for purposes of introduction to the concepts of Grid Computing, are as follows:

- A financial organization processing wealth management application collaborates with the different departments for more computational power and software modeling applications. It pools a number of computing resources, which can thereby perform faster with real-time executions of the tasks and immediate access to complex pools of data storage, all while managing complicated data transfer tasks. This ultimately results in increased customer satisfaction with a faster turnaround time.

- A group of scientists studying the atmospheric ozone layer will collect huge amounts of experimental data, each and every day. These scientists need efficient and complex data storage capabilities across wide and geographically dispersed storage facilities, and they need to access this data in an efficient manner based on the processing needs. This ultimately results in a more effective and efficient means of performing important scientific research.

- Massive online multiplayer game scenarios for a wide community of international gaming participants are occurring that require a large number of gaming computer servers instead of a dedicated game server. This allows international game players to interact among themselves as a group in a real-time manner. This involves the need for on-demand allocation and provisioning of computer resources, provisioning and self-management of complex networks, and complicated data storage resources. This on-demand need is very dynamic, from moment-to-moment, and it is always based upon the workload in the system at any given moment in time. This ultimately results in larger gaming communities, requiring more complex infrastructures to sustain the traffic loads, delivering more profits to the bottom lines of gaming corporations, and higher degrees of customer satisfaction to the gaming participants.

- A government organization studying a natural disaster such as a chemical spill may need to immediately collaborate with different departments in order to plan for and best manage the disaster. These organizations may need to simulate many computational models related to the spill in order to calculate the spread of the spill, effect of the weather on the spill, or to determine the impact on human health factors. This ultimately results in protection and safety matters being provided for public safety issues, wildlife management and protection issues, and ecosystem protection matters: Needles to say all of which are very key concerns.

Today, Grid Computing offers many solutions that already address and resolve the above problems. Grid Computing solutions are constructed using a variety of technologies and open standards. Grid Computing, in turn, provides highly scalable, highly secure, and extremely high-performance mechanisms for discovering and negotiating access to remote computing resources in a seamless manner. This makes it possible for the sharing of computing resources, on an unprecedented scale, among an infinite number of geographically distributed groups. This serves as a significant transformation agent for individual and corporate implementations surrounding computing practices, toward a general-purpose utility approach very similar in concept to providing electricity or water. These electrical and water types of utilities, much like Grid Computing utilities, are available "on demand," and will always be capable of providing an always-available facility negotiated for individual or corporate utilization.

In this new and intriguing book, we will begin our discussion on the core concepts of the Grid Computing system with an early definition of grid. Back in 1998, it was defined, "A computational grid is a hardware and software infrastructure that provides dependable, consistent, pervasive, and inexpensive access to high-end computational capabilities" (Foster & Kesselman, 1998).

The preceding definition is more centered on the computational aspects of Grid Computing while later iterations broaden this definition with more focus on coordinated resource sharing and problem solving in multi-institutional virtual organizations (Foster & Kesselman, 1998). In addition to these qualifications of coordinated resource sharing and the formation of dynamic virtual organizations, open standards become a key underpinning. It is important that there are open standards throughout the grid implementation, which also accommodate a variety of other open standards-based protocols and frameworks, in order to provide interoperable and extensible infrastructure environments.

Grid Computing environments must be constructed upon the following foundations:

- *Coordinated resources.* We should avoid building grid systems with a centralized control; instead, we must provide the necessary infrastructure for coordination among the resources, based on respective policies and service-level agreements.

- *Open standard protocols and frameworks.* The use of open standards provides interoperability and integration facilities. These standards must be applied for resource discovery, resource access, and resource coordination.

Another basic requirement of a Grid Computing system is the ability to provide the quality of service (QoS) requirements necessary for the end-user community. These QoS validations must be a basic feature in any Grid system, and must be done in congruence with the available resource matrices. These QoS features can be (for example) response time measures, aggregated performance, security fulfillment, resource scalability, availability, autonomic features such as event correlation and configuration management, and partial fail over mechanisms.

There have been a number of activities addressing the above definitions of Grid Computing and the requirements for a grid system. The most notable effort is in the standardization of the interfaces and protocols for the Grid Computing infrastructure implementations. We will cover the details later in this book. Let us now explore some early and current Grid Computing systems and their differences in terms of benefits.

EARLY GRID ACTIVITIES

Over the past several years, there has been a lot of interest in computational Grid Computing worldwide. We also note a number of derivatives of Grid Computing, including compute grids, data grids, science grids, access grids, knowledge grids, cluster grids, terra grids, and commodity grids. As we explore careful examination of these grids, we can see that they all share some form of resources; however, these grids may have differing architectures.

One key value of a grid, whether it is a commodity utility grid or a computational grid, is often evaluated based on its business merits and the respective user satisfaction. User satisfaction is measured based on the QoS provided by the grid, such as the availability, performance, simplicity of access, management aspects, business values, and flexibility in pricing. The business merits most often relate to and indicate the problem being solved by the grid. For instance, it can be job executions, management aspects, simulation workflows, and other key technology-based foundations.

Earlier Grid Computing efforts were aligned with the overlapping functional areas of data, computation, and their respective access mechanisms. Let us further explore the details of these areas to better understand their utilization and functional requirements.

Data

The data aspects of any Grid Computing environment must be able to effectively manage all aspects of data, including data location, data transfer, data access, and critical aspects of security. The core functional data requirements for Grid Computing applications are:

- The ability to integrate multiple distributed, heterogeneous, and independently managed data sources.
- The ability to provide efficient data transfer mechanisms and to provide data where the computation will take place for better scalability and efficiency.
- The ability to provide data caching and/or replication mechanisms to minimize network traffic.
- The ability to provide necessary data discovery mechanisms, which allow the user to find data based on characteristics of the data.
- The capability to implement data encryption and integrity checks to ensure that data is transported across the network in a secure fashion.
- The ability to provide the backup/restore mechanisms and policies necessary to prevent data loss and minimize unplanned downtime across the grid.

Computation

The core functional computational requirements for grid applications are:

- The ability to allow for independent management of computing resources
- The ability to provide mechanisms that can intelligently and transparently select computing resources capable of running a user's job
- The understanding of the current and predicted loads on grid resources, resource availability, dynamic resource configuration, and provisioning
- Failure detection and failover mechanisms
- Ensure appropriate security mechanisms for secure resource management, access, and integrity

Let us further explore some details on the computational and data grids as they exist today.

Computational and Data Grids

In today's complex world of high speed computing, computers have become extremely powerful as to that of (let's say) five years ago. Even the home-based PCs available on the commercial markets are powerful enough for accomplishing complex computations that we could not have imagined a decade prior to today.

The quality and quantity requirements for some business-related advanced computing applications are also becoming more and more complex. The industry is now realizing that we have a need, and are conducting numerous complex scientific experiments, advanced modeling scenarios, genome matching, astronomical research, a wide variety of simulations, complex scientific/business modeling scenarios, and real-time personal portfolio management. These requirements can actually exceed the demands and availability of installed computational power within an organization. Sometimes, we find that no single organization alone satisfies some of these aforementioned computational requirements.

This advanced computing power applications need is indeed analogous to the electric power need in the early 1900s, such that to provide for the availability of electrical power, each user has to build and be prepared to operate an electrical generator. Thus, when the electric power grid became a reality, this changed the entire concept of the providing for, and utilization of, electrical power. This, in turn, paved the way for an evolution related to the utilization of electricity. In a similar fashion, the computational grids change the perception on the utility and availability of the computer power. Thus the computational Grid Computing environment became a reality, which provides a demand-driven, reliable, powerful, and yet inexpensive computational power for its customers.

As we noted earlier in this discussion, a computational Grid Computing environment consists of one or more hardware- and software-enabled environments that provide dependable, consistent, pervasive and inexpensive access to high-end computational capabilities (Foster & Kesselman, 1998).

Later in this book, in the "Grid Anatomy" section, we will see that this definition has evolved to give more emphasis on the seamless resource sharing aspects in a collaborative virtual organizational world. But the concept still holds for a computational grid where the sharable resource remains a computing power. As of now, the majority of the computational grids are centered on major scientific experiments and collaborative environments.

The requirement for key data forms a core underpinning of any Grid Computing environment. For example, in data-intensive grids, the focus is on the management of data, which is being held in a variety of data storage facilities in geographically dispersed locations. These data sources can be databases, file systems, and storage devices. The grid systems must also be capable of providing data virtualization services to provide transparency for data access, integration, and processing. In addition to the above requirements, security and privacy requirements of all respective data in a grid system is quite complex.

We can summarize the data requirements in the early grid solutions as follows:

- The ability to discover data
- The access to databases, utilizing meta-data and other attributes of the data
- The provisioning of computing facilities for high-speed data movement
- The capability to support flexible data access and data filtering capabilities

As one begins to realize the importance of extreme high performance-related issues in a Grid Computing environment, it is recommended to store (or cache) data near to the computation, and to provide a common interface for data access and management.

It is interesting to note that upon careful examination of existing Grid Computing systems, readers will learn that many Grid Computing systems are being applied in several important scientific research and collaboration projects; however, this does not preclude the importance of Grid Computing in business-, academic-, and industry-related fields. The commercialization of Grid Computing invites and addresses a key architectural alignment with several existing commercial frameworks for improved interoperability and integration.

As we will describe in this book, many current trends in Grid Computing are toward service-based architectures for grid environments. This "architecture" is built for interoperability and is (again) based upon open standard protocols. We will provide a full treatment including many of the details toward this architecture throughout subsequent sections in this book.

CURRENT GRID ACTIVITIES

As described earlier, initially, the focused Grid Computing activities were in the areas of computing power, data access, and storage resources.

The definition of Grid Computing resource sharing has since changed, based upon experiences, with more focus now being applied to a sophisticated form of coordinated resource sharing distributed throughout the participants in a virtual organization. This application concept of coordinated resource sharing includes any resources available within a virtual organization, including computing power, data, hardware, software and applications, networking services, and any other forms of computing resource attainment. This concept of coordinated resource sharing is depicted in Figure 1.1.

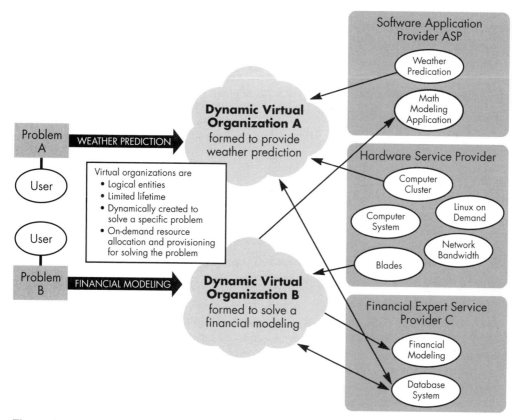

Figure 1.1
Dynamic benefits of coordinated resource sharing in a virtual organization.

As depicted in the previous illustration, there are a number of sharable resources, hardware and software applications, firmware implementations, and networking services, all available within an enterprise or service provider environment. Rather than keeping these resources isolated within an atomic organization, the users can acquire these resources on a "demand" basis. Through implementing this type of Grid Computing environment, these resources are immediately available to the authenticated users for resolving specific problems. These problems may be a software capability problem (e.g., modeling, simulation, word processing, etc.) or hardware availability and/or computing capacity shortage problems (e.g., processor computing resources, data storage/access needs, etc.). While on another level, these problems may be related to a networking bandwidth availability problem, the need for immediate circuit provisioning of a network, a security event or other event correlation issue, and many more types of critical environmental needs.

Based upon the specific problem dimension, any given problem may have one or more resolution issues to address. For example, in the above case there is two sets of users, each with a need to solve two different types of problems. You will note that one has to resolve the weather prediction problem, while the other has to provide a financial modeling case. Based upon these problem domains noted by each of the user groups, their requirements imply two types of virtual organizations. These distinct virtual organizations are formulated, sustained, and managed from a computing resource viewpoint according to the ability to access the available resources. Let us further explore this concept of "*virtualization*" by describing in more detail the usage patterns found within each of the virtual organizations.

- *A virtual organization for weather prediction.* For example, this virtual organization requires resources such as weather prediction software applications to perform the mandatory environmental simulations associated with predicting weather. Likewise, they will require very specific hardware resources to run the respective software, as well as high-speed data storage facilities to maintain the data generated from performing the simulations.
- *A virtual organization for financial modeling.* For example, this virtual organization requires resources such as software modeling tools for performing a multitude of financial analytics, virtualized blades[1] to run the above software, and access to data storage facilities for storing and accessing data.

These virtual organizations manage their resources and typically will provision additional resources on an "as-needed" basis. This on-demand approach provides tremendous values toward scalability, in addition to aspects of enhanced reusability. This approach is typically found in any "on-demand" environment. This capability is based upon a *utility* infrastructure, where resources are allocated as, and when, they are required. Likewise, their utility pricing scenarios are always based upon the capturing of usage metrics.

The following discussion introduces a number of requirements needed for such Grid Computing architectures utilized by virtual organizations. We shall classify these architecture requirements into three categories. These resources categories must be capable of providing facilities for the following scenarios:

- The need for dynamic discovery of computing resources, based on their capabilities and functions.
- The immediate allocation and provisioning of these resources, based on their availability and the user demands or requirements.
- The management of these resources to meet the required service level agreements (SLAs).
- The provisioning of multiple autonomic features for the resources, such as self-diagnosis, self-healing, self-configuring, and self-management.
- The provisioning of secure access methods to the resources, and bindings with the local security mechanisms based upon the autonomic control policies.

Virtual organization must be capable of providing facilities for:

- The formation of virtual task forces, or groups, to solve specific problems associated with the virtual organization.
- The dynamic collection of resources from heterogeneous providers based upon users' needs and the sophistication levels of the problems.
- The dynamic identification and automatic problem resolution of a wide variety of troubles, with automation of event correlation, linking the specific problems to the required resource and/or service providers.
- The dynamic provisioning and management capabilities of the resources required meeting the SLAs.
- The formation of a secured federation (or governance model) and common management model for all of the resources respective to the virtual organization.
- The secure delegation of user credentials and identity mapping to the local domain(s).
- The management of resources, including utilization and allocation, to meet a budget and other economic criteria.

Users/applications typically found in Grid Computing environments must be able to perform the following characteristics:

- The clear and unambiguous identification of the problem(s) needing to be solved
- The identification and mapping of the resources required solve the problem
- The ability to sustain the required levels of QoS, while adhering to the anticipated and necessary SLAs
- The capability to collect feedback regarding resource status, including updates for the environment's respective applications

The above discussion helps us now to better understand the common requirements for grid systems. In the subsequent chapters in this section, and moreover throughout this book, we discuss the many specific details on the Grid Computing architecture models and emerging Grid Computing software systems that have proven valuable in supporting the above requirements.

The following section will provide treatment toward some of the more common Grid Computing business areas that exist today, and those areas that will typically benefit from the above concepts of Grid Computing. It is worthy to mention that these business areas are most often broadly classified, and based upon the industry sector where they reside.

AN OVERVIEW OF GRID BUSINESS AREAS

One of the most valuable aspects of all Grid Computing systems are that they attract the business they are intended to address. In an "on-demand" scenario, these Grid Computing environments are the result of autonomic provisioning of a multitude of resources and capabilities, typically demonstrating increased computing resource utilization, access to specialized computer systems, cost sharing, and improved management capabilities.

IBM BUSINESS ON DEMAND INITIATIVE

Business On Demand (in the rest of the book we will refer to this as On Demand) is not just about utility computing as it has a much broader set of ideas about the transformation of business practices, process transformation, and technology implementations. Companies striving to achieve the Business On Demand operational models will have the capacity to sense and respond to fluctuating market conditions in real-time, while providing products and services to customers in a Business On Demand operational model. The essential characteristics of on-demand businesses are responsiveness to the dynamics of business, adapting to variable cost structures, focusing on core business competency, and resiliency for consistent availability. This is achieved through seamless integration of customers and partners, virtualization of resources, autonomic/dependable resources, and open standards.

There have been a significant number of commercialization efforts, which support Grid Computing in every sector of the marketplace. In general terms, the utilization of Grid Computing in business environments provides a rich and extensible set of business benefits. These business benefits include (but are not limited to):

- Acceleration of implementation time frames in order to intersect with the anticipated business end results.
- Improved productivity and collaboration of virtual organizations and respective computing and data resources.
- Allowing widely dispersed departments and businesses to create virtual organizations to share data and resources.
- Robust and infinitely flexible and resilient operational infrastructures.
- Providing instantaneous access to massive computing and data resources.

- Leveraging existing capital expenditures investments, and operational expenditure investments, which in turn help to ensure optimal utilization and costs of computing capabilities.
- Avoiding common pitfalls of overprovisioning and incurring excess costs.

Many organizations have started identifying the major business areas for Grid Computing business applications. Some examples of major business areas include (but are not limited to):

- Life sciences, for analyzing and decoding strings of biological and chemical information
- Financial services, for running long, complex financial models and arriving at more accurate decisions
- Higher education for enabling advanced, data- and computation-intensive research
- Engineering services, including automotive and aerospace, for collaborative design and data-intensive testing
- Government, for enabling seamless collaboration and agility in both civil and military departments and other agencies
- Collaborative games for replacing the existing single-server online games with more highly parallel, massively multiplayer online games

Let us now introduce and explore the analytics of each of these industry sectors by identifying some of the high-level business-area requirements for Grid Computing systems. In doing so, we will look at the facilities necessary for grid systems in order to meet these requirements.

Life Sciences

This industry sector has noted many dramatic advances in the life sciences sector, which have in turn provided rapid changes in the way that drug treatment and drug discovery efforts are now being conducted. The analytics and system efforts' surrounding genomic, proteomics, and molecular biology efforts provides the basis for many of these Grid Computing advancements in this sector. These advances have now presented a number of technical challenges to the information technology sector, and especially the Grid Computing disciplines.

Grid Computing efforts have realized that these challenges include huge amounts of data analysis, data movement, data caching, and data mining. In addition to the complexity of processing data, there needs to be additional requirements surrounding data security, secure data access, secure storage, privacy, and highly flexible integration. Another area that requires attention is the querying of nonstandard data formats and accessing data assets across complex global networks.

The above requirements presented by life sciences require a Grid Computing infrastructure to properly manage data storage, providing access to the data, and all while performing complex analysis respective to the data. The Grid Computing systems can provide a common infrastructure for data access, and at the same time, provide secure data access mechanisms while processing the data. Today, life sciences utilizes the Grid Computing systems to execute sequence comparison algorithms and enable molecular modeling using the above-collected secured data.

This now provides the Life Sciences sector the ability to afford world-class information analysis respective to this discussion, while at the same time providing faster response times and far more accurate results.

Financial Analysis and Services

This industry sector has noted many dramatic advances in the financial analysis and services industry sector. The technological and business advances are most noted in the information technology areas, the emergence of a competitive market force customer satisfaction, and reduction of risk as the most competitive areas financial communities continually strive to achieve. The requirements related to sophistication, accuracy, and faster execution are among the more salient objectives across financial communities. These objectives are now achieved by real-time access to the current and historical market data, complex financial modeling based on the respective data, and faster response times to user queries.

Grid Computing provides the financial analysis and services industry sector with advanced systems delivering all the competitive solutions in Grid Computing. These solutions exemplify the infrastructure and business agility necessary to meet and exceed the uniqueness that the financial analysis and services industry sector requires. This particular value statement is accomplished by the fact that many of these solutions in this industry are dependent upon providing increased access to massive amounts of data, real-time modeling, and faster execution by using the grid job scheduling and data access features. For this to be most successful, these financial institutions tend to form virtual organizations with participation from several different departments and other external organizations. In addition to the use of existing resources, a grid system can provide more efficiency by easily adapting to the rapidly changing algorithms pertaining to the financial analytics.

Research Collaboration

Research-oriented organizations and universities practicing in advanced research collaboration areas require the analysis of tremendous amounts of data. Some examples of such projects are subatomic particle and high energy physics experiments, remote sensing sources for earth simulation and modeling, and analysis of the human genome sequence.

These virtual organizations engaged in research collaboration activities generate petabytes[2] of data and require tremendous amounts of storage space and thousands of computing processors. Researchers in these fields must share data, computational processors, and hardware instrumentation such as telescopes and advanced testing equipment. Most of these resources are pertaining to data-intensive processing, and are widely dispersed over a large geographical area.

The Grid Computing discipline provides mechanisms for resource sharing by forming one or more virtual organizations providing specific sharing capabilities. Such virtual organizations are constituted to resolve specific research problems with a wide range of participants from different regions of the world. This formation of dynamic virtual organizations provides capabilities to dynamically add and delete virtual organization participants, manage the "on-demand" sharing of resources, plus provisioning of a common and integrated secure framework for data interchange and access.

Engineering and Design

The enormous competitive pressure in the business and industry sectors today afford most engineering and design far less turnaround time. They need mechanisms to capture data, speed up the analysis on the data, and provide faster responses to market needs. As we already know, these engineering activities and design solutions are inherently complex across several dimensions, and the processing requirements are much more intense than that of traditional solutions of the past.

These complexities fall into several areas of solutions in Grid Computing that span across industry sectors all over the world. These complexities are described (but are not limited to) the following areas:

- The analysis of real-time data to find a specific pattern within a problem
- The parametric studies to verify different aspects of the systems
- The modeling experiments to create new designs
- The simulation activities to verify the existing models for accuracy

Grid Computing systems provide a wide range of capabilities that address the above kinds of analysis and modeling activities. These advanced types of solutions also provide complex job schedulers and resource managers to deal with computing power requirements. This enables automobile manufacturers (as an example) to shorten analysis and design times, all while minimizing both capital expenditures and operational expenditures.

Collaborative Games

There are collaborative types of Grid Computing disciplines that are involving emerging technologies to support online games, while utilizing on-demand provisioning of computation-intensive resources, such as computers and storage networks. These resources are selected based on the requirements, often involving aspects such as volume of traffic and number of players, rather than centralized servers and other fixed resources.

These on-demand-driven games provide a flexible approach with a reduced up-front cost on hardware and software resources. We can imagine that these games use an increasing number of computing resources with an increase in the number of concurrent players and a decrease in resource usage with a lesser number of players. Grid Computing gaming environments are capable of supporting such virtualized environments for enabling collaborative gaming.

Government

The Grid Computing environments in government focus on providing coordinated access to massive amounts of data held across various agencies in a government. This provides faster access to solve critical problems, such as emergency situations, and other normal activities. These key environments provide more efficient decision making with less turnaround time.

Grid Computing enables the creation of virtual organizations, including many participants from various governmental agencies (e.g., state and federal, local or country, etc.). This is necessary in order to provide the data needed for government functions, in a real-time manner, while performing the analysis on the data to detect the solution aspects of the specific problems being addressed. The formation of virtual organizations, and the respective elements of security, is most challenging due to the high levels of security in government and the very complex requirements.

GRID APPLICATIONS

Based on our earlier discussion, we can align Grid Computing applications to have common needs, such as what is described in (but not limited to) the following items:

- Application partitioning that involves breaking the problem into discrete pieces
- Discovery and scheduling of tasks and workflow
- Data communications distributing the problem data where and when it is required
- Provisioning and distributing application codes to specific system nodes
- Results management assisting in the decision processes of the environment
- Autonomic features such as self-configuration, self-optimization, self-recovery, and self-management

Let us now explore some of these Grid applications and their usage patterns. We start with schedulers, which form the core component in most of the computational grids.

Schedulers

Schedulers are types of applications responsible for the management of jobs, such as allocating resources needed for any specific job, partitioning of jobs to schedule parallel execution of tasks, data management, event correlation, and service-level management capabilities. These schedulers then form a hierarchical structure, with meta-schedulers that form the root and other lower level schedulers, while providing specific scheduling capabilities that form the leaves. These schedulers may be constructed with a local scheduler implementation approach for specific job execution, or another meta-scheduler or a cluster scheduler for parallel executions. Figure 1.2 shows this concept.

The jobs submitted to Grid Computing schedulers are evaluated based on their service-level requirements, and then allocated to the respective resources for execution. This will involve

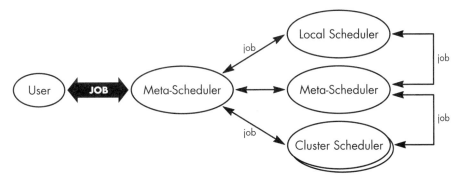

Figure 1.2
The scheduler hierarchy embodies local, meta-level, and cluster schedulers.

complex workflow management and data movement activities to occur on a regular basis. There are schedulers that must provide capabilities for areas such as (but not limited to):

- Advanced resource reservation
- Service-level agreement validation and enforcement
- Job and resource policy management and enforcement for best turnaround times within the allowable budget constraints
- Monitoring job executions and status
- Rescheduling and corrective actions of partial failover situations

Later in this book, full treatment is provided for many of the most notable scheduler and meta-scheduler implementations.

Resource Broker

The resource broker provides *pairing* services between the service requester and the service provider. This pairing enables the selection of best available resources from the service provider for the execution of a specific task. These resource brokers collect information (e.g., resource availability, usage models, capabilities, and pricing information) from the respective resources, and use this information source in the pairing process.

Figure 1.3 illustrates the use of a resource broker for purposes of this discussion. This particular resource broker provides feedback to the users on the available resources. In general cases, the resource broker may select the suitable scheduler for the resource execution task, and collaborate with the scheduler to execute the task(s).

The pairing process in a resource broker involves allocation and support functions such as:

- Allocating the appropriate resource or a combination of resources for the task execution
- Supporting users' deadline and budget constraints for scheduling optimizations

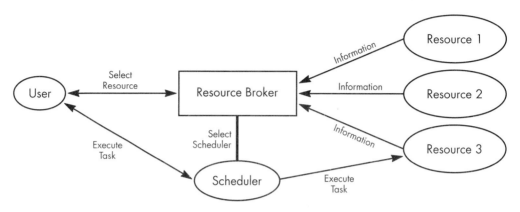

Figure 1.3
The resource broker collects information from the respective resources, and utilizes this
information source in the pairing process.

Load Balancing

The Grid Computing infrastructure load-balancing issues are concerned with the traditional
load-balancing distribution of workload among the resources in a Grid Computing environment.
This load-balancing feature must always be integrated into any system in order to avoid processing delays and overcommitment of resources. These kinds of applications can be built in connection with schedulers and resource managers.

The workload can be pushed outbound to the resources, based on the availability state and/or
resources, and can then pull the jobs from the schedulers depending on their availability. This
level of load balancing involves partitioning of jobs, identifying the resources, and queueing of
the jobs. There are cases when resource reservations might be required, as well as running multiple jobs in parallel.

Another feature that might be of interest for load balancing is support for failure detection and
management. These load distributors can redistribute the jobs to other resources if needed.

Grid Portals

Grid portals are similar to Web portals, in the sense they provide uniform access to the grid
resources. For example, grid portals provide capabilities for Grid Computing resource authentication, remote resource access, scheduling capabilities, and monitoring status information.
These kinds of portals help to alleviate the complexity of task management through customizable and personalized graphical interfaces for the users. This, in turn, alleviates the need for end
users to have more domain knowledge than on the specific details of grid resource management.

Some examples of these grid portal capabilities are noted in the following list:

- Querying databases or LDAP servers for resource-specific information

- File transfer facilities such as file upload, download, integration with custom software, and so on
- Manage job through job status feedbacks
- Allocate the resources for the execution of specific tasks
- Security management
- Provide personalized solutions

In short, these grid portals help free end users from the complexity of job management and resource allocation so they can concentrate more on their domain of expertise. There are a number of standards and software development toolkits available to develop custom portals. The emerging Web services and Web service portal standards will play a more significant role in portal development.

Integrated Solutions

Many of the global industry sectors have witnessed the emergence of a number of integrated grid application solutions in the last few years. This book focuses on this success factor.

These integrated solutions are a combination of the existing advanced middleware and application functionalities, combined to provide more coherent and high performance results across the Grid Computing environment.

Integrated Grid Computing solutions will have more enhanced features to support more complex utilization of grids such as coordinated and optimized resource sharing, enhanced security management, cost optimizations, and areas yet to be explored. It is straightforward to see that these integrated solutions in both the commercial and noncommercial worlds sustain high values and significant cost reductions. Grid applications can achieve levels of flexibility utilizing infrastructures provided by application and middleware frameworks.

In the next section we introduce and explain the grid infrastructure. Today, the most notable integrated solutions in the commercial and industry sectors are utility computing, on-demand solutions, and resource virtualizations infrastructures. Let us briefly explore aspects of some of these infrastructure solutions. We will provide an additional, more focused treatment in subsequent chapters of this book.

GRID INFRASTRUCTURE

The grid infrastructure forms the core foundation for successful grid applications. This infrastructure is a complex combination of a number of capabilities and resources identified for the specific problem and environment being addressed.

In initial stages of delivering any Grid Computing application infrastructure, the developers/service providers must consider the following questions in order to identify the core infrastructure support required for that environment:

1. What problem(s) are we trying to solve for the user? How do we address grid enablement simpler, while addressing the user's application simpler? How does the developer (programmatically) help the user to be able to quickly gain access and utilize the application to best fit their problem resolution needs?

2. How difficult is it to use the grid tool? Are grid developers providing a flexible environment for the intended user community?

3. Is there anything not yet considered that would make it easier for grid service providers to create tools for the grid, suitable for the problem domain?

4. What are the open standards, environments, and regulations grid service providers must address?

In the early development stages of grid applications, numerous vertical "towers" and middleware solutions were often developed to solve Grid Computing problems. These various middleware and solution approaches were developed for fairly narrow and limited problem-solving domains, such as middleware to deal with numerical analysis, customized data access grids, and other narrow problems. Today, with the emergence and convergence of grid service-oriented technologies,[3] including the interoperable XML[4]-based solutions becoming ever more present and industry providers with a number of reusable grid middleware solutions facilitating the following requirement areas, it is becoming simpler to quickly deploy valuable solutions. Figure 1.4 shows this topology of middleware topics.

In general, a Grid Computing infrastructure component must address several potentially complicated areas in many stages of the implementation. These areas are:

- Security
- Resource management
- Information services
- Data management

Let us further examine the significance of each of these above components.

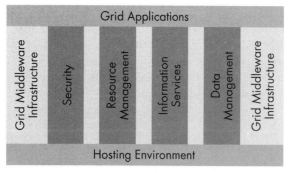

Figure 1.4
Grid middleware topic areas are becoming more sophisticated at an aggressive rate.

Security

The heterogeneous nature of resources and their differing security policies are complicated and complex in the security schemes of a Grid Computing environment. These computing resources are hosted in differing security domains and heterogeneous platforms. Simply speaking, our middleware solutions must address local security integration, secure identity mapping, secure access/authentication, secure federation, and trust management.

The other security requirements are often centered on the topics of data integrity, confidentiality, and information privacy. The Grid Computing data exchange must be protected using secure communication channels, including SSL/TLS and oftentimes in combination with secure message exchange mechanisms such as WS-Security. The most notable security infrastructure used for securing grid is the Grid Security Infrastructure (GSI). In most cases, GSI provides capabilities for single sign-on, heterogeneous platform integration and secure resource access/authentication.

The latest and most notable security solution is the use of WS-Security standards. This mechanism provides message-level, end-to-end security needed for complex and interoperable secure solutions. In the coming years we will see a number of secure grid environments using a combination of GSI and WS-Security mechanisms for secure message exchanges. We will discuss the details of security mechanisms provided by these standards later in this book.

Resource Management

The tremendously large number and the heterogeneous potential of Grid Computing resources causes the resource management challenge to be a significant effort topic in Grid Computing environments. These resource management scenarios often include resource discovery, resource inventories, fault isolation, resource provisioning, resource monitoring, a variety of autonomic capabilities,[5] and service-level management activities. The most interesting aspect of the resource management area is the selection of the correct resource from the grid resource pool, based on the service-level requirements, and then to efficiently provision them to facilitate user needs.

Let us explore an example of a job management system, where the resource management feature identifies the job, allocates the suitable resources for the execution of the job, partitions the job if necessary, and provides feedback to the user on job status. This job scheduling process includes moving the data needed for various computations to the appropriate Grid Computing resources, and mechanisms for dispatching the job results.

It is important to understand multiple service providers can host Grid Computing resources across many domains, such as security, management, networking services, and application functionalities. Operational and application resources may also be hosted on different hardware and software platforms. In addition to this complexity, Grid Computing middleware must provide efficient monitoring of resources to collect the required matrices on utilization, availability, and other information.

One causal impact of this fact is (as an example) the security and the ability for the grid service provider to reach out and probe into other service provider domains in order to obtain and reason about key operational information (i.e., to reach across a service provider environment to ascertain firewall and router volume-related specifics, or networking switch status, or application server status). This oftentimes becomes complicated across several dimensions, and has to be resolved by a meeting-of-the-minds between all service providers, such as messaging necessary information to all providers, when and where it is required.

Another valuable and very critical feature across the Grid Computing infrastructure is found in the area of provisioning; that is, to provide autonomic capabilities for self-management, self-diagnosis, self-healing, and self-configuring. The most notable resource management middleware solution is the Grid Resource Allocation Manager (GRAM). This resource provides a robust job management service for users, which includes job allocation, status management, data distribution, and start/stop jobs.

Information Services

Information services are fundamentally concentrated on providing valuable information respective to the Grid Computing infrastructure resources. These services leverage and entirely depend on the providers of information such as resource availability, capacity, and utilization, just to name a few. This information is valuable and mandatory feedback respective to the resources managers discussed earlier in this chapter. These information services enable service providers to most efficiently allocate resources for the variety of very specific tasks related to the Grid Computing infrastructure solution.

In addition, developers and providers can also construct grid solutions to reflect portals, and utilize meta-schedulers and meta-resource managers. These metrics are helpful in service-level management (SLA) in conjunction with the resource policies. This information is resource specific and is provided based on the schema pertaining to that resource. We may need higher level indexing services or data aggregators and transformers to convert these resource-specific data into valuable information sources for the end user.

For example, a resource may provide operating system information, while yet another resource might provide information on hardware configuration, and we can then group this resource information, reason with it, and then suggest a "best" price combination on selecting the operating system on other certain hardware. This combinatorial approach to reasoning is very straightforward in a Grid Computing infrastructure, simply due to the fact that all key resources are shared, as is the information correlated respective to the resources.

Data Management

Data forms the single most important asset in a Grid Computing system. This data may be input into the resource, and the results from the resource on the execution of a specific task. If the infrastructure is not designed properly, the data movement in a geographically distributed system can quickly cause scalability problems. It is well understood that the data must be near to the computation where it is used. This data movement in any Grid Computing environment requires absolutely secure data transfers, both to and from the respective resources. The current advances surrounding data management are tightly focusing on virtualized data storage mechanisms, such as storage area networks (SAN), network file systems, dedicated storage servers, and virtual databases. These virtualization mechanisms in data storage solutions and common access mechanisms (e.g., relational SQLs, Web services, etc.) help developers and providers to design data management concepts into the Grid Computing infrastructure with much more flexibility than traditional approaches.

Some of the considerations developers and providers must factor into decisions are related to selecting the most appropriate data management mechanism for Grid Computing infrastructures. This includes the size of the data repositories, resource geographical distribution, security requirements, schemes for replication and caching facilities, and the underlying technologies utilized for storage and data access.

So far in this introductory chapter we have been discussing the details surrounding many aspects of the middleware framework requirements, specifically the emergence of service provider-oriented architectures[6] and, hence, the open and extremely powerful utility value of XML-based interoperable messages. These combined, provide a wide range of capabilities that deal with interoperability problems, and come up with a solution that is suitable for the dynamic virtual organizational grids. The most important activity noted today in this area is the Open Grid Service Architecture (OGSA) and its surrounding standard initiatives. Significant detail is recorded on this architecture, and will be given full treatment in subsequent chapters in this book. The OGSA provides a common interface solution to grid services, and all the information has been conveniently encoded using XML as the standard. This provides a common approach to information services and resource management for Grid Computing infrastructures.

This introductory chapter has discussed many of the chapters and some of their detail that will be presented throughout this book. This introductory discussion has been presented at a high level, and more detailed discussions with simple-to-understand graphics will follow.

CONCLUSION

So far we have been describing and walking through overview discussion topics on the Grid Computing discipline that will be discussed further throughout this book, including the Grid Computing evolution, the applications, and the infrastructure requirements for any grid environment.

In addition to this, we have discussed when one should use Grid Computing disciplines, and the factors developers and providers must consider in the implementation phases. With this introduction we can now explore deeper into the various aspects of a Grid Computing system, its evolution across the industries, and the current architectural efforts underway throughout the world.

The proceeding chapters in this book introduce the reader to this new, evolutionary era of Grid Computing, in a concise, hard-hitting, and easy-to-understand manner.

NOTES

1. The term "blades" refers to a smaller circuit inserted into a larger machine footprint, with many other blades, where each blade is performing, as it's own distinct computer. This notion is commonly referred to as "blade computing."

2. A *petabyte* is a term that indicates a unit of computer memory or data storage capacity equal to 1,024 terabytes (or 2^{50} bytes): one quadrillion bytes.

3. Please refer to the book *Business On Demand: Technology and Strategy Perspectives* (Fellenstein, 2004) for further details and precision on important technologies, Grid Computing, and key strategy perspectives.

4. XML (Extensible Markup Language) is a meta-language written in SGML (Standardized Markup Language) that allows one to design a markup language used to allow for the easy interchange of documents and data across the World Wide Web.

5. Please refer to Fellenstein (2004) for further details and precision on important technologies, Grid Computing, and key strategy perspectives.

6. Please refer to Fellenstein (2004) for further details and precision on important service provider technologies, Grid Computing, and key strategy perspectives on both topics.

Grid Computing Worldwide Initiatives

The last decade has introduced a number of changes to the way that computing facilities have been traditionally utilized. The emergence of distributed computing and its widespread acceptance has had an unprecedented impact on the utility of computing facilities.

Internet computing emerged as the strong motivating factor to decentralize these computing facilities. As of now, the Internet, and hence wide area networking, has become the ubiquitous standard for the electronic world. By the beginning of this century, the wide area distributed computing discipline has taken a new turn with more emphasis on controlled and coordinated resource sharing among dynamic groups of organizations and/or individuals.

In Chapter 2, we discuss the contributions of the major Grid Computing organizations that are working on an agreeable open process, standardization, and interoperable implementation of the grid to enable the community for manageable resource sharing and coordination. The focus of Chapter 3 is the so-called "grid problem," a real grid problem, and how the grid architecture is defined to solve the problem.

In this part of the book, we explore the concepts around virtual organizations and how the new grid architecture is adequate to understand and solve the complex problems of virtualization of resources and organizational grouping. In Chapter 4, we go through the grid computing road map where we will discuss how the grid is evolving with more emphasis on open standard process, service orientation, and knowledge sharing. This includes an overview on the existing technology fabric for the grid, the evolving service-oriented architecture model with more interoperable solutions, and finally the knowledge-based semantic grid with more focus on interchangeable metadata.

Grid Computing Organizations and Their Roles

G rid Computing organizations and their roles can be broadly classified into four categories based on their functional role in Grid Computing. These roles are best described as:

- Organizations developing grid standards and best practices guidelines
- Organizations developing Grid Computing toolkits, frameworks, and middleware solutions
- Organizations building and using grid-based solutions to solve their computing, data, and network requirements
- Organizations working to adopt grid concepts into commercial products, via utility computing, and Business On Demand[1] computing

Figure 2.1 shows these categories, while also noting the technologies involved in the many areas of Grid Computing. In subsequent chapters of this book, we will explain these technologies in

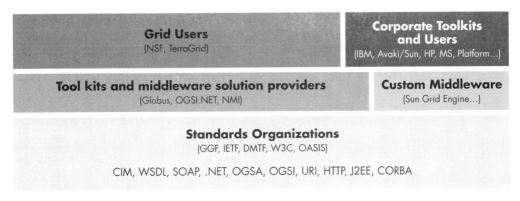

Figure 2.1
The basic classifications of Grid Computing organizations.

Figure 2.2
Some of prominent Grid Computing organizations worldwide.

greater detail. There is also another book in this IBM Business On Demand book series which goes into deeper discussions on the subject: *Business On Demand: Technology and Strategy Perspectives* (Fellenstein, 2004).

There are many organizations in the world striving to achieve new and innovative Grid Computing environments. In this chapter we will explore not only the world-class examples of Grid Computing environments, but we will also explore those organizations involved in the plight. The IBM Corporation is a leader in the pursuit of Business On Demand Grid Computing environments and the corporation itself has enabled a global Business On Demand environment. IBM is, today, working with a large number of global customers in the same endeavor.

ORGANIZATIONS DEVELOPING GRID STANDARDS AND BEST PRACTICE GUIDELINES

These organizations are responsible for refining the grid standardization process and defining the best practice guidelines for the scientific and industry usage of grid.

The most prominent among such organizations is Global Grid Forum (GGF). There are other standards organizations working closely with GGF in this process, including OASIS (Organization for the Advancement of Structured Information Standards), W3C (World Wide Web Consortium), IETF (the Internet Engineering Task Force), and DMTF (the Distributed Management Task Force).[2] GGF is mainly working in the Grid arena while others have more broad-based programs covering other parts of the computing industry such as network, resource, business, and Internet standards. For example, W3C is working on the standardization of Web and Web-related technologies, including Web services, eXtensible Markup Language (XML), and Semantic Web. GGF is working closely with these organizations in defining the grid standards aligned with the other open standard processes and providing inputs and requirements to other standards organizations.

Global Grid Forum (GGF)

The GGF[3] was established a couple of years ago as a public community forum for the discussion of grid technology issues. The GGF enables a means of coordinating Grid Computing technology efforts, promoting reuse and interoperability, and sharing the results. As of now, there are more than 400 organizations involved with GGF from around the world. This includes scientific research institutions, universities, and commercial organizations.

The GGF's primary objective is to promote and support development, deployment, and implementation of grid technologies and applications via creation and documentation of best practices—specifications, use cases, architecture, and implementation guidelines.

The basic goals of the GGF are to:

- Create an open process for the development of grid agreements and specifications
- Create grid specifications, architecture documents, and best practice guidelines
- Manage and version controls the documents and specifications
- Handle intellectual property policies
- Provide a forum for information exchange and collaboration
- Improve collaboration among the people involved with grid research, grid framework builders, grid deployment, and grid users
- Create best practice guidelines from the experience of the technologies associated with Grid Computing
- Educate on advances in the grid technologies and share experiences among the people of interest

The organization consists of different work areas, with research groups and work groups for each area. The work groups are the main activity centers of the GGF. These work groups are created to address a research, implementation, and operational area related to the infrastructure for building any "grid."

The major work areas of the GGF are as follows:

- Application and programming environments
- Architecture
- Data
- Information systems and performance
- Peer-to-peer: Desktop grids
- Scheduling and resource management
- Security

As of today, one of the major activities in GGF that is attracting the grid community is the architecture model based on the open standard Web service architecture, called Open Grid Service Architecture (OGSA). A detailed discussion on this emerging standard is a necessity which we will undertake in a subsequent chapter. With open standards as the foundation and software integration, OGSA has emerged as the core grid technology for future resource sharing, especially with the newly added commercial dimension to Grid solutions.

ORGANIZATIONS DEVELOPING GRID COMPUTING TOOLKITS AND THE FRAMEWORK

To achieve a successful adoption of Grid Computing requires an adequate infrastructure, security services, key services, applications, and portals. Let us now explore and identify some of the most prominent organizations responsible for the toolkits, middleware, and framework for Grid Computing.

Globus

The Globus[4] project is a multi-institutional research effort to create a basic infrastructure and high-level services for a computational grid. A computational grid is defined as hardware and software infrastructure that provides dependable, consistent, pervasive, and inexpensive access to high-end computational capabilities (Foster & Kesselman, 1998). They have now evolved into an infrastructure for resource sharing (hardware, software, applications, and so on) among heterogeneous virtual organizations. These grids enable high creativity by increasing the average and peak computational performance available to important applications regardless of the spatial distribution of both resources and users.

The details on Globus infrastructure provided in Figure 2.3 are based on the latest release from Globus called Globus GT3. Globus provides layered software architecture with a low-level infrastructure to host high-level services defined for grid. These high-level services are related to resource discovery, allocation, monitoring, management, security, data management, and access. The lower layer infrastructure (GT3 Core) provides a framework to host the high-level services.

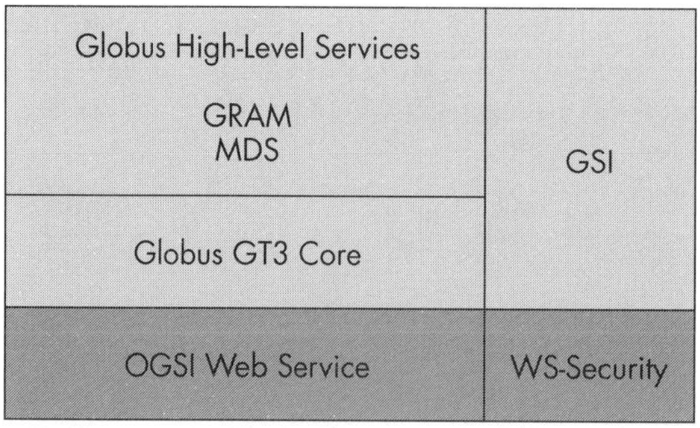

Figure 2.3
Globus GT3 middleware, core, and high-level services present a wide variety of capabilities.

Some of the core high-level services included with the existing Globus toolkit are found in the following discussion.

Globus Resource Allocation Manager (GRAM)

GRAM provides resource allocation, process creation, monitoring, and management services. GRAM simplifies the use of remote systems by providing a single standard interface for requesting and using remote system resources for the execution of "jobs." The most common use of GRAM is the remote job submission and control facility. However, GRAM does not provide job scheduling or resource brokering capabilities. We could see that the job scheduling facilities are normally provided by the local system. GRAM uses a high-level Resource Specification Language (RSL) to specify the commands and maps them to the local schedulers and computers.

Grid Security Infrastructure (GSI)

GSI provides a single-sign-on, run anywhere authentication service with support for local control over access rights and mapping from global to local user identities. While keeping the existing GSI mechanisms, the current GSI3 standard is in alignment with the Web service security standards by defining a GSI profile for WS-Security.[5]

Information Services

A GT3 Information service provides information about grid resources, for use in resource discovery, selection, and optimization.

The Monitoring and Discovery Service (MDS) is an extensible grid information service that combines data discovery mechanisms with the Lightweight Directory Access Protocol (LDAP). The MDS provides a uniform framework for providing and accessing system configuration and status information such as computer server configuration, network status, or the locations of replicated datasets. The current GT3 framework merges the MDS with the XML data framework for better integration with existing Web services and OGSA.

The latest Globus Toolkit (GT3) is a java implementation of the OGSI specification. The discussion on the architecture and programming model of the GT3 infrastructure software and the details on the high-level services are deferred to the last section of this book.

Legion

Legion,[6] a middleware project initiated by the University of Virginia, is object-based metasystems software for grid applications. The goal of the Legion project is to promote the principled design of distributed system software by providing standard object representations for processors, data systems, file systems, and so on. Legion applications are developed in terms of these standard objects. Groups of users can construct a shared virtual workspace to collaborate on research and exchange information.

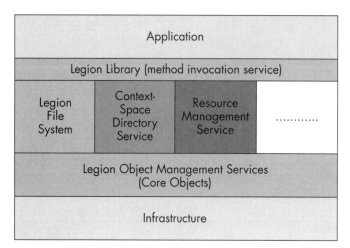

Figure 2.4
Legion application architecture.

Figure 2.4 shows the architecture of a Legion system. Legion sits on top of the user's operating system and acts as mediator between its own host(s) and other required resources. Legion's scheduling and security policies act on behalf of the user in undertaking time-consuming negotiations with outside systems and system administrators. To allow users to take advantage of a wide range of possible resources, Legion offers a user-controlled naming system called *context space*, so that users can easily create and use objects in distributed systems.

An Interface Definition Language (IDL) is defined to describe the method signatures (name, parameter, and return values) supported by the object interface. We could see that these objects provide a scalable persistence mechanism by storing the inactive objects (objects in "inert" state) to the secondary storage.

Some of the important characteristics of Legion systems are summarized below.

Everything is an object.   In a Legion system, *Legion Object* represents a variety of hardware and software resources, which respond to member function invocations from other objects in the system. Legion defines the message format and high-level protocol for object interaction (through IDL), but not the programming language or the communications protocol.

Classes manage their own instances.   Every Legion object is defined and managed by its *class object*. Class objects are given system-level responsibility; classes create new instances, schedule them for execution, activate and deactivate them, and provide information about their current location to client objects. These classes whose instances are themselves classes are called *metaclasses*.

Users can provide their own classes.   Legion allows its users to define and build their own "class" objects. This enables the Legion programmers to have a flexible architecture model for their "metaclasses" with the capabilities to determine and even change the system-level mechanisms of their objects.

Core objects implement common services. Legion defines the interface and basic functionality of a set of core object types that support basic system services, such as naming, binding, object creation, activation, deactivation, and deletion.

Some of the core objects defined by the Legion system are:

- Host objects: Abstractions of processing resources which may represent a single processor or multiple hosts and processors
- Vault objects: Provide persistent storage for scalable persistence of the objects
- Binding object: Maps the object IDs to the physical addresses
- Implementation objects: Allow legion objects to run as processes in the systemand contain a machine code that is executed on a request to create the object or activate it.

Figure 2.5 shows Legion object A with its class object (metaclass) and the corresponding basic system services.

In 1997, the first Legion toolkit was released, and in the following year, Applied Metacomputing (later relaunched as Avaki Corporation) was established to exploit the toolkit for commercial purposes.

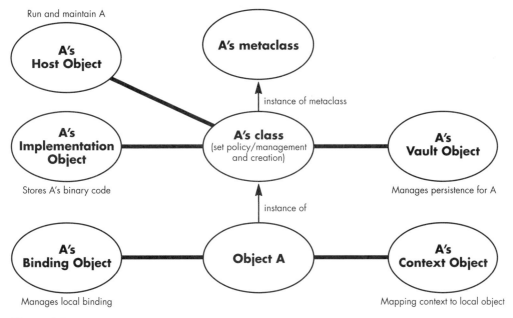

Figure 2.5
Legion core object and relationship.

Condor and Condor-G

Condor[7] is a tool for harnessing the capacity of idle workstations for computational tasks. Condor is well suited for parameter studies and high throughput computing, where jobs generally do not need to communicate with each other.

We can classify Condor as a specialized workload management system for computation-intensive jobs. Like other full-featured batch systems, Condor provides a job queuing mechanism, scheduling policy, priority scheme, resource monitoring, and resource management. Upon receiving serial or parallel jobs from the user, the Condor system places them into a queue, chooses when and where to run the jobs based upon a policy, carefully monitors their progress, and ultimately informs the user upon completion.

We can make use of Condor to manage a cluster of dedicated compute nodes. It is suitable for effectively harnessing the CPU power from idle workstations. Condor has mechanisms for matching resource requests (jobs) with resource offers (machines).

While Condor software tools focus on harnessing the power of opportunistic and dedicated resources, Condor-G is a derivative software system, which leverages the software from Condor and Globus with major focus on the job management services for grid applications. This is a combination of interdomain resource management protocols of Globus (GRAM, Index Services) with the intradomain resource management methods of Condor. Figure 2.6 shows a sample usage of Condor-G in combination with Globus. As shown, Condor-G contains a GASS Server,

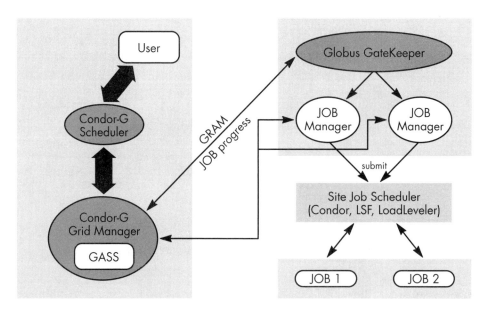

Figure 2.6
Remote execution of Condor-G on Globus-managed resource using Globus Job manager.

which is used to transfer jobs to and from the execution center. The Condor-G Grid manager uses GRAM to get the Job progress information from Globus Gate Keeper.

Condor software is used by both scientific and commercial organizations. The major scientific initiative that uses Condor includes NSF Middleware Initiative (NMI), Grid Physics Network (GriPhyN), International Virtual Data Grid laboratory (iVDGL), TerraGrid, and so on. Some of the prominent commercial uses of condor software involve solving computational Grid Computing problems, as done by Micron Technologies, CORE Digital Pictures, and NUG30 Optimization Problem Solver.

Nimrod

Nimrod[8] provides a user interface for describing the "parameter sweep" problems, with resulting independent jobs being submitted to a resource management system.

Nimrod-G is a derivative software system, which harnesses the software from Nimrod and Globus to harness multi-domain resources as if they all belong to the one personal domain. It provides a simple *declarative parametric language* for expressing the parameters for execution. This system exposes novel resource management and job scheduling algorithms based on the economic principles of computing. Such a set of resource trading services is called GRACE (Grid Architecture for Computational Economy). GRACE provides mechanisms to negotiate on the QoS parameters, deadlines, and computational costs. In addition, it offers incentive for relaxing requirements. We could see that depending on users' QoS requirements, these resource brokers dynamically lease Grid services at runtime depending on their cost, quality, and availability.

Leveraging the services provided by grid middleware systems develops the Nimrod-G toolkit and resource broker. These middleware systems include Globus, Legion, GRACE, and so forth.

As illustrated in Figure 2.7, the Nimrod architecture defines the following components:

1. Nimrod-G clients, which can provide tools for creating parameter sweep applications, steering and control monitors, and customized end-user applications and GUIs
2. The Nimrod-G resource broker, which consists of a Task farming engine (TFE), a scheduler that performs resource discovery, trading and scheduling features, a dispatcher and actuator, and agents for managing the jobs on the resource

It is important to note that the Nimrod-G broker provides its services by leveraging the grid middleware systems including Globus, Legion, Condor, and so on.

As we have previously discussed, the core feature of the Nimrod-G toolkit is the support for user-defined deadlines. For example: "Get this simulation done in 10 minutes with a budget of USD $200." Also, budget constraint for scheduling optimizations is a part of the core features.

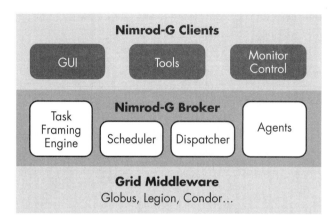

Figure 2.7
Architecture of Nimrod-G.

Nimrod-G facilitates the execution of the user requirement by managing supply and demand of resources in the grid using a set of resource trading services.

The most important scheduling algorithms used in Nimrod-G are:

- Cost optimization—uses the cheapest resource
- Time optimizations—results in parallel execution of the job
- Cost-time optimization—similar to cost optimization but if there are multiple jobs with the same cost, then the time factor is taken into consideration
- Conservative time strategy—similar to time optimization, but guarantees that each unprocessed job has a minimum budget per job

---

PARAMETRIC COMPUTATIONAL EXPERIMENTS

Parametric computational experiments are becoming increasingly important in science and engineering as a means of exploring the behavior of complex systems. For example, a flight engineer may explore the behavior of a wing by running a computational model of the airfoil multiple times while varying key parameters such as angle of attack, air speed, and so on.

The results of these multiple experiments yield a picture of how the wing behaves in different parts of parametric space.

Many practitioners of Grid Computing believe that economic policy/criteria-driven Grid Computing, as depicted by Nimrod-G, is a major interest to the utility computing world.

UNICORE (UNiform Interface to COmputer REsource)

The UNICORE[9] project is funded by the German Ministry of Education and Research with the design goal including a uniform and easy-access graphical user interface (GUI), open architecture based on the concept of an abstract job, a consistent security architecture, minimal interface with local administrative procedures, and exploitation of the existing and emerging technologies including Web and Java.

UNICOREpro was produced within the UNICORE to provide a uniform interface for job preparation and secure submission of the job similar to a portal. This enables users to create workflow for job execution and control execution behaviors. This is an open source project developed using Java technology. The UNICOREpro server provides capabilities for authorization, job management, data transfer, and batch interface.

A project called GRIP (GRid Interoperability Project) was started in 2002 to achieve the interoperability between UNICORE and Globus. The EUROGRID software is based on the UNICORE system developed and used by the leading German HPC centers.

NSF Middleware Initiative (NMI)

NMI[10] was created by the National Science Foundation (NSF) to help scientists and researchers use the Internet to effectively share instruments, laboratories, and data and to collaborate with each other. Middleware is software that connects two or more otherwise separate applications across the Internet or local area networks.

Middleware makes resource sharing seem transparent to the end user, providing capabilities, consistency, security, and privacy.

NMI consists of two teams:

> **Grid Research Integration Deployment and Support (GRIDS) Center.** The
> GRIDS[11] center is responsible for defining, developing, deploying, and supporting an
> integrated and stable middleware infrastructure created from a number of open source
> grid and other distributed computing technology frameworks. It intends to support 21st-
> century science and engineering applications by working closely with a number of uni-
> versities and research organizations.
> Some of the open source packages included in this middleware are Globus Toolkit, Con-
> dor-G, GSI-OpenSSH, Network Weather service, Grid Packaging Tools, GridConfig,
> MPICH-G2, MyProxy, and so on.
> **Enterprise and Desktop Integration Technologies (EDIT) Consortium.** EDIT[12]
> develops tools, practices, and architectures to leverage campus infrastructures to facili-
> tate multi-institutional collaboration.
> EDIT provides software to support a wider variety of desktop security, video, and enter-
> prise uses with a directory schema. This facilitates the federated model of directory-

enabled interrealm authentication and authorization. In addition, they are responsible for conventions and best practice guidelines, architecture documents, policies, and to provide services to manage the middleware. Some of the open sources packages included in this middleware are: LDAP Operational ORCA Kollector (LOOK), Privilege and Role Management Infrastructure Standards Validation (PERMIS), openSAMIL, and others.

The latest release (Release 3) of the NMI middleware consists of 16 software packages. The above two teams of the NMI is creating production-quality middleware using open-source and open-standards approaches. They continue to refine processes for team-based software development, documentation, and technical support. The software packages included in the NMI solution have been tested and debugged by NMI team members, so that various users, campuses, and institutions can easily deploy them. In addition, it helps to facilitate directory-enabled (LDAP) sharing and exchanging of information to support authentication and authorization among campuses and institutions.

The aforementioned best practices and policy deliverables have been reviewed and deployed by leading campuses and institutions. Some of the major initiatives using this middleware suite include NEESgrid (Network for Earthquake Engineering Simulation), GriPhyN, and the iVDGL.

ORGANIZATIONS BUILDING AND USING GRID-BASED SOLUTIONS TO SOLVE COMPUTING, DATA, AND NETWORK REQUIREMENTS

These organizations and individuals are the real users of Grid Computing. They are benefiting from resource sharing and virtualization. As of now these projects are mostly in the scientific areas. We will be discussing some of the major grid projects and infrastructures around the world. In general, these grid users need:

- On-demand construction of virtual computing system with the capabilities to solve the problems at hand including scarcity of computing power, data storage, and real-time processing
- A provision for collaborative visualization of the results of the above process
- A dynamic construction of virtual organizations to solve certain specific problems at hand

United States Department of Energy: Science Grid (DOE)

The DOE Science Grid[13] aims to provide an advanced distributed computing infrastructure based on Grid Computing middleware and tools to enable a high degree of scalability in scientific computing. The vision is to revolutionize the use of computing in science by making the construction and use of large-scale systems of diverse resources as easy as using today's desktop environments.

The following describes characteristics of DOE:

- Most of the DOE projects are widely distributed among collaborators and non-collaborators. It requires a cyberinfrastructure that supports the process of distributed science with sharable resources including expensive and complex scientific instruments.
- All of the science areas need high-speed networks and advanced middleware to discover, manage, and access computing and storage systems.

The DOE Science Grid is an integrated and advanced infrastructure that delivers:

- Computing capacity adequate for the tasks in hand
- Data capacity sufficient for scientific tasks with location independence and manageability
- Communication power sufficient for the above tasks
- Software services with rich environments that let scientists focus on the science simulation and analysis aspects rather than on management of computing, data, and communication resources

The construction of grids across five major DOE facilities provides the computing and data resources. To date major accomplishments include the following:

- Integration of DOE's Office of Science supercomputing center providing large-scale storage systems into the grid
- Design and deployment of a grid security infrastructure for collaboration with U.S. and European High Energy Physics projects, helping to create a single-sign-on solution within the grid environment

The following work is used by the DOE's Particle Physics Data Grid, Earth Systems Grid, and Fusion Grid projects:

- A resource monitoring and debugging infrastructure for managing these widely distributed resources
- Several DOE applications use this grid infrastructure including computational chemistry, ground water transport, climate modeling, bio informatics, and so on.

European Union: EUROGRID Project

The EUROGRID[14] project is a shared-cost Research and Technology Development project (RTD) granted by the European Commission, with the participation of 11 partners and 6 European Union countries, in order to create an international network of high performance computing centers. This project will demonstrate the use of GRIDs in selected scientific and industrial communities in order to address the specific requirements of these communities, and highlight the benefits of using GRIDs.

The major objectives of the EUROGRID project are:

- To establish a European GRID network of leading high performance computing centers from different European countries

- To operate and support the EUROGRID software infrastructure
- To develop important GRID software components and to integrate them into EUROGRID (fast file transfer, resource broker, interface for coupled applications, and interactive access)
- To demonstrate distributed simulation codes from different application areas (biomolecular simulations, weather prediction, coupled CAE simulations, structural analysis, real-time data processing, etc.)
- To contribute to the international GRID development and work with the leading international GRID projects

The application-specific work packages identified for the EUROGRID project are described in the following areas:

Bio Grid. The BioGRID project develops interfaces to enable chemists and biologists to submit work to high performance center facilities via a uniform interface from their workstations, without having to worry about the details of how to run particular packages on different architectures.

Metro Grid. The main goal of the Metro Grid project is the development of an application service provider (ASP) solution, which allows anyone to run a high resolution numerical weather prediction model on demand.

Computer-Aided Engineering (CAE) Grid. This work project focuses on industrial CAE applications including automobile and aerospace industries. It aims at providing services to high performance computing (HPC) customers who require huge computing power to solve their engineering problems.

The major partners in this work package are Debis SystemHaus and EADS Corporate Research Center. They are working to exploit the CAE features like code coupling (to improve system design by reducing the prototyping and testing costs) and ASP-type services (designing application-specific user interfaces for job submission).

High Performance Center (HPC) Research Grid. This HPC research grid is used as a test-bed for the development of distributed applications, and as an arena for cooperative work among major scientific challenges, using computational resources distributed on a European scale. The major partners in this work-package are the HPC centers.

The EUROGRID software is based on the UNICORE system developed and used by the leading German HPC centers.

European Union: Data Grid Project

DataGrid[15] is a project funded by the European Union that aims to enable access to geographically distributed computing power and storage facilities belonging to different institutions. This will provide the necessary resources to process huge amounts of data coming from scientific experiments in different disciplines.

The three real data-intensive computing applications areas covered by the project are:

- High Energy Physics
- Biology and Medical Image Processing
- Earth Observations

High Energy Physics (led by CERN, Switzerland)

One of the main challenges for High Energy Physics is to answer longstanding questions about the fundamental particles of matter and the forces acting between them. In particular, the goal is to explain *why some particles are much heavier than others, and why particles have mass at all.* To that end, CERN is building the *Large Hadron Collider (LHS)*, one of the most powerful particle accelerators.

The search on LHS will generate huge amounts of data. The DataGrid Project is providing the solution for storing and processing this data. A multitiered, hierarchical computing model will be adopted to share data and computing power among multiple institutions. The Tier-0 center is located at CERN and is linked by high-speed networks to approximately 10 major Tier-1 data-processing centers. These will fan out the data to a large number of smaller ones (Tier-2).

Biology and Medical Image Processing (led by CNRS, France)

The storage and exploitation of genomes and the huge flux of data coming from post-genomics puts growing pressure on computing and storage resources within existing physical laboratories. Medical images are currently distributed over medical image production sites (radiology departments, hospitals).

Although there is a need today, as there is no standard for sharing data between sites, there is an increasing need for remote medical data access and processing.

The DataGrid project's biology test-bed is providing the platform for the development of new algorithms on data mining, databases, code management, and graphical interface tools. It is facilitating the sharing of genomic and medical imaging databases for the benefit of international cooperation and health care.

Earth Observations (led by ESA/ESRIN, Italy)

The European Space Agency missions download *100 gigabytes of raw images per day* from space. Dedicated ground infrastructures have been set up to handle the data produced by instruments onboard the satellites. The analysis of atmospheric ozone data has been selected as a specific test-bed for the DataGrid. Moreover, the project will demonstrate an improved way to access and process large volumes of data stored in distributed European-wide archives.

TeraGrid

The TeraGrid[16] project was first launched by the NSF and was a multiyear effort to build and deploy the world's largest, fastest distributed infrastructure for open scientific research. The TeraGrid includes 20 teraflops[16] of computing power distributed at five sites, facilities capable of managing and storing nearly 1 petabyte of data, high-resolution visualization environments, and toolkits for Grid Computing. These components will be tightly integrated and connected through a network that will operate at 40 gigabits per second—this is the fastest research network on the planet today.

The major objective of this project includes creation of a high-speed network; grid services that provide data sharing, computing power, and collaborative visualization; and to provide facilities that create the technology requirements (e.g., data storage, bandwidth, etc.).

The five sites in the project are:

- National Center for Supercomputing Applications (NCSA) at the University of Illinois
- San Diego Supercomputer Center (SDSC) at the University of California
- Argonne National Laboratory in Argonne, Illinois
- Center for Advanced Computing Research (CACR) at the California Institute of Technology in Pasadena
- Pittsburgh Supercomputer Center (PSC)

The TeraGrid project is sometimes called a "cyberinfrastructure" that brings together distributed scientific instruments, terascale and petascale data archives, and gigabit networks. Figure 2.8 shows different layers of the TeraGrid architecture.

Base Grid Services Layer (Resource Layer)

Some of the base services required for the TeraGrid are authentication and access management, resource allocation and management, data access and management, resource information service, and accounting. This layer forms the building block for the other high-level services.

Figure 2.8
TeraGrid architecture.

Core Grid Services (Collective Layer)

With a main focus on coordination of multiple resources, core grid services include functionalities for data movement, job scheduling, monitoring, and resource discovery.

Advanced Grid Services

These are high-level application services, which provide super schedulers, repositories, categorization, resource discovery, and distributed accounting.

Based on the above architecture, the TeraGrid is defining protocols, schema, and interfaces at each layer of the above architecture but not implementation-specific details. These interfaces provide interoperability between the sites implementing the TeraGrid project.

NASA Information Power Grid (IPG)

NASA's Information Power Grid[18] (IPG) is a high-performance computational and data grid. Grid users can access widely distributed heterogeneous resources from any location, with IPG middleware adding security, uniformity, and control.

Some of the major projects undertaken by IPG are:

Resource Broker

A grid user has to make a resource selection from a large number and variety of resources that they could use for an application. For each potential resource, the resource selection system considers the following factors:

- Computer system characteristics, such as amount of memory, amount of disk space, CPU speed, number of CPUs, type of operating system, available software, and so on
- The time required for the execution of the job
- The cost to use that resource or computer system

Performance Prediction

There are several types of predictions that are useful when deciding where to run applications. These include job/application execution time on different computer systems, wait time in scheduling queues before the job begins executing, and the time to transfer files between computer systems.

Job Manager

Job Manager is used to reliably execute jobs and maintain information about jobs. These jobs consist of file operations (i.e., copy a file between machines, create a directory, delete a file or directory, and so on) and execution operations (i.e., execute an application on a specific computer system).

Portability Manager (PM)

Portability is a key issue with the grid environment and PM is responsible for the establishment of a suitable environment for the execution of the user application by automatically identifying the dependencies of each user program.

Framework for Control and Observation in Distributed Environments (CODE)

The CODE project provides a secure, scalable, and extensible framework for making observations on remote computer systems. It then transmits this observational data to where it is needed, performing actions on remote computer systems and analyzing observational data to determine what actions should be taken. Observational data is transmitted using a distributed event service.

Test and Monitoring Service

The IPG Test and Monitoring Service will provide a framework for examining the health of the grid, so that problems with, or degradation of, grid resources are promptly detected; the appropriate organization, system administrator, or user is notified; and solutions are dispatched in a timely manner.

Dynamic Accounting System (DAS)

DAS provides the following enhanced categories of accounting functionality to the IPG community:

- Allows a grid user to request access to a local resource via the presentation of grid credentials
- Determines and grants the appropriate authorizations for a user to access a local resource without requiring a preexisting account on the resource to govern local authorizations
- Exchanges allocation data between sites to manage allocations in a grid-wide manner instead of a site-specific manner
- Provides resource pricing information on the grid
- Collects and reports the necessary data to ensure accountability of grid users for the use of resources and to enable resource providers to better manage their grid resources

CORBA-IPG Infrastructure

The CORBA-IPG infrastructure gives CORBA-enabled applications, such as object-oriented propulsion systems being developed at NASA Glenn Research Center, the ability to utilize the widely distributed resources made available by the NASA IPG.

COMMERCIAL ORGANIZATIONS BUILDING AND USING GRID-BASED SOLUTIONS

In the last couple of years we have seen a tremendous commercial interest in Grid Computing solutions. These commercial aspects are centered on the concept of resource sharing and resource virtualization principles.

Every computing resource including clusters, servers, blades, operating systems, and applications are viewed as *utilities*. The advancement of Grid Computing through the principles of open technologies, standard-based integration, and hardware and software technology maturity are behind these utility concepts.

The key strategy areas of grid applicability in the commercial world are utility computing, resource virtualization, and on-demand computing. Some of the prominent technologies helping the commercial organizations in their vision are:

- Advancement of service-oriented architectures, in particular Web services, enables organizations to start working on interoperable software solutions
- Hardware virtualizations capabilities including clusters, blades, and so forth
- Software capabilities in resource management and provisioning including policy-driven architectures to meet quality of service, usage and accounting measurements, and so on
- Autonomic computing principles enable high availability of resources

Some of the core concepts introduced by the major commercial organizations include Business On Demand solutions by IBM, the Utility computing and Data centers of HP, N1 technology initiative from Sun Microsystems, and Microsoft's '.Net' strategies. There are other organizations already playing a major role in Grid Computing infrastructure deployment. These participants include IBM Corporation, Avaki, Platform, and others.

The emerging Grid Computing technologies, especially the Open Grid Service Architecture (OGSA), is playing a major role in the standardization of the activities in the grid space. We will see the details on these standards later on in this book.

NOTES

1. For a detailed account of Business On Demand, refer to the book *Business On Demand: Technology and Strategy Perspectives* (Fellenstein, 2004).

2. For more information, visit *www.w3c.org, www.oasis-open.org, www.ietf.org, www.dmtf.org.*

3. For more information on the Global Grid Forum, refer to their website at *www.ggf.org.*

4. For more information on the Globus toolkit and middleware services, refer to their website at *www.globus.org.*

5. For more information, go to *www-106.ibm.com/developerworks/library/ws-secure.*

6. You can get information on the Legion toolkit and middleware services by visiting Legion on the Web at *http://legion.virginia.edu.*

7. You can get information on Condor and Condor-G toolkit and middleware services by visiting Condor at *www.cs.wisc.edu/condor/*.

8. You can find more information on this system at *www.csse.monash.edu.au/~davida/nimrod/*.

9. You can find more information about UNICORE at *www.unicore.org*.

10. For more information on this middleware suite, you can visit *www.nsf-middleware.org*.

11. For more information on the GRIDS center, visit *www.grids-center.org*.

12. For more information on EDIT, visit *www.nmi-edit.org*.

13. For more information, you can visit *http://doesciencegrid.org*.

14. You can find more information on the European Union Grid project at *www.eurogrid.org/*.

15. For more information, visit *http://eu-datagrid.web.cern.ch/eu-datagrid/*.

16. You can find the details of this project and its implementation status on the Web at *www.teragrid.org*.

17. A *teraflop* is a measure of computing speed equal to one trillion floating-point operations per second.

18. For more details on IPG projects, visit *www.ipg.nasa.gov*.

The Grid Computing Anatomy

I n Foster (1998), the Grid concept is defined as the *controlled and coordinated resource sharing and problem solving in dynamic, multi-institutional virtual organizations.* This sharing of resources, ranging from simple file transfers to complex and collaborative problem solving, is accomplished within controlled and well-defined conditions and policies. The dynamic grouping of individuals, multiple groups, or organizations that defined the conditions and rules for sharing are called *virtual organizations.*

In this chapter, we will define the "grid problem," the core concepts of a "virtual organization," and the architecture defined to solve the "grid problem."

THE VIRTUAL ORGANIZATION CONCEPT IN GRID COMPUTING IS KEY

One of the significant operational concepts in Grid Computing is the notion of the *virtual organization.* This involves the dynamic computation-oriented task of defining groupings of individuals, such as multiple groups or organizations. Although this is perhaps simple to understand, in theory, it remains complex across several dimensions. The complexities involved in this dynamic assembly revolve around identifying and bringing in those humans that initially defined the conditions in order to instantiate the grid. For instance, automated consideration of the rules, the policies, and the specific conditions affecting operations in the grid are, hence, the generating force for processing and sharing the information with those individuals in any virtual organization of a grid.

The simplest way of thinking about this advanced Grid Computing concept is captured in the term *virtual organizations.* This type of computation-oriented grouping serves as the basis for identifying and managing the grid computer groups, associated with any particular grid community of end users.

THE GRID PROBLEM

Grid Computing has evolved as an important field in the computer industry by differentiating itself from the distributed computing with an increased focus on the resource sharing, coordination, and high-performance orientation. Grid Computing is trying to solve the problems associated with resource sharing among a set of individuals or groups.

These Grid Computing resources include computing power, data storage, hardware instruments, on-demand software, and applications. In this context, the real problems involved with resource sharing are resource discovery, event correlation, authentication, authorization, and access mechanisms. These problems become proportionately more complicated when the Grid Computing solution is introduced as a solution for utility computing, where industrial applications and resources become available as sharable. The best example of this is in the IBM Corporation's Business On Demand resource implementations in Grid Computing.

This commercial on-demand utility concept spanning across Grid Computing services has introduced a number of challenging problems to the already complicated grid problem domains. These challenging problems include service-level management features, complex accounting, utilization metering, flexible pricing, federated security, scalability, open-ended integration, and a multitude of very difficult arrays of networking services to sustain. It is key to understand that the networking services can no longer be taken for granted, as these very important services now become the central nervous system for the enablement of all worldwide Grid Computing environments.

The Concept of Virtual Organizations

The concept of a virtual organization is the key to Grid Computing. It is defined as a dynamic set of individuals and/or institutions defined around a set of resource-sharing rules and conditions (Foster, Kesselman, & Tuecke). All these virtual organizations share some commonality among them, including common concerns and requirements, but may vary in size, scope, duration, sociology, and structure.

The members of any virtual organization negotiate on resource sharing based on the rules and conditions defined in order to share the resources from the thereby automatically constructed resource pool. Assigning users, resources, and organizations from different domains across multiple, worldwide geographic territories to a virtual organization is one of the fundamental technical challenges in Grid Computing. This complexity includes the definitions of the resource discovery mechanism, resource sharing methods, rules and conditions by which this can be achieved, security federation and/or delegation, and access controls among the participants of the virtual organization. This challenge is both complex and complicated across several dimensions.

Let us explore two examples of virtual organizations in order to better understand their common characteristics. The following describes these two examples in simple-to-understand terms.

1. Thousands of physicists from different laboratories join together to create, design, and analyze the products of a major detector at CERN, the European high energy physics laboratory. This group forms a "data grid," with intensive computing, storage, and network services resource sharing, in order to analyze petabytes of data created by the detector at CERN. This is one example of a virtual organization.

2. A company doing financial modeling for a customer based on the data collected from various data sources, both internal and external to the company. This specific virtual organization customer may need a financial forecasting capability and advisory capability on their investment portfolio, which is based on actual historic and current real-time financial market data. This financial institution customer can then be responsive by forming a dynamic virtual organization within the enterprise for achieving more benefit from advanced and massive forms of computational power (i.e., application service provider) and for data (i.e., data access and integration provider). This dynamic, financially oriented, virtual organization can now reduce undesirable customer wait time, while increasing reliability on forecasting by using real-time data and financial modeling techniques. This is another example of a virtual organization.

With a close observation of the above-mentioned virtual organizations, we can infer that the number and type of participants, the resources being shared, duration, scale, and the interaction pattern between the participants all vary between any one single virtual organization to another. At the same time, we can also infer that there exist common characteristics among competing and sometimes distrustful participants that contributed to their virtual organization formation. They may include (Foster, Kesselman, & Tuecke) some of the following items for consideration:

1. *Common concerns and requirements on resource sharing.* A virtual organization is a well-defined collection of individuals and/or institutions that share a common set of concerns and requirements among them. For example, a virtual organization created to provide financial forecast modeling share the same concerns on security, data usage, computing requirements, resource usage, and interaction pattern.

2. *Conditional, time-bound, and rules-driven resource sharing.* Resource sharing is conditional and each resource owner has full control on making the availability of the resource to the sharable resource pool. These conditions are defined based on mutually understandable policies and access control requirements (authentication and authorization). The number of resources involved in the sharing may dynamically vary over time based on the policies defined.

3. *Dynamic collection of individuals and/or institutions.* Over a period of time a virtual organization should allow individuals and/or groups into and out of the collection; provided they all share the same concerns and requirements on resource sharing.

4. *Sharing relationship among participants is peer-to-peer in nature.* The sharing relation among the participants in a virtual organization is peer-to-peer, which emphasizes that the resource provider can become a consumer to another resource. This introduces a

number of security challenges including mutual authentication, federation, and delegation of credentials among participants.

5. *Resource sharing based on an open and well-defined set of interaction and access rules.* Open definition and access information must exist for each sharable resource for better interoperability among the participants.

The above characteristics and nonfunctional requirements of a virtual organization lead to the definition of an architecture for establishment, management, and resource sharing among participants. As we will see in the next section, the focus of the grid architecture is to define an interoperable and extensible solution for resource sharing within the virtual organization.

Grid Architecture

A new architecture model and technology was developed for the establishment, management, and cross-organizational resource sharing within a virtual organization. This new architecture, called *grid architecture,* identifies the basic components of a grid system, defines the purpose and functions of such components and indicates how each of these components interacts with one another (Foster, Kesselman, & Tuecke). The main attention of the architecture is on the interoperability among resource providers and users to establish the sharing relationships. This interoperability means common protocols at each layer of the architecture model, which leads to the definition of a grid protocol architecture as shown in Figure 3.1. This protocol architecture defines common mechanisms, interfaces, schema, and protocols at each layer, by which users and resources can negotiate, establish, manage, and share resources.

Figure 3.1 illustrates the component layers of the architecture with specific capabilities at each layer. Each layer shares the behavior of the component layers described in the next discussion. As we can see in this illustration, each of these component layers is compared with their corresponding Internet protocol layers, for purposes of providing more clarity in their capabilities.

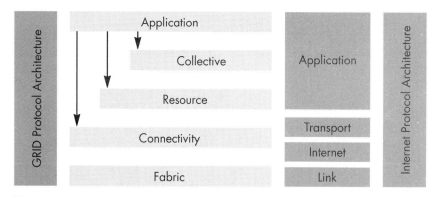

Figure 3.1
This illustrates a layered grid architecture and its relationship to the Internet protocol architecture (Foster, Kesselman, & Tuecke).

Now let us explore each of these layers in more detail.

Fabric Layer: Interface to Local Resources

The Fabric layer defines the resources that can be shared. This could include computational resources, data storage, networks, catalogs, and other system resources. These resources can be physical resources or logical resources by nature.

Typical examples of the logical resources found in a Grid Computing environment are distributed file systems, computer clusters, distributed computer pools, software applications, and advanced forms of networking services. These logical resources are implemented by their own internal protocol (e.g., network file systems [NFS] for distributed file systems, and clusters using logical file systems [LFS]). These resources then comprise their own network of physical resources.

Although there are no specific requirements toward a particular resource that relates to integrating itself as part of any grid system, it is recommended to have two basic capabilities associated with the integration of resources. These basic capabilities should be considered as "best practices" toward Grid Computing disciplines. These best practices are as follows:

1. Provide an "inquiry" mechanism whereby it allows for the discovery against its own resource capabilities, structure, and state of operations. These are value-added features for resource discovery and monitoring.
2. Provide appropriate "resource management" capabilities to control the QoS the grid solution promises, or has been contracted to deliver. This enables the service provider to control a resource for optimal manageability, such as (but not limited to) start and stop activations, problem resolution, configuration management, load balancing, workflow, complex event correlation, and scheduling.

Connectivity Layer: Manages Communications

The Connectivity layer defines the core communication and authentication protocols required for grid-specific networking services transactions. Communications protocols, which include aspects of networking transport, routing, and naming, assist in the exchange of data between fabric layers of respective resources. The authentication protocol builds on top of the networking communication services in order to provide secure authentication and data exchange between users and respective resources.

The communication protocol can work with any of the networking layer protocols that provide the transport, routing, and naming capabilities in networking services solutions. The most commonly used Network layer protocol is the TCP/IP Internet protocol stack; however, this concept and discussion is not limited to that protocol. The authentication solution for virtual organization environments requires significantly more complex characteristics. The following describes the characteristics for consideration:

Single sign-on.   This provides any multiple entities in the grid fabric to be authenticated once; the user can then access any available resources in the grid Fabric layer without further user authentication intervention.

Delegation.   This provides the ability to access a resource under the current users permissions set; the resource should be able to relay the same user credentials (or a subset of the credentials) to other resources respective to the chain of access.

Integration with local resource specific security solutions.   Each resource and hosting has specific security requirements and security solutions that match the local environment. This may include (for example) Kerberos security methods, Windows security methods, Linux security methods, and UNIX security methods. Therefore, in order to provide proper security in the grid fabric model, all grid solutions must provide integration with the local environment and respective resources specifically engaged by the security solution mechanisms.

User-based trust relationships.   In Grid Computing, establishing an absolute trust relationship between users and multiple service providers is very critical. This accomplishes the environmental factor to which there is then no need of interaction among the providers to access the resources that each of them provide.

Data security.   The data security topic is important in order to provide data integrity and confidentiality. The data passing through the Grid Computing solution, no matter what complications may exist, should be made secure using various cryptographic and data encryption mechanisms. These mechanisms are well known in the prior technological art, across all global industries.

Resource Layer: Sharing of a Single Resource

The Resource layer utilizes the communication and security protocols defined by the networking communications layer, to control the secure negotiation, initiation, monitoring, metering, accounting, and payment involving the sharing of operations across *individual resources.*

The way this works is the Resource layer calls the Fabric layer functions in order to access and control the multitude of local resources. This layer only handles the individual resources and, hence, ignores the global state and atomic actions across the other resource collection, which in the operational context is the responsibility of the Collective layer.

There are two primary classes of resource layer protocols. These protocols are key to the operations and integrity of any single resource. These protocols are as follows:

Information Protocols.   These protocols are used to get information about the structure and the operational state of a single resource, including configuration, usage policies, service-level agreements, and the state of the resource. In most situations, this information is used to monitor the resource capabilities and availability constraints.

Management Protocols.   The important functionalities provided by the management protocols are:

- Negotiating access to a shared resource is paramount. These negotiations can include the requirements on quality of service, advanced reservation, scheduling, and other key operational factors.
- Performing operation(s) on the resource, such as process creation or data access, is also a very important operational factor.
- Acting as the service/resource policy enforcement point for policy validation between a user and resource is critical to the integrity of the operations.
- Providing accounting and payment management functions on resource sharing is mandatory.
- Monitoring the status of an operation, controlling the operation including terminating the operation, and providing asynchronous notifications on operation status, is extremely critical to the operational state of integrity.

It is recommended that these resource-level protocols should be minimal from a functional overhead point of view and they should focus on the functionality each provides from a utility aspect.

The Collective Layer: Coordinating Multiple Resources

While the Resource layer manages an individual resource, the Collective layer is responsible for all global resource management and interaction with a collection of resources. This layer of protocol implements a wide variety of sharing behaviors (protocols) utilizing a small number of Resource layer and Connectivity layer protocols.

Some key examples of the common, more visible collective services in a Grid Computing system are as follows:

Discovery Services.   This enables the virtual organization participants to discover the existence and/or properties of that specific available virtual organization's resources.

Coallocation, Scheduling, and Brokering Services.   These services allow virtual organization participants to request the allocation of one or more resources for a specific task, during a specific period of time, and to schedule those tasks on the appropriate resources.

Monitoring and Diagnostic Services.   These services afford the virtual organizations resource failure recovery capabilities, monitoring of the networking and device services, and diagnostic services that include common event logging and intrusion detection. Another important aspect of this topic relates to the partial failure of any portion of a Grid Computing environment, in that it is critical to understand any and all *business impacts* related to this partial failure are well known, immediately, as the failure begins to occur—all the way through its corrective healing stages.

Data Replication Services.   These services support the management aspects of the virtual organization's storage resources in order to maximize data access performance with respect to response time, reliability, and costs.

Grid-Enabled Programming Systems.   These systems allow familiar programming models to be utilized in the Grid Computing environments, while sustaining various Grid Computing networking services. These networking services are integral to the environment in order to address resource discovery, resource allocation, problem resolution, event correlation, network provisioning, and other very critical operational concerns related to the grid networks.

Workload Management Systems and Collaborative Frameworks.   This provides multi-step, asynchronous, multicomponent workflow management. This is a complex topic across several dimensions, yet a fundamental area of concern for enabling optimal performance and functional integrity.

Software Discovery Services.   This provides the mechanisms to discover and select the best software implementation(s) available in the grid environment, and those available to the platform based on the problem being solved.

Community Authorization Servers.   These servers control resource access by enforcing community utilization policies and providing these respective access capabilities by acting as policy enforcement agents.

Community Accounting and Payment Services.   These services provide resource utilization metrics, while at the same time generating payment requirements for members of any community.

As we can observe based on the previous discussion, the capabilities and efficiencies of these Collective layer services are based on the underlying layers of the protocol stack. These collective networking services can be defined as general-purpose Grid Computing solutions to narrowed-domain and application-specific solutions. As an example, one such service is accounting and payment, which is most often very specific to the domain or application. Other notable and very specialized Collective layer services include schedulers, resource brokers, and workload managers (to name a few).

Application Layer: User-Defined Grid Applications

These are user applications, which are constructed by utilizing the services defined at each lower layer. Such an application can directly access the resource, or can access the resource through the Collective Service interface APIs (Application Provider Interface).

Each layer in the grid architecture provides a set of APIs and SDKs (software developer kits) for the higher layers of integration. It is up to the application developers whether they should use the collective services for general-purpose discovery, and other high-level services across a set of resources, or if they choose to start directly working with the exposed resources. These user-defined grid applications are (in most cases) domain specific and provide specific solutions.

Grid Architecture and Relationship to Other Distributed Technologies

It is a known fact that in the technology of art that there are numerous well-defined and well-established technologies and standards developed for distributed computing. This foundation has been a huge success (to some extent) until we entered into the domain of heterogeneous resource sharing and the formation of virtual organizations.

Based on our previous discussions, grid architectures are defined as a coordinated, highly automated, and dynamic sharing of resources for a virtual organization. It is appropriate that we turn our attention at this stage toward the discussion regarding how these architecture approaches differ from the prior art of distributed technologies, that is, how the two approaches compliment each other, and how we can leverage the best practices from both approaches.

Our discussion will now begin to explore notions of the widely implemented distributed systems, including World Wide Web environments, application and storage service providers, distributed computing systems, peer-to-peer computing systems, and clustering types of systems.

World Wide Web

A number of open and ubiquitous technologies are defined for the World Wide Web (TCP, HTTP, SOAP, XML) that in turn makes the Web a suitable candidate for the construction of the virtual organizations. However, as of now, the Web is defined as a browser–server messaging exchange model, and lacks the more complex interaction models required for a realistic virtual organization.

As an example, some of these areas of concern include single-sign-on, delegation of authority, complex authentication mechanisms, and event correlation mechanisms. Once this browser-to-server interaction matures, the Web will be suitable for the construction of grid portals to support multiple virtual organizations. This will be possible because the basic platforms, fabric layers, and networking connectivity layers of technologies will remain the same.

Distributed Computing Systems

The major distributed technologies including CORBA, J2EE, and DCOM are well suited for distributed computing applications; however, these do not provide a suitable platform for sharing of resources among the members of the virtual organization. Some of the notable drawbacks include resource discovery across virtual participants, collaborative and declarative security, dynamic construction of a virtual organization, and the scale factor involved in potential resource-sharing environments.

Another major drawback in distributed computing systems involves the lack of interoperability among these technology protocols. However, even with these perceived drawbacks, some of these distributed technologies have attracted considerable Grid Computing research attention toward the construction of grid systems, the most notable of which is Java JINI.[1] This system, JINI, is focused on a platform-independent infrastructure to deliver services and mobile code in order to enable easier interaction with clients through service discovery, negotiation, and leasing.

Application and Storage Service Providers

Application and storage service providers normally outsource their business and scientific applications and services, as well as very high-speed storage solutions, to customers outside their organizations. Customers negotiate with these highly effective service providers on QoS requirements (i.e., hardware, software, and network combinations) and pricing (i.e., utility-based, fixed, or other pricing options).

Normally speaking, these types of advanced services arrangements are executed over some type of virtual private network (VPN), or dedicated line, by narrowing the domain of security and event interactions. This is oftentimes somewhat limited in scope, while the VPN or private line is very static in nature. This, in turn, reduces the visibility of the service provider to a lower and fixed scale, with the lack of complex resource sharing among heterogeneous systems and inter-domain networking service interactions.

This being said, the introduction of the Grid Computing principles related to resource sharing across virtual organizations, along with the construction of virtual organizations yielding inter-domain participation, will alter this situation. Specifically, this will enhance this utility model of application service providers and storage service providers (ASP/SSP) to a more flexible and mature value proposition.

Peer-to-Peer Computing Systems

Similar to Grid Computing, peer-to-peer (P2P) computing is a relatively new computing discipline in the realm of distributed computing. Both P2P and distributed computing are focused on resource sharing, and are now widely utilized throughout the world by home, commercial, and scientific markets. Some of the major P2P systems are SETI@home[2] and file sharing system environments (e.g., Napster, Kazaa, Morpheus, and Gnutella).

The major difference between Grid Computing and P2P computing is centered on the following notable points:

1. They differ in their target communities. Grid communities can be small with regard to number of users, yet will yield a greater applications focus with a higher level of security requirements and application integrity. On the other hand, the P2P systems define collaboration among a larger number of individuals and/or organizations, with a limited set of security requirements and a less complex resource-sharing topology.

2. The grid systems deal with more complex, more powerful, more diverse, and a highly interconnected set of resources than that of the P2P environments.

The convergence of these areas toward Grid Computing is highly probable since each of the disciplines are dealing with the same problem of resource sharing among the participants in a virtual organization. There has been some work, to date, in the Global Grid Forum (GGF) focused on the merger of these complimentary technologies for the interests of integrating the larger audience.

Cluster Computing

Clusters are local to the domain and constructed to solve inadequate computing power. It is related to the pooling of computational resources to provide more computing power by parallel execution of the workload. Clusters are limited in scope with dedicated functionality and local to the domain, and are not suitable for resource sharing among participants from different domains. The nodes in a cluster are centrally controlled and the cluster manager is aware of the state of the node. This forms only a subset of the grid principle of more widely available, intra/interdomain, communication, and resource sharing.

SUMMARY

This chapter introduced the grid problem in the context of a virtual organization and the proposed Grid Computing architecture as a suggested solution to the grid problem. The overall grid architecture is designed for controlled resource sharing with better interoperability among the participants.

This introduction on the anatomy of Grid Computing helps us understand aspects of architecture and design, while understanding the grid protocols for resource sharing with the maximum interoperability between users and resources. In addition to this, this chapter discussed the relationships between grid systems and distributed systems by providing emphasis toward the understanding of exactly how these varying disciplines compliment, while at the same time, differ in some degrees to each other.

NOTES

1. For more details on JINI and related projects, visit *www.jini.org*.
2. Details on the SETI@home project can be found at *http://setiathome.ssl.berkeley.edu/*.

The Grid Computing Road Map

The last decade has noted a substantial change in the ways global industries, businesses, and home users apply computing devices, including a wide variety of ubiquitous computing resources and advanced Web services. Initially, the focus was on localized computing resources and respective services; however, the capabilities have changed over time and we are now in an environment consisting of sophisticated, virtualized, and widely distributed Business On Demand utility services.

Major global organizations, solutions providers, service providers, and technology innovators, whom we have already discussed in the earlier chapters (and even those we have not yet discussed), have absolutely contributed to this technology evolution. In the previous chapter, we explored several grid architecture points, and the architectural relationships between grid and other distributed computing technologies. As we can see from this discussion and the following illustration, the evolution of Grid Computing is progressing at a very rapid rate. This computing evolution is tightly aligned with the incredible and very rapid evolution of the Internet and other open standards architectures.

As shown in Figure 4.1, the evolution of Grid Computing is broadly classified into three generations. This Grid Computing evolution is discussed in detail by Roure, Baker, Jennings, and Shadbolt.

In previous chapters, we explored some of the major projects and organizational initiatives that contributed to the first generation and second generation of Grid Computing. The first two phases were concentrating on large-scale resource discovery, utilization, and sharing within the virtual organizational boundaries. The major drawback in these two phases was the lack of transparency among the middleware, which contributed to monolithic and noninteroperable solutions for each grid environment.

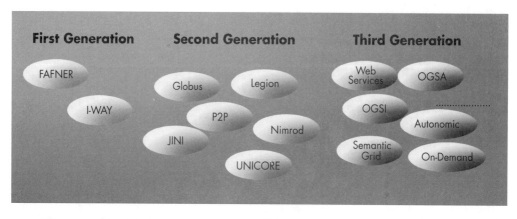

Figure 4.1
The Grid Computing technology road map is simply illustrated in terms of generations.

This difference in the first two stages results in a vertical tower of solutions and applications for resource sharing among organizations. Today, we are in the third generation of Grid Computing where the applications and solutions are focusing on open technology-based, service-oriented, and horizontally-oriented solutions that are aligned with the other global industry efforts. The grid infrastructures are clearly transitioning from *information aware* to that of *knowledge-centric* frameworks.

In this chapter we begin to explore a detailed discussion on the third generation of technologies, and the respective grid architectures and the road map that is guiding the next generation of grid technology initiatives.

The next generations of Grid Computing technologies that are channeling this third generation of grid initiatives are noted as:

- Autonomic computing
- Business On Demand and infrastructure virtualization
- Service-oriented architecture and grid
- Semantic grids

AUTONOMIC COMPUTING

The term "autonomic" comes from an analogy to the autonomic central nervous system in the human body, which adjusts to many situations automatically without any external help. With the increasing complexity in dealing with distributed systems, solutions, and shared resources in grid environments, we require a significant amount of autonomic functions to manage the grid.

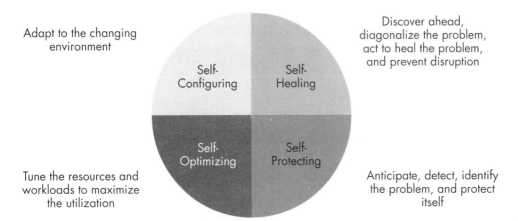

Adapt to the changing environment

Discover ahead, diagonalize the problem, act to heal the problem, and prevent disruption

Tune the resources and workloads to maximize the utilization

Anticipate, detect, identify the problem, and protect itself

Figure 4.2
Autonomic computing vision is robust across several complimentary dimensions.

As detailed in Figure 4.2, basic autonomic computing systems must follow the four basic principles:[1]

- Self-configuring (able to adapt to the changes in the system)
- Self-optimizing (able to improve performance)
- Self-healing (able to recover from mistakes)
- Self-protecting (able to anticipate and cure intrusions)

Orchestrating complex connected problems on heterogeneous distributed systems is a complex job and requires a number of autonomic features for the infrastructure and resource management. Thus, it is important that our systems be as self-healing and self-configuring as possible in order to meet the requirements of resource sharing and to handle failure conditions. These autonomic enhancements to the existing grid framework at the application and middleware framework level provide a scalable and dependable grid infrastructure.

IBM, the pioneer in worldwide autonomic computing initiatives, has already implemented a number of projects around the world in this general concept, while keeping in mind the synergies to create global grid solutions. These global grid solutions are continuously being enhanced to include autonomic computing capabilities. Grid Computing and autonomic computing disciplines will continue to work closely together to develop highly reliable, efficient, self-managing grids. It is these two computing disciplines that alone serve as the basis for the IBM Corporation's global strategies underpinning Business On Demand.[2]

BUSINESS ON DEMAND AND INFRASTRUCTURE VIRTUALIZATION

Utility-like computing is one of the key technology resources that help businesses to develop Business On Demand capabilities. However, Business On Demand is not just about utility com-

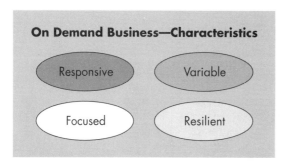

Figure 4.3
Business On Demand characteristics are shared across four distinct areas.

puting, as it has a much broader set of ideas about the transformation of business practices, process transformation, and technology implementations. Companies striving to achieve the Business On Demand operational models will have the capacity to sense and respond to fluctuating market conditions in real time, while providing products and services to customers in a Business On Demand operational model.

In general, on-demand business has four essential characteristics (Figure 4.3):[3]

1. *Responsive.* Business On Demand has to be responsive to dynamic, unpredictable changes in demand, supply, pricing, labor, and competition.

2. *Variable.* Business On Demand has to be flexible in adapting to variable cost structure and processes associated with productivity, capital, and finance.

3. *Focused.* Business On Demand has to focus on their core competency, its differentiating tasks and assets along with closer integration with its partners.

4. *Resilient.* A Business On Demand company has to be capable of managing changes and competitive threats with consistent availability and security.

In order to achieve the above core capabilities, a Business On Demand operating environment, as shown in Figure 4.4, must possess the following essential capabilities:

1. *Integrate.* Integrated systems enable seamless linkage across the enterprise and across its entire range of customers, partners, and suppliers.

2. *Virtualization.* Resource virtualization enables the best use of resources and minimizes complexity for users. We can achieve the virtualization of resources through the use of a number of existing and emerging technologies including clusters, LPARs, server blades, and grid. Based on our earlier discussions, we know that grids provide the best use of the virtualized resources for its virtually organized customers within the constraints of service-level agreements and policies.

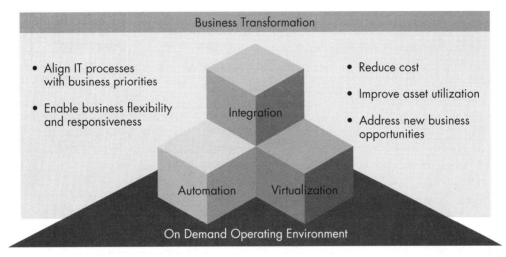

Figure 4.4
The Business On Demand operating environment is rich with autonomic process enablement combined with advanced concepts in Grid Computing, like virtualization.

> **3.** *Automation.* As we discussed in the last section, the *autonomic* capabilities provides a dependable technology framework for an on-demand operating environment.
>
> **4.** *Open standards.* An open, integrateable technology allows resource sharing to be more modular. Some of the most notable open standards are XML, Web services, and OGSA standards.

As previously discussed, we have seen that the infrastructure virtualization transformation can be achieved by the utilization of the Grid Computing infrastructure. These sharable virtualized resources form the backbone for a Business On Demand environment. Beyond the need for virtualization of hardware resources, the virtualization of data and software applications must also occur. This enables access to resources as a single entity, and enabling applications to respond quickly to the dynamic needs of the enterprise. This virtualization provides computational and/or data grids for high computation-intensive throughput, as well as a uniform data access mechanism.

SERVICE-ORIENTED ARCHITECTURE AND GRID

A distributed system consists of a set of software agents that all work together to implement some intended functionality. Furthermore, the agents in a distributed system do not operate in the same processing environment, so they must communicate by hardware/software protocol stacks that are intrinsically less reliable than direct code invocation and shared memory. This has important architectural implications because distributed systems require that developers of infrastructure and applications consider the unpredictable latency of remote access, and take into account issues of concurrency and the possibility of an unplanned partial failure (Kendall, Waldo, Wollrath, & Wyant, 1994).

A *service-oriented architecture (SOA)* is a specific type of distributed system in which the agents are "software services" that perform some well-defined operation (i.e., it provides a service), and this type of architecture can be invoked outside of the context of a larger application. By this, we can infer a service is acting as a user-facing software component of a larger application. This separation of functionality helps the users of the larger application to be concerned only with the interface description of the service.

In addition, the SOA stresses that all services have to be a network-addressable interface that communicates via standard protocols and data formats called *messages*. The major functionality of an SOA is the definition of the messages (i.e., its format, content, and exchange policies) that is exchanged between the users and the services. The Web architecture[4] and the Web Services Architecture[5] are instances of a service-oriented architecture (SOA).

Grid is a distributed system for sharing of resources among participants. As we have seen in the first paragraph of this chapter, grid, being a distributed architecture, has to deal with problems of the distributed computing grid, including latency, concurrency, and partial failures. We have discussed in earlier chapters of the grid architecture section that the current Grid Computing architecture is built upon the existing distributed technologies with a major focus on resource sharing, interoperation, and virtual organizational security. The SOA is a distributed architecture with more focus on the service interoperability, easier integration, and extensible and secure access.

The Web services architecture is gaining the most attention in the industry as an open, standards-based architecture with a main focus on interoperability. The W3C is leading this initiative. The core components of the Web service architecture are shown in Figure 4.5.

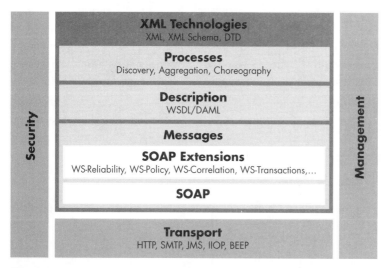

Figure 4.5
Web services architectures are a key enabler in the overall computing discipline of Grid Computing.

From a closer look at the above figure we can infer that XML and related technologies (XML, DTD, XML Schema) form the base technologies of the Web services. Web services are invoked and results are provided via messages that must be exchanged over some communications medium, where a communication medium can be a low-level networking services transport protocol (e.g., telecommunications protocol [TCP]), and/or a high-level communication protocol (HTTP), and/or a combination of both.

The message format can be specified through the Simple Object Access Protocol (SOAP) and its extensions, but this capability is not just limited to SOAP. The SOAP functionality provides a standard way for exchanging the messages.

Interoperability across heterogeneous systems requires a mechanism to define the precise structure and data types of the messages that has to be exchanged between a message producer and a consumer. The Web Service Description Language (WSDL) is another desirable choice to describe the message and exchange pattern.

The SOAP specification provides the definition of the XML-based information that can be used for exchanging structured and typed information between peers in a decentralized, distributed environment. SOAP is fundamentally a stateless, one-way message exchange paradigm, but applications can create more complex interaction patterns (including request/response and request/multiple responses). SOAP is silent on the semantics of any application-specific data it conveys. At the same time SOAP provides a framework (SOAP header) by which application-specific information may be conveyed in an extensible manner. Also, SOAP provides a full description of the required actions taken by a SOAP node on receiving a SOAP message. In short, a SOAP message is a SOAP envelope with a SOAP header and a SOAP body where the header contains semantic and metadata information about the contents of the SOAP body, which form the message. Most of the Web service vendors today uses SOAP as their message payload container.

The WSDL provides a model and an XML format for describing Web services. WSDL enables one to separate the description of the abstract functionality offered by a service from concrete details of a service description.

Grid Computing is all about resource sharing by integrating services across distributed, heterogeneous, dynamic virtual organizations formed from disparate sources within a single institution and/or external organization. This integration cannot be achieved without a global, open, extensible architecture agreed upon by the participants of the virtual organization.

The OGSA achieves these integration requirements by providing an Open Service-Oriented model for establishing Grid Computing architectures. The OGSA is described in detail in the "physiology" paper (Foster, Kesselman, Nick, & Tuecke). The OGSA is aligned with the service-oriented architecture as defined by the W3C and utilizes a Web service as its framework and message exchange architecture. Thanks to the valuable and innovative concepts of the OGSA, and the open nature of the standard, the GGF formed an architecture work area to discuss the OGSA and its programming model.

The basic approach the OGSA has taken is to integrate itself with the Web services architecture and define a programming model using this emerging architecture. The Open Grid Service Infrastructure (OGSI) uses WSDL as its service description mechanism and Web service infrastructure for the message exchange. We will further explore the details surrounding the OGSA and its core components that constitute this architecture in a later section of the book.

SEMANTIC GRIDS

The W3C initiated a "metadata activity," which defines a standard for a metadata definition surrounding a Semantic Web. The Semantic Web is defined as the next generation of Web services.

THE SEMANTIC WEB DEFINES THE NEXT GENERATION OF WEB SERVICES

The Semantic Web is an extension of the current Web in which information is given well-defined meaning, better enabling computers and people to work in cooperation. It's the idea of having data on the Web defined and linked in a way that it can be used for more effective discovery, automation, integration, and reuse across various applications.

The Web can reach its full potential if it becomes a place where data can be shared and processed by automated tools as well as critical people skills (W3C-SEM).

Figure 4.6 shows the semantic evolution. We will start exploring this evolution with the understanding of the Semantic Web.[6]

The two most important technologies for building Semantic Webs are XML and Resource Description Framework (RDF). XML allows users to add arbitrary structure to documents through markup tags, but says nothing about the meaning of the structures. Meaning is expressed by the RDF, which encodes itself in sets of triples, wherein each triple represents the subject, object, and the predicate of an elementary sentence. These triples can be written using XML tags. The subject and object are each identified by a Universal Resource Identifier (URI).

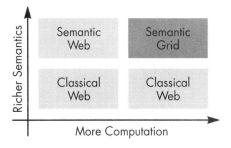

Figure 4.6
The Semantic Web and grid evolution is straightforward across several dimensions, as shown in this illustration.

An RDF document makes assertions that particular things, for instance, people and Web pages, have properties (e.g., "is a sister of" or "is the author of") with certain values (e.g., another person, another Web page). For further clarification consider the example, "Jeff is the author of the book *ABC*." In this example, the subject is "Jeff," the predicate is "the author of," and the object is "the book." This structure turns out to be a natural semantic, meaning to describe the vast majority of the data processed by machines. The RDF has, hence, evolved as a data model for logic processing.

Another important aspect of the Semantic Web is the use of "ontology" to describe collections of information like concepts and relationships that can exist in many semantic situations. This semantic taxonomy defines classes of objects and relations among them.

Figure 4.7 illustrates the Semantic Web architecture layers. The real power of the Semantic Web will be realized when people create many programs that collect data from diverse sources, process the information, and exchange the results with other programs.

The Semantic Grid[7] is a natural evolution in Grid Computing, toward a knowledge-centric and metadata-driven computing paradigm. The Semantic Grid is an effort to utilize Semantic Web technologies in Grid Computing development efforts, from the grid infrastructure to the delivery of grid applications.

These concepts will enhance more automated resource and knowledge/information-based resource sharing. Knowing this importance of the evolution of a Semantic Web and its usability in Grid Computing, the GGF has created a research group for Semantic Grid under the Grid Architecture area. We can find a number of Semantic Grid projects including Corporate Ontology Grid,[8] grid-enabled combinatorial chemistry,[9] Collaborative Advanced Knowledge Technologies[10] in the Grid, and many other significant initiatives.

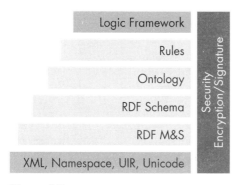

Figure 4.7
The Semantic Web architecture is shown in this illustration with the necessary security and encryption required across all levels.

SUMMARY

The Grid Computing technology road map leads the natural evolution of distributed computing with more emphasis on open architecture models, knowledge-centric solutions, and simpler forms of integration. This Grid Computing evolution will enable easier resource discovery, virtualization, and autonomic enhancements for grid solutions.

In the subsequent sections of this book, we discuss the details of these highly ambitious operating environments, software standards, and innovative programming models.

NOTES

1. For more information, go to IBM's Web site at *www-3.ibm.com/autonomic/index.html*.

2. For more detailed discussions on the IBM Corporation's Business On Demand strategies, please refer to the book *Business On Demand: Technology and Strategy Perspectives* (Fellenstein, 2004).

3. For more information, go to IBM's Web site at *www-3.ibm.com/e-business/index.html*.

4. For more information, go to *www3.org/TR/webarch/*.

5. For more information, go to *www3.org/2002/WS/arch/*.

6. For more information on Semantic Web, visit *www.w3.org/2001/sw/*.

7. For more information on Semantic Grid, visit *www.semanticgrid.org*.

8. For more information, visit *www.cogproject.org/*.

9. More information is available at *www.combechem.org/*.

10. For more information, visit *www.aktors.org/coakting/*.

The New Generation of Grid Computing Applications

In today's new generation of services, almost weekly we find new emerging approaches to applications processing and service delivery. Along with these new innovative applications are the open-ended architectures required to sustain these advanced forms of systematic operations. Along with these new and innovative services delivery approaches are the incredible applications serving multiple continents of end users.

In this part of the book, we will further explore in greater detail the service architecture models, the service delivery models, advanced languages, advanced messaging schemes, innovative Web services paradigms, and more aspects of Grid Computing disciplines. Several of the discussions will become rather technical as related to computer language implementations. These are important, low-level details to understand, as it is by virtue of these language implementations that Grid Computing implementations are instantiated. Detailed aspects of security will also be discussed. Examples of language implementations will be shown, at the coding level, to afford readers a clear understanding of the deep complexity in establishing the grid, from the language implementation view.

This part of the book on the new generation of Grid Computing applications, discusses in great detail an unprecedented series of capabilities never before realized in computing solutions. This, in turn, has enabled for the first time a unique opportunity for the transformation of business enterprises, research capabilities, and academic endeavors.

Merging the Grid Services Architecture with the Web Services Architecture

The computer programming and software modeling disciplines have gone through an incredible number of changes during the last two decades. We started with structured programming models, then moved on to object-oriented programming models, and then moved to component-oriented programming and software design.

Each level of this progression was seemingly built on top of the other. Software design concepts then emerged from simple monolithic software design into a state of highly collaborative and distributed software design. The latest approach in this progression is service-oriented architecture (SOA) (see Figure 5.1).

In the earlier periods of software development, the basic premise of the component software ignores the details on interoperable messages and exchange patterns, while concentrating on the cohesive abstraction on software models. However, SOA is concerned with interoperable message interchange to and/or from a message producer to a message consumer, while hiding the details of the message processing. There are a number of derivatives of this message exchange pattern, based upon the synchronous/asynchronous nature, the protocol exchange model, the data format, and the end points.

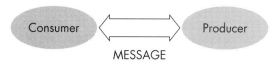

Figure 5.1
In the SOA, the exchange of messages is quite straightforward as a high-level concept.

SERVICE-ORIENTED ARCHITECTURE

A service-oriented architecture is intended to define loosely coupled and interoperable services/ applications, and to define a process for integrating these interoperable components.

In SOA, the system is decomposed into a collection of network-connected components. Applications and resources within a service-oriented architecture should not be built as a tightly coupled monolithic model. Rather, these applications are composed dynamically from the deployed and available services in the network.

These services are dynamically discovered and bound together in a loosely coupled manner. This dynamic construction allows the system to quickly respond to new business requirements. Because these applications are not tightly coupled to their components, they provide increased stability and availability to users, reacting to component failure by finding and binding to equivalent components without requiring human intervention.

The most commonly understood SOA architectures are Web and Web services. The Web architecture has evolved even before we started talking about the SOA. On careful examination of the interaction model exhibited by the Web, it is inherent that it is a medium for message exchange between a consumer and producer using a common, well understandable, and interoperable data model, HTML/XHTML. There is no tight coupling that exists between the client and service.

Figure 5.2
Messaging interaction between the Web browser end user and the services producer.

The above model (Figure 5.2) was adequate for the common user agent-based interaction. But when the interaction pattern becomes complex, such as business-to-business, the above Web architecture model needs more polished message exchange patterns to adapt to any user agent and/or applications of choice. There comes the concept of a more generalized solution, Web services. The Web service architecture extends the above interaction pattern further by adding the power and expressiveness of XML.

Figure 5.3
Messaging interaction between the end user and the producer.

As we can see in Figure 5.3, the exchange messages centered on XML and the interaction pattern have evolved to an any-to-any scenario. This flexible interaction pattern using XML messages as the core data format increases the value of SOAs. This produces the interaction request–response patterns, asynchronously, for better interoperability between consumers and any of its producers. This is a very loosely coupled system.

In order to better align with SOA principles, this architecture is polished with more emphasis on standard definitions of the service description, registration, discovery, and interactions. Figure 5.4 shows a commonly used interaction pattern.

Figure 5.4 shows the following concepts:

- A service provider creates a service for interaction and exposes the service's description for the consumers with the necessary message format and transport bindings.
- The service provider may decide to register this service and its description with a registry of choice.
- The service consumer can discover a service from a registry or directly from the service provider and can start sending messages in a well-defined XML format that both the consumer and service can consume.

This is a simple yet powerful concept of providing message interactions. Each of these interactions can be further broken down into different layers. As an example, the interaction pattern between the consumer and the service is a combination of message, message packaging, and transport protocols. This architecture needs to further extend by adding QoS requirements, security, and management aspects. We will cover these details in the coming pages. Let us now open discussion on the Web services architecture as our example candidate to explore SOA.

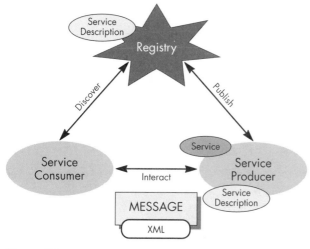

Figure 5.4
The SOA interaction pattern.

WEB SERVICE ARCHITECTURE

A Web service is a software system identified by a URI, whose public interfaces are defined and described using XML. The other software systems can interact with these systems using XML messages. This definition closely matches the W3C Web service architecture group's definition.[1] Figure 5.5 explains this architectural definition.

The core information projected by Figure 5.5 includes:

- The Web service architecture is built around the XML technologies.
- The Web service is independent of the underlying transport mechanism.
- The messages exchanged between a customer and services forms the base layer of this architecture.
- These messages may be packaged and exchanged using envelopes including SOAP and its extension models.
- The SOAP extension models provide a number of SOAP header messages for message correlation, transactional capabilities, message reliability, and service addressing.
- There is a high-level description on the messages to exchange and the interaction pattern. This description can be given through any description language of choice. The most notable among these description languages are the Web Service Description Language, or simply WSDL.
- We can build a number of technologies around this architectural model. These technologies can be high-end applications, infrastructure software, and middleware solutions.
- Other notable features are the vertical pillars for security and management, which are needed for all the horizontal architecture components.

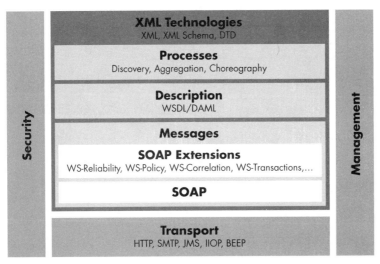

Figure 5.5
The Web service architecture.

Now we will go through the details of these layers. We will start our discussion on the core technology builder, XML.

XML, RELATED TECHNOLOGIES, AND THEIR RELEVANCE TO WEB SERVICES

We have seen earlier that the Web service agents (requesters and providers) exchange information in the form of messages. These messages are defined in terms of XML Infoset.[2] The importance of XML lies on the concepts of a standard-based, flexible, and extendable data format. The Web service messages are defined using XML Infoset, XML Schema, and XML Namespace standards. Understand that these base concepts of XML messages is important to adhere to in order to develop interoperable solutions.

The XML Infoset defines a set of information items and their properties, which describes an XML document. These definitions help the standards and tools to validate the XML documents created. For example, the WSDL standard must conform to the XML Infoset definition of an XML document. This is also valid for the messages exchanged between agents. A well-formed XML message enables interoperation and easier integration. One important concern that may arise is the serialization format of the XML documents for transport and binding. There are many serialization formats available for XML including simple XML text streams to binary XML streams. Note that the wire format of the message is transport and binding dependent.

The other notable XML construct is the message schema or message format definition. These schemas can be defined using the XML schema[3] standard, but may not be sufficient for more complex types and assertions. As of today, most of the XML systems tend to use XML schema as the standard for type definition. In the coming years we will witness more evolution in this area with the maturity and intermingling of XML schema with other standards such as RDF,[4] RELAX-NG.[5]

We can observe in many implementation situations that the complexities of the XML messages are growing with numerous applications and standards. A proper partitioning of XML documents is needed for the correct description and exchange of the messages. The XML community addresses this document versioning and partitioning problem with XML namespace[6] definitions.

As we have seen in the previous illustration, these XML technologies form the basis for all Web services-related standards and messages. This list can be extended to other XML family suites of protocols such as XML Base,[7] XPath,[8] and XPointer.[9]

XML MESSAGES AND ENVELOPING

In this section we will see how XML Web service messages are packaged and enveloped. The most notable mechanism available is SOAP. However, we must be aware that this is not the only enveloping mechanism available for Web services. There are other technologies available including BEEP,[10] HTTP,[11] and IIOP.[12] For example, we could send XML messages over HTTP operations (GET/POST/PUT/DELETE, etc.), which provide some basic enveloping constructs. Since SOAP is the most prominent for XML Web services, we will concentrate our discussion on that protocol and its supported extension mechanisms.

SOAP

SOAP[13] is a simple and lightweight XML-based mechanism for creating structured data packages that can be exchanged between network applications. Our discussion on SOAP is based on the latest SOAP specification, SOAP 1.2, which passes the recommendation criteria of the W3C organization.

The SOAP specification defines the following fundamental components:

- An envelope that defines a framework for describing message structure
- A set of encoding rules for expressing instances of application-defined data types
- A convention for representing remote procedure calls (RPC) and responses
- A set of rules for using SOAP with HTTP
- Message exchange patterns (MEP) such as request–response, one-way, and peer-to-peer conversations

SOAP can be used in combination with a variety of network protocols, such as HTTP, SMTP, BEEP, FTP, and RMI/IIOP. As we have noted from previous implementation of Web services, SOAP is currently being used as the de facto standard for XML messaging including enveloping and exchanging messages.

SOAP provides a simple enveloping mechanism and is proven in being able to work with existing networking services technologies, such as HTTP. SOAP is also very flexible and extensible. It provides capabilities to add-on standards and application-defined extensions. The wide acceptance of SOAP is based on the fact that it builds upon the XML infoset.

The format of a SOAP message is formally defined in SOAP 1.2 Part 1; specifically, the Messaging Framework specification.[14] Figure 5.6 illustrates a simple SOAP message structure, as defined by this specification.

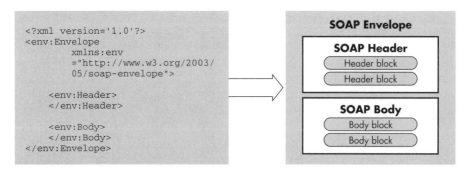

Figure 5.6
SOAP message formats.

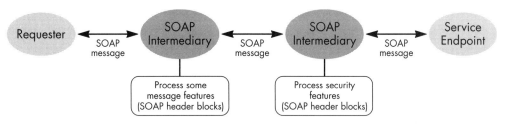

Figure 5.7
SOAP intermediaries.

As illustrated in Figure 5.6, a SOAP message is packaged in a SOAP:Envelope, which consists of zero or more SOAP:Header and exactly one SOAP:Body. The SOAP body and header can be further divided into blocks. While the SOAP body blocks are intended for the final receiver, the header blocks can be interpreted by the SOAP intermediaries. Figure 5.7 illustrates such a message exchange pattern.

The SOAP header blocks carry information such as security, transactional information, correlation, and so on. These intermediaries may act on these header blocks, add more blocks, change them, or leave them untouched. These header blocks can be targeted to some intermediary or final receiver by the use of "roles" attributes ("actors" in SOAP 1.1). The value (specified by URI) of the "roles" attribute can be an address or a standard role name as defined by the SOAP specification, which are:

- "next"—each SOAP intermediary and the ultimate receiver must act on this role
- "none"—the SOAP nodes must not act in this role
- "ultimateReceiver"—the ultimate receiver must act in this role

A sample SOAP message with roles is defined in Listing 5.1.

Listing 5.1 Sample SOAP message with roles.

```xml
<?xml version="1.0" ?>
 <env:Envelope xmlns:env="http://www.w3.org/2003/05/soap-envelope">
   <env:Header>
     <a:firstheaderBlock xmlns:a="http://ph.com"
           env:role="http://ph.com/example/role">
     ...
     </a:firstheaderBlock>
     <q:secondBlock xmlns:q="http://ph.com"
       env:role="http://www.w3.org/2003/05/soap-envelope/role/next">
     ...
     </q:secondBlock>
   </env:Header>
   <env:Body >
     ...
   </env:Body>
 </env:Envelope>
```

Here <a:firstheaderBlock> is targeted to SOAP nodes who are acting on the role *http:// ph.com/example/role*, whereas the <q:secondBlock> must need to be processed by all SOAP nodes in the path, and finally by the ultimate receiver. If no "role" is specified, it is assumed for the ultimate receiver.

We must be cautious in the distinction of these roles, in that we must identify the actor on a message header for the correct processing of the message. There are two other attributes that we must combine with the "role" attribute. They are "mustUnderstand" and "relay." We will note the details in the processing model in the following section.

Thus far, we are discussing topics regarding the format of the message. However, SOAP is much more than simply a message format, it also provides a simple framework for extensible messages and message processing features.

The SOAP Processing Model

The processing of a SOAP message is dependent on the role assumed by the processor. As we have mentioned above, the SOAP headers are targeted using a "role" attribute. If the SOAP intermediary plays the role as defined by the SOAP message, it can then process the message.

There are two options related to processing. If the SOAP header is targeted to this node and specifies a "mustUnderstand" flag set to "true," then the processing node must process that header. If there is no such requirement (i.e., mustUnderstand flag is not set), it is up to the processing node to decide on the processing of the message. Once the processing is completed, the message will be directed to the next node. The decision on the next node selection is not specified by the SOAP specification. Therefore, it is now the choice of the processing node to make such a decision. However, there are some standards that exist to specify common routing mechanisms, such as WS-Routing[15] and WS-Addressing.[16]

Another interesting aspect of this message-forwarding paradigm is the concept of relaying SOAP headers. A header can have a "relay" attribute value (i.e., true or false) to indicate that nonprocessed headers get forwarded to the next node. The default value is "false." This indicates a SOAP node, which is targeted by this header, will not forward this header to the next node.

If we refer back to the SOAP 1.1 specification (SOAP1.1), we could see that there is no standard processing rules for SOAP extensions (header) processing. This causes a number of interoperability problems. However, the SOAP 1.2 specification introduces the following core SOAP constructs in order to support SOAP extensions.

SOAP Features

A SOAP feature is an extension to the SOAP messaging framework. These features are common in distributed computing such as reliability, security, correlation, routing, and message exchange patterns such as request/response, one-way, and peer-to-peer conversations. Readers must be aware that this is an abstract concept with the indication that there is some processing needs to be done in the SOAP nodes but it does not specify how this processing is done.

A SOAP feature has the following characteristics:

1. A unique name used to identify the feature and its properties. This enables us to identify whether a SOAP node supports a specific feature. For example, if we have a feature called "secure-ssl-channel," then we can ask the SOAP nodes, including the ultimate receiver, whether they support that feature or not.

2. A set of properties associated with a feature that can be used to control, constrain, or identify a feature. For example, we can see in the SOAP request–response message exchange pattern there are properties for accessing the inbound or outbound messages, the immediate sender, and next destination.

It is important to understand that SOAP provides two mechanisms for implementing these features:

1. *SOAP header blocks*. In this kind of implementation SOAP header blocks are used to specify a feature. These headers are processed by the SOAP nodes. As we have seen, the SOAP processing model defines the behaviors of a single processing SOAP node in order to process an individual message. The most common example of such a feature is the security features as defined by WS-Security specifications.

2. *SOAP binding protocol*. In this case the features are directly implemented in the protocol binding level. For example, a binding extension to support the SOAP over SSL protocol.

As we have noted, in the first case it is more protocol independent and flexible, but this may cause unnecessary processing overhead. The second case is protocol dependent and the flexibility is limited.

In addition to the extensions as specified in the above cases, the SOAP specification defined a standard feature for the message exchange pattern called MEP. Let us now explore in further detail exactly how this is defined.

Message Exchange Pattern

One special type of SOAP feature is the MEP. A SOAP MEP is a template that establishes a pattern for the exchange of messages between SOAP nodes. Some examples of MEPs include request/response, one-way, peer-to-peer conversation, and so on. To clarify further, we could consider a special MEP, a request for proposal (RFP) MEP, where we could define a message exchange pattern for the RFP such as submitting a request to the service provider, getting a response from the provider at a later period, and other subpatterns. We can envision building these kinds of message exchange patterns.

MEP, similar to other features, is implemented either as headers or using protocol bindings. A MEP may be supported by one or more underlying protocol binding instances either directly or indirectly with support from the software. This software implements the required processing to support the SOAP feature, expressed as a SOAP module.

SOAP Modules

The combined syntax and semantics of a set of SOAP headers are known as a SOAP module. A SOAP module realizes one or more SOAP features. This enables us to specify a more general-purpose concept such as a secure purchase order, with a combination of one or more features, including the purchase order MEP as described above, the security feature, and more.

So far we have discussed message packaging, transmission, and processing in a transport in a rather independent manner. These SOAP messages can be transported through different transport bindings, such as HTTP, TCP, and BEEP. The SOAP defined some protocol bindings for its transport methods. The most notable one is SOAP over HTTP utilizing the GET and POST operations.

SERVICE MESSAGE DESCRIPTION MECHANISMS

A service description (Figure 5.8) is a set of documents that collectively describe the interface to a service (i.e., service expectations and functionalities). In addition to the interface definition, and as it implies in the name, it must describe the semantics of a service, such as the relationship between operations on a service, the meaning of an interface, and/or the basic behavior of an operation.

A service must be cohesive, and it must provide service descriptions with the details on its utilization syntax and semantics. Normally speaking, these service descriptions are intended for programmatic processing rather than human processing.

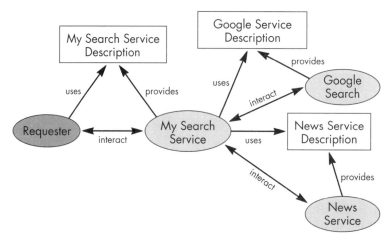

Figure 5.8
Service description for Web services.

A sample service description and its usage is shown in Figure 5.8, where a search engine service is exposing some of its capabilities to the external world so that its clients can understand the syntax and semantics of that service, and interact with the service. This service may then interact with other services using the description provided by those services, such as other search engines or news services.

This description can be expressed in any available description languages, such as Web Service Description Language (WSDL), Dynamic Agent Markup Language (DAML[17]), or Resource Description Framework (RDF). However, we should note that this description can be expressed in a combination of languages. One such example combination may be using WSDL for service syntax description while using RDF for service semantic description in association with WSDL. Figure 5.9 shows how this can be expressed for the above search service.

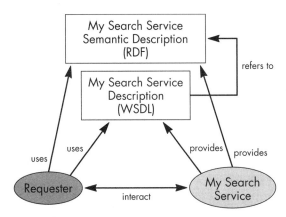

Figure 5.9
Sample service description with semantic information.

Let us now explore WSDL to understand the basic constructs provided to describe a Web service.

Web Service Description Language (WSDL)

This discussion is based on the WSDL 1.1 specification.[18] We will cover some core concepts of WSDL 1.2, which is a work activity in the W3C.[19] Some of the WSDL 1.2 constructs are of importance to the grid services community.

Quick Overview of WSDL 1.1

WSDL is an XML Infoset-based document, which provides a model and XML format for describing Web services. This enables services to be described, and enables the client to consume these services in a standard way without knowing much on the lower level protocol exchange binding including SOAP and HTTP. This high-level abstraction on the service limits human interaction and enables the automatic generation of proxies for Web services, and these proxies can be static or dynamic. WSDL allows the description of both document-oriented and RPC-oriented messages.

As shown in Figure 5.10, a WSDL document can be divided into abstract definitions and agreed-upon definitions. The abstract section defines the SOAP messages in a platform-independent language and a neutral manner. The abstract definitions help to extend service definitions and enhance the reusability where the agreed-upon definition enables multiple protocol bindings such as HTTP and SMTP and end points of choice (e.g., service end points). The abstract service definition components are Types, Messages, Operations, PortType, and Binding. Agreed-upon definition components are Service, Port, and Binding. These agreed-upon definitions specify the wire message serialization, transport selection, and other protocol implementation aspects. The WSDL binding elements are used to specify the agreed-upon grammar for input, output, and fault messages. There are specific binding extensions defined by WSDL for SOAP and HTTP.

There can be two kinds of message encoding; that is, literal encoding and SOAP encoding. *Literal encoding* specifies that the messages will be constructed according to the XML schema "literal," and SOAP encoding occurs according to the SOAP-encoding rules "encoded," defined in

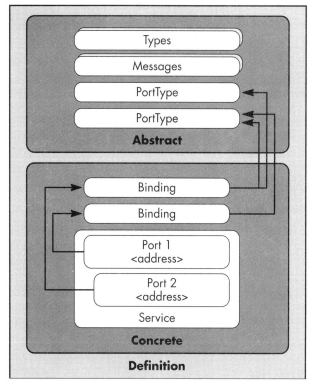

Figure 5.10
The WSDL 1.1 abstract and agreed-upon components.

the SOAP specification. The other important concepts in WSDL are the message transfer format; messages can be transferred as "document" or "rpc" parameters. *Document* means that the message part is the body of the message, while RPC means that the parts are just parameters of the call, with specific signatures that are wrapped in an element. These transfer formats confirm to the SOAP semantic of the SOAP message exchange.

There has been a number of limitations with this model including service semantic clarifications, extension mechanisms, and the support for new constructs in the SOAP 1.2 specification. WSDL 1.2 is trying to resolve these problems.

Quick Overview of WSDL 1.2

Some of the major changes are introduced to align the WSDL 1.1 specification with the SOAP 1.2 specification, and the overall service-oriented architecture standards such as Web architecture and Web service architecture.

One of the major semantic clarifications we can discuss is regarding the concept of the *service*. Let us explore the semantic details of this concept. We will start with the concept of a resource. A resource is anything that can be addressable by a URI. These resources can be software applications, hardware abstractions, or Web resources (e.g., HTML pages or forms). Every resource can be logically represented by a set of interfaces, such as manageability interfaces, operational interfaces, and other such interfaces. A service is then treated as a realization of a single interface of a resource. This is represented in Figure 5.11.

Note that a service can have any number of end points and bindings. But every service is a representation of a single interface. This interface may be a combination of multiple interfaces through derivation. We discuss the details of the interface inheritance toward the end of this section on WSDL 1.2.

This view is different from the WSDL 1.1's view, where a single service can be bound to multiple interfaces through bindings. This causes confusion on the semantic of a service. It is a fact that in WSDL 1.1, it is difficult to express service semantics through the description language. A binding may select to implement any interfaces of choice. This confusion is later clarified in WSDL 1.2 by having a service as a representation of a single interface of a resource. A service may then have multiple end points with different addresses and bindings, however, always bound to the same resource using the same interface.

There is another construct introduced to clarify the resource that a service is implementing. This is done using a new construct called "targetResource." This "targetResource" is an attribute of a service element, with a URI value representing the resource URI.

Based on the above discussion, a service element is defined in Listing 5.2:

Listing 5.2   A service element definition in WSDL 1.2.

```
<definitions>
..................................................................
<service name="xs:NCName" interface="xs:QName" targetResource="xs:anyURI"? >
        <end-point />*
  </service>
</definitions>
```

We can see the WSDL 1.2 description information elements in the following illustration. The concept of "Resource" is logical. As shown in Figure 5.11, the service developers have to define the abstract concepts of a service and attach a service to the target resource and the corresponding interface. The binding selection must then be a runtime activity.

In addition to the clarification on the semantic of a service, WSDL 1.2 has introduced the concept of features, properties, and so on. These concepts are in line with the SOAP 1.2 counterparts and can be extended to other protocols of choice.

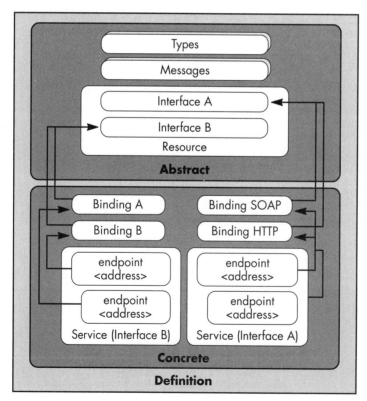

Figure 5.11
The WSDL 1.2 abstract and agreed-upon components.

By defining features and properties in WSDL, a reader (i.e., software agents or humans) can identify the following characteristics:

1. Some requirements on the interface/operations for its successful execution. For example, some operations need to provide a WS-Security assertion of type XML signature.
2. Some indications on the availability of some feature so that we can rely on them. For example, a service can state that a feature called "privacy policy" is available for verification.
3. General information on the values of the features and its properties.

These features may oftentimes appear at the interface level or at the binding level. In addition to these extensions for features and modules, there are some major changes that have been introduced, as described below.

1. Operation overloading is removed from WSDL. Note that WSDL 1.1 supports the operation overloading facilities. Thus, we have to take care when designing WSDL, especially with interface inheritance.
2. As we have noticed, the "PortType" construct in WSDL 1.1 is now changed to "interface" to align with the existing distributed technologies and IDL. This interface supports the inheritance capability. It is worthy to note that this extensibility of interfaces is one of the core concepts in the grid service specification. Listing 5.3 shows a sample interface hierarchy.

Listing 5.3   A sample interface hierarchy provided in WSDL 1.2.

```
<Definitions .............>
. . . . . . . . . . . . . . . . . . . . . . . . . . . . . . . . . . . . . . . . . . . . . . . . . . . . .
        <interface name="A">
                <operation name="add">
                </operation>
        </interface>

        <interface name="B" extends="A">
                <operation name="subtract">
                </operation>
        </interface>
. . . . . . . . . . . . . . . . . . . . . . . . . . . . . . . . . . . . . . . . . . . . . . .
</definitions>
```

We will see the details on this interface hierarchy and its usage pattern in the next chapter during our discussion on Grid Computing.

- The "ports" construct in WSDL 1.1 has changed to "end points" in WSDL 1.2.

- Another feature that is valuable is the "mechanisms" to include other schema languages to describe the types of the message. Most notable works in this area are inclusion of DTD and RELAX-NG.
- A number of MEPs has been defined to support complex message exchange scenarios, such as request–response, input, and output. WSDL 1.2 defined these MEPs as well-defined features with specific properties.

The Global XML Architecture Vision

We have discussed earlier in this chapter that Web services are trying to unify software integration among partners, through advanced networking services and methods of interoperable messaging. These interoperability and integration points can be achieved only through the definition of interoperable messages, exchange patterns, and processes.

The IBM Corporation, Microsoft, and a number of other vendors are working on a Global XML Architecture (GXA), which provides a modular, XML-based, open standards-based, and federated XML Web services suite. These are infrastructure-level protocols for building Web service applications. These protocols include standards for security, reliability, addressing, transactions, and multiparty agreements.

The vision behind such an XML architecture includes:

1. Providing standards-based and interoperable protocol definitions
2. Reducing development efforts by separating infrastructure protocols from application and transport protocols
3. Providing open standards-based designs for interoperable messaging across multiple vendors

Based on Figure 5.12, we can further explore the basic principle of GXA.

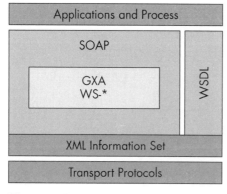

Figure 5.12
The GXA and dependencies.

The XML Data Model

The core of Web services is the XML data model or the XML information set. This is defined by the W3C and forms the core of all XML specifications including SOAP and WSDL. This common base allows creation of adaptable tools and XML processors.

Modularity

In an earlier section, we have discussed that SOAP provides an enveloping and processing mechanism, respective to the messages being exchanged. The most common problem found with the existing protocols is the lack of the interoperable wire format. SOAP is trying to adopt a transport-independent wire format for XML messages. This is based on the SOAP encoding format as specified by the SOAP specification, or using XML schema as the wire format. The XML schema encoded messages are recommended and often called "document/literal" messages. Since XML schema is an industry standard, and based on *infoset*, the interoperability is essentially guaranteed.

The GXA architecture is building on top of SOAP. The GXA protocols (for the most part) are SOAP extensions based on SOAP headers or features. The architecture makes use of the knowledge of SOAP intermediaries and supports SOAP actors (e.g., "role" in SOAP 1.2).

Decentralization and Federation

An observation we could make at this stage is that there exists the concept of *constraint agreement* between the parties involved in Web service integration. This agreement is on the syntax and semantics of the messages being exchanged. They may disagree on the software accepting the message, programming languages used to build the system, operating system utilized, and the database system utilized.

The GXA accepted the concept of *decentralization*, allowing the parties involved to make their own decision on all parts of message processing including: security, policies requirements, and processing. Therefore, this concept of "federation" still allows these parties to exchange information in meaningful formats. For example, a party can exchange a message with another party, even though both disagree on the security implementation mechanisms.

Application and Transport Neutral

SOAP and hence GXA does not dictate on the transport mechanism for message exchange. This is a binding-level decision done by the agreement between the service and the requester. This binding agreement is independent of the message being exchanged. The application neutrality comes from the fact that it is not defining any specific message exchange protocol but instead defining standards-based XML messages that needed to be exchanged.

Open Standards Initiatives

Today, many of the specifications and standard protocol definitions are being submitted to various standards organizations, including OASIS and W3C. This standardization process will help to further refine these specifications and their adoptability across various heterogeneous application and protocol stacks. These standards organizations, together with the Web Service Interoperability Organization (WS-I), can provide the desired infrastructure standards the industries require to continue demonstrating progress in this area of Grid Computing and Web services.

The major building blocks identified by the GXA includes facilities for:

1. Message-level security
2. Exchanging transaction-aware messages
3. Message exchange coordination among participants
4. Reliable message exchange patterns
5. Message routing and referral processes
6. Addressing mechanisms to dispatch messages to the intended party
7. Service and message policies for proper message handling
8. Attachments to foreign bodies that won't fit with regular XML messages
9. Metadata information exchange

Since these components are leading the way to becoming the core technology building blocks and interoperability solutions, we next explore the most commonly used components and its internal design details. In this next discussion, we explore policies, security, and addressing.

Service Policy

The Web service policy framework provides a general-purpose model and the corresponding syntax to describe and communicate the respective policies of a Web service.

It is important to understand that this policy framework does not provide a negotiation framework for Web services. We have to use these policy building blocks in conjunction with other Web service standards and specific application-level policy negotiation services.

Basically, WS-Policy enables a model and framework to express policy assertions about a Web service. These assertions are extensible grammar for expressing capabilities, requirements, and the general characteristics of a service. Note that some of these assertions may manifest into wire messages (e.g., security credentials), while some others are just information and checkpoints for service users (e.g., privacy policy).

This policy model and framework defines the following components:

- *Policy expression.* An XML Infoset representation of one or more policy assertions.
- *Policy subject.* An entity (e.g., an end point, object, or resource) to which a policy can be bound.

- *Policy assertion*. An individual preference, requirement, capability, or other property (e.g., security, privacy, and so on).
- *Policy attachment*. The mechanism for associating policy with one or more subjects is referred to as a policy attachment.

The following discussion will introduce us to the above components of this policy model. List-ing 5.4 shows a sample policy expression, with two policy statements containing the names "QA" and "QB," respectively. It is important to pay close attention to the XML elements defined in this listing. We will also reuse this listing as a reference for the following discussion on the policy language features.

Listing 5.4   A sample policy expression.

```
<wsp:Policy xmlns:wsp="..." xmlns:wsu="..." xmlns:x="..."
            xml:base="http://www.acme.com/policies"
            wsu:Id="A"
            Name="QA"
            TargetNamespace="http://www.acme.com/policies">
<wsse:SecurityToken>
<wsse:TokenType>wsse:Kerberosv5TGT</wsse:TokenType>
</wsse:SecurityToken>

<wsse:Integrity>
        <wsse:Algorithm Type="wsse:AlgSignature"
                URI="http://www.w3.org/2000/09/xmlenc#aes" />
    </wsse:Integrity>
</wsp:Policy>

<wsp:Policy xmlns:wsp="..." xmlns:wsu="..." xmlns:x="..."
            xml:base="http://www.acme.com/policies"
            wsu:Id="B"
            Name="QB"
        wsp:Preference ="1"
            TargetNamespace="http://www.acme.com/policies">
<x:ExpeditedDelivery wsp:Usage="wsp:Required" />
  </wsp:Policy>
```

Policy Expressions and Assertions

A policy expression is a mechanism to convey a set of policy assertions (e.g., security, privacy, and other policy-related items). In the above listing we are specifying a security policy assertion.

A policy expression is an XML Infoset with a combination of a top level <wsp:policy> container element, the policy operators (<wsp:all>, <wsp:ExactlyOne>, <wsp:OneorMore>, and <wsp:Policy>), and some attributes (wsu:Id, Name, wsp:Preference, and so on) to distinguish the policy usage. The attributes Name and ID are used to uniquely identify the policy expression. This expression contains zero or more domain-specific assertions.

These assertions can be standard defined (WS-Security assertions) and/or service provider defined (as shown in Listing 5.4). It is important to understand that the evaluations of these expressions are application-specific behavior for a given subject. We will explore later, in the policy attachment section, explanations on exactly how we can associate a policy subject with a policy expression. In the previous listing, the policy expression "QA" contains two assertions: "wsse:SecurityToken" and "wsse:Integrity."

As described in the previous listing, there are two policy expressions with a default operation of <wsp:all>. This indicates that with all the policy assertions expressed, there is a present need to be satisfied. This means that for the first policy expression "QA," both the assertions "wsse:SecurityToken" and "wsse:Integrity" must be satisfied.

A Mechanism for Policy Expression Attachment

There are two mechanisms by which we can attach a policy expression with one or more subjects or resources. First is the XML-based resources to attach policy expressions as part of the definition. This can be done by the definition of two global XML schema attributes, as shown in Listing 5.5.

Listing 5.5 A global schema attribute to define policy expression references.

```
<xs:schema>
  <xs:attribute name="PolicyURIs" type="wsp:tPolicyURIs" />
  <xs:attribute name="PolicyRefs" type="wsp:tPolicyRefs" />
</xs:schema>
```

We can use the above-defined attributes to attach the policy references with a resource XML definition, as shown in Listing 5.6.

Listing 5.6 An instance of a resource with the policy expression references.

```
<MyElement xmlns:wsp="http://schemas.xmlsoap.org/ws/2002/12/policy"
           wsp:PolicyURIs="http://www.acme.com/policies#A
                           http://www.acme.com/policies#B" />
```

This shows how to attach policy expressions to resources independently from their definition. In the above case we know the XML resource element and can change its representation. However, this may not be possible in all cases. In such cases, we need to define the policy attachment and apply that to the subject or resource of interest. Listing 5.7 shows how we can do this using the wsp:PolicyAttachment element.

Listing 5.7 Policy attachment.

```
<wsp:PolicyAttachment>
  <wsp:AppliesTo>
    <wsa:End-pointReference >
<!—can be any resource/service - ->
    </wsa:End-pointReference>
  </wsp:AppliesTo>
  <wsp:PolicyReference URI="http://www.acme.com/my-policy.xml" />
</wsp:PolicyAttachment>
```

Listing 5.7 shows how we can attach a policy reference XML file (my-policy.xml), which contains the policy expressions to any resource identifiable through WS-Address specification EndpointReference.

The developer will discover this is a more flexible approach. Interested readers could discover how these policy expressions are attached to WSDL and UDDI definition elements in WS-PolicyAttachment.[20] Also, there is some work underway to standardize some of the common sets of assertions (WS-PolicyAssertions).[21]

Security

Most of the existing security is dealing with point-to-point security solutions. This point-to-point security can be achieved by different ways, including SSL/TLS and IPSec as examples. Figure 5.13 shows point-to-point security establishment.

Figure 5.13
Point-to-point security establishment.

As shown in Figure 5.14, Web services security involves achieving end-to-end message security between the initial sender of the message to the final receiver of the message. These messages may go through many intermediaries on the way.

Figure 5.14
End-to-end security.

This message security is a combination of different levels of security requirements including end-point authentication and authorization, message integrity, message confidentiality, privacy, trust, and federation among collaborators.

In general, to achieve the end-to-end security, the following points must be accommodated:

- A Web service end point can ask the requester to submit the necessary claims.
- A requester can send the message along with proof of the claim, which is normally called "security tokens" such as username/password, Kerberos tickets, and X509 certificates.
- If the requester does not have the required claims, the requestor can obtain the claims from some other trusted agency and pass these claims along with the message. These trusted authorities are called "security token services."

We know that achieving the above level of security is a challenge. The GXA architecture tries to address the previous problem of security with a set of interoperable and industry-accepted standards. The following diagram shows the core security standards identified by GXA in order to achieve the required end-to-end security.

Our discussions will be focused on WS-Security,[22] which forms the base security standard as illustrated in Figure 5.15.

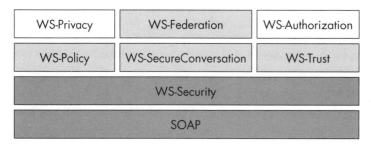

Figure 5.15
WS-Security stack with the highlighted boxes indicating the available standards.

There are a number of distributed technologies that exist today, including Kerberos, public key, and others. The widespread acceptance of these technologies helps the creators of the WS-Security specifications decide how to use them effectively in the Web services environment, instead of creating new security technologies.

This decision paved the way for creating XML standards that uses existing technologies and future ones. With these requirements in mind, the WS-Security standard defines a SOAP header with a number of security assertions and meta-information. This provides quality of protection through message integrity and message confidentiality.

In general, the base WS-Security specification addresses

- Security credential exchange
- Signatures
- Encryption

First, we will explore a basic SOAP header annotated with WS-Security information. Then, we will use this sample WS-Security header, as shown in Listing 5.8, to explain the previous add-on security constructs.

Listing 5.8   WS-Security header in SOAP message.

```
<?xml version="1.0" encoding="utf-8"?>
<s:Envelope
  xmlns:s="http://schemas.xmlsoap.org/soap/envelope/"
  xmlns:wsse="http://schemas.xmlsoap.org/ws/2002/12/secext">
  <s:Header>
   <wsse:Security>
      ...
   </wsse:Security>
  </s:Header>
  <s:Body>
      ...
  </s:Body>
</s:Envelope>
```

As we can infer from the sample skeleton, WS-Security defined its own namespace and a SOAP header with <Security> as its root element.

We have previously mentioned that WS-Security addresses message integrity, which allows a receiver to be sure that the data is not tampered with in any way, and the message confidentiality and integrity is maintained. This ensures that the data cannot be compromised while in transit. WS-Security allows us to send security tokens, such as user name/password combinations, Kerberos tickets, or an X.509 certificate. We will explore each of these in the following sections.

MESSAGE INTEGRITY IS A PRACTICE TO ENSURE INTEGRITY

Message integrity allows a receiver to be sure that the data is not tampered with on the way to and from its origin/destination. This is normally achieved using digital signatures created using public key technologies. XML signature allows public key mechanisms. In addition, it also allows the concept of encrypting the message digest using a symmetric key (known to both parties). A message digest is a checksum on the message content created using different algorithms such as MD5.

Message confidentiality means that only the intended receiver(s) can decode the received message. Others on the way cannot decode the information in the message. This confidentiality of the message exchange can be achieved using encryption mechanisms.

Exchanging the Security Credential Information

For proper authentication of the sender and receiver to occur, there needs to be an exchange of tokens showing their identity. This enables the parties to verify with whom they are exchanging information. There are a number of security tokens available, including Kerberos, signatures, and user name/password. WS-Security provides a standard mechanism for exchanging any of these credentials, along with the messages. It is important to understand that WS-Security does not address the application/service authentication process, which is an application/service run-time specific issue.

While it is legal to exchange any kind of token with WS-Security, it specifies two possible kinds of tokens, summarized below.

UsernameToken. Listing 5.9 presents an example of how we can pass a username and password with a WS-Security header.

Listing 5.9   Passing username token with WS-Security.

```
<wsse:Security
 xmlns:wsse="http://schemas.xmlsoap.org/ws/2002/12/secext">
 <wsse:UsernameToken>
  <wsse:Username>bob</wsse:Username>
  <wsse:Password>x4%78r</wsse:Password>
 </wsse:UsernameToken>
</wsse:Security>
```

This is a very simple process of security management but may get compromised on the network transfer. In most situations these tokens are passed in an encrypted transport network connection similar to Secure Socket Layer (SSL).

BinarySecurityToken. Binary tokens send tokens encoded as binary streams. These binary encoding schemes may be of different types, such as Base64 encoding. Let us explore how we can use this mechanism to send Kerberos tickets and X.509 digital signatures. These message formats are specified by the WS-Security specifications.

Kerberos Tokens

Listing 5.10 provides an example of how the BinarySecurityToken can be utilized to send a Kerberos ticket.

Listing 5.10   Passing binary tokens with WS-Security—Kerberos.

```
<wsse:Security
 xmlns:wsse="http://schemas.xmlsoap.org/ws/2002/12/secext">
 <wsse:BinarySecurityToken
  ValueType="wsse:Kerberosv5ST"
```

Listing 5.10   Passing binary tokens with WS-Security—Kerberos. (Continued)

```
  EncodingType="wsse:Base64Binary">
    WsEdUtt...
  </wsse:BinarySecurityToken>
</wsse:Security>
```

The above listing shows a Kerberos ticket security token embedded with the <BinarySecurityToken> element. As we can see from this example, this is not much different from the previously mentioned username token. This element ValueType attribute indicates that this is a Kerberos Version 5 service ticket, which (in this example) is utilized to authenticate this client to a particular service.

X509 Certificates

Listing 5.11 provides an example of how the BinarySecurityToken can be utilized to send an X509 certificate.

Listing 5.11   Passing binary tokens with WS-Security—X509 certificate.

```
<wsse:Security
 xmlns:wsse="http://schemas.xmlsoap.org/ws/2002/12/secext">
 <wsse:BinarySecurityToken
  ValueType="wsse:X509v3"
  EncodingType="wsse:Base64Binary">
    XdfTr ...
 </wsse:BinarySecurityToken>
</wsse:Security>
```

The above listing illustrates how to embed an X509 certificate within the <BinarySecurityToken> element. This element ValueType attribute indicates that this is an X509 Version 3 certificate, which is used to authenticate this client to a particular service.

Let us now explore a discussion regarding how to achieve message integrity using the WS-Security mechanism.

Attaining Message Integrity

To maintain the integrity of the SOAP message, it is required to digitally sign the XML document. The XML Signature[23] mechanism provides a standard to digitally sign XML documents (or a fragment of) the XML document. WS-Security utilizes this capability of XML Signature to maintain its message integrity. Let us discover how XML Signature works, and how WS-Security utilizes this feature to protect messages.

XML Signature defines a signature element whose contents include the digital signature and the information related to that specific signature. Normally speaking, the <Signature> element used with SOAP contains the <SignedInfo>, < SignatureValue>, and <KeyInfo> elements.

Listing 5.12   Using WS-Security and XML Digital Signature to protect the message integrity.

```
<s:Envelope ...........
<s:Header>
  <wsse:Security>
        <wsse:BinarySecurityToken ValueType="wsse:X509v3"
                EncodingType="wsse:Base64Binary" wsu:Id="X509Cert">
                XdfTr...
        </wsse:BinarySecurityToken>

        <ds:Signature xmlns:ds="http://www.w3.org/2000/09/xmldsig#">
        <ds:SignedInfo>
                <ds:CanonicalizationMethod
                    Algorithm="http://www.w3.org/2001/10/xml-exc-c14N"/>
                <ds:SignatureMethod
                    Algorithm="http://www.w3.org/2000/09/xmldsig#rsa-sha1"/>
                <ds:Reference URI="#MessageBody1">
                <ds:DigestMethod Algorithm=
                    "http://www.w3.org/2000/09/xmldsig#sha1"/>
                <ds:DigestValue>
                            iUtr6ou...
                </ds:DigestValue>
                </ds:Reference>
        </ds:SignedInfo>
        <ds:SignatureValue>
                SDRT7bHY...
        </ds:SignatureValue>
        <ds:KeyInfo>
                <wsse:SecurityTokenReference>
                        <wsse:Reference URI="#X509Cert"/>
                </wsse:SecurityTokenReference>
        </ds:KeyInfo>
        </ds:Signature>
  </wsse:Security>
 </s:Header>
<s:Body wsu:Id="MessageBody1">
  ...
 </s:Body>
</s:Envelope>
```

Listing 5.12 shows a sample XML digital signature utilized with the WS-Security SOAP header in order to protect the integrity of the SOAP body identified by "MessageBody1." Considering the above listing sample, we can list the core elements of XML Signature and discover how well it fits with WS-Security and the overall SOAP message.

As shown in Listing 5.12, <CanonicalizationMethod> identifies the XML canonicalization algorithm.

CANONICAL XML

The rules for XML authoring are flexible so that the same document structure and the same piece of information can be represented by different XML documents, and even XML schema or DTD can be validated from them. For example, the following two XML documents are semantically equal. However, they contain the attributes in a different order. Another item that can be noted in these documents is that the second listing contains more white space.

```
<?xml version="1.0" ?>
- <address type="US">
  <zipcode value="12345"  type="us-zip"/>
  </ address >

<?xml version="1.0" ?>
- <address type="US">

<zipcode  type="us-zip" value="12345"/>
  </ address >
```

This is a major problem with XML, as it is a text-based document and the treatment of each character may have a significant effect on the bit-by-bit validity of the document even though the document may be semantically equal. This causes problems especially when dealing with message integrity.

The XML canonicalization algorithm is used to convert the XML document to a standards format, bit by bit, to avoid problems by ensuring the document will be identifiable as the same document, bit by bit, by everyone.

In the previously illustrated example of code, you will note we are using the algorithm identified as "http://www.w3.org/2001/10/xml-exc-c14N" and defined by the W3C XML Signature working group. The <SignatureMethod> identifies the algorithm used to create the digital signature. These algorithms include the Secure Hash Algorithm (SHA) along with DSA or RSA. In the above example code we are using "RSA." The <Reference> identifies the resource to be signed. This reference may be SOAP body parts identified through message part ids (wsu:id). In addition, the reference carries the algorithm used and the digest value. In this specific example we are creating a digest using the SHA algorithm and signing the SOAP body identified as

"MessageBody1." <SignatureValue> contains the real signature of the message. <KeyInfo> identifies the key that should be used to validate the above signature. This is optional provided that the recipient of the message knows how to obtain the key.

In the previous discussion we mentioned that a flexible and efficient approach to achieve the XML message integrity has some problems, especially regarding the processing overhead on converting the messages to canonical format, creating the digest on that format, and adding signatures using that digest. In short, the processing required to support XML Signatures is highly process intensive. This can become complicated when we start checking the integrity of the message parts with the same (or different) algorithms. Another challenging problem is the creation of certificates and the exchange of them among the parties of interest. It is important to understand that we must exert the highest degree of care regarding these circumstances, and when we should use the XML signature.

Let us now explore the topic of attaining a message exchange with confidentiality, especially in the context of end-to-end messaging transfers.

How to Transfer Messages with Confidentiality

The above discussed message integrity mechanism will tell us whether the message is tampered with on the way or not; however, it won't prevent someone on the message path from peeking into the message. For that we need to encrypt the XML message or fragments of the message using some standard mechanism. The XML encryption[24] standard helps us achieve this level of confidentiality. Let's discuss how the XML encryption works and how WS-Security uses that to protect our private messages. Listing 5.13 illustrates a sample SOAP message encryption mechanism using WS-Security.

Listing 5.13   An encrypted XML message using WS-Security.

```
<s:Envelope   xmlns:s="http://schemas.xmlsoap.org/soap/envelope/"
              xmlns:wsse="http://schemas.xmlsoap.org/ws/2002/12/secext"
              xmlns:wsu="http://schemas.xmlsoap.org/ws/2002/07/utility"
              xmlns:ds="http://www.w3.org/2000/09/xmldsig#"
              xmlns:xenc="http://www.w3.org/2001/04/xmlenc#">
<s:Header>
 <wsse:Security>
      <xenc:EncryptedKey>
            <xenc:EncryptionMethod
                  Algorithm="http://www.w3.org/2001/04/xmlenc#rsa-1_5"/>
            <ds:KeyInfo>
                  <ds:KeyName>
                        CN=Key13, C=US
                  </ds:KeyName>
            </ds:KeyInfo>
            <xenc:CipherData>
```

Listing 5.13   An encrypted XML message using WS-Security. (Continued)

```
                            <xenc:CipherValue>
                                    utyf^7sdf . .
                            </xenc:CipherValue>
                    </xenc:CipherData>
                    <xenc:ReferenceList>
                            <xenc:DataReference URI="#EncryptedBody1"/>
                    </xenc:ReferenceList>
            </xenc:EncryptedKey>
    </wsse:Security>
</s:Header>
<s:Body>
        <xenc:EncryptedData wsu:Id="EncryptedBody1">
                <xenc:EncryptionMethod
                    Algorithm='http://www.w3.org/2001/04/xmlenc#tripledes-cbc'/>
                <xenc:CipherData>
                        <xenc:CipherValue>
                            WSDG^9unsV . . .
                        </xenc:CipherValue>
                </xenc:CipherData>
        </xenc:EncryptedData>
    </s:Body>
</s:Envelope>
```

WS-Security utilizes three parts of the XML encryption: <EncryptedData>, <EncryptedKey>, and <ReferenceList>. Let us further examine each of these parts.

<EncryptedData>.   As shown in Listing 5.13, this element contains the actual encrypted data in a subelement called <CipherData>. This element can also contain subelements that indicate the encryption algorithm that was used, the key that was used in order to perform the encryption. Normally, the keys are again encrypted and will be added to the header, as shown in < Encrypt-edKey>. This is the case we have presented in the above sample listing.

<EncryptedKey>.   Similar to <EncryptedData> and in Listing 5.13, it has three subelements: <EncryptionMethod>, <KeyInfo>, and <CipherData>. The main difference lies in the fact that what is being encrypted here is a symmetric key. This header's <EncryptionMethod> describes how this key was encrypted rather than how the actual data was encrypted. The data is encrypted using the <EncryptedData> mechanism, as we have noted earlier in the text.

As defined by WS-Security, XML encryption can be used in a number of ways with SOAP messages. We can encrypt the entire body, some body parts, and certain header elements, or even attachments sent with the message. The intermediaries on the path of the SOAP message can add their own encrypted headers or decryption, and process parts intended solely for themselves.

Now we can define some of the higher-level security standards. We are not planning to go into details; however, we will present their usage and relationship with WS-Security.

Some High-Level GXA Security Standards

The high-level security standards associated with GXA are further explored in this discussion.

WS-Trust

We have seen earlier that the requester must possess a secure token to establish a secure message channel to the Web service end point. There may be cases where the requestor or the service may need to request tokens from other trusted parties, called secure token services. These requests for tokens, and the issuance of security tokens and trust relationship management aspects, are specified in the WS-Trust specification.[25]

As shown in Figure 5.16, the WS-Trust deals with different aspects of secure token services, including how to request a token and the issuing of tokens in a trusted manner. This issuance of tokens must be secure and built on top of WS-Security. The secure token services can be a contact point for secure negotiation through delegation and impersonation.

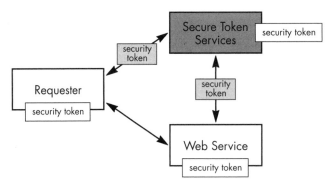

Figure 5.16
Secure Token services and the security token exchange.

WS-SecureConversation

This specification defines extensions that build on WS-Security to provide secure communication. The mechanisms provided include provisions for establishing and sharing security contexts, and deriving session keys from security contexts (see Figure 5.17).

WS-Federation

WS-Federation defines mechanisms that are used to enable identity, attribute, authentication, and authorization federation across different trust environments.

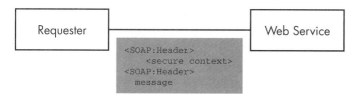

Figure 5.17
A secure conversation using the WS-SecureConversation header.

Thus far, we have been discussing how to achieve end-to-end security in Web service applications. Now we will explore one of the latest specifications in the GXA related to this, which addresses the end-point identification mechanism. The end-point identification is simple in most of the cases (i.e., stateless services); however, this may become more complex when the end points are stateful instances, or a realization of a combination of custom properties. We need to have a deep understanding of this specification since it is going to be utilized in all other specifications to address the end points.

Addressing (WS-Addressing)

WS-Addressing (WSA)[26] provides transport-neutral mechanisms to address Web services and messages.

This capability is provided by the specification using two constructs:

1. A flexible and extendable end-point reference description model
2. A set of SOAP message headers (SOAP features) and rules to map the above reference elements to the header elements

Normally speaking, Web services are invoked by the WSDL-provided service end-point information. For example, WSDL service ports have a location address, which identifies the end point. This information is suitable in most of the cases until we start exploring stateful Web services and/or adding more dynamic information to the address (e.g., instance information, policy constructs, etc.).

This requires a client or runtime system to uniquely identify a service at runtime based on this runtime information. These elements of binding specific information on the address may include a primary key, unique identifier, and other key elements. Currently, there is no standard way that this information can be exchanged, and the mapping of that exchanged information to the runtime engine while accessing the service.

In general, the current WSDL 1.1 is not suitable for the following situations:

1. Dynamic generation and customization of the service end-point descriptions

2. Identification and description of specific service instances that are created as the result of stateful interactions

3. Flexible and dynamic exchange of end-point information

The WS-Addressing specification tries to solve the above problem by providing a lightweight mechanism for identifying and describing end-point information, and mapping that information to the SOAP message headers.

Listing 5.14 illustrates how to define a sample end-point description using the WS-Addressing specification.

Listing 5.14   A sample WS-Address end-point identification mechanism.

```
<wsa:End-pointReference xmlns:wsa="..." xmlns:acme="..."
xmlns:ogsi="...">
    <wsa:Address>http://www.acme.com/base</wsa:Address>
    <wsa:ReferenceProperties>
        <ogsi:instanceOf>myService</ogsi: instanceOf >
    </wsa:ReferenceProperties>
  <wsa:PortType>acme:AcmeSearchPortType</wsa:PortType>
</wsa:End-pointReference>
```

As shown in the preceding listing, a WSA-defined End-pointReference contains a number of subelements, such as <Address>, <ReferenceProperties>, <PortType>, <ServiceName>, and WS-Policy. The <Address> element is a URI that identifies the end point. This end point may be a network address or logical address. We can infer from the specification that with the exception of the <Address> subelement, all other subelements are optional. Based on the service end point requirements, these elements may appear in the description.

As shown in the above sample listing, our Acme service end point needs some reference properties, which uniquely identifies this instance of Acme service. We can have any number of reference properties and the usability of these properties is binding and runtime specific. For example, in the above case the OGSI runtime directs the calls to the specific Acme service instance identified by "myService." The PortType is another optional parameter but may help the client-side binding stubs for validation on the operation, prior to making the call to the destination. We can also attach any number of WS-Policy expressions, along with this end point, to further qualify the end point.

The above discussion helps to clarify that WS-Addressing provides much more information, and is rather dynamic in nature, when compared to the normal WSDL service location address.

In addition to the description language, there needs to be a mechanism to bind this information with a SOAP message. In the next section, we will examine the WSA-defined message headers and how the mapping is occurring from an end point to SOAP headers.

Listing 5.15 illustrates how to add a SOAP header with WSA constructs and end-point mapping.

Listing 5.15 WSA with SOAP header.

```
<S:Envelope xmlns:S="http://www.w3.org/2002/12/soap-envelope"
        xmlns:acme="..." xmlns:ogsi="...">
   <S:Header>
     ...
     <wsa:To> http://www.acme.com/base</wsa:To>
     <ogsi:instanceOf>123456789</ogsi: instanceOf >
     ...
   </S:Header>
   <S:Body>
     ...
   </S:Body>
</S:Envelope>
```

The preceding listing shows how the service end-point description, defined in the previous listing, is actually mapped into the SOAP headers. The most important mapping is the mapping of <Address> maps to <To> element, which is a required element. The reference properties are copied as header elements. This, in turn, enables the SOAP processors to handle them.

The Significance of WS-Addressing in the Context of Grid Services

Grid services created using the OGSI standard, which we will cover later in the book in greater detail, faces the same problem of instance addressing.

Currently, the grid service instance lookup is handled in two steps. First, the resolution process where it is establishing a handle resolution to convert the grid service unique handle (GSH) to a service reference. This may result in a dynamic grid service reference (GSR) with the current address of the service instance information embedded in the SOAP address location, and in some cases, in the newly defined <instanceOf> WSDL element.

This dynamic is an OGSI platform-specific solution, and the tools have to be built to handle and map this dynamically generated address to the stub. WS-Addressing can avoid this problem when the end-point reference is constructed such that it is rich enough to carry the specific instance address with its associated properties. These can be directly mapped to SOAP headers as specified by the WSA specification. This enables any client-side framework that is capable of working with the stateful service.

RELATIONSHIP BETWEEN WEB SERVICE AND GRID SERVICE

Throughout this chapter, we have been discussing Web services, and the respective technical underpinnings of Web services. The basic premise of this architecture is the creation of interoperable services and their respective applications.

Readers are by now aware that Grid Computing is the process of resource sharing among a collection of participants: This involves interoperable access to sharable resources. The architectural evolution of Grid Computing selects Web services as the technology for defining these interoperable resources. The main criteria on this selection are the open protocol base and the interoperable messaging solutions, as proposed by the Web services architecture. We have already discussed the evolution of grid services and its adaptability to the emerging technologies. In the next section, we will explore the details on how grid services are defined around Web services architectures, and the standardization process of grid services.

Given the previous discussion, we can now spend some time in exploring the relation between Web services and grid services, how we can differentiate each of them, and in what situations they share similarities.

An application or service may have the ability to maintain a state, and that state may be pertaining to the user of that application. For example, a purchase order system keeps a user's order information between the interaction, the user, and the system (i.e., verify order, change order, update order, etc.), until the order is submitted for delivery. This state information (i.e., purchase order) may be local to the application or the service, or it may be stored in an external state machine(s) such as databases, other resources, local session state, and the resource/service object.

It is noteworthy to understand how the above state is managed in Web service scenarios. Generally speaking, we can classify service state management into two forms. These two forms are as follows:

1. *Interaction aware state.* Normally, in the world of the Web and Web services, a client may interact with a service for a long period of time, as we have discussed in the above purchase order case. These interactions are correlated using some information passed from the client to the service, along with the message. This can be a simple cookie, a session ID, or complex correlation information. The advantage of this architecture design point is that the server side is not managing any specific client state information, or creating a specific instance for a client. The server-side implementation is very scalable and stateless in nature. It is not preventing the real state being persisted in a state machine external to the application; instead, this is correlated to a specific client's state using the session ID. This is, typically, how normal Web and Web services are defined.

2. *Application aware state.* In these situations, services are aware of its client and create a specific instance of the service for the specific client, and pass that instance information (e.g., primary key) back to the client for interaction. At this stage, the client is holding a reference to the specific instance of the service/application, and hence, can interact with the service instance without passing any correlation information. These services are typically referred to as stateful services, because the state information is held in the service itself and not passed back to the client. One important item to notice about this state management, similar to the above case, is that the service need not sustain the

state; rather, the service may delegate the state to other state machines. The only requirement is that the client owns a reference to the service instance.

Grid services are stateful Web services with a well-defined set of interfaces and behaviors for interaction. The following discussion explores the above concepts.

Interaction Aware State Information

This discussion addresses the previous introductory topic, interaction aware state information, which is related to state management. Figure 5.18 depicts these state machine scenarios we have just introduced, and subsequent discussions further examine this concept.

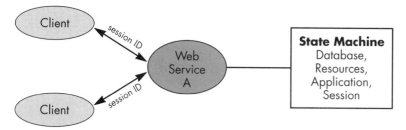

Figure 5.18
Information aware stateless Web services.

Figure 5.18 depicts a client talking to a Web service named "A." In this scenario, the client is maintaining some session ID, and each time it interacts with the Web service, it passes that correlation information (e.g., purchase order key) to the service end point. This enables the runtime function to dispatch the calls to any Web service of the type "A." The service is then able to handle the request for the client, based upon the session ID passed along with the respective request. This is a very scalable approach.

Application Aware State Information

This discussion addresses the previous introductory topic, application aware state information, which is related to state management. Figure 5.19 depicts these state machine scenarios we have just introduced, and subsequent discussions further examine this concept.

Stateful Web Services

In this case, the service itself maintains some state information for the client. Hence, each client is provided a specific instance of a Web service to engage. This is analogous to the object-based system, whereby the object clients create an object instance of the type of object class, and then maintains a pointer to that instance, and subsequently interacts with that instance. Each object instance maintains its nonstatic state information in its memory location.

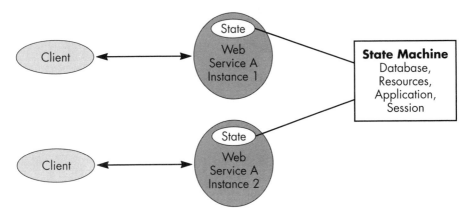

Figure 5.19
Application-based stateful Web services.

Similarly, the Web service client maintains a reference to an instance of the service, and then communicates to that specific service instance. The instance holds the state of the client, and can make and execute the business decision based on that current state information. For example, the service instances maintaining a purchase order within a given instance.

Grid Services

This discussion provides information related to grid services, and the comparisons to stateful Web services. Figure 5.20 shows the OGSI interaction with the stateful Web services machine(s).

Grid services are, in fact, stateful Web services. The service itself maintains some state information, and it exposes a set of standard interfaces to enable interactions with its client. These exposed interfaces enable the client to get/set the state information, in addition to the normal

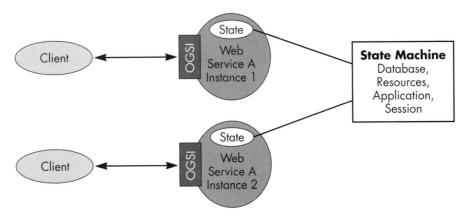

Figure 5.20
Grid services.

service behaviors. These exposed interfaces are defined in the OGSI specification. This specification provides mechanisms to:

- Service lifecycle management
- Instance state introspection and discovery
- Instance state change event notification

In addition to the above behaviors, OGSI provides for a unique handle for the stateful Web service, called the grid service handle (GSH). Generally speaking, a grid service can be accessed through a grid service reference (GSR), which then forms the binding-level information to access a service instance. This interface-enabled access to a stateful Web service then provides interoperability at the message level.

WEB SERVICE INTEROPERABILITY AND THE ROLE OF THE WS-I ORGANIZATION

We conclude our discussions on emerging Web services with some form of introduction to the works initiated by the Web Service Interoperability (WS-I[27]) organization.

This important organization is an open-standards industry organization that is responsible for handling the interoperability issues of Web services by defining well-defined profiles for Web services interoperability. These profiles can be treated as best practice guidelines for most service interoperability concerns.

However, these profiles are not necessarily standards by themselves; rather, these profiles are based on the existing standards, such as SOAP, WSDL, and UDDI. The term "guidelines" may be a more appropriate form of understanding.

In addition to these interoperable profile guidelines from WS-I, the organization provides tools to validate the messages to verify their conformity with the defined profiles. As of today, this organization defined a basic profile[28] for an XML message exchange, using SOAP 1.1, WSDL 1.1, and XML schema as the core standards. Since this is appearing to maintain its form as the major interoperability guideline for Web service messages, we will spend some time in reviewing these details related to these best practices in order to better understand how they are defined.

Introduction to Basic Profile Guidelines

The current released version of basic profile is version 1.0. The WS-I board already accepted this Web service basic profile 1.0 as a candidate recommendation. This basic profile 1.0 is built upon the following specifications:

- SOAP 1.1, including material related to
  - Namespaces in XML
  - XML 1.0 Second Edition

- WSDL 1.1, including material related to
  - XML Schema 2001 Part 1: Structures
  - XML Schema 2001 Part 2: Datatypes
- UDDI 2.0 (which includes support for UDDI 1.0 interfaces)
- SOAP Messages with Attachments, W3C note, 11 December 2000

It is important to understand the basic profile version and its base standards, including their respective versions. Based upon prior discussion, we are aware that these standards are evolving. The best practice usage model may, therefore, differ regarding combinations of these standards. The actual scope of the profile is bound by the standards it depends upon. It should be further understood that at development and test time, one may need to select a profile that matches the environment. Let us now begin to review more of the details surrounding this topic.

Some Details on the Basic Profile, with Samples

The basic premise of this profile is to ensure that Web services are able to communicate. The basic profile does not define any application semantics; rather, it ensures that the messages can be exchanged between any requester and the provider. The requirements are numbered (e.g., R2001) such that the validation tools and readers can refer to them as appropriate.

The basic profile provides interoperability in the following areas.

Messaging

The messaging aspect of Web service requires the most attention in order to achieve the required level of interoperability.

Web service messages are specified as XML messages. These XML messages are packaged into the SOAP envelope, and then transported through SOAP nodes to the final end-point destination. These messages may go through a number of intermediaries and processors.

This complexity requires a high level of interoperability among all the parties involved. The basic profile defines some core requirements around this message exchange pattern, including XML representation of SOAP messages, encoding requirements, SOAP processing model requirements, SOAP fault handling semantics, and SOAP binding over transport protocols.

The profile prefers the use of "literal" (nonencoded) XML messages rather than "encoded" XML messages. If we are using encoding, we must specify a soap:encodingStyle attribute to specify the required encoding schemes, including any restrictions such as "encodingStyle" which must not be present in <soap:envelope>, and in the child elements of the <soap:body>.

The "soap:mustUnderstand" attribute must accept only a "0" or a "1" value. The aforementioned sample validation rule helps us understand the depth and details of the profile. We will review a real validation using the profile tool later in the book in order to understand the details.

Service Description

The profile defines the best usable scenarios for WSDL to describe interoperable messages. This section defines a number of correct usage scenarios for WSDL. This is to be considered an extended set of requirements.

WSDL Document Structure

This section covers a wide number of requirements on the possible construction of a WSDL document as a whole. This includes document validation, importing other schemas, encoding, placement of elements, and namespace management. The following example rules explain the correct usage patterns.

The R2007 requirement specifies that the <wsdl:import> must specify a location attribute. It must not be empty.

The above example relates to the importing of other XML schemas from other locations. The next example specifies the requirements on the above import statement placement.

The R2022 requirement defines that the <wsdl:import> elements must precede all other elements from the WSDL namespace, except <wsdl:documentation>.

There are a number of such mandatory, optional, and required rules on the document structure.

Best Practices Usage of WSDL Types, Messages, portTypes, and Bindings

There are a lot of mandatory and optional rules that have been specified in this section related to the areas of WSDL portType definitions, message usage, and message type construction. The binding area covers the best usage pattern over different bindings, such as HTTP.

An incorrect example of a declaration for <wsdl:message> is shown below:

```
<message name="GetTradePriceInput">
    <part name="tickerSymbol" element="xsd:string"/>
    <part name="time" element="xsd:timeInstant"/>
  </message>
```

or, another form of the same declaration is shown below:

```
<message name="GetTradePriceInput">
    <part name="tickerSymbol" element="xsd:string"/>
  </message>
```

As mentioned, the above <wsdl:message> usage is incorrect, even though it is valid with reference to WSDL. Based on R2206, a wsdl:message in a <wsdl:description> containing a wsdl:part that uses the element attribute must refer to a global element declaration.

The correct implementation of the declaration is shown below:

```
<types xmlns:test="http://example.org/test/">>
    <xsd:element name="SubscribeToQuotes" type="test:SubscribeToQuotesType" />
</types>
<message name="GetTradePriceInput">
    <part name="body" element="test:SubscribeToQuotes"/>
 </message>
```

WSDL 1.1 has not clearly specified the child element structure in the case of a document-literal approach. The basic profile avoids confusion by clearly mandating the requirements on the <soap:body> message. The child element of <soap:body> must be an instance of the global element declaration referenced by the corresponding <wsdl:message> part. Based upon the above declaration of the "SubscribeToQuotes" message, the correct SOAP message must be constructed as shown below:

```
<s:Envelope xmlns:s="http://schemas.xmlsoap.org/soap/envelope/"
xmlns:xsi="http://www.w3.org/2001/XMLSchema-instance"
xmlns:xsd="http://www.w3.org/2001/XMLSchema"
xmlns:test=" http://example.org/test/">
  <s:Header/>
    <s:Body>
       <test: SubscribeToQuotes xmlns:test=" http://example.org/test/">
              ..............
       </test: SubscribeToQuotes>
    </s:Body>
</s:Envelope>
```

Similar to the above examples, there are about 60–70 requirements listed in the basic profile to clarify the WSDL description mechanism.

Use of XML Schema

WSDL 1.1 uses the XML schema as one of its type systems. The basic profile mandates the use of XML schema in accordance with the XML schema 1.0 recommendation.

Service Publication and Discovery.   The use of registries in Web service is an optional feature. The most common registry suitable for Web service publication is Universal Description Discovery and Integration (UDDI).[29] The basic profile lists some common rules for this publication; however, the usage model is not (yet) always compatible with UDDI 2.0.

Security.   The basic profile incorporates the networking services transport-level securities, such as HTTPS. The requirement is simple, in that it requires the SOAP address to specify an "https" address, rather than normal "http." The rest of the processing is a binding-level functionality.

Tools.   The tools play an important role in the basic profile validation. The basic profile requirements are complex for a service developer to verify, related to its accuracy. The tools should help in each stage of the development effort. The service developer can validate the

WSDL for interoperability concerns. Furthermore, runtime efforts should provide for the facilities to introspect the XML messages, through the wire, for interoperability concerns, and accordingly advise as to any situations encountered in this stage.

These tools provide some interesting capabilities:

- They validate the XML SOAP message against its corresponding WSDL and schema.
- They log the response on validation in a conformance report for review (normally an HTML file).
- On review we can determine each of the tests and validation results.
- If there is a validation failure or a need for some explanation or any recommendation, they may point us to the corresponding basic profile recommendation.

The current specification for tools defines two important aspects.

Monitoring SOAP messages. This allows tools to monitor the SOAP messages from a requester to a Web service. These SOAP messages are redirected to another port through tunneling mechanisms. As we can see, these monitors output the data in format as needed by the analyzer.

Analyzing SOAP messages. These tools are responsible for analyzing the logged messages in conjunction with the service WSDL, XML schema, and UDDI profiles. These messages are validated against the test assertion document, and finally a conformance report is produced. These types of analytical tools provide powerful validation capabilities when properly combined with these basic profile recommendations. This overall tools architecture is depicted in Figure 5.21.

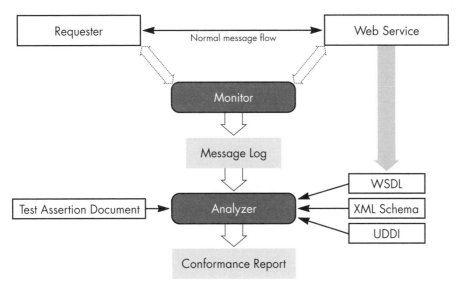

Figure 5.21
The basic profile validation tools.

Security Profiles and Other Areas to Consider

In addition to the basic profile we have just discussed, there are other important works underway throughout the global technical communities to define a common interoperable security profile that matches the WS-Security standards. This work is also intended to define other testing tools to validate secure message exchange interactions. Another notable area is the development of sample applications and their usage scenarios.

We recommend using WS-I-defined tools to validate the XML message for better interoperability. In the coming years, we will most likely witness that many of the existing Web service vendors will be incorporating these tools in their products for the purpose of testing interoperability.

NOTES

1. For more information, go to *www.w3.org/2002/ws/arch/*.

2. XML-INFO: *www.w3.org/TR/XML-infoset/*

3. XML-Schema: *www/w3.org/XML/Schema*

4. More information on RDF and related specifications are available in *www.w3.org/RDF/*.

5. RELAX-NG is an ongoing schema effort from OASIS. Visit *www.oasis-open.org*.

6. XML-Namespace: *www.w3.org/TR/XML-names11/*

7. XML Base: *www.w3.org/TR/xmlbase/*

8. XPath: *www.w3.org/TR/xpath*

9. XPointer: *www.w3.org/TR/xptr*

10. BEEP: *www.beepcore.org/*

11. HTTP: *www.w3.org/Protocols/*

12. IIOP: *www.omg.org/technology/documents/corba_spec_catalog.htm*

13. SOAP: *www.w3.org/2000/xp/Group/*

14. For more information, go to *www.w3.org/TR/2003/REC-soap12-part1-20030624/*.

15. WS-Routing: *http://msdn.microsoft.com/ws/2001/10/Routing/*

16. WS-Addressing: *http://www-106.ibm.com/developerworks/webservices/library/ws-add/*

17. DAML information can be found at *www.daml.org/*.

18. For more information, go to *www.w3.org/TR/wsd/*.

19. For more information, go to *www.w3.org/2002/ws/desc/*.

20. For more information, go to *http://msdn.microsoft.com/ws/2002/12/PolicyAttachment/*.

21. For more information, go to *http://msdn.microsoft.com/ws/2002/12/PolicyAssertions/*.

22. For more information, go to *http://www-106.ibm.com/developerworks/library/ws-secure*.

23. For more information, go to *www.w3.org/signature*.

24. For more information, go to *www.w3.org/Encryption/2001/*.

25. For more information, go to *http://www-106.ibm.com/developerworks/library/ws-trust/*.

26. For more information, go to *http://msdn.microsoft.com/ws/2003/03/ws-addressing/*.

27. For more information on the activities of the WS-I organization, visit *www.ws-i.org*.

28. For more information, go to *www.ws-i.org/Profiles/Basic/2003-06/BasicProfile-1.0-BdAD.html*.

29. For more information on UDDI, visit *www.uddi.org*.

The Grid Computing Technological Viewpoints

In today's world of high technology achievements, there are none more impressive than the global movement into Grid Computing. Grid Computing accomplishments can now prove to be able to present a virtual computing environment that appears to be more powerful, and sustain more processing power, than the world's largest computer.

In Part 4, we explore the vast number of complex technologies that comprise the realm of Grid Computing. We describe exactly how, through specific combinatorial designs, the world is able to leverage these innovative solutions to assist in the resolution of some of the most difficult, computation-intensive problem-solving activities.

Also in this part of the book, full treatment will be provided to allow the reader to better understand how to achieve "true" distributed resource sharing across heterogeneous and dynamic "virtual organizations." Grid Computing technologies require several improvements in alignment with many of the traditional computing technologies.

In the early days of Grid Computing, a number of custom middleware solutions were created to solve the "grid problem" (as we defined the so-called "grid problem" in earlier parts of the book). However, this resulted in non-interoperable solutions, while at the same time, integration among the participants became a challenging experience. As we have also discussed earlier, the third wave of the Grid Computing era is now focusing on the easier integration, security, and quality of control aspects of resource sharing.

Foster, Kesselman, Nick, and Tuecke describe the Open Grid Service Architecture (OGSA) as a solution to the above problem. This architectural concept is a result of the alignment of existing grid standards with the emerging service-oriented architecture as well as the Web. The Web service standards define an open standard mechanism for service creation, service naming, and service discovery. It provides an interoperable message exchange pattern between client and service by using XML as the message format. The OGSA defines standard message formats and message exchange patterns for Grid Computing.

This standardization of messages and exchange patterns enables interoperability among grid services. Also, this eliminates the need to worry about the underlying operating system where the IT resources are hosted, and/or transport level networking services, and/or protocols used for message exchange. These are treated as the fundamental runtime binding issues.

The OGSA provides a uniform way to describe grid services and defines a common pattern of behavior for all grid services. In short, this architecture defines grid service behaviors, service description mechanisms, and protocol binding information by using Web services as the technology enabler. The architecture thus developed uses the best features from both the grid and Web services community.

The core technologies that forms the basis of OGSA are:

- *eXtensible Markup Language (XML). This markup language is used to define the message exchange format and structure.*

- *Web Service Description Language (WSDL). This is a service description language for Web services; the same is used for describing grid services.*

The companion technologies that are of interest for our discussion are:

- *Simple Object Access Protocol (SOAP). This is a standard-based message enveloping mechanism. In addition to this message format, it defines a set of standard message exchange patterns.*

- *Universal Description, Discovery, and Integration (UDDI). A standard and interoperable platform that enables companies and applications to quickly, easily, and dynamically find and use Web services over the Internet.*

Refer to the last chapter for a detailed discussion on these technologies. These core technologies are the basic building blocks for the Open Grid Service Infrastructure (OGSI) that forms the base layer of the grid service architecture. In the opening two chapters we explore details of the OGSA and the platform components including the OGSI specification.

Open Grid Services Architecture (OGSA)

INTRODUCTION

T he grid infrastructure is mainly concerned with the creation, management, and the application of dynamic coordinated resources and services. These dynamic and coordinated
resources and services are complex. They may be individual or a collection of entities with a
short or long lifespan. These resources may be constituted from single or from multiple institutions so as to provide a homogeneous or heterogeneous set of functionalities. Even though the
complexity and difference in resources and services may vary within every virtual organization,
they are all agreed to deliver a set of QoS features including common security semantics, workflow, resource management, problem determination, failover, and service-level management.
These QoS features require a well-defined architecture to achieve the desired level of service
quality. This prompted for the introduction of Open Grid Service Architecture (OGSA) to support the creation, maintenance, and application of ensembles of services maintained by virtual
organizations (VO) (Foster, Kesselman, & Tuecke).

CLARIFICATION OF THE USAGE OF RESOURCE AND SERVICE

In most of the technology papers and specifications, the definition of the term
"resource" and "service" are used interchangeably to represent anything that is sharable and/or can be used by an external user. Even though this may look conceptually
correct for the specific scenarios they may be representing, for our discussion we
would like to further clarify the resource and service concepts.

A resource is something sharable or a representation of a logical or physical entity
(e.g., software application, hardware, operating system, cluster, etc.) and has a number
of interfaces or application provider interfaces (API) to mange, access, and monitor

---

the resource. A service is a realization of one of the interfaces with the necessary binding and message exchange pattern information for the use of the client. This is represented in Figure 6.1.

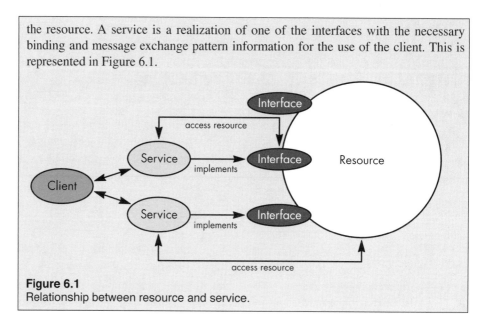

Figure 6.1
Relationship between resource and service.

OGSA Architecture and Goal

OGSA architecture is a layered architecture, as shown in Figure 6.2, with clear separation of the functionalities at each layer. As you can see from the figure, the core architecture layers are OGSI, which provides the base infrastructure, and OGSA core platform services, which are a set of standard services including policy, logging, service-level management, and so on. The high-level applications and services use these lower layer core platform components and OGSI that become part of a resource-sharing grid.

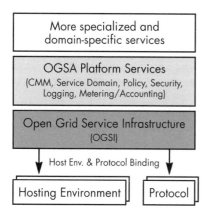

Figure 6.2
OGSA platform architecture.

The major OGSA goals are:

- Identify the use cases that can drive the OGSA platform components
- Identify and define the core OGSA platform components
- Define hosting and platform-specific bindings
- Define resource models and resource profiles with interoperable solutions

As of today there have been a lot of activities in the GGF to define the use cases and core platform services. We are going to concentrate most of our discussion on these two areas. As you can see, there is not much activity going on in the platform binding and resource models/profile areas. We are assuming that these areas will become more active when people start implementing more OGSA-based grid solutions in their environments and more sharable resources become exposed to the grid community.

In addition to the broad goals defined above, OGSA defines more specific goals, including:

- Facilitating distributed resource management across heterogeneous platforms
- Providing seamless quality of service delivery
- Building a common base for autonomic management solutions
- Providing common infrastructure building blocks to avoid "stovepipe solution towers"
- Open and published interfaces and messages
- Industry-standard integration solutions including Web services
- Facilities to accomplish seamless integration with existing IT resources where resources become on-demand services/resources
- Providing more knowledge-centric and semantic orientation of services

We start with some use cases that drive the architecture behind OGSA. We then explore core services that are developed as part of the platform solutions for the requirements gathered during the "use case" phase. In the chapter "Introduction to OGSI Specification," we cover the details of the OGSI specification through examples.

Some Sample Use Cases That Drive the OGSA

The OGSA architecture working group defines a number of use cases from a wide variety of application scenarios including those related to e-science and e-business applications.

The main purposes of these use cases are:

- To identify and define core OGSA platform functionalities
- To define core platform components based on the functionality requirements
- To define the high-level requirements on these core components and identify their interrelationship

These use cases are defined as part of the OGSA-WG charter definition specified by GGF, which says, "To produce and document the use cases that drive the definition and prioritization of OGSA platform components, as well as document the rationale for our choices."

As we can see, some of these use cases defined below from the e-business and e-science world helps identify the general OGSA platform features, components, and their interrelationships. This will pave the way for the detailed discussion on the OGSA architecture platform components.

Here are the representational use cases from the OGSA Architecture working group,[1] which we will use in our discussion:

- Commercial Data Center (Commercial Grid)
- National Fusion Collaboratory (Science Grid)
- Online Media and Entertainment (Commercial Grid)

We will discuss the core aspects, scenarios, and the requirements drawn from these use cases. This will form the basis for our discussion on the OGSA core platform component.

COMMERCIAL DATA CENTER (CDC)

Summary

Data centers are common in most of the big enterprises in order to consolidate the huge number of servers to reduce the total cost of ownership. Data centers play a key role in the outsourcing business where major businesses outsource their IT resource management to concentrate on their core business competence and excellence. These data centers are required to manage a huge number of IT resources (servers, storages, and networks). Since these data centers are providing resource-sharing capabilities across virtual organization, grid computing forms the technology of choice for their resource management.

In order to support such a commercial grid, the grid technology platform, middleware, and applications should possess a number of core functionalities. We identify and enlist these functionalities by defining the customers of this data center and their usage scenarios.

Customers/Providers (Actors)

- **Grid Administrator.** An administrator wants to get the maximum utilization of the resources in the data center and the management of the resource sharing to be controlled through resource policies.
- **IT System Integrator.** A system integrator wants to reduce the complexity of the distributed and heterogeneous system. Also, they are responsible for the construction of the heterogeneous system and management of service changes.
- **IT Business Activity Manager.** A business manager needs a scalable and reliable platform at a lower cost and an agreed-upon quality of service.

Scenarios

- **Multiple in-house systems support within the enterprise.** Consolidate all the in-house systems in one place and make resources available on an on-demand basis. This reduces the cost of ownership and increases resource utilization. This scenario is suitable for human resource services, customer resource management, finance, and accounting systems.
- **Time-constrained commercial campaign.** Provides the resources on demand in order to run time-constrained campaigns and levy charges on the basis of usage. Examples of these campaigns include sales promotion campaigns, game ticket sales, and so on.
- **Disaster recovery.** An essential part of the major IT systems today. Commercial GRID system could provide standard disaster recovery frameworks across remote CDC at low cost.
- **Global load balancing.** Geographically separated data centers can share high workload and provide scalable systems.

Functional Requirements on OGSA

After a thorough and careful examination of the static and dynamic behavior present in this use case, the following functional requirements of the grid architecture can be identified:

- Discovery of the available resources
- Secure authentication, authorization, and auditing on resource usage
- Resource brokering services to better utilize and use the resources and to achieve the level of quality requirements
- Scalable and manageable data-sharing mechanisms
- Provisioning of resources based on need
- Scheduling of resources for specific tasks
- Advanced reservation facilities to achieve the scale of QoS requirements
- Enable metering and accounting to quantify the resource usage into pricing units
- Enable system capabilities for fault handling and partial failure detection/correction
- Use static and dynamic policies
- Manage transport and message levels and end-to-end security
- Construct dynamic virtual organizations with common functionalities and agreements
- Facilitate resource monitoring
- Enable the facilities for disaster recovery in case of outages

Now let us move on to another use case where we will discuss a scientific research project with geographically distributed participants.

NATIONAL FUSION COLLABORATORY (NFC)

Summary

The NFC project defines a virtual organization devoted to fusion research and provides the "codes" developed by this community to the end users (researchers). Earlier, this "code" software was installed in the end user's machine. This became a complex and unmanageable process of software management, distribution, versioning, and upgrade. Due to this change management and configuration problem the fusion community decided to adopt the ASP model, known as "network services model," where the "code" is maintained by the service provider and made accessible to the remote clients. This eliminates the burden on the end user but adds some QoS requirements on the service provider, including executing the "code" as efficiently as possible, executing within a certain time frame, and producing the results with accuracy. As you can imagine, this is the best-case usage model for a computational grid. Now, we can drill down into the usage scenarios of this grid and derive the functional requirements on Grid Computing architecture.

Customers (Actors)

Scientists. They are customers of the fusion code provided by the fusion service provider. Some of the customer requirements are:

- The ability to run the "code" in remote resources on the condition of end-to-end quality of service with a guarantee of time-bound execution.
- Availability of the resource (code execution) in the computational grid.
- A policy-based management of resources; including who can run the code, how many hardware resources are available, etc.
- Ability to use community services by getting accredited with the community rather than an individual service provider. This is a form of "dynamic account" creation and usage.

Scenarios

- A remote client (scientist at an NFC facility) can run code on a remote site within a time frame. The service provider downloads the necessary data and executes a workflow script.
- A monitoring agent starts and watches the submitted job for service-level agreement (SLA) validation. This helps the service provider to provision more resources or recover from failure conditions, etc.
- Integrate with external applications and resources for data and/or code execution and flexible delegation of rights.

Functional Requirements on OGSA

After a thorough and careful examination of the static and dynamic behavior present in this use case, the following functional requirements of the grid architecture can be identified:

- Discovery of available resources
- Workflow management for job distribution across resources
- Scheduling of service tasks
- Enabling the facilities for disaster recovery in case of outages
- Provisioning of resources based on the need
- Resource brokering services to better utilize and use the resources and to achieve the level of quality requirements
- Load balancing to manage workloads
- Network transport management
- Integration with legacy applications and their management
- Handling application and network-level firewalls
- Service-level agreement and agreement-based interaction
- Providing end-to-end security and security authorization and use policies

Next we discuss an online media and entertainment project with some highly interactive content and data sharing among participants. This is an on-demand media and entertainment system, which can be a classic representation of the next generation of on-demand applications.

ONLINE MEDIA AND ENTERTAINMENT

Summary

The entertainment contents may consist of different forms (e.g., movie on demand or online games) with different hosting capacity demands and lifecycle properties. One of the primary goals of this use case is the ability to dynamically manage the resources based on workload demand and current system configuration. Another observation with media entertainment is the change of the content during its lifecycle and changes in the roles of the actors involved.

User involvement and responsiveness with the entertainment content drives this use case into two categories:

- The consumption of the media content, movie on demand, with very limited user interaction
- Frequent user interaction with the content, as we can see in online games.

A number of new commercial consumer experiences will emerge from the economic factors of content subscription, usage-based pricing, content availability, and differentiation among competitors.

Most of online media entertainment (games and video on demand) are designed based on a stovepipe solution for each media entertainment and each solution is managed separately. This will become a cumbersome solution because of the lack of reusability and overprovisioning of the resources. The grid architecture should provide mechanisms for on-demand provisioning, new business models (pricing models), and resource-sharing models.

Actors

1. A customer who consumes the entertainment content
2. A service provider who hosts the entertainment content
3. A publisher who offers the entertainment content
4. A developer who consumes the entertainment content

Scenarios

- A consumer, for example a game player, accesses the game portal and authenticates with the game server and starts the game.
- There are several providers that are working in concert to provide the required service for the consumer. For example, the network service provider offers the required

bandwidth, the hosting provider provides the server and storage, and the application service provider offers common services like game engine, accounting and billing applications, and help.
- The content provider or media studio provides the content for the customer experience.

Each of the above activities is an interaction between actors.

Functional Requirements on OGSA

After a thorough and careful examination of the static and dynamic behavior present in this use case, the following functional requirements of the grid architecture can be identified:

- Discovery of resources
- Instantiating new service
- Service-level management to meet user expectations
- Enabling metering and accounting to quantify resource usage into pricing units
- Monitoring resource usage and availability
- Managing service policies
- Providing service grouping and aggregation to provide better indexing and information
- Managing end-to-end security
- Servicing lifecycle and change management
- Failure management
- Provisioning management
- Workload management
- Load balancing to provide a scalable system

We can see that the requirements enlisted in each of the use cases are complex. Providing a solution to these complex requirements is a challenging task. We will see in the coming chapter how the OGSA architecture is trying to provide some basic solutions to the above requirements.

SUMMARY

The above use cases introduced some of the core scientific and commercial usage patterns for grid computing. After going through the above representative use cases and the functional requirements exhibited by each of them, we can classify them into four categories:

1. Basic functions
2. Security functions
3. Resource management functions
4. System properties

Discussion of the details of these classifications will be covered when we discuss the platform components. Based on the above functional requirements, Open Grid Service Architecture WG started identifying the platform services and the component model definitions for each of the identified services.

NOTE

1. For more information, go to *https://forge.gridforum.org/projects/ogsa-wg*.

The OGSA Platform Components

T he job of the OGSA is to build on the grid service specification (Open Grid Service Infrastructure, or OGSI) to define architectures and standards for a set of "core grid services" that are essential components to every grid. As we have discussed in the previous chapter, a set of core OSGA use cases are developed, which forms a representative collection from different business models (e.g., business grids and science grids) and are used for the collection of the OGSA functional requirements. We have identified some core basic functions across all the grid services.

Let us now further explore the details of these core platform services and their definitions in the context of OGSA and their interrelationships. We are assuming that these core grid service components must be present in every OGSA-based interoperable Grid Computing framework for the best quality of control features.

As shown in Figure 8.1, the basic OGSA architectural organization can be classified into five layers:

- native platform services and transport mechanisms
- OGSA hosting environment
- OGSA transport and security
- OGSA infrastructure (OGSI)
- OGSA basic services (meta-OS and domain services)

The above defined OGSA layers form the foundation for new high-level management applications and middleware Grid solutions and new class of Grid applications.

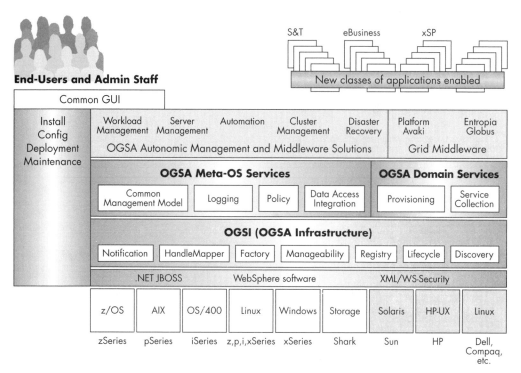

Figure 8.1
OGSA core platform components—an IBM vision on OGSA and integrated software components.

NATIVE PLATFORM SERVICES AND TRANSPORT MECHANISMS

The native platforms form the concrete resource-hosting environment. These platforms can be host resources specific to operating systems or hardware components, and the native resource managers manage them. The transport mechanisms use existing networking services transport protocols and standards.

OGSA HOSTING ENVIRONMENT

We will cover in subsequent chapters exactly how the standard interface definitions defined by the grid service specification allows for two services/resources interoperating together. These definitions do not, however, address the portability of services implementations. Portability across hosting environments still needs to be addressed by both grid communities and other hosting environments, including J2EE or .NET. These communities are working together on this, and solutions will be forthcoming over the next relatively short period of time.

CORE NETWORKING SERVICES TRANSPORT AND SECURITY

An OGSA standard does not define the specific networking services transport, nor the security mechanisms in the specification. Instead, it assumes use of the platform-specific transport and security at the runtime instance of operation. In other words, these properties are defined as service binding properties, and they are dynamically bound to the native networking services transport and security systems at runtime. These binding requirements are flexible; however, the communities in collaboration with the hosting and platform capabilities must work together to provide the necessary interoperability aspects.

OGSA INFRASTRUCTURE

The grid service specification developed within the OGSI working group has defined the essential building block for distributed systems. This is defined in terms of Web service specifications and description mechanisms (i.e., WSDL). This specification provides a common set of behaviors and interfaces to discover a service, create service instance, service lifecycle management, and subscribe to and deliver respective notifications.

OGSA BASIC SERVICES

Some of the most notable and interesting basic services are as follows:

- Common Management Model (CMM)
- Service domains
- Distributed data access and replication
- Policy
- Security
- Provisioning and resource management
- Accounting/metering
- Common distributed logging
- Monitoring
- Scheduling

These representational services are derived from the use cases, which we have discussed in the last chapter. In subsequent chapters we will cover each of the above core services in greater detail. This discussion will include these services and their behaviors, the interfaces and information model, and their relevance to the grid community and OGSA in particular. Some of these basic services have already been defined and others are still evolving. However, we believe these services are representational services and, hence, require a more thorough discussion.

SUMMARY

This chapter introduced us to the platform components of the OGSA architecture and their relationships. In addition, we identified some of the core services that should be presented for consideration. The next chapter will introduce us to the base infrastructure components of the OGSA, entitled the Open Grid Service Infrastructure (OGSI). This OGSI discussion is one of detail, covering all aspects of the specification and its relationship with other core technologies.

Open Grid Services Infrastructure (OGSI)

INTRODUCTION

Grid Computing has attracted global technical communities with the evolution of Business On Demand computing and Autonomic Computing. Grid Computing is a process of coordinated resource sharing and problem solving in dynamic, multi-institutional virtual organizations. In the context of Business On Demand and Autonomic Computing (i.e., self-regulating), Grid Computing deserves special attention.

It is a technical challenge to achieve a highly ambitious interaction among resources being shared across virtual organizations with less centralized control, while at the same time ensuring the highest quality of service. The GGF is striving to standardize this process of resource sharing through a set of software architecture standards and other important framework initiatives. The GGF started a number of architecture standardization efforts in order to provide better software interoperability, higher levels of security, more encompassing resource definitions, discovery capabilities, policy management, and overall environmental manageability aspects. One such architecture standardization process is theOGSA, discussed in the previous chapter.

The base component of that architecture is the OGSI. The OGSI is a grid software infrastructure standardization initiative, based on the emerging Web services standards that are intended to provide maximum interoperability among OGSA software components.

GRID SERVICES

Based on the OGSI specification,[1] a grid service instance is a Web service that conforms to a set of conventions expressed by the WSDL as service interfaces, extensions, and behaviors. A grid service provides the controlled management of the distributed and often long-lived state that is commonly required in sophisticated distributed applications. According to the definition of OGSI, every grid service is a Web service; however, the converse need not be true.

The OGSI specification defines the following:

- How grid service instances are named and referenced
- How the interfaces and behaviors are common to all GRID services
- How to specify additional interfaces, behaviors, and their extensions

The grid services specification does not address the common service hosting behaviors, including how grid services are created, managed, and destroyed in a hosting environment. Rather, the specification recommends message-level interoperability, whereby any grid service client following the OGSI standard can interact with every grid service hosted by any hosting environment. This message-level interoperability is the core feature of this standard, and it is achieved by using XML as the core message format and schema.

THE GRID SERVICE SPECIFICATION DOES NOT ADDRESS COMMON SERVICE HOSTING

This discussion is based on the proposed final draft published by the GGF OGSI WG, dated June 27, 2003. This specification has gone through the GGF 60-day public review process and incorporated public recommendation and will soon be accepted by the GGF as a grid standard.

The acceptance of this specification will provide significant effects across global Grid Computing communities.

For purposes of this particular discussion, the OGSI, and the concepts introduced by the specification, we will now introduce a sample from the management aspect of grid services, as specified through the Meta-OS service of the Common Management Model.[2] This sample is an operating system resource implementation with its associated factory service implementation. We will be focusing on the OGSI concepts used by this sample service implementation, and not on the manageability features. Since OGSI is layered on top of the Web service standard, familiarity with the core Web service concepts, including XML, XML schema, WSDL, SOAP, and the Web services programming model, (i.e., client and server side) will help us to better understand the OGSI in greater depth. We can find greater details on these technologies in the previous discussion and by visiting their Web sites.

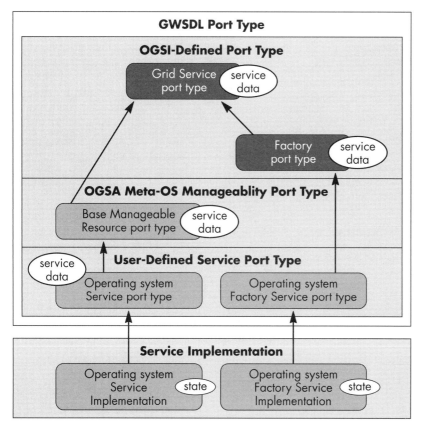

Figure 9.1
The OGSI Port Type Inheritance model for operating system service and the operating system
factory service sample (the solid arrow indicates the inheritance).

The interface inheritance diagram, as shown in Figure 9.1, introduces the following concepts of
a grid service, enabled by:

- Providing a stateful Web service implementation of the operating system service with
  public interface (OperatingSystem portType) to access the service and its state.

- Supporting interface inheritance. The operating system service implements
  OperatingSystem portType, which is derived from the BaseManageableResource
  interface, which in turn extends the GridService interface.

- Specifying the common grid service behaviors (public "state data" and "operations")
  using GridService portType as defined by the OGSI.

- Allowing the operating system services to inherit the public state data and operations
  from its parent port types.

- Manipulating the state of a service through the GridService operations such as "findServiceData" and "setServiceData."
- Enabling the client so that it can discover the state and meta-data of the service through "findServiceData" of the GridService interface. We will see the common OGSI-defined service meta-data later in this chapter.
- Establishing a pattern implementation for the operating system service, whereby the factory service inherits from the OGSI factory interface. This is an optional feature and hence may not present itself in the real grid service implementation environments.

One of the requirements of services defined by the OGSI is the ability to describe the preceding concepts using an OGSI description model, which is a combination of Web service WSDL and OGSI GWSDL. We will see the details in later sections.

A HIGH-LEVEL INTRODUCTION TO OGSI

This high-level introduction will set the stage for the detailed technical discussion on OGSI. The OGSI specification defines a component model using a Web service as its core base technology, with WSDL as the service description mechanism and XML as the message format. As we know, Web services in general are dealing with stateless services, and their client interaction is mostly stateless. On the other hand, grid services are a long-running process, maintaining the state of the resource being shared, and the clients are involved in a stateful interaction with the services. There are two dimensions to the stateful nature of a Web service:

1. *A service is maintaining its state information.* These are normally classified as application state and in the case of grid service it directly maps to the state of the resource.
2. *The interaction pattern between the client and service can be stateful.* There are numerous architecture styles and programming models for defining these stateful interactions including BPEL4WS[3] and REST (Fielding).

As of now, the OGSI is attempting to answer the first dimension of the state problem by creating a programming model for how and where an application/service resource state can be logically maintained, and how these states are exposed to the client. This does not mean, however, that the service contains all its physical state. The physical state may be held in the real resource being modeled as the grid service. This publicly known state can be a subset of the overall application state. We believe that the OGSI should address the stateful message exchange pattern in coordination with the stateful interaction specifications.

Figure 9.2 introduces a number of concepts surrounding OGSI, and its relation to Web services. The following list describes points of interest related to this model.

- Grid services are layered on top of Web services.
- Grid services contain application state factors, and provide concepts for exposing the state, which is referred to as the service data element.

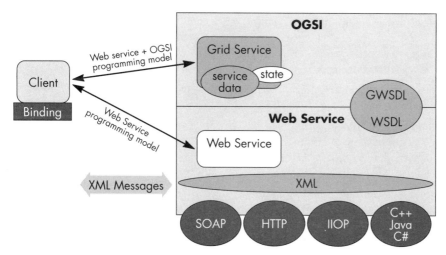

Figure 9.2
Typical Web service and grid service layers.

- Both grid services and Web services communicate with its client by exchanging XML messages.
- Grid services are described using GWSDL, which is an extension of WSDL. GWSDL provides interface inheritance and open port type for exposing the service state information—referred to as service data. This is similar to interface properties or attributes commonly found in other distributed description languages.
- The client programming model is the same for both grid service and Web service. But grid services provide additional message exchange patterns such as the handle resolution through OGSI port types.
- The transport bindings are selected by the runtime. Message encoding and decoding is done for the specific binding and high-level transport protocol (SOAP/HTTP).

SOME OF THE TERMINOLOGIES WE MUST BE FAMILIAR WITH FOR THESE DISCUSSIONS ARE:

Web service: A software component identified using a URI, whose public interfaces and binding are described using XML. These services interact with its clients using XML message exchanges.

Stateful Web service: A Web service that maintains some state information between clients' interactions.

Grid service: This is a stateful Web service with a common set of public operations and state behaviors exposed by the service. These services are created using the OGSI-defined specification.

> **Grid service description**: A mechanism to describe the public operations and behaviors of a grid service. This is expressed using a combination of WSDL and GWSDL language specifications. The WSDL is a language specified by W3C, whereas GWSDL is an extension mechanism for WSDL and is specified by OGSI specification.
>
> **Grid service instance**: An instance of a grid service created by the hosting container and identified by a unique URI called grid service handle (GSH).
>
> **Grid service reference**: A temporal binding description of a grid service endpoint. This binding lists the interfaces, endpoint address, protocol for communication, and message encoding rules. In addition, it may contain service policies and other metadata information. Some examples of GSR are WSDL, IOR, and so forth.
>
> **Service data element**: These are publicly accessible state information of a service included with the WSDL portType. These can be treated as interface attributes.

With this high-level information on OGSI and the grid service, let us move on to the technical details of the specification. We will try to explain the core concepts through some simple code snippets. Later in subsequent sections of the book, we will be discussing some of the framework implementation of OGSI standards, and then we will discuss how we can implement real samples based on the OGSI specification.

TECHNICAL DETAILS OF OGSI SPECIFICATION

The last section provides us with the basic concepts of grid service, the terminologies used, relationships with distributed technologies, and how we can align grid services and Web services. Let us now explore the core technical underpinnings of the OGSI specification with more elaborate samples and explanations. This discussion helps grid services developers, and tool vendors, to get detailed information on the OGSI usage model. We recommend referring to the OGSI specification for more clarification on these concepts. We will start with the OGSI extensions on WSDL.

OGSI and Its Use of WSDL

OGSI is based on Web services and it uses WSDL as a mechanism to describe the public interfaces of the grid service. There are two core requirements for describing Web services based on the OGSI:

- The ability to describe interface inheritance
- The ability to describe additional information elements (state data/attributes/properties) with the interface definitions

Similar to most Web services, OGSI services use WSDL as a service description mechanism, but the current WSDL 1.1[4] specification lacks the above two capabilities in its definition of portType. The WSDL 1.2[5] working group has agreed to support these features through portType (now called "interface" in WSDL 1.2) inheritance and an open content model for portTypes. As an interim solution, OGSI developed a new schema for portType definition (extended from normal WSDL 1.1 schema portType Type) under a new namespace definition, GWSDL.

This being one of the most important and challenging parts of the OGSI specification, we need to spend some time analyzing the GWSDL schema and its relation to WSDL.

Listing 9.1   The WSDL PortType definition schema in the GWSDL namespace.

```
...
<schema targetNamespace =    http://www.gridforum.org/namespaces/2003/
03/gridWSDLExtensions
xmlns:gwsdl       = http://www.gridforum.org/namespaces/2003/03/
gridWSDLExtensions
xmlns:wsdl="http://schemas.xmlsoap.org/wsdl/"
...
<import namespace="http://schemas.xmlsoap.org/wsdl/"/>

<element name="portType" type="gwsdl:portTypeType"/>
<complexType name="portTypeType">
   <complexContent>
      <extension base="wsdl:portTypeType">
         <sequence>
            <any namespace="##other"
                 minOccurs="0" maxOccurs="unbounded"/>
         </sequence>
         <attribute name="extends" use="optional">
            <simpleType>
               <list itemType="QName"/>
            </simpleType>
         </attribute>
         <anyAttribute namespace="##other"/>
      </extension>
   </complexContent>
</complexType>
</schema>
```

Listing 9.1 shows the WSDL schema definition in the GWSDL namespace. The important information conveyed by this schema definition includes:

- An XML element "portType" is defined in the GWSDL namespace ("gwsdl:portType").
- The XML element "portType" is extending (XML schema extension) the "wsdl:portTypeType," which is defined by WSDL 1.1 schema.

- An open content element model for port type content from any other namespace using <any namespace="##other".../>. This enables us to embed any XML elements from namespaces other than "gwsdl" inside the gwsdl:portType element.

- This new element adds an optional attribute called "extends," which takes the QName list. Note that these QNames must be either a wsdl:portType or gwsdl:portType name.

- An open content attribute model by using <anyAttribute.../>. This provides us with the flexibility of adding any attributes to "gwsdl:portType."

Based on the previous discussion regarding the GWSDL portType declaration, let's create a sample GWSDL port type definition.

Listing 9.2   A sample GWSDL portType.

```
<gwsdl:portType name="OperatingSystem"
extends="crm:BaseManageableResource ogsi:GridService">

<wsdl:operation name="reboot"/>
<wsdl:operation name="shutdown"/>

<sd:serviceData name="lifecycleModel"    ..... />
<sd:serviceData name="serviceGroupType"  ..... />
</gwsdl:portType>
```

In Listing 9.2, we are utilizing the "gwsdl:portType" with the name "OperatingSystem" and it extends two other port types, crm:BaseManageableResource and ogsi:GridService, respectively. The open content model of the gwsdl:portType now allows new elements into the portType definition from other namespaces such as "sd:serviceData," as shown in the listing.

Significance of Transforming GWSDL to WSDL Definition

It is, however, a known fact that none of the WSDL 1.1 tools can handle these extensions. Most of them will fail on WSDL validation. The current WSDL 1.1 manipulation tools are used to create native language interfaces, stubs, and proxies from WSDL, and for the converse process of creating WSDL from the services implemented in native language. These functions have to be *intelligent* in order to handle these extensions. Basically, GWSDL extensions are to be transformed to WSDL 1.1 artifacts. This includes:

- All the "extends" port types, and their operations, which are brought down to a single most derived portType. This process is called "flattening" of the interface hierarchy to the most derived type.

- All the service data elements and GWSDL extensions are retained for the reverse transformation process.

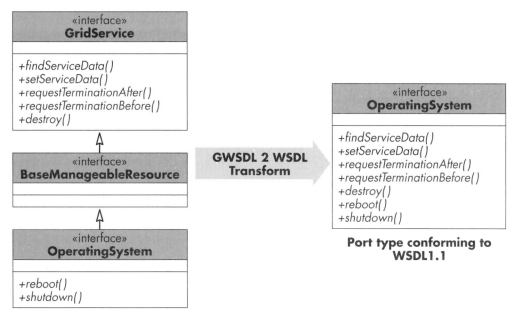

Figure 9.3
The WSDL 2 WSDL transformation process.

Some work has been accomplished in the GGF OGSI WG to define a normal process of defining the above transformation process.[6] Let us explore and illustrate this transformation process through the following discussion and example illustration.

Figure 9.3 shows a simple transformation process (i.e., port type flattening), where the GWSDL portType OperatingSystem extends the BaseManageableResource and GridService declarations. These declarations are subsequently flattened to a WSDL portType OperatingSystem, with all operations from its parent. It is worthy to note that the WSDL 1.1 tools can all work on this newly emerged portType definition.

Operator Overloading Support in OGSI Port Type

Another important aspect of the OGSI is the naming convention adopted for the portType operations, and the lack of support for operator overloading. In these situations, the OGSI follows the same conventions as described in the suggested WSDL 1.2 specification. This now becomes rather complex across several different dimensions, especially in the context of interface inheritance, and the process of transformation to a single inheritance model as previously described. In these kinds of situations, we have to adhere to the OGSI recommendation.

The OGSI recommends that if two or more port type operation components have the same value for their name and target namespace, then the component model (i.e., the semantic and operation signature) for these operations must be identical. Furthermore, if the port type operation components are equivalent, then they can be considered as candidates to collapse into a single operation.

> ### PORT TYPE OPERATION CONSIDERATIONS ARE KEY
>
> There is a consensus among OGSI work group members to follow the WSDL 1.2 specification in all respects. This agreement may eliminate the new schema and namespace (GWSDL) introduced by the OGSI when WSDL 1.2 reaches the recommendation stage.
>
> Therefore, related to current utilization and for backward compatibility, developers of tools and applications should consider the use of the GWSDL extensions. In addition to the WSDL 1.2 recommendation, one should become familiar with the Web Services-Interoperability (WS-I) basic profile best practices guidelines for interoperable Web services and grid services.

Let us now explore one of the most interesting concepts of a somewhat common approach to describe the publicly available state information of a service and its architectural model.

INTRODUCTION TO SERVICE DATA CONCEPTS

A grid service is a *stateful* Web service. Because of this architecture model design fact, the service data concept requires the OGSI to identify a common mechanism to expose the state data of the service instance to the service requestor of the query, the update action itself, and finally enable the change notification to occur. In this case, the OGSI utilized the "service data declaration" as a mechanism for publicly expressing the available state information of a service. This concept, however, is not limited to grid services.

The service data concept can be extended to any stateful Web service for declaring its publicly available state information through the service data concepts. Therefore, developers that were exposed to some of the more traditional distributed technologies, and their interface declaration (IDL) approaches, will be familiar with this somewhat similar concept. Some of the object-oriented distributed language interfaces use attributes declaration to indicate the exposed state/properties of the services they describe.

The following describes the service data concepts introduced by the OGSI specification:

- Service data declaration (SDD) is a mechanism to expose a publicly available state of a service.
- Service data elements (SDE) are accessible through the common grid service interfaces ("findServiceData" and "setServiceData").
- The internal state of a service should not be a part of the service data declaration.

Provided that we have now discussed the usability of service data, let us now explore the concepts, semantics, and usage model of service data in the context of a grid service.

How to Declare Service Data with a portType

Listing 9.3   The service data element declaration and some static service data values.

```
<gwsdl:portType name="OperatingSystem"
               extends="crm:BaseManageableResource ogsi:GridService">
<wsdl:operation name="reboot">
        . . . . . . . . . . . . . . . . . . . . . . . . . . . . .
</wsdl:operation>
. . . . . . . . . . . . . . . . . . . . . . . . . . . . . . . .
<sd:serviceData name="lifecycleModel"
                                    type="crm:lifecycleModelType"
                                    minOccurs="1"
                                    maxOccurs="1"
                                    nillable="true"
                                    mutability="static"/>

<sd:serviceData name="serviceGroupType"  . . . . . />
. . . . . . . . . . . . . . . . . . . . . . . . . . . . . . . . . . . . . . . . . . . . . .
<sd:staticServiceDataValues>
            <crm:lifecycleModel>
            <lifecycleState name="down">
                <subState name="restartable"/>
                <subState name="recovered"/>
            </lifecycleState>
            <crm:lifecycleModel/>
. . . . . . . . . . . . . . . . . . . . . . . . . . . . . . . . . . . . . . . . .
        </sd:staticServiceDataValues>
. . . . . . . . . . . . . . . . . . . . . . . . . . . . . . . . . . . . . . . . .
</gwsdl:portType>
```

Listing 9.3 shows how we can extend the GWSDL portType (name="OperatingSystem") with the contents of serviceData, which is used to define service data elements (SDE). Static service data values are defined in the WSDL portType and are available to all services that implement this portType.

FOUR SERVICE DATA CONCEPTS

Service Data Elements (SDE). The publicly accessible service data XML elements that are defined inside gwsdl portTypes are called service data elements, or SDEs (e.g., as shown in the above listing, there are two SDEs, lifecycleModel and service-GroupType).

Service Data Declaration (SDD). The SDEs in the port type are referred to as service data declaration, or SDD (e.g., the above listing indicates that there are two SDDs available in the OperatingSystem portType).

Service Data Element Values (SD values). These are values of the service data elements. These values are XML fragments. There may be a schema for the XML element fragment as defined by the SDE "type" attribute. There are two types of SD values based on service data element's mutability attribute value "static" and "dynamic" (e.g., the above listing shows that two service data elements and their values as static service data values, which are declared in the port type using <sd:static-ServiceDataValues> element).

Service Data Set (SD set). This can be a logical or physical collection of service data elements and their values for a service instance. This set is exposed through GridService portType public interfaces ("findServiceData," "setServiceData").

This is an aggregated collection of SDEs from all the port types in the interface hierarchy, which the service implements.

Service Data Structure

Service data is clearly modeled in the OGSI-defined namespace attribute, which is elaborated in the Web site *www.gridforum.org/namespaces/2003/03/serviceData.* This new OGSI schema type for service data ("sd:serviceData") contains seven predefined attributes, including name, type, minOccurs, maxOccurs, modifiable, mutability, and nilable. Most of these attributes are standard XSD types, with the exception of the "mutability" attribute. This is further defined by OGSI as an enumerated type, with values of "static," "constant," "extendable," and "mutable."

Note that this schema allows us to always add additional attributes of choice. There is another notable, yet often underutilized feature in this instance provided by this type of definition. It is the open content model related to content from any other namespace. This feature may be utilized in the future to expose some policies or meta-data about the service data, including security profiles.

Table 9.1 lists these attributes of service data and their default values.

Table 9.1   Defines the details of the Service Data Element Attributes

SDE Attributes	Description and Default Values
Name	This is a required attribute with a uniquely identifiable name of the service data element in the target namespace.
Type	This is the other required attribute, which defines the XML schema type of the service data value, the SD value. The SD value is based upon this schema and can be defined as simple or complex in a manner related to XSD schema types, and/or one may define this in terms of other complex types.

Table 9.1   Defines the details of the Service Data Element Attributes (Continued)

SDE Attributes	Description and Default Values
maxOccurs	This indicates the maximum number of SDE values that can appear in the service instance's SDE value set, or the portType staticServiceData Values. Default value = 1
minOccurs	This indicates the minimum number of SDE values that can appear in the service instance's SDE value set or the portType staticServiceDataValues. If minOccurs = 0, then this SDE is optional. Default value = 1

nilable	This indicates whether an SD value can have a nil value. One can declare this SDE as:
	
	`<sd:serviceData name="lifecycleModel"`
	`        type="crm:lifecycleModelType" nillable="true"/>`
	
	Another valid SDE value is:
	
	`<sd: lifecycleModel xsd:nil="true" />.`
	
	Default value = false

modifiable	This is a mechanism to specify a read-only and changeable service data element. If changeable, you can use "setServiceData" operation to change its SDE value based on the other attribute (mutability, min, and max) constraints. This modifiable attribute is applicable to the service requestor only. Internally a service can change its SDE values if other constraints are met. Default value = false (all SDEs are by default "read only")
mutability	This is an indication of whether and how the values of a service data element can change. Possible values are "static" | "constant" | "extendable" | "mutable" (see Table 9.4 for detailed information). Default value = "extendable"

This attribute set is extensible through the open attribute declaration of the schema's SDE. Therefore, the service can add more semantic information about a service data through attribute extensibility. An example of this extensibility is presented later with life cycle attributes for a service data element.

Remembering the default values of these attributes will help us to understand and define a good state management framework for grid services. Based on the SD definition, and as shown in the above table, the required attributes for an SDE are "name" and "type" attributes and the service developer is expected to provide them. The other attributes have default values assigned to them.

How Mutability Attributes Affect Service Data

One of the most complex concepts of the service data element is its mutability attribute. Table 9.2 below shows the possible mutability attributes and the resulting SDE values. It also shows how we can define and initialize those values.

Table 9.2   Service data element mutability attributes

SDE Mutability Attribute Value	Description of SDE Value	How to Define and Initialize This SDE Value
Static	Analogous to a language class member variable. All portType declarations carry this service data value.	Inside GWSDL portType using <static-ServiceDataValues>. We can see this example in the previous listing.
Constant	This SDE value is constant and must not change.	This SDE value is assigned on the creation of grid service (runtime behavior).
Extendable	Similar to the notion of appending values. Once added, these values remain with the SDE, while new values are appended.	Programmatically speaking, we can append new SDE values. The new values are appended while the old ones remain.
Mutable	The SDE values can be removed and others can be added.	Programmatically speaking, we can change these SDE values and add new ones.

Types of Service Data Elements and Service Data Values

Every service instance has a collection of service data elements it exposes through public interfaces. These service data elements can be classified into two types of attributes, based upon the creation semantics. These are:

1. *Static*. Declared as part of the service's interface definition (GWSDL portType definition).
2. *Dynamic*. Added to a service instance dynamically. This behavior is implementation specific. The client may know the semantics (type and meaning) of the service data, or can acquire that information from somewhere (service or third party) through meta-data exchange.

For example, in order to process the dynamic SDE values, you may need to get the schema type information for the SDE values from a remote location.

HOW TO DISCOVER AVAILABLE SERVICE DATA ELEMENTS (STATIC AND DYNAMIC) IN A SERVICE

To support both types of service data, the client must get the complete list of service data elements in a service during runtime. The client can query a service to get the current list of service data elements using the findServiceData method of the grid service (the service instance keeps a list of SDE elements, both static and dynamic, in its "serviceDataName" service data SDE).

We will see the details later when we discuss the GridService portType.

We have already noted that the initial values of the service data element are specified in WSDL, yet only for SDEs with a mutability value of "static." We can see that in the aforementioned listing example.

SERVICE DATA IMPLEMENTATION NOTES

The OGSI specification did not direct how the service data values for an SDE are stored in a service instance. The service implementation can make this decision, based upon the dynamic, persistence, and other constraints of the SD values.

For real-time data behavior in a service, one may implement a "pull" mechanism for the respective service data value, whereas caching of SD values in a logical service data set can provide faster response.

Even though the specification does direct the need for a prescribed SDE storage mechanism in the service side, it necessitates the need for a logical XML document model with "serviceDataValues" as the root element. This root element may contain service data element values in any encoding format. This is an implementation-specific behavior.

The GWSDL portType Inheritance Affects the Service Data

A grid service can support the portType inheritance model as defined by the GWSDL. We have already discussed this in this interface hierarchy. Let us now explore the causal impacts of how this inheritance model can affect the service data declarations that are associated with each portType in the inheritance chain.

Listing 9.4 describes how the portType hierarchy and service data declarations work together.

Listing 9.4   A port type hierarchy example to explain the service data aggregation scenarios.

```
<gwsdl:portType name="base">
    <sd:serviceData name="base_sd" type="xsd:string" minOccurs="1"
    maxOccurs="1" mutability="static" />
```

Listing 9.4   A port type hierarchy example to explain the service data aggregation scenarios.

```
        <!—local SDE declaration and not abstract- ->
        <sd:serviceData name="local_sd" type="xsd:string" minOccurs="0"
         mutability="static" />

        <sd:staticServiceDataValues>
                < base_sd>base</ base_sd>
        </sd:staticServiceDataValues>
</gwsdl:portType>


<gwsdl:portType name="derived_A" extends="base">
        <sd:serviceData name="derived_A_sd" type="xsd:string"
         minOccurs="1" maxOccurs="1" mutability="static" />
        <sd:staticServiceDataValues>
                < derived_A_sd >derived 1</derived_A_sd >
        </sd:staticServiceDataValues>
</gwsdl:portType>


<gwsdl:portType name=" derived _B" extends="base">
        <sd:serviceData name="derived B_sd" type="xsd:string"
         minOccurs="1" maxOccurs="1" mutability="static" />
        <sd:staticServiceDataValues>
                < derived B_sd> derived 2</derived B_sd >
        </sd:staticServiceDataValues>
</gwsdl:portType>


<gwsdl:portType name="most_derived" extends="derived_A  derived_B">
        <sd:serviceData name="most_derived_sd" type="xsd:string"
         minOccurs="1" maxOccurs="1" mutability="static" />
        <sd:serviceData name="local_sd" type="xsd:string"
         mutability="static" />
        <sd:staticServiceDataValues>
                < most_derived_sd >most derived</ most_derived_sd >
                <local_sd> local value D </local_sd>
        </sd:staticServiceDataValues>
</gwsdl:portType>
```

The service contains a union of all the service data elements defined in the portTypes that it implements. Table 9.3 shows how a service data aggregation occurred, with the inheritance hierarchy based on the above listing. This aggregation is based on the name of the service data element (QName) and, hence, only one service data element with the same QName is present in the service.

Table 9.3   Service Data Element Attributes

If a service implements:	The service data set then must contain:
Base	base_sd, local_sd
Derived_A	base_sd, derived_A_sd, local_sd
Derived_B	base_sd, derived_B_sd, local_sd
most_derived	base_sd, derived_A_sd, derived_A_sd, most_derived_sd, local_sd (with a value of 'local value D')

For example, Listing 9.4 utilizes only one <local_sd> element in the most_derived portType because the base portType's <local_sd> and most_derived portType's <local_sd> has the same local name, and they belong to the same targetNamespace.

Another important aspect to pay close attention to is on the static service data value aggregation model in the case of port type inheritance. This process adds the following conclusions:

The values of the static elements are aggregated down the interface hierarchy:

- If a portType contains a static SD element, yet does not specify a static service data value, then that portType can be treated as:
  - Abstract if the minOccurs is not 0, and we must provide some value in our derived port types.
  - If minOccurs is 0, then the static service data will not be initialized.
- The cardinality requirements (i.e., minOccurs and maxOccurs) on service data elements must be preserved. This is especially true in the case of static inheritance. For example, if the maximum service data element values allowed is set to 1, then the derived types must conform to that rule, as it cannot set more than a single value.

We should refer to the OGSI specification for more examples, and best practices guidelines, on these cardinality constraints. We can also see information on how to define an abstract portType with the SDE, how the implementation and tools should check for cardinality violation, and so on.

Qualifying Service Data Element with Lifetime Attributes

In addition to the expressed features of the service data as previously discussed, there is also a "hidden" concept in the specification with respect to the lifetime properties associated with the service data elements. The concept is hidden because it is just a recommendation that the service/client implementation could possibly ignore. However, good designs, programs, and tools should be aware of this feature.

The service data element represents the real-time observations of the dynamic state of a service instance. This real-time observation forces the clients to understand the validity and availability of the state representation. That is, certain service data elements, especially within dynamic

SDEs, may have a limited lifetime. If there is lifetime information associated with the SDE, it can help the client to make decisions on whether an SDE is available, has validity, and when it is to revalidate the SDE. The most helpful development implementation of this concept may be the client-side service data cache, and an associated revalidation mechanism.

Based on the preceding requirements, the specification provides three kinds of lifetime properties:

- The time from which the contents of this element are valid (ogsi:goodFrom)
- The time until which the contents of this element are valid (ogsi:goodUntil)
- The time until which this element itself is available (ogsi:availableUntil)

The first two properties are related to the lifetime of the contents, while the third, the availableUntil attribute, defines the availability of the element itself. For example, we may see a dynamic SDE with availability until a specific time, and thereafter, it ceases to exist. This is a good indication for the users of this specific service data element not to use that SDE after that specified time.

According to the specification, these values are optional attributes of the SDE element and the SDE values; however, it is always recommended to include the optional attributes in the XML schema design of the types for the service data elements.

Listing 9.5 includes a service data declaration (myPortType), its type (myType), and these lifetime attributes, through open content XML schema type attribute declarations (##any).

Listing 9.5   An SDE "myPortType" and the SDE type "myType" with the open content attributes (anyAttribute) for a lifetime attribute declaration.

```
<wsdl:types>
      <xsd:complexType name="myType">
      <xsd:sequence>
            <xsd:element name="myElem" type="xsd:string"/>
      </xsd: sequence >
      <anyAttribute namespace="##any" />
      </xsd:complexType>
</wsdl:types>


<gwsdl:portType name ="myPortType">
      <sd:serviceData name="mySDE" type="myType" />
      ..........
</gwsdl:portType>
```

Based on the service data declaration in the above listing, one may assume that an instance of a service data element may contain the following values (Listing 9.6):

Listing 9.6 Instantiated service data values for an SDE based on the lifetime service data declaration (in Listing 9.5), and its possible lifetime properties.

```
<sd:serviceDataValues>
      < mySDE goodFrom="2003-04-01-27T10:20:00.000-06:00"
                goodUntil="2003-05-20-27T10:20:00.000-06:00"
                availableUntil="2004-05-01-27T10:20:00.000-06:00">
            <myElem goodUntil="2003-04-20-27T10:20:00.000-06:00" >
                test
            </ myElem>
      </ mySDE>
</sd:serviceDataValues>
```

Listing 9.6 has instantiated service data values inside of the service instance, for the "mySDE" SDE, grouped under the logical <serviceDataValues> root element.

Listing 9.6 shows that the subelements in the SDE values (myElem) can override the goodUntil lifetime property to a new time earlier than that of the parent (mySDE). The attribute extension (anyAttribute) of the SDE element schema and the XML schema type of the SDE (shown in Listing 9.5) values makes this override feature possible.

This is a best practice recommendation for service developers and modelers for fine-grain control of lifetime properties of a service data element value. If the service data element and its value do not contain the declaration of these properties, then the goodFrom, goodUntil, and availableUntil properties are unknown.

Summary on OGSI-Defined Service Data Concepts

To conclude our discussion on service data, we list the core advantages of using this programming model:

- Provides an aggregated view of the service state rather than individual state values or properties
- Gives a document-centric view (XML documents) of the data, thereby avoiding specific methods for state access
- Shows flexibility in supporting dynamic state information and service state introspection
- Provides lifetime and subscription support on the state properties
- Enables dynamic construction of state data information elements and values and the declaration of static values for the state

GRID SERVICE: NAMING AND CHANGE MANAGEMENT RECOMMENDATIONS

This is a critical area in distributed systems where a service may undergo changes, including the publicly available interface and/or implementation, over some specified period of time. Let us now explore how these changes are handled in OGSI Grid services, and what best practices one should adhere to when dealing with such dynamics.

One should contend with the semantics of grid services as follows:

- The semantic of a grid service instance must be well defined by its interface definition; a combination of portTypes, operations, messages, types, and service data declarations.
- The implementation semantics must be consistent with the interface semantics; otherwise, it may confuse the client and may result in wayward behavior.

Based on the previous observations, here are some important best practices to consider:

- Service interfaces and implementations should agree on the semantics of the service.
- If there is a change to the interface (e.g., syntax and/or semantics) it is recommended to provide a new interface to the client, as opposed to changing the existing interface.
- All the elements of a grid service element must be immutable. This means that the QName of the portType, operation, message, service data declaration, and associated types are immutable. Any changes in any of these should result in a new interface portType.
- New interfaces should always be created using a new portType QName (i.e., a local name and a namespace combination).

GRID SERVICE INTERFACE CHANGE MANAGEMENT

Based on the above best practices, the port Type designs (i.e., the grid service public interfaces) are to be accomplished by taking into account that once a service interface is published to the customers, one cannot change it; instead, one can only provide a new interface with a new name.

This is one of many best practices identified in this chapter.

Grid Service Instance Handles, References, and Usage Models

Every grid service implemented utilizing the OGSI specification should adhere to certain practices, which are important to the overall integrity of the service.

One or more GSHs must be unique. This is key due to the fact that these handles uniquely identify a grid service instance that is valid for the entire life of a service. However, handles do not carry enough information to allow a client to communicate directly with the service instance. The service's GSH is based on a URI scheme[7] (e.g., http://) and the specific information (e.g, abc.com/myInstance).

A client must resolve the GSH information to a service specific to the GSR discussed in the next section, in one of three ways: by itself, by using the mechanisms provided from the service provider (e.g., a HandleResolver service, which implements a Handle-Resolver portType), or by delegating to a third-party handle resolving service (e.g. www.handle.net).

One or more GSRs are key to access integrity. A client can access a grid service through the use of a GSR, which can be treated as a pointer to a specific grid service instance. A GSR is a remote service "reference" and contains all the information to access the service. The format of a GSR is specific to the binding mechanism used by the client to communicate with the service.

Some examples of these binding formats include the following:

- Interoperable object reference (IOR) for clients utilizing the Remote Method Invocation/Internet Inter-ORB Protocol (RMI/IIOP)
- WSDL for clients utilizing the SOAP protocol
- .NET remoting reference

A grid service instance may have one or more GSRs available to it. The GSRs are associated with a lifecycle that is different from the service lifecycle. When the GSR is no longer valid, the client should get a reference to the service using an available GSH. It is important to note that the specification recommends a WSDL encoding of a GSR for a service. Thus, we may find that most of the grid service implementers will support WSDL encoding as the default encoding, and based upon the performance and quality, can switch to other encoding.

Listing 9.7　OGSI schema definition for GSR.

```
targetNamespace = "http://www.gridforum.org/namespaces/2003/03/OGSI"
<xsd:element name="reference" type="ogsi:ReferenceType"/>

<xsd:complexType name="ReferenceType" abstract="true">
  <xsd:attribute ref="ogsi:goodFrom" use="optional"/>
  <xsd:attribute ref="ogsi:goodUntil" use="optional"/>
</xsd:complexType>
```

Listing 9.7 shows the schema definition for the GSR. The optional lifetime attributes defined by the GSR schema provide the validity of that specific GSR.

Recommended GSR Encoding in WSDL

As of today, most of the accomplishments on binding are performed around the WSDL encoding of a GSR. This fact is of interest to the developers now faced with the construction of grid services. A discussion on WSDL encoding of a GSR with some samples is important. Listing 9.8 depicts this point of interest.

Listing 9.8 XML schema for WSDL encoding of a GSR.

```
targetNamespace = http://www.gridforum.org/namespaces/2003/03/OGSI"
<xsd:complexType name="WSDLReferenceType">
   <xsd:complexContent>
      <xsd:extension base="ogsi:ReferenceType">
         <xsd:sequence>
            <xsd:any namespace="http://schemas.xmlsoap.org/wsdl/"
                  minOccurs="1" maxOccurs="1" processContents="lax"/>
         </xsd:sequence>
      </xsd:extension>
   </xsd:complexContent>
</xsd:complexType>
```

Listing 9.8 depicts the XML schema for WSDL encoding of a GSR. The best practices on this encoding scheme are:

- The GSR reference must contain a WSDL definition element (i.e., with one service) as the child element.
- The WSDL definition element must contain only one WSDL service element, and may contain other elements from the "wsdl" namespace.
- The XML processing is set to "lax," which means XML parser validation is completed on this content element, based upon the availability of the "wsdl" definition schema; otherwise, no validation will be performed. This is accomplished by a runtime parser configuration, or by including "schemaLocation" for WSDL's XSD definition along with the XML message.

Listing 9.9 A sample WSDL encoding schema of a GSR.

```
<ogsi:reference xsi:type="ogsi:WSDLReferenceType">
     < wsdl:definitions name="OperatingSystemDefinition"
     xmlns="http://schemas.xmlsoap.org/wsdl/"
     xmlns:wsdl="http://schemas.xmlsoap.org/wsdl/">
           ..........................................................
           <wsdl:service name="OperatingSystemService">
                < wsdl:port.........................</ wsdl:port>
           </ wsdl:service>
     </wsdl:definitions>
</ogsi:reference>
```

As the developer of the grid service, one should be aware of another helpful practice defined by the specification called *service locator*. This is a grid service locator class with zero or more GSHs, GSRs, and portTypes (identified by portType QName) implemented by the service. All of the GSHs and GSRs must refer to the same grid service, and the service must implement all of the defined port types. This logical grouping helps client devices have a unique view of any given service instance.

Life Cycle of a Grid Service Instance

The hosting environment manages the lifecycle of a grid service by determining how and when a service is created, and how and when a service is destroyed. It is important to understand that the OGSI specification does not direct that behavior. For example, a grid service based on an Enterprise Java Bean (EJB) has the same lifecycle properties and manageability interfaces and policies as defined by that EJB specification.

The following describes lifecycle service creation patterns, as defined by the OGSI, to assist the clients of a grid service:

- A common grid service creation pattern is defined through the grid service factory interface (as discussed in the next sections) and through a createService operation. The service can decide whether or not to support this behavior, based upon the respective policies defined for the service.
- Two destruction mechanisms are defined:
  1. Calling an explicit destruction operation (i.e., destroy the operation on a specific GridService portType)
  2. Using a service-supported soft-state mechanism, based on the termination time attribute of a service

Service Lifecycle Management Using a Soft-State Approach

The soft-state lifetime management approach is a recommended method in the grid service lifecycle management process. Every grid service has a termination time set by the service creator or factory. A client device with appropriate authorization can use this termination time information to check the availability (i.e., lease period) of the service, and can request to extend the current lease time by sending a keep-alive message to the service with a new termination time. If the service accepts this request, the lease time can be extended to the new termination time requested by the client.

This soft-state lifecycle is controlled by appropriate security and policy decisions of the service, and the service has the authority to control this behavior. For example, a service can arbitrarily terminate a service, or a service can extend its termination time, even while the client holds a service reference. Another point to keep in mind is whether or not to actually destroy a service, or just to make it unavailable. This is a service hosting environment decision. Some of the behaviors that we can infer from the specification are:

- A grid service can send lifetime event notifications using the standard grid service notification process.

- A grid service's support for the lifetime is implementation dependent, and one must consult the service documentation for the details on this behavior.
- A Client with proper authority can request for an early termination of a grid service.
- A grid service can extend the service termination time, or terminate itself, at any time during its lifecycle.

Service Operation Extensibility Features of Grid Services

Another interesting feature introduced by the specification is the concept of extensible operations through the use of untyped parameters using the XML schema xsd:any construct. This feature allows grid service operations maximum flexibility by allowing "any" parameters (i.e., XML fragments) for that operation. However, this feature introduces confusion on the client side regarding the kind of parameters it can pass to the service. To avoid that confusion, the specification provides the client base with a mechanism (i.e., query capabilities) to ask the service about the supported extensible parameter and its type (XML schema) information.

This example will make the preceding idea clearer. We have already discussed that we can use findServiceData of GridService to query the service data of a service instance. A service can support different types of queries, including query by service data names and query by XPath. The specification defines the input parameter of findServiceData as extensible, utilizing ogsi:ExtensibilityType. In this example, one can retrieve all the possible queries supported by the service instance from the SDE values of the service's "findserviceDataExtensibility" service data element. By default, a service provides a static query type value called "queryByServiceDataNames" defined by utilizing the staticServiceDataValue. These static SDE values are defined for GridService portType in the ogsi.gwsdl. We will see more details on the operation extensibility features when we discuss the grid service portTypes.

Service Fault Handling in OGSI

A <wsdl:operation> can define a fault message in the case of an operation failure. In many cases, a service developer decides on the message format and the contents. The OGSI defines a common fault message type to simplify the problem of different fault message types being defined. The OGSI defines a base XSD fault type (ogsi:faultType) that every grid service must return. Listing 9.10 explains the usage model of this fault type.

Listing 9.10 Fault definitions in OGSI.

```
<definitions name="OperatingSystem" ....>
<types>
    <element name="targetInvalidFault"
        type="TargetInvalidFaultType"/>
    <complexType name="TargetInvalidFaultType">
      <complexContent>
        <extension base="ogsi:FaultType"/>
```

Listing 9.10 Fault definitions in OGSI. (Continued)

```
        </complexContent>
      </complexType>
        ...........................................
  </types>
  <message name="TargetInvalidFaultMessage">
    <part name="fault" element="targetInvalidFault"/>
  </message>
  ...................
  <gwsdl:portType name="OperatingSystem">
          <operation name="reboot">
                  <input...>
                  <output...>
                  <fault name=" TargetInvalidFaultMessage "
                              message="TargetInvalidFaultMessage "/>
                  <fault name="Fault" message="ogsi:faultMessage"/>
          </operation>
  </gwsdl:portType>
  .........................
  <definitions>
```

Here our reboot operation returns a fault message of the type TargetInvalidFaultType, which is of the OGSI-defined common fault type ogsi:FaultType. This provides applications to define and process a common model for all the fault messages. It is a mandatory recommendation that all grid service in addition to the operation-specific fault messages must return a "ogsi:faultMessage." This fault message is to return all the faults that are not defined by the service developer. Listing 9.10 above shows these requirements.

Grid Service Interfaces

The grid service interfaces and their associated behaviors are described by the OGSI specification.

The UML interface hierarchy diagram, as shown in Figure 9.4, describes the OGSI-defined interfaces. Let us now explore the basic and essential information pertaining to service interface behaviors, message exchanges, and interface descriptions.

We can classify OGSI interfaces into three sets of interfaces based upon their functionality. These are the OGSI core, notification, and service groups. Table 9.4 describes the interface name, description, and service data defined for these interfaces, as well as the predefined static service data elements.

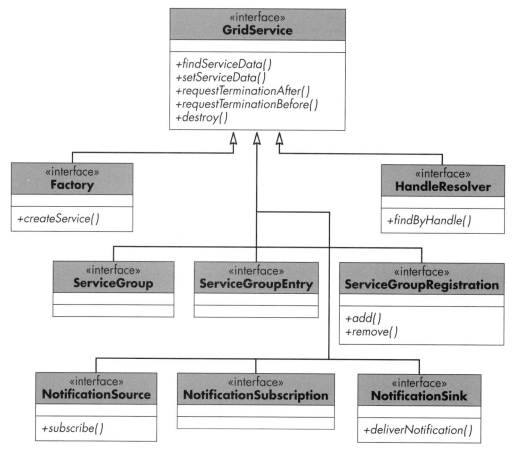

Figure 9.4
OGSI-defined portTypes.

As noted in the interfaces in Table 9.4, all grid services are required to implement the GridService portType and its respective behaviors. This interface and its associated service data set provide service-specific meta-data and information that one can use for dynamic service introspection, and being the core component of the OGSI specification, this interface warrants more attention.

Table 9.4 portTypes That Support Grid Service Behaviors, Service Data Elements, and Static Service Data Values

PortType Name	Interface Description and Operations	Service Data Elements Defined by This portType	Default Service Data (static) Values

GridService (required)	All Grid services implement this interface and provides these operations and behaviors.
	
	Operations:
	1. findServiceData
	2. setServiceData
	3. requestTerminationTimeAfter
	4. requestTerminationTimeBefore
	5. destroy
		1. interfaces
		2. serviceDataName
		3. factoryLocator
		4. GridServiceHandle
		5. GridServiceReference
		6. findServiceDataExtensibility
		7. setServiceDataExtensibility
		8. terminationTime
			`<ogsi: findServiceDataExtensibility`
			`inputElement="queryByServiceDataNames" />`
			`<ogsi: setServiceDataExtensibility`
			`inputElement="setByServiceDataNames" />`
			`<ogsi: setServiceDataExtensibility`
			`inputElement="deleteByServiceDataNames" />`

Factory (optional)	To create a new grid service. Operations: 1. createService	1. createServiceExtensibility	None
HandleResolver (optional)	A service-provided mechanism to resolve a GSH to a GSR. Operations: 1. FindByHandle	1. handleResolverScheme	None

159

Inside the GridService portType

The UML notations in Figure 9.5 show the details of this interface.

GridService
–interface : QName –serviceDataName : QName –factoryLocator : LocatorType –gridserviceHandle : ReferenceType –gridServiceReference : ReferenceType –findServiceDataExtensibility : OperationExtensibilityType –setServiceDataExtensibility : OperationExtensibilityType –terminationTime : TerminationTimeType
+findServiceData(in queryExpression : ExtensibilityType) : ExtensibilityType +setServiceData(in updateExpression : ExtensibilityType) : ExtensibilityType +requestTerminationAfter(in requestTerminationAfter : TerminationTimeType) +requestTerminationTimeBefore(in requestTerminationTimeBefore : TerminationTimeType) +destroy()

Figure 9.5
The UML representation of GridService PortType.

As shown in Figure 9.5, this interface provides a number of service state attributes, and a number of operations common to all grid services. Focusing attention on the above interface definition, one can infer that the "findServiceData" and "setServiceData" are both extensible operations. They also provide the basic capability of passing any input parameters and returning any output parameter from the service. We will see the specific semantics in the following sections.

Grid Service–Provided Service Data Query Capabilities: Syntax and Semantics

The OGSI is provided as a common approach for discovering the state information from a grid service. Every grid service implements the GridService portType, and thereby a client can use the "findServiceData" operation on a grid service passing a query expression. The format and semantics of the query expression parameter is based upon the query support provided by the service.

By default, every grid service must support the "queryByServiceDataName" query expression. This is a simple query, utilized by "findServiceData" by passing the QName of the service data element of interest to get the service data element values for that SDE. A grid service may support other query expressions, including XPath/XQuery. All query types including the predefined query types are stored in the "findServiceDataExtensibility" and "setServiceDataExtensibility" service data element values. Table 9.5 lists the predefined static extensibility types ("queryBy-ServiceDataNames," "setByServiceDataNames," and "deleteByServiceDataNames").

The grid service implementation team must provide both the semantic and message formats of the extended query expressions. Consult the service and interface documentation to find out the specific details on this additional query support.

Based on the previous discussion, let us now examine some examples of using the find operation. Let us first find all the supported query expressions from a service (a read-only query).

The query syntax for this operation is as follows:

findServiceData (ExtensibilityType queryByServiceDataNames), where the extensibility type contains the input message as shown in Listing 9.11.

Listing 9.11   A query by a service data input message.

```
<ogsi:queryByServiceDataNames>
  <name>ogsi:findServiceDataExtensibility</name>
                          <!— name of the service data element - ->
</ogsi:queryByServiceDataNames>
```

As described in Listing 9.11, note that the example is passing a known type of query expression "queryByServiceDataNames" and the service data name of interest in this query. In this case, the example is utilizing the "findServiceDataExtensibility" serviceData name, which is the holder of the read-only queryExpressions type supported by this specific service.

The above operation may return an output message as shown in Listing 9.12:

Listing 9.12   A query by service data output message.

```
<sd:serviceDataValues>
  <ogsi:findServiceDataExtensibility
      inputElement="ogsi:queryByServiceDataNames"/>
                              <!—this is a mandatory return - ->
  <ogsi:findServiceDataExtensibility
      inputElement="ogsi:queryByXPath"/> <!—may present - ->
</sd:serviceDataValues>
```

Listing 9.12 suggests that the service supports the default "queryByServiceDataNames" and a service-specific additional query expression "queryByXPath."

It is also possible to dynamically determine all of the interfaces exposed by the grid services. The query syntax for this operation is utilizing *findServiceData (ExtensibilityType interfaceSD),* where extensibility type contains the input message; this is shown in Listing 9.13.

Listing 9.13   A query by service data input message.

```
<ogsi:queryByServiceDataNames>
    <name>ogsi:interface</name>
</ogsi:queryByServiceDataNames>
```

The above operation may result in an output message as shown in Listing 9.14.

Listing 9.14   The result of a find query for all support interfaces.

```
<sd:serviceDataValues>
   <ogsi:interface>
        ogsi:GridService   <!—always will be present - ->
        cmm:BaseManageableResource
        cmm:OperatingSystem
   </ogsi:interface>
..............................................................
</sd:serviceDataValues>
```

Listing 9.14 suggests that this service implements interfaces, including the ogsi:GridService, cmm:BaseManageableResource, and the cmm:OperatingSystem.

Grid Service–Provided Service Data Update Capabilities: Syntax and Semantics

The previous section explains the "read-only" behavior of the service state. Some state information in a grid service is updateable or changeable by the client. This is similar to using set operations to update object properties in Java Beans or other language objects.

As discussed earlier in this book, an OGSI service can specify whether a state data value is changeable by explicitly setting the modifiable attribute to "true."

Every grid service must support the "setServiceData" operation with the "updateExpression" extensibility type parameter. The format and semantics of the update expression parameter are based on the update feature support provided by the service. For example, a service can provide simple state data, update data, or a complex XUpdate[8] update expression.

We have noted that by default, every grid service provides two update expressions of type "setByServiceDataNames," and "deleteByServiceDataNames."

Let us now explore some additional utilization examples. Let us find all the update expressions supported by the service. The query syntax is *findServiceData (ExtensibilityType queryByServiceDataNames)*, where the extensibility type contains the input message as shown in Listing 9.15:

Listing 9.15   A query by service data input message.

```
<ogsi:queryByServiceDataNames>
   <name>ogsi:setServiceDataExtensibility</name>
   <!—this is a mandatory update expression type for all service - ->
</ogsi:queryByServiceDataNames>
```

The above operation may result in an ExtensibilityType, with an output message as shown in Listing 9.16:

Listing 9.16 Supported update expressions.

```
<sd:serviceDataValues>
    <ogsi:setServiceDataExtensibility
        inputElement="ogsi:setByServiceDataNames"/>
    <ogsi:setServiceDataExtensibility
        inputElement="ogsi:deleteByServiceDataNames"/>
</sd:serviceDataValues>
```

As shown in Listing 9.16, this service supports two types of updates, "setByServiceDataNames" and "deleteByServiceDataNames."

Let us now apply a set operation on service data, with a "mutable" attribute of "true," using the supported "updateExpression" retrieved from the above step. The query syntax is *setServiceData (ExtensibilityType updateByServiceDataNames)*, where the extensibility type contains the input message as shown in Listing 9.17:

Listing 9.17 An input message for the set operation.

```
<ogsi:setByServiceDataNames>
    <someServiceDataElement NameTag>
        new SDE value(s)
    </someServiceDataElement NameTag>
</ogsi:setByServiceDataNames>
```

The service handling of the set operation on service data is based upon a number of rules defined by OGSI. These rules include:

- The serviceData must be modifiable; the SDE-modifiable attribute must be "true."
- The serviceData mutability attribute should not be "static" or "constant."
- If the serviceData mutability attribute is "extendable," the set operation must append the new SDE values to the existing SDE values.
- If the serviceData mutability attribute is "mutable," the set operation must replace the existing SDE values with the new SDE values.
- The SDE values, "append" and "replace", must adhere to the minOccurs and maxOccurs attributes on SDE values.

The partial failure on update and delete operations involving service data elements may be common due to the distributed nature of grid services and lack of concurrency in the distributed model. Therefore, the grid service provides partial failure indication faults and the client should be aware of dealing with that. This fault type extends "ogsi:FaultType" and must contain all the service data elements that cannot be updated with the one or more fault cause information schemas.

Grid Service Factory Concepts

This is an abstract concept or pattern that can be utilized to create a service instance by the client. This is an optional interface and provides an operation called "createService."

Figure 9.6 illustrates the basic service creation pattern for a grid service instance. Once the creation process has been successfully executed, the factory returns the grid service locator (GSH and GSR) information, which can then be utilized by the client to locate the service.

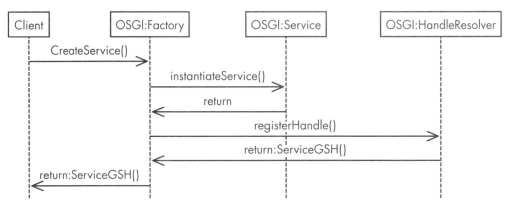

Figure 9.6
The grid service factory usage pattern.

The pattern does not mandate the creation of the instance; in the case of lazy creation, it may just return a GSH for the service; however, it will postpone the creation of the actual service instance. Another point to note regarding creation semantics is the dependency on the hosting environments; the specification does not mandate any implementation semantics. For example, we can infer that if the grid service instance is an EJB entity, the factory may correspond to the EJB home, which is responsible for the creation of an EJB entity bean.

Grid Service Handle Resolution Concepts

Handle resolving is a standard mechanism to resolve a GSH into a GSR. This is an optional feature based on the HandleResolver portType. A grid service instance that implements the HandleResolver portType is called a "handle resolver."

This handle resolution process is implementation dependent and may be tied to the hosting environment. For example, in a J2EE environment, this handle resolution can be tied to the J2EE JNDI lookup, and hence, a JNDI server can be a HandleResolver service. Another example may be a global handle resolution service provider that can resolve the handle to any services regis-

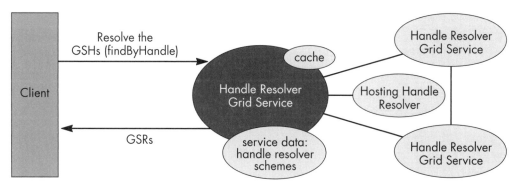

Figure 9.7
A simple handle resolution process.

tered with it. In some cases, a client can perform the resolution of service instance handle to a service reference.

Figure 9.7 shows a simple handle resolution process. These resolving services may contain a cache of handles and GSRs and are capable of collaborating with other "resolvers" in order to resolve the handle. Once the handle is resolved, it returns a GSR for the service instance.

OGSI-Defined Grid Service Notification Framework

Let us now explore some of the asynchronous messaging capabilities provided by the grid services. Notification is required in the process of sending asynchronous one-way messages from a service to the interested client. The OGSI defined a set of standard mechanisms for sending notification messages. This specification defines a rich set of concepts.

> ### OGSI MESSAGE NOTIFICATION CONCEPTS ARE ROBUST
>
> A *notification source* is a grid service instance that implements the Notification-Source portType and is the source of the notification.
>
> A *notification sink* is a grid service instance that receives the notification messages from any number of sources. A sink must implement the Notification sink portType.
>
> A *notification message* is an XML element sent from the source to sink and the type of this element is based on the subscription expression.
>
> A *subscription expression* is an XML element that describes what messages should be sent from the notification source to the sink and when the message was sent.
>
> A *subscription* grid service is created on a subscription request and helps the clients manage the lifetime of the subscription. These subscription services are created on subscription and these services should implement NotificationSubscription portType.

This form of messaging is key in Grid Computing discipline, and is described in Table 9.5.

Table 9.5 portTypes That Support Grid Service Notification Framework, Service Data Elements, and Static Service Data Values

PortType Name	Interface Description and Operations	Service Data Elements Defined by This portType	Default Service Data (Static) Values
NotificationSource (optional)	This enables a client to subscribe for notification based on a service data value change. Operations: 1. subscribe	notifiableServiceDataName subscribeExtensibility	`<ogsi: subscribeExtensibility inputElement="subscribeByServiceDataNames" />`
NotificationSink (optional)	Implementing this interface enables a grid service instance to receive notification messages based on a subscription. Operations: 1. deliverNotification	None	None
NotificationSubscription (optional)	Calling a subscription of a Notification Source results in the creation of a subscription grid service. Operations: None defined	SubscriptionExpression sinkLocator	None

The OGSI-defined notification portTypes and their associated service data are shown in Table 9.5. Figure 9.8 depicts the notification flow.

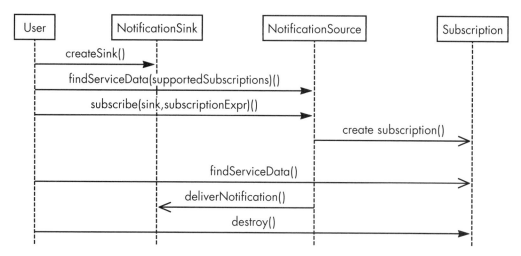

Figure 9.8
The simple sequence notification flow.

A sample notification process, as illustrated in Figure 9.8, involves the client creating a sink object to receive notification. This sink object is implementing the NotificationSink interface. The client discovers the available subscription types supported by the notification source by the query syntax findServiceData (ExtensibilityType subscribeByServiceDataNames), where the extensibility type contains the input message as shown in the following XML fragment.

Listing 9.18   A query by service data input message.

```
<ogsi:queryByServiceDataNames>
   <name>ogsi:subscribeExtensibility</name>
</ogsi:queryByServiceDataNames>
```

The operation in Listing 9.18 may result in an ExtensibilityType response message, with an XML message as shown in Listing 9.19:

Listing 9.19   Subscription expressions.

```
<sd:serviceDataValues>
   <ogsi:subscribeExtensibility
        inputElement="ogsi:subscribeByServiceDataName"/>
</sd:serviceDataValues>
```

As shown in Listing 9.18, this service supports a "subscribeByServiceDataName" subscription type.

> **SUBSCRIBEBYSERVICEDATANAME SUBSCRIPTION**
>
> This subscription results in notification messages being sent whenever any of the named service data elements change. This subscription results in messages being sent based on two important attributes of this subscription, minInterval and maxInterval.
>
> As shown in this example, the message sent contains all the service data element values.

Let us now explore where the client calls the service to subscribe for the service data name to pass the subscription expression of the type "subscribeByServiceDataName" with the associated interval properties and the GSH to where the messages must deliver the value. The service receiving this "subscribe" operation initiates the following actions:

- This subscription results in the creation of a subscription grid service.
- The service returns the locator for this subscription service.

Whenever there is a service data change, and the criteria set for minimum and maximum interval meets acceptance, the source delivers an XML message to the sink after formatting the message based on the subscription criteria.

Finally, when the client operation is completed with the service, it can kill the subscriptions by calling destroy on the subscription service. The behavior of this operation, such as removing the subscription, is a service implementation specific.

Service Grouping Concepts in OGSI

The third set of portTypes provides the grouping concepts for grid services. The grid services can be grouped based on certain classification schemes, or they can utilize simple aggregation mechanisms.

Some example of grouping includes:

- Simple registries or index services where there is no specific classification scheme but are aggregated collections of services for discovery purposes.
- A federated service group to solve some specific problems including weather prediction, distributed load balancing, service cluster, and so on.

Table 9.6 lists the OGSI-defined service group related to port types, operations, and service data elements.

Table 9.6 portTypes That Support the Grid Service Grouping Behavior, Service Data Elements, Static Service Data Values

PortType Name	Interface Description and Operations	Service Data Elements Defined by This portType	Default Service Data (Static) Values
ServiceGroup (optional)	An abstract interface to represent a grouping of zero or more services. This interface extends the GridService portType. Operations: No operations are defined but can use operations defined in a GridService portType.	MembershipContentRule entry	None
ServiceGroupRegistration (optional)	This interface extends the ServiceGroup interface and provides operations to manage a ServiceGroup including add/ delete a service to/from a group. Operations: 1. add 2. remove	addExtensibility removeExtensibility	`<ogsi: removeExtensibility inputElement="matchByLocatorEquivalence" />`
ServiceGroupEntry (optional)	This is a representation of an individual entry of a Service-Group and is created on Service-GroupRegistration "add." Each entry contains a service locator to a member grid service, and information about the member service as defined by the service group membership rule (content). Operations: None defined	memberServiceLocator content	

The service group concepts introduced by OGSI are useful to build registries for grid services. Table 9.6 lists the OGSI-defined interfaces associated with this grouping. Based upon the observation on OGSI interfaces, and their service data, there can be two types of registries. These registries are locally managed registries and grid managed registries.

Locally managed registries are created for internal use inside a grid system. These registries are derived from serviceGroup portType, and the registry entries (grid services) are created at start-up. The entries are added through configuration or using custom APIs. This grouping is "local" because no external grid operations are exposed from ServiceGroup portType. One typical use of such a registry is for the creation of a registry with a collection of service factories.

Grid managed registries are derived from the ServiceGroupRegistration portType. This interface provides external operations to add and delete group entries into the registry. This portType is derived from ServiceGroup, and hence provides a private registry to hold the group contents. Figure 9.9 illustrates this concept. The ServiceGroupRegistrion is derived from ServiceGroup and the broken line indicates a logical operation.

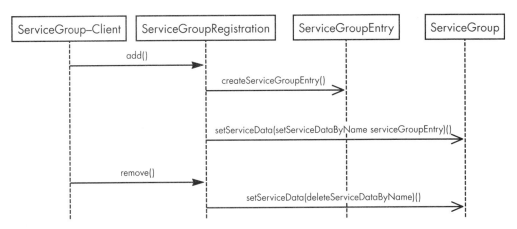

Figure 9.9
A sequence diagram showing the service group in action.

The best practice is applied for the registries to be externally managed, to create a service group deriving from ServiceGroupRegistration, and for all other cases (i.e., private, static, and internal) to create registries derived from ServiceGroup.

Let us now explore the internal concepts introduced by the service group, including membership rules, service entries, and management.

Membership Rules for a Service Group

Deriving a service from the ServiceGroup portType, and utilizing the "MembershipContentRule" service data for the classification mechanisms can create a grouping concept similar to a registry.

This "rule" (MembershipContentRule) service data is used to restrict the membership of a grid service in the group.

This rule specifies the following:

- A list of interfaces that the member grid services must implement.
- Zero or more contents, identifiable through QName, that are needed to become a part of this group. The contents of QName are listed with the ServiceGroupEntry utilizing the "content" service data element.
- This service data has a mutability value of "constant," and hence these rules are created by the runtime on ServiceGroup service startup (i.e., in most of the cases).

What follows is a sample rule definition with two rules:

Listing 9.20   A service group membership rule sample.

```
<memberShipContentRule>
    <memberInterface>
        crm:OperatingSystemFactory
    </memberInterface>
    <content>
        ogsi:CreateServiceExtensibilityType
    </content>
</memberShipContentRule>
< memberShipContentRule>
    <memberInterface> crm:OperatingSystem<memberInterface>
    <content>
        ogsi:CreateServiceExtensibilityType
    </content>
</memberShipContentRule>
```

Based upon the above rules, this service group contains grid services that implement either OperatingSystemFactory or OperatingSystem interfaces. In addition, the above rules specify a content rule, which states that the corresponding ServiceGroupEntry, created for each service in the group, must define the content with QName "ogsi:CreateServiceExtensibilityType." We will later explore this content information.

The specific as to exactly how this rule is validated is an implementation decision. For example, using runtime type checking on the service can test the interface validity.

Service Entries in a Service Group

Another very important construct in the registry is the storage for the collection of services. The ServiceGroup provides a service data element called "entry," which provides a structure for the constituent members of the ServiceGroup.

Each of these SDE values contains:

- A locator pointer to the serviceGroupEntry grid service instance that manages the constituent grid service instance—a proxy to the real service instance
- A locator pointer to the member grid service instance
- The contents of the entry

An example of such an entry is shown in Listing 9.21.

Listing 9.21   A ServiceGroupEntry sample.

```
<ogsi:EntryType>
    <serviceGroupEntryLocator>
        <ogsi:handle>
            http://localhost/ogsi/ServiceGroupEntry/osEntry
        </ogsi:handle>
    </serviceGroupEntryLocator>
    <memberServiceLocator>
        <ogsi:handle>
            http://localhost/ogsi/crm/OperatingSystemFactory
        </ogsi:handle>
    </memberServiceLocator>
    <content>
        <ogsi:CreateServiceExtensibilityType>
            <createsInterface>OperatingSystemFactory</createsInterface>
        </ogsi:CreateServiceExtensibilityType>
    </content>
</ogsi:EntryType>
```

ServiceGroupEntry

This portType defines the interface through which the individual entries in ServiceGroup can be effectively managed. Every service in the group contains a corresponding ServiceGroupEntry instance. In fact, this can be treated as a "proxy" of a sort to the service instance. In the UML diagram shown earlier, a service client using a ServiceGroupRegistration service creates this proxy, and then adds the proxy to the ServiceGroup collection.

A Simple Registry Utilizing the OGSI Service Group Concepts

Let us now explore how a simple private registry holds factories responsible for the creation of grid services in a container. This is a locally managed registry for the factories of the services running in a container. An example is simply constructed, based upon the OperatingSystemFactory service, which is responsible for OperatingSystem creation.

This registry implements the ServiceGroup portType. The meta-data in the registry comes from ogsi:Factory portType, where the service data specifies all the services that a factory can create.

The following discussion is focused on creating this grouping service. Since most of the meta-data for the factory registry is well defined and quite static in nature, the data can be defined in a GWSDL description as static service data values.

Listing 9.22 A service group containing grid service factories.

```
<gwsdl:portType name="factoryServiceGroup" extends="ServiceGroup"/>
<sd:staticServiceDataValues>
    <ogsi:EntryType>
        <serviceGroupEntryLocator nil="true"/>
        <memberServiceLocator>
            <ogsi:handle>
                http://localhost/ogsi/crm/OperatingSystemFactory
            </ogsi:handle>
        </memberServiceLocator>
        <content>
            <ogsi:CreateServiceExtensibilityType>
            <createsInterface>OperatingSystem</createsInterface>
            <createsInterface>GridService</createsInterface>
            </ogsi:CreateServiceExtensibilityType>
        </content>
    </ogsi:EntryType>

    <ogsi:EntryType>
        <serviceGroupEntryLocator nil="true"/>
        <memberServiceLocator>
            <ogsi:handle>
                http://localhost/ogsi/policy/PolicyEnforcementFactory
            </ogsi:handle>
        </memberServiceLocator>
        <content>
            <ogsi:CreateServiceExtensibilityType>
            <createsInterface>PolicyService</createsInterface>
            <createsInterface>GridService</createsInterface>
            </ogsi:CreateServiceExtensibilityType>
        </content>
    </ogsi:EntryType>

<sd:staticServiceDataValues>
```

The important information we can derive from the above listing is:

- Since these services are managed locally, the serviceGroupEntryLocator is not utilized.
- The memberLocator rule provides the handle to the factory instance, where we have two factories registered with this registry.
- The content rule states what type of services each factory can create. These services must conform to the interfaces identified in the logic.

This registry, upon startup, loads this information and updates ServiceGroup's "membership-Rules" and "entry" service data fields.

The client can utilize the standard grid service calls to discover the factory instances that can be utilized for creating the "operating system" services. The client can query the registry for all the ServiceGroup entries using the "findServiceData" operation, and passing the query expression as shown in Listing 9.23.

Listing 9.23   A query to the registry.

```
<ogsi:queryByServiceDataNames>
<name> ogsi:entry </name>
<ogsi:queryByServiceDataNames>
```

The preceding query may result in the following result:

Listing 9.24   Service group query results.

```
<sd:serviceDataValues>
    <ogsi:EntryType>
        <serviceGroupEntryLocator nil="true"/>
        <memberServiceLocator>
            <ogsi:handle>
                http://localhost/ogsi/crm/OperatingSystemFactory
            </ogsi:handle>
        </memberServiceLocator>
        <content>
            <ogsi:CreateServiceExtensibilityType>
            <createsInterface>OperatingSystem</createsInterface>
            <createsInterface>GridService</createsInterface>
            </ogsi:CreateServiceExtensibilityType>
        </content>
    </ogsi:EntryType>
</sd:serviceDataValues>
```

The clients can now run an XPath query on the above results to find out the factory that can be used to create an "OperatingSystem" service using the XPath expression in the following logic: // ogsi:EntryType[content/ogsi:CreateServiceExtensibilityType/createInstance="OperatingSystem"].

This results in a list of EntryTypes that will create an operating system service. Again, to obtain the specific handle to the factory execution, this XPath query is: //ogsi:handle.

The client can utilize this GSH to the factory, obtained by execution of the above step, in order to create the operating system service.

We can now reduce the number of client-side XPath operations if the service supports a query by the XPath "operationExtensibility" type. In these cases, the client can issue the "findService-Data" call with the XPath information, and can then directly obtain the factory handle.

Grid Services and Client Programming Models

As presented in previous discussions, the details surrounding the concepts of OGSI are rich and robust across several dimensions. Let us now focus on exactly how to define the client-side programming patterns that interact with an OGSI-defined grid service.

Earlier discussions were focused on how the OGSI is based upon Web services concepts, and how the core direction of this standardization process is on the interoperability between grid services and Web services. This interoperability can be achieved by using the OGSI standards-driven XML messages and the exchange patterns. The OGSI is not defining a new programming model, rather the OGSI is grounding itself upon the existing Web service programming model. At the same time, the OGSA provides some standard interaction pattern including conversion of the GSH to the GSR.

The grid services are uniquely identified by the GSH. A client should convert the GSH (i.e., a permanent network-wide pointer) to a GSR prior to accessing the services. The GSH does not convey tremendous amounts of information; instead, the GSH provides the identity of a service. Once the client retains a GSR, it can access the service.

There are two types of clients:

> *Static*. These kinds of clients have plurality of a priori knowledge on the runtime binding information. This includes aspects of native host system message mapping capabilities, the language maps, types for marshalling/de-marshalling of messages, creation of service helpers, and proxies. Normally speaking, the client uses the WSDL/GWSDL information to create these artifacts. These kinds of clients are faster, yet less flexible in operations. Any change in service description requires the recreation of the above artifacts.
>
> *Dynamic*. These types of clients are flexible and they are not bound to any predefined artifacts. They start from the service description discovery and runtime creation of interaction artifacts, including binding and type-mapping information. These types of clients are highly flexible, yet may perform with less efficiencies.

The locator helper class, as defined by OGSI, provides an abstraction for the service binding process and handle resolution process. Most of the grid toolkits today may generate this artifact to help the client deal with GSHs, GSRs, and interactions between the two entities.

The client framework is, in theory, simple, as illustrated in Figure 9.10.

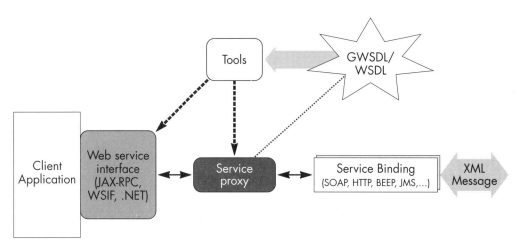

Figure 9.10
The client-side framework.

The client always needs to be aware of the GWSDL extension, and should rely on the tools for the transformation of GWSDL portTypes to WSDL portTypes for simplified aspects involving interoperability with existing WSDL 1.1 tools and frameworks. In the next section, we introduce specific implementations of the client-side artifacts from the perspectives of different grid toolkits.

Grid Services and Service Programming Model

The OGSI specification does not dictate particular service implementation architectures. There are numerous ways by which a developer can achieve this architectural environment, ranging from implementing grid services as operating system services, to the more sophisticated server-side component model as specified by J2EE or COM+. The OGSI services can be hosted in the smaller footprint pervasive devices, all the way up to the more sophisticated mainframe environments.

A grid services implementation can provide host service protocol termination, and service behaviors, in the same executable or operating system service environments. Figure 9.11 shows an application providing protocol termination and the grid service implementation.

Grid services can be implemented as components (e.g., Servlets, EJB, etc.) that can be hosted in a container, and the container along with the host environment provides the service protocol termination points and marshalling and de-marshalling of the messages. In this scenario, there may be requirements to adapt to the container behaviors and the models. For example, if a service is

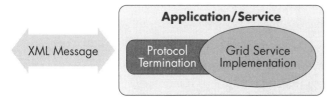

Figure 9.11
A simple grid service implemented as an application.

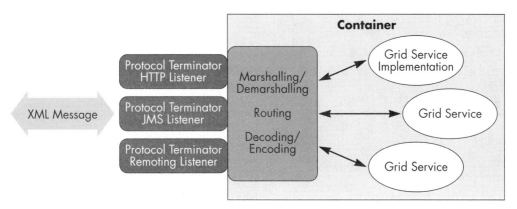

Figure 9.12
A container model for a service implementation.

implementing itself as an EJB, the service lifecycle may need to be coherent with the EJB lifecycle model. Most of the grid toolkits tend to use this model for their middleware implementation. Figure 9.12 shows such a service implemented in J2EE Web containers.

Some of the key core service implementation requirements are as follows:

- Ability to provide a well-defined service description in GWSDL/WSDL
- Adhere to the XML message formats, as defined in the service description based on the OGSI specification
- Leverage the Web service infrastructure (and standards) for achieving message-level interoperability

SUMMARY

The OGSI specification successfully addresses a number of very important issues associated with distributed systems (i.e., lifecycle, naming, references, and state management). At the same time, some incoherence exists when the specification adopts some of the Web services concepts: instance addressing, stateful services concepts (i.e., referencing and state representation), and Web services best practices guidelines (e.g., the document-centric view). These issues can be sorted out with the emergence of stateful Web services and correlations, in addition to the maturity of WS-Addressing and related specifications.

The OGSI specification handles many key grid services required behaviors, it is extensible, and it achieves maximum interoperability across service implementations. Several software frameworks available today are based on the OGSI specification. The Globus GT3 is the most prominent and practical implementation of this specification. In a later chapter, we will explore in great detail exactly how the Globus Grid Toolkit and other middleware providers have implemented the OGSI specifications.

NOTES

1. For more information, go to *www.forge.gridforum.org/projects/ogsi-wg/*.

2. For more information, go to *www.forge.gridforum.org/projects/cmm-wg/*.

3. For more information, go to *http://www-106.ibm.com/developerworks/library/ws-bpel/*.

4. For more information, go to *www.w3.org/TR/wsdl/*.

5. For more information, go to *www.w3.org/2002/ws/desc/*.

6. For more information, go to *https://forge.grid/orum.org/projects/ogsi.wg*.

7. For more information, go to *www.w3.org/Addressing/*.

8. For more information, go to *www.xmldb.org/xupdate*.

OGSA Basic Services

COMMON MANAGEMENT MODEL (CMM)

The Open Grid System Architecture (OGSA) Common Management Model[1] (CMM) is an abstract representation of real IT resources such as disks, file systems, operating systems, network ports, and IP addresses. The CMM can also be an abstract representation of logical IT resources, which can be a composition of the physical IT resources to build services and complete business applications.

Some of the most important and commonly utilized terms in the management of resources are "manageable resource," "manageability," and resource "management."

KEY TERMS TO UNDERSTAND

Manageable resource is any IT entity that has some state to which the management operations can be applied. A manageable resource can be any entity, hardware (hard drives), software components (a database), complete applications (help desk system), and even transient things such as print jobs.

Manageability is a concept whereby a resource defines information that can be utilized to manage the resource. Manageability details all the aspects of a resource that support management, including interaction with a resource from the management applications.

Management is the process of monitoring, modifying, and making decisions about a resource, including the capabilities that use manageability information, to perform activities or tasks associated with managing IT resources.

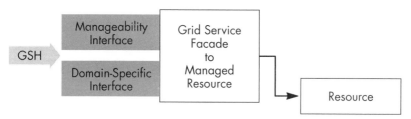

Figure 10.1
The manageable resource grid services facade.

The CMM is a "single" model for management that can be utilized with, and extended for, multiple grid resource models; however, it does not define a resource information model (e.g., CIM, SNMP, JMX), which is the job of the other standards organizations (e.g., DMTF, JCP). The CMM defines a set of common management interfaces by which these manageable resources are exposed to the external management applications for the sole purposes of managing these resources.

In CMM, every management resource is represented as a grid service instance that possesses a state, a unique instance identifier, and operational interfaces. Figure 10.1 depicts the grid services facade.

Figure 10.1 shows a manageable resource and its facade grid service that provides CMM-specific manageability interfaces and domain-specific interfaces. One must be certain on the difference between manageability interfaces and domain-specific interfaces.

Manageability Interfaces

Every resource represented by CMM has a grid service facade that represents the underlying resource, and exposes a set of canonical interfaces and behaviors common to all the CMM services. This grid service has a state that corresponds to the resource state and a managed lifecycle model.

Domain-Specific Interfaces

Every CMM resource exposes a number of domain-specific interfaces, in addition to the canonical manageability interfaces for its management applications. These domain-specific interfaces are tightly coupled to the domain in which these resources are defined. As an example, we can consider the case of a resource instrumented in CIM. This resource exposes a standard CMM manageability interface and, in addition, exposes some CIM-specific interfaces (e.g., a CIM Operating System interface) to deal with the resources. These interfaces provide access to the resources but do not represent the CMM-managed resource behavior.

The OGSA CMM specification defines three aspects of manageability:

   1. An XML schema (XSD) for modeling the resource manageability information
   2. A collection of manageability portTypes
   3. Guidelines for modeling resource

New Constructs for Resource Modeling

A resource's manageability information is modeled using the XML schema. CMM-defined extensions and additional data types (i.e., XML attributes) allow those manageable resources to provide additional information to the management applications.

In order to better capture the data, CMM defined the following new data types: counter and gauge. In addition to these data types, CMM defined XML attributes that are classified as:

- Versioning related
  - Version
  - Deprecated
  - Experimental
- Unit related
  - Units
- Lifecycle characteristics
  - Valid
  - Changeable
  - Volatile
  - Latency

Let us now examine the core port types exposed by the common management model.

CMM-Defined Manageability Interfaces

The CMM-defined manageability interfaces are the WSDL portTypes that are defined as part of the management interfaces of a manageable resource. We can see that CMM is trying to factor out the common set of interfaces that can function against all the resources. These interfaces are called "canonical port types" that provide a consistent behavior and functionality to the management applications (Figure 10.2).

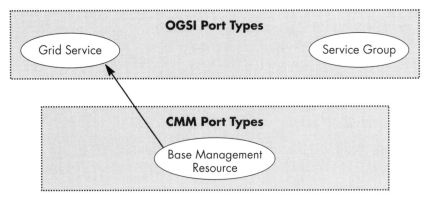

Figure 10.2
CMM manageability port types.

There are two most important canonical port types defined for CMM. As we have previously seen in the OGSI specification, the GridService port type is the core interface and is present in all grid services, and it provides a set of common behaviors and operations. The other interface defined by CMM is the BaseManageablePortType. This contains common behaviors (e.g., service data) that must be implemented by all manageable resources. The behaviors represented by this port type include resource lifecycle data, relationships to other resource types and data, searchable resource properties, and resource groups to which this resource instance belongs within the respective environment.

In addition to these standard canonical port types, a CMM resource can utilize other grid service port types as defined by the OGSI specification. One commonly utilized port type is service group; it is utilized to represent a grouping and collection behavior for a certain group of resources, or for enumeration of resources of the same types.

Resource Modeling Concepts

The primary components of the Common Management Model are data types (i.e., existing and new), additional XML attributes, service data, and their associated service data descriptions and port types.

In general, a resource type is represented as a port type, the managed properties of the resource are represented as service data of the port type, and methods on the resource are port type operations.

Let us now explore an important modeling concept of the CMM service composition, and how it models the granular resource models. The resources defined using CMM are generally coarse-grained services rather than granular or normalized resource model definitions. In other words, the service is self-contained with normalized resource models, and contains a few relationships to other services.

We further explore this concept by using the case of a disk resource that has a model for manage-ability containing characteristics of the disk, a model for a set of error statistics, a model for its disk metrics, and a relationship model to a computing system resource. When we set forth to model this as a CMM service, all these behaviors are aggregated into the service; a CMM service is composed of manageability characteristics, error statistics, and metric models. In addition to this notion, all of this expresses a containment relationship to a computer system.

Let us now explore further to better understand some of the core concepts defined in the CMM specification. These concepts are as follows:

- *Service data and resource properties.* Properties of a manageable resource are expressed as service data and grid service port type operations. "findServiceData" and "setServiceData" can be utilized to access and modify these properties.
- *Base management port type and its behavior.* This (BaseManageableResource) canonical port type contains service data elements that must be implemented by all

manageable resources. This port type extends the OGSI GridService port type and adds service data that has valuable information about a manageable resource. Table 10.1 lists the common service data elements of this port type.

Table 10.1   Service Data Elements in Base Management portType

Service Data Name	Description
lifeCycleModel	Describes the states of the resource and/or substates through which the resource will transition. These are static service data values, which we will further explore later in "CMM Resource Lifecycle model."
currentLifeCycleState	The current state of the resource and substate information, which we will further explore later in "CMM Resource Lifecycle model."
serviceGroupType	The portType of the manageable resource that provides the service group function for manageable resource of this type. This static value is set in WSDL and must present only with the primary apex-derived port type in the hierarchy. This helps to "locate" a service group that holds these resource instances.
searchProperty	Zero (or more) service data elements (i.e., properties) that are utilized for searching for a manageable resource. A service can use these values for caching and for searching. These are static service data values.
relatedInstance	Expresses the relationship between management resources "instance," which we will further explore in the "Relationship and Dependency" section.
relatedType	Expresses the relationship between management resources "type," which we will further explore in the "Relationship and Dependency" section.

As previously discussed, these service data values are accessed by the grid service port type's "findServiceData" and "setServiceData" operations. The "relatedInstance" service data is the only service data value in the BaseManageableResource port type that is mutable, and hence, the setServiceData operation is applicable to that service data for adding new related instances to the current resource instance.

Resource Lifecycle Modeling

For purposes of this discussion, a lifecycle is a set of states that a resource can sustain, including the valid transitions between those states. In CMM, this lifecycle is represented by the lifecycle model service data of the base management port type. This is the most complex modeling process in the CMM; the resource exists from the time they are created until they are destroyed, and they transition through a variety of states in between these two states.

This complexity forces CMM to come up with a recommendable and generic lifecycle model for all the resources. Let us now explore this lifecycle model recommended by the CMM. It is important to understand that this is not the only possible model based on the resource complexity, lifecycle states, and transition logic; there may be other lifecycle models. This lifecycle model is different from a grid service lifecycle model, and there is no effort (as of today) to merge these models together.

Let us now explore the proposed lifecycle model.

Based on the proposed CMM common lifecycle model, there are five possible lifecycle states for a resource and the proposed operational state of that resource. These are noted as follows:

- **Down**

   In this state, a resource is created but cannot do useful work until it is up.
   Operational states are:
   - Restartable: This resource is stopped but can be restarted.
   - Recovered: This resource is down but can be restarted.
- **Starting**

   This is a transient state indicating that the resource is starting and the next state may be either up or failed.
   Operational states are:
   - OK: The resource is expected to attain the up state soon.
   - Error: The resource is expected to attain the failed state soon.
- **Up**

   In this state, the resource is available and ready to perform the work.
   Operational states are:
   - Idle: The resource is ready but is now not processing any job.
   - Busy: The resource is ready but is busy with another job.
   - Degraded: The resource is ready but is in a degraded condition where we cannot meet the expected quality of service requirements.
- **Stopping**

   This is a transient state where the resource is in the process of stopping. The next state may likely be either Failed or Down.
   Operational states are:
   - OK: The resource is expected to attain the down state soon.
   - Error: The resource is expected to attain the failed state soon.
- **Failed**

   In this state, the resource is not available except for problem determination.
   Operational states are:
   - dependencyFailure: This resource cannot be restarted because of the loss of a supporting/hosting resource.
   - nonRecoverableError: This resource is not capable of being restarted because of critical errors.

Based upon the above observations and conditions of the resource state, the following artifacts are defined by the CMM:

- An XSD that describes the structure of the lifecycle state element
- A service data element that defines the lifecycle model utilized by a resource
- A service data element that holds the current lifecycle value of a resource
- The XML attributes that describe the lifecycle characteristics of a service, including changeability, validity, volatility, and latency. These values are critical for management applications.

The following XSD (Listing 10.1) describes the lifecycle model type as defined by the CMM:

Listing 10.1 The schema definition for a lifecycle model.

```
<xsd:complexType name="lifecycleModelType">
    <xsd:sequence>
        <xsd:element ref="crm:lifecycleState" minOccurs="1"
            maxOccurs="unbounded"/>
        </xsd:sequence>
</xsd:complexType>
<xsd:element name="lifecycleState" type="crm:lifecycleStateType"/>

<xsd:complexType name="lifecycleStateType">
<xsd:sequence>
    <xsd:element name="subState" minOccurs="0" maxOccurs="unbounded">
    <xsd:complexType>
        <xsd:attribute name="name" type="xsd:NCName"/>
    </xsd:complexType>
    </xsd:element>
</xsd:sequence>
<xsd:attribute name="name" type="xsd:NCName"/>
</xsd:complexType>
```

The GWSDL port type defines the service data description for a lifecycle model, as shown in Listing 10.2.

Listing 10.2 The service data definition for a lifecycle model.

```
<sd:serviceData name="lifecycleModel"
                type="crm:lifecycleModelType"
                minOccurs="1"
                maxOccurs="1"
                nillable="true"
                mutability="static"/>
```

As one will notice by observing the above constructs, this lifecycle model for service data is static, and hence, the GWSDL constructs contain the possible values of this service data description in the <staticServiceDataValues> section of GWSDL portType.

A commonly utilized lifecycle value and its substates for the lifecycle model service data are described in Listing 10.3.

Listing 10.3 The static service data values.

```
<sd:staticServiceDataValues>
<crm:lifecycleModel>
      <lifecycleState name="down">
            <subState name="restartable"/>
            <subState name="recovered"/>
            </lifecycleState>
            <lifecycleState name="starting">
                <subState name="OK"/>
                <subState name="error"/>
            </lifecycleState>
            <lifecycleState name="up">
                <subState name="idle"/>
                <subState name="busy"/>
                <subState name="degraded"/>
            </lifecycleState>
            <lifecycleState name="stopping">
                <subState name="OK"/>
                <subState name="error"/>
            </lifecycleState>
            <lifecycleState name="failed">
                <subState name="dependencyFailure"/>
                <subState name="nonrecoverableError"/>
            </lifecycleState>
   </crm:lifecycleModel>
</sd:staticServiceDataValues>
```

This concludes our introduction to the resource lifecycle modeling. It should be noted that based on what has been previously discussed, the lifecycle model is a general-purpose lifecycle model, and we may need to also deal with new lifecycle state models for CMM.

Resource Grouping Concepts in CMM

The management applications need to locate manageable resources in the system. This manageable resource collection size may vary depending on the system and the environment. There is a problem of locating fine-grained resources in the system, as normal "registries" are not sophisticated enough to retain that much information. The service domain concept, which we will cover later in this book, will address this problem of service location with a federation of information across registries. However, it is still not sufficient to address the fine-grained resource problem.

The CMM works to resolve this fine-grained resource problem by utilizing the natural grouping of resource concepts that exist in the system. To appropriately explain this natural grouping, based on resource types, we can consider the sample of a database server hosting some databases, and these databases in turn contain the tables. We can also infer that these containers are responsible for the management of the resources that it contains. The CMM container resource and the contained resource form a resource group. The CMM then uses the Service Group concept in the OGSI for managing these resources.

Every manageable resource defined by CMM must implement the BaseManageableResource port type. As we have previously discussed, it is possible that a resource can be a container, which holds the same type of resources instance, in addition to the regular management port type. This use case is explained in Figure 10.3.

In this example, the database, the table, and the database server are manageable resources; however, the database server has more functionality and acts as a container (i.e., implementing OGSI ServiceGroup) for the resources belonging to that server.

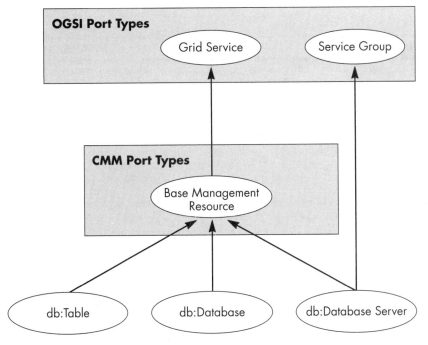

Figure 10.3
Example of a manageable port type.

Relationship and Dependency among Resources

There may oftentimes be relationships existing among many instances of manageable resources. This relationship model is not specific to the CMM; the service relationships exist in the grid and Web service environments. Let us take a look at these ideas in order to better familiarize ourselves with the two core concepts here:

1. Relationships describe which resources are connected to each other and what type of connection exists; however, they do not describe the details of how one resource depends on the other.
2. Dependencies add additional information to the relationship on exactly how one resource depends on another. For example, a database resource indicates that it uses a storage device and provides more details on the needs such as storage space.

We will begin our discussion on the CMM relationship model with a simple example on relationships. Processes are created by operating system and the operating system is hosted by the computer system, which is a part of a cluster. CMM provides mechanisms to model these types of resource relationships (see Table 10.2).

In CMM, the BaseManageableResource port type provides two service data definitions (relatedInstance and relatedType) to deal with a relationship.

Table 10.2 CMM-defined relationship types.

Relationship Type	Description
Hosts	Any resource "A" hosts another resource "B" if resource "A" provides an environment in which resource "B" is created and runs. The lifecycle of resource "B" is a subset of the lifecycle of resource "A" and resource "B" cannot exist without resource "A." For example, a database hosts the table within it.
Contains	Any resource may consist of a number of other resources. Any contained resource has the same lifetime as the containing resource. If resource "A" contains resource "B," then if "A" installs "A," "B" gets installed and if "A" stopped "B" gets stopped. For example, a deployed J2EE application containing various modules.
Federates	Any numbers of resources are in different hosting environments and are utilized together to form another resource. For example, an application includes a database and queue and they do not know each other but work together in the application.
Aggregates	A number of resources are grouped together. For example, a resource that represents all computers in a department.
Uses	A resource uses another resource. It is different from federates. For example, a security system uses a LDAP registry to hold user information.
Implements	One resource is utilized to implement the function of another. For example, a database server is implemented as a Linux or Windows service.

These types of relationships exist in current programming environments and are explained quite well by the UML relationship model and dependency graphs. We believe that this CMM-specific relationship model should be elevated to the grid service and Web service worlds, with the appropriate modifications.

We have now discussed the new concepts and canonical information provided by CMM. The resource's manageability information can be implemented using any of the existing management instrumentation methods, such as Common Information Model (CIM), Simple Network Management Protocol (SNMP), and Lightweight Directory Access Protocol (LDAP).

The CMM resource model and management grid service are independent of the underlying service implementation and resource instrumentation. One important question that may come across is: What is the value CMM provides over a normal service interface to any existing resource instrumentation models? The answer lies in the fact that CMM is not just an algorithmic mapping from a grid service to resource instrumentation. Instead, CMM contains a more behavior-specific and self-contained resource management model. Also, the same resource model may map to multiple instrumentation choices, and this is a binding choice.

Summary

We can summarize the CMM discussion with the characteristics it exposes to the resource management world. These characteristics are as follows:

- CMM provides an abstract representation of the real-world physical resource or logical resources.
- CMM provides common manageability operations.
- CMM can overlay multiple resource instrumentations.
- Resources are now grid services containing four capabilities.
    1. Common lifecycle management
    2. Common resource discovery
    3. Common event notification
    4. Common resource attribute query
- CMM provides well-defined resource states.

Two areas where the architecture needs to mature are as follows:

- Provisions to plug in new lifecycle models into the CMM base
- Elevating the relationship model presence in CMM to the core grid service level architecture

SERVICE DOMAINS

The OGSA service domain architecture[2] proposes a high-level abstraction model to describe the common behaviors, attributes, operations, and interfaces to allow a collection of services to function as a single unit. This is accomplished through collaboration with others in a fully distributed, heterogeneous, grid-enabled environment. This provides the users of any service domain access environment to be aggregated into the appropriate services operations, simply, as if they are merely a part of a single service.

In general, the services in a service domain can be thought of as the following:

- Resource oriented, including CPU, storage space, and network bandwidth
- Systems and infrastructure oriented, including security, routing, and management
- Application-oriented services such as purchase orders, stock transactions, insurance, etc.

These domains can be homogeneous or heterogeneous, compute intensive, transactional, and business process function providers. Multiple service domains can be composed and mixed for the requirement of the enterprise.

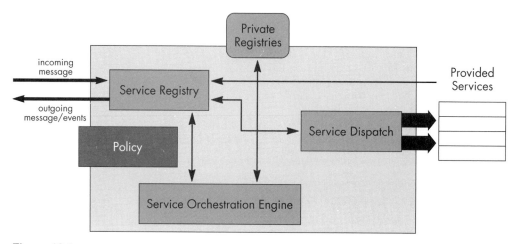

Figure 10.4
The service domain and orchestration.

As depicted in Figure 10.4, service domain components provide the following functionalities:

- Service registration and collection
- Service routing and selection
- Service interoperation and transformation
- Flexible service composition
- Automatic service orchestration

Based upon this discussion, we can see that the OGSA architecture for service domain defines an OGSI ServiceCollection port type and provides functionalities for register (add) and unregister (remove) service instances from the service domain. The core concept of service domain surrounds these interfaces and behaviors that it exposes.

Let us now further explore some of these behaviors and interfaces. These behaviors can be thought of as:

- Filter: Supports choosing/selecting a service instance as part of a service collection.
- Selection: Enables choosing a particular service instance as part of the service collection.
- Topology: Allows a service collection to impose some topological order for the instances of the services.
- Enumeration: Enumerates the services in a service domain and/or across other service domains.
- Discovery: Allows a service domain to discover services from one or more registries and/or other service domains. These discovered services are included as part of their collection.
- Policy: Provides some "intelligence" on the service domain operations. These types of policy rules include (but are not limited to) service-level definitions, recovery, event handling, discovery/selection, service mapping, and business guidelines.

Summary

As of today, there is no standard or architecture-driven process for efficient building block components that enable grid services and Web services to be organized, filtered, deployed, grouped, discovered, dispatched, recovered, and optimized dynamically in real time. This OGSA-driven service domain concept addresses these shortcomings by providing a service collection model that includes the domain schema, attributes, and operations to control the behaviors of service registration, automatic service routing, heterogeneous service interoperability, policy rule-based operations, dynamic service sharing, and aggregation of the collections.

POLICY ARCHITECTURE

The definition of the term "policy" is often confusing and contextual. In the context of the OGSA, we can define "policy" as a definitive goal, course, or method of action based on a set of conditions to guide and determine present and future decisions. Policies are implemented and utilized in a particular context. For example, there are policies for security, workload, networking services, business processes, and a multitude of other areas. In the context of grid services, the OGSA policy service provides a set of rules or policies to administer, manage, and control access to any grid service.

The OGSA-defined policy service provides a framework for creating, managing, validating, distributing, transforming, resolving, and enforcing policies in a distributed grid environment. The OGSA policy work uses a derivative of the IETF[3]/DMTF[4] Policy Core Information Model (IETF RFC 3060 /DMTF DSP0108) as its information model. By getting polished by the resource management teams across the industry, these policies are naturally most suitable for IT resource management. OGSA policies are based on an XML schema, which is a derivative of the CIM

Policy Core Information Model Extension (PCIMe) and is suitable for most of the known policy representations. The UML diagram, in Figure 10.5, explains the policy information model.

POLICY MANAGEMENT IS SIMPLE IN CONCEPT, YET INCREDIBLY IMPORTANT

The definition of the term "policy" is often ambiguous and rather contextual. In the context of the OGSA, we can define "policy" as a definitive goal, course, or method of action based on a set of conditions to guide and determine present and future decisions. This, in part, affords autonomic decision support aspects in Grid Computing solutions.

Policies are implemented and utilized in a particular context. For example, there are policies for security, workload, networking services, business processes, and a multitude of other areas.

In the context of grid services, the OGSA policy service provides a set of rules or policies to administer, manage, and control access to any grid service.

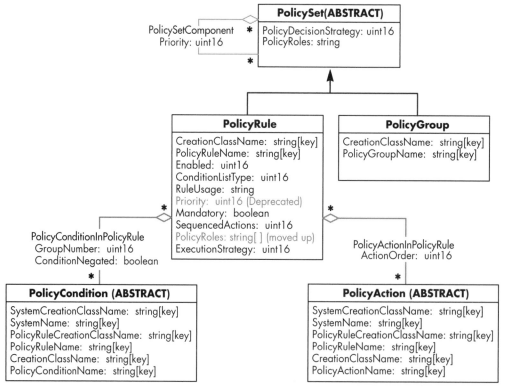

Figure 10.5
The DMTF/IETF Policy Information Model.

The OGSA policy model is a collection of rules based on conditions and actions. In general, policies are expressed as "if <condition> then <action>" rule-type of syntax. In addition to the policy schema definition, it provides classification and grouping of rules and scope of policies, based upon the management discipline and rules. Another important aspect is the support for notification on policy state changes, whereby a client is notified of the policies when it becomes effective, expired, or updated.

The following shows sample policies that are in the context of this discussion:

- QoS policy example:
  If (customers are "executives") then (provide a "gold" [always available] level service)
- Workload policy example:
  If (today is the Government tax return lastWeek) then (allocate 10,000 more servers from server pool to Farm1, Farm2 to provide better response time)
  If (today is the Government tax return lastDay) then (allocate 25,000 more servers from server pool to Farm1, Farm2, Farm3 to provide better response time)

Levels of Policy Abstraction

The multiple levels of policy abstraction helps the policy service to differentiate the roles of the policy actors (i.e., policy administrators who are responsible for policy creation and maintaining), policy enforcement points (i.e., the consumer of policies), and policy transformation requirements. As illustrated in Figure 10.6, these levels of abstraction are business level, domain level, and device level. The policies are created as high-level business definitions, such as SLA, event management, and are then translated to a canonical form as prescribed by the OGSA policy framework, based on the IETF extension model. These domain-level policies are transformed to specific device-level formats understandable to the enforcement points where they are applied in the decision-making process.

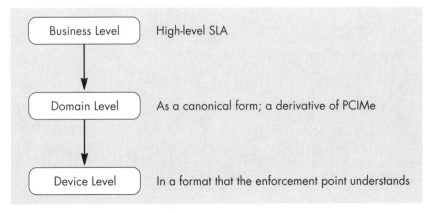

Figure 10.6
The conceptual levels of policy abstraction.

AUTOMATED POLICY ENFORCEMENT IS KEY TO AUTONOMIC BUSINESS OPERATIONS

Policies are created as high-level business definitions, such as SLA, event management, and networking services (monitoring, etc.) They are then translated to a canonical form as prescribed by the OGSA policy framework, based on the IETF extension model. These domain-level policies are transformed to specific device-level formats understandable to the enforcement points where they are applied in the decision-making process.

Programmatic director tools for policy enforcement are then able to ascertain, sustain, and manage business operations based on dynamic policies dictated by business leaders involved in specific operational aspects of the business enterprise.

A Sample Policy Service Framework

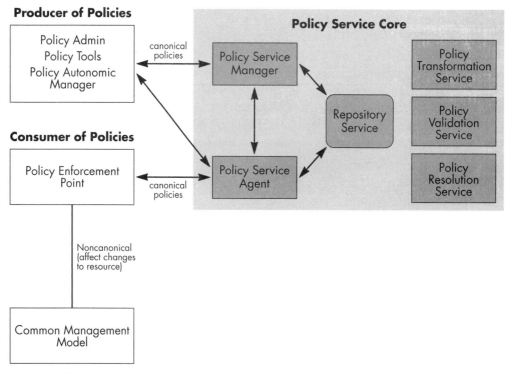

Figure 10.7
The defined OGSA Policy Service Core.

Figure 10.7 shows some of the core policy service components. These very important autonomic elements can be further understood according to the following definitions.

POLICY MANAGERS ARE VERY POWERFUL AUTONOMIC COMPONENTS IN GRID COMPUTING

Policy Manager

This is a manager service responsible for controlling access to the policy repository for the creation and maintenance of policy documents. This manager is expecting policies in a canonical form as defined by the standard. There should be only one manager in a policy service infrastructure.

Policy Repository

This is a repository service, which provides a set of abstract interfaces to store the policy documents. In reality, this can be any type of storage (e.g., remote/local disk, database, file system, memory, etc.) accessed and abstracted through the Data Access Interfaces Service (DAIS). We will cover this data access and integration service interface and framework in detail in a later section of this book.

Policy Enforcement Points

These are the framework and software components that are executing the policy enforcement decisions. They work in conjunction with the policy service agent to retrieve, transform, and resolve any conflict resolution of the policy.

Policy Service Agent

These are the policy decision maker agents, and they work with the policy enforcement points and the policy manager. They expect and inspect the data in a canonical format.

Policy Transformation Service

These services are responsible for transforming the business objectives and the canonical policy document to the device-level configurations.

Policy Validation Service

These services act as administrators and tools; the act of validating the policy changes is accomplished using these services.

Policy Resolution Service

These services act as "guardians" of the policy resolution process, and evaluate the policies in the context of business SLAs.

Policy Tools and Autonomic Managers

These tools are responsible for the creation of policy documents, and registering them with the policy manager.

Policy Service Interfaces

The OGSA Policy framework defines some core interfaces and functionalities to implement a robust, end-to-end, distributed policy management set of services. As we have previously discussed high-level elements of this framework, this framework should always include the following:

- A canonical representation for expressing the policy (i.e., the Policy Information Model [PIM] and the core XML schema)
- A management control point for defining and sustaining the policy lifecycle (i.e., the Policy Service Manager Interface)
- An interface for policy consumers to retrieve policies (i.e., the Policy Service Agent Interface)
- A means to ensure that a service is fully policy aware, and will validate a policy as required (i.e., the Policy Enforcement Point Interface)
- A means to effect changes on a resource (i.e., utilizing the Common Management Model)

WS-Policy Overview and Its Relation to OGSA Policy

In an earlier chapter we covered the WS-Policy Language and its utilization in the Web service environment. At the current point in time, the grid communities are unable to identify much activity in the GGF to align the OGSA Policies with the WS-Policy(s).

Summary

The policy work in OGSA is primarily derivative work from the IETF and DMTF policy work, with added elements of grid service abstractions and behaviors. This policy work is mostly suitable for IT resource management. We are expecting more works on defining the relationship between different policy standards including WS-Policy, OASIS-initiated business-level policy works, and service-level agreements and how these policy information models can collaborate and compliment the OGSA policy.

SECURITY ARCHITECTURE

In this section, we will approach grid service security[5] with a detailed discussion on the security challenges faced by the grid community in general, and then explore the details of security solutions provided by the OGSA. Resource sharing among heterogeneous virtual organization participants is a complex process because of the challenges faced in integration, interoperability, and trust relationship.

We can further explain this by examining the following factors:

Integration Challenge. There are numerous security frameworks, comprehensive standards, and implementation available today. The majority of these organizations, individuals, and/or resources have their own preferences about the security requirements that are most suitable for their own environment. We cannot replace all these security frameworks, nor are we able to come up with a common alternative. This places the burden on the participants to honor the existing security frameworks and/or seamlessly integrate with them. This, in turn, requires that the OGSA security architecture be "implementation agnostic," so that it can be instantiated in terms of the existing security mechanisms; that is, "extensible" so that it can incorporate new security services when available; and capable of integration with the existing security services.

Interoperability Challenge. The resource sharing of these interoperable resources may extend into many domains of security realms, and their respective needs security interoperability at each layer of service implementation. Let us examine these various levels in the following points:

- At protocol level, different domains need to exchange messages across their protocol layers and they need to have interoperability at each layer of the protocol stack.
- At the policy level, secure interoperability requires each party to specify any policy it may wish to enact in order to enter into a secure conversation, and these policies need to be interoperable and mutually comprehensible.
- At identity level, we require mechanisms for identifying a user from one domain to another domain. For any cross-domain invocation to succeed in a secure environment, the mapping of identities and credentials to the target domain identity is absolutely required.

Trust Relationship Challenge. The trust among the participants in a dynamic virtual organization is the most complex thing to achieve, and this trust must be evaluated for each session or request. This requires federation of a trust relationship among the participants.

To summarize, for the security challenges in a grid environment, one must ensure the following points are addressed while categorizing the solution areas:

- Integration solutions where interfaces should be abstracted to provide an extensible architecture.
- Interoperable solutions, to enable services to invoke each other even when they are hosted by different virtual organizations with different security mechanisms and policy requirements.
- Define, manage, and enforce trust policies within a dynamic grid environment.

Figure 10.8 depicts these security items.

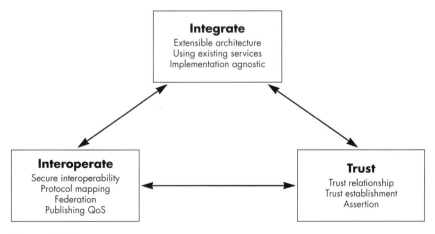

Figure 10.8
The categories of security challenges are complex in a grid environment.

Figure 10.8 emphasizes the security challenges we have discussed earlier in this discussion, and their solution dependency. As indicated by the relationship arrows, a solution within a given category will often depend on another category.

OGSA Security Architecture

The OGSA security architecture addresses the above problems and challenges through security mechanisms that are plug-and-play at the client and service side. These design points are discoverable by the service requester from a service description. The grid environment requires an OGSA platform security mechanism to support, integrate, and unify popular security models, mechanisms, protocols, platforms, and technologies.

COMMON SECURITIES ELEMENTS REQUIRED FOR A GRID ENVIRONMENT

Authentication

Provide integration points for multiple authentication mechanisms and the means for conveying the specific mechanisms utilized in any given authentication operation.

Delegation

Provide facilities for delegation of access rights from requestors to the services. These delegated access rights must be transferred to the tasks to be performed, and for a limited time, framed in order to limit the risk of misuse.

Single Sign On

This capability allows a service user to utilize multiple resources with one explicit logon process, and thereafter, automatically delegate the same authenticated credential for the next resource access without user intervention, within a specific period of time. These single-sign-on sessions may include accessing of resources in other domains using a service credential delegation.

Credential Lifespan and Renewal

Credentials have a limited time span associated with them, and most of the grid jobs may take more time to execute. This may cause credentials to get invalidated, rendering the system to an invalid state. In order to avoid this, a grid system must support credential expiry notifications to the users and credential revalidation facilities.

Authorization

This model allows for controlling access to OGSA services based on authorization policies (i.e., who can access a service, and under what conditions) attached to each service. In addition, it allows the requesters to specify invocation policies (i.e., to whom does the client trust to provide the requested service). Authorization should accommodate various access control models and implementations.

Privacy

Privacy policies may be treated as a type of authorization policy that brings privacy semantics to a service usage session. Similar to authorization, OGSA security must allow both a requester and a service to enforce privacy policies, for instance, taking into account things like personally identifiable information (PII), purpose of invocation, etc.

Confidentiality

Protect the confidentiality of the underlying communication (networking services transport) mechanism, and the confidentiality of the messages or documents that flow over the transport mechanisms in an OGSA-compliant infrastructure. The confidentiality requirement includes point-to-point transport, as well as store-and-forward mechanisms.

Message Integrity

This provides mechanisms to detect the unauthorized changes to messages. The use of message- or document-level integrity checking is determined by one or more policies, which are determined by the QoS of the service.

Policy Exchanges

Allow clients and services to dynamically exchange policy information to establish a negotiated security context between them. Such policy information will contain authentication requirements, supported functionality, constraints, privacy rules, etc.

Secure Logging

For nonrepudiation, notarization, and auditing; provide logging facilities for all secure conversations, especially logging negotiations.

Assurance

Provide a means to qualify the security assurance level that can be expected from a hosting environment. This can be utilized to express protection characteristics of the environment, such as virus protection, firewall utilization, internal VPN access, etc.

Manageability

Provide manageability of security functions, such as identity management, policy management, security key management, and other critical aspects.

Firewall Traversal

Security firewalls are present in most of the distributed systems network to prevent unwanted messages from entering into a respective domain. The grid, being a virtual organization, realizes firewalls may cause challenges on message transfers between participants. This forces the OGSA security model to circumvent the firewall protection without compromising the local host security.

Securing the OGSA Infrastructure

Securing the OGSA infrastructure secures the OGSI itself. The model must include securing components like Grid HandleMap, discovery service, etc.

Security Services

The OGSA security architecture has an insurmountable task of establishing a security model to capture all the above requirements. As a natural progression, the OGSA security architecture is aligned with the Web services security model. Figure 10.9 shows the security architecture model of the OGSA.

Figure 10.9 shows the core security models utilized in the grid environment. All grid services communicate with each other based on a set of bindings specified by the services. These bindings must deal with the security details including message confidentiality, integrity, and authentication.

Normally speaking, these bindings are initialized on a runtime-based set of policies, specified by the service providers. These security policies can be specified as static documents, such as WSDL or WS-Policy documents, or can be negotiated at runtime based on the capabilities of the client and service.

The common policies specified include supported elements such as authentication mechanisms, required integrity/confidentiality, trust policies, privacy policies, and security assertions (e.g., policy assertions). Once the grid service client and service providers discover the receptive security policy, they can then enter into a secure conversation mode and establish a secure channel for the messaging exchange. This channel must then also enforce all of the agreed-upon security QoS guarantees.

Let us now explore the details of each of these components in more detail, and better understand the technologies of interest in each layer of the security component model.

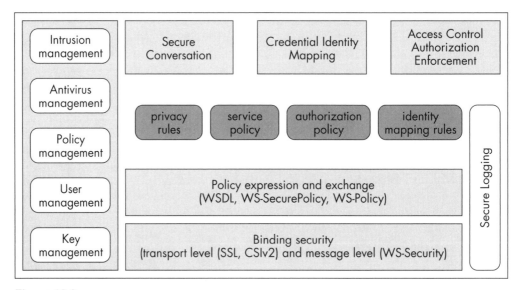

Figure 10.9
The OGSA security architecture.

Binding Security

The binding transport includes SOAP, IIOP, JMS, HTTP, and so on, and each of these transport protocols have different security requirements for authentication, message integrity, and confidentiality. For example, HTTP and SSL combined comprises "https" as its secure conversation channel, guaranteeing message integrity and confidentiality, yet with the limitation of a point-to-point protocol channel. This networking services protocol may also require higher-level coordination services for end-to-end flow across intermediaries (e.g., firewalls, proxy servers, etc.).

In the case of SOAP messages, the WS-Security model[6] provides a secure message exchange pattern utilizing the SOAP headers as the security information exchange carrier. The integrity and confidentialities of SOAP messages can then be protected utilizing XML digital signatures and encryption standards,[7] and WS-Security then provides secured profiles for exchange of this information. Other binding level security infrastructure includes CSIv2 for IIOP-based communications adopted by CORBA vendors, and the J2ee 1.4 as a mandatory standard for secure IIOP messages.

Policy Expression and Exchange

In order for a secure message exchange to exist, both the service requester and service provider must agree on the certain policies for the receptive secure message and conversation to occur. This policy agreement can be accomplished a priori (i.e., static information) or at runtime (i.e., dynamic), and the best possible security binding selections must be performed at both the service provider and service requester sides of the conversation. The grid, being a highly dynamic environment, also requires dynamic policies and decisions to be executed at runtime. These dynamic policies can be associated with the service WSDL, service's service data, or can be exchanged through collaborative negotiations. In addition to the conversational requirements, there may often be a requirement for the respective policy information to be present in order to provide secure binding to native platform services.

One of the notable technology candidates in policy exchange areas is WS-Policy, which specifies how service providers and service requesters can, in turn, specify their respective requirements and capabilities.

At this stage of the discussion, we have explored the binding and policy exchange layers, which allows the service requester and service provider to discover the policies they require for a secure conversation to occur. The next layer is related to the nature and enforcement of these policies. That is, a secure association between service endpoints; mapping of identities and translation of credentials; and authorization policies and privacy policies, which provide access control to services.

Secure Association

In the grid context, the communications between a service requester and the service provider are oftentimes long-running conversations through various message exchanges. The OGSA security architecture specifies creating a secure context during the initial negotiation between the client and the service, while utilizing the same context for protecting the subsequent messages.

The secure context is then coupled with networking services transport binding, and this concept is already available with most of the security protocols (e.g., SSL and IIOP-CSIv2). For the OGSA Grid Computing environment, the secure conversation support is provided using the WS-SecureConversation protocol. Recalling from an earlier chapter discussion, the WS-SecureConversation describes how a mutual authentication between service requester and service provider is accomplished and how to establish mutually authenticated security context.

Identity and Credential Mapping/Translation

A grid environment consists of multiple trusts (i.e., virtual organizations) and security domains. To cross the domain boundaries requires a mutual authentication. Therefore, a requirement exists to map and/or translate the credentials from one domain into another. This interoperation needs a "federation" of domains and their security mechanisms.

This federation can be accomplished through the mapping and/or translation of identities and/or credentials from one domain to another utilizing some trusted intermediary services, gateways, or proxies. In the context of Web services, there is some ongoing work to define this federation message exchange pattern and model. The grid community of practitioners can expect the WS-Federation to become a published approach for OGSA-based grid services some time in the not too distant future.

Authorization Enforcement

Authorization to access a resource is controlled by policies enforced in the resource provider side of the environment. Today, there are several different commercial authorization mechanisms available across the industries. The most prominent ones are role-based authorization, rule-based authorization, and identity-based authorization. The selection of these mechanisms is entirely based on the service requirements, hosting platform capabilities, and the application domain (e.g., B2B, B2C, G2C, etc.).

WS-Authorization provides more specific details on how access policies for grid services and Web services are specified and managed. In today's grid scenarios, most of the access to the resources is controlled, based upon the identity of the requester. This requires the resource to maintain an access control list (ACL) with the identity of the end user, or with the mapped identity of the end user. In the second case, a mapping or translation of identity must occur before the end user can access the resource(s).

Privacy Enforcement

Maintaining anonymity, or the ability to withhold private information, is one of the core requirements in many grid service environments. Organizations involved in the grid environment may need to declare their privacy requirements, and conversely may need to monitor the privacy policy enforcement results. The WS-Privacy specification provides mechanisms to describe a model for embedding privacy information and exchanging this information in conjunction with the messages. In the case of protecting privacy requirements, and declaring them to customers, the grid environment must adhere to the WS-Policy model, and therefore align with the W3C's P3P efforts.[8]

Trust

Every member of a VO is likely to have a security infrastructure that includes authentication service, user registry, authorization engine, firewalls, network-level protection, and other security services. These security policies are defined to the security domain in which they exist. This self-containing security model requires a trust among the VO members before they can access the above services. This trust relation can be called "membership in the VO" and will enable a set of policies among the VO participants, identity and credential mapping policies, and/or a membership with the trusted party through some proxies or gateways. The grid trust model is based on the WS-Trust specification.

Core Security Services for OGSA

In previous sections of the book we have discussed the security features and these requirements for a grid environment. We have discussed how we can achieve many of these security requirements, and the specific details of each of the security models. We have already noted that in a grid domain, the interoperability and integration among the existing security technologies is an absolute requirement.

In order to achieve these aforementioned capabilities, the OGSA grid security standard has defined a set of abstract services on the top of the existing security platforms and framework. These services are exposed through the WSDL.

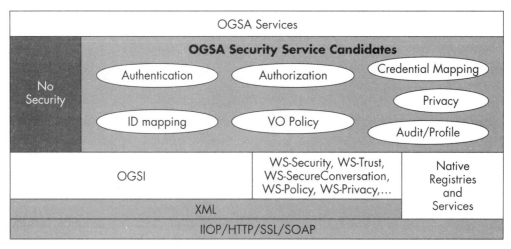

Figure 10.10
The OGSA Platform security components.

Figure 10.10 details the OGSI security platform services and their relationship with other OGSA components. Let us now explore the possible OGSA security service candidates in greater detail:

- Authentication service. Validates the service requester's identity. One example can be the basic authentication mechanism where user identity and password are validated within the user registry.
- Identity mapping service. Provides an identity mapping function where one service's identity can be mapped to another service's identity in another domain. These services are not concerned with the authentication to the service.
- Authorization service. Resolves the request to access a service by verifying the access policies associated with the requester. The OGSA security service relies on the hosting environment's access control mechanisms using the service requestor's identity and policies associated with the service.
- Virtual organization policy service. The OGSA security service can utilize the OGSA policy framework in order to provide policy storage, policy enforcement, and policy validation.
- Credential conversion service. Responsible for the conversion of user credentials to another type and/or form of credentials.
- Audit service. Responsible for producing the records of the security activities and logging them based upon the specified policies.
- Profile service. Concerns the creation and storage of profiles, including personalization data.
- Privacy service. Concerns the policy-driven classification of PII. These services can be utilized to enforce the privacy requirements for a service requester and provider.

Summary

In summary, the grid security model must be able to leverage these existing security standards for their QoS requirement on secure message exchange. The OGSA security architecture asserts that the OGSA security model needs to be consistent with the Web service security model. Many practitioners in the Grid Computing discipline believe that the WS-Security model, and its core components, are going to become the default standard for interorganizational and interenterprise secure messaging exchange brokering services. This WS-Security model is not simply limited to SOAP bindings, and can always be extended to any message protocols that can exchange XML messages, while having an associated information model.

METERING AND ACCOUNTING

There is a general requirement that resource utilization should be monitored for cost allocation, capacity analysis, dynamic provisioning, grid-service pricing, fraud and intrusion detection, and/or billing. The OGSA platform architecture is defining a common set of interfaces and behaviors for these metering and accounting requirements. One presumption inherent in this architecture approach is the utilization of the CMM (Common Management Model) as a provider for resource performance and utilization information models, this is related directly with the metering and accounting architecture. For example, an operating system resource implemented as a CMM service can provide critical information, including average CPU utilization, I/O activities, file system utilization, interprocess communications, memory buffer utilization, and more. This information is mandatory for determining the metrics for metering and accounting services.

Let us now explore the concepts of metering, rating, accounting, and bill payment in the context of the OGSA grid platform environment, and analyze what critical information it provides, and how the OGSA utilizes this information.

Metering Service Interface

Grid services will oftentimes consume multiple resources, and these resources will often be shared by multiple service instances. We know that most of the current operating systems have metering subsystems for measuring the resource consumption and aggregating their own respective utilization measurements.

The OGSA metering service provides access to systems (i.e., operating system and/or system-level software) providing aggregated utilization data (i.e., monitored data). This aggregated data is exposed through a metering service data element. The most common factor affecting this aggregated data is the time window for aggregation (e.g., days, hours, seconds) and may vary between the data producers (i.e., the services) and enforcers (i.e., the administrators, operating systems, etc.).

Metering involves the capability to measure the resource consumption in a workflow model executing on widely distributed, loosely coupled servers, storages, and network resources. The OGSA provides these end-to-end metering capabilities involving a number of resources and associated workflows. These measurements are valuable for dynamic resource provisioning and grid pricing.

The above OGSA metering explanations are associated with resource consumption, and the metering of that consumption. There is a need to provide aggregated application-level consumption measurement, for example, a service fee for each service invocation across a worldwide enterprise.

METERING IS KEY TO THE BUSINESS ON DEMAND SERVICES MODEL

Metering involves the capability to measure the resource consumption in a workflow model executing on widely distributed, loosely coupled servers, storages, and network resources. This workflow can be directly involved with Business On Demand services (for example) and may be key to the operations of any enterprise.

The OGSA provides these end-to-end metering capabilities involving a number of resources and associated workflows. These measurements are valuable for dynamic resource provisioning and grid pricing.

Rating Service Interface

A rating interface is responsible for the following:

- Converting the metered resource information into financial measurements.
- Providing valuable financial information to the business service (i.e., financial advice) including the cost of the components utilized to deliver the service. This helps the service to advertise its estimated cost and usage pricing schemes, and enables customers to make the best economic decision.

Accounting Service Interface

Accounting services can make use of the rated financial information retrieved through rating services in order to calculate user subscription costs over a specific period of time, per use (i.e., On Demand), or on a monthly basis. This service provides user subscription and account-related information to other services for decision making on user subscription (e.g., suspend, revoke, activate, etc.), bill payment, and other relevant business operational expenses.

Billing/Payment Service Interface

These services work in collaboration with the accounting service to collect the payments, provide mediation capabilities, and a wide variety of financial interface requirements.

Summary

As we have described in an earlier chapter, the grid economy is still in its evolutionary stages, and to get successful adoption of Grid Computing environments, we need a grid with a variety of cost models that are based on cost and time models. A best recommendation on the economy of grid can be arrived at only if we can measure the resource utilization in such an environment.

To complicate the situation, in a grid environment, these resources may be involving a complicated and complex workflow, involving other resources across one or more virtual organizations. This involves the accurate correlation of resource metrics.

The OGSA is working to provide a solution, and common pattern, to these challenges through the above services and interfaces. We can find this information extremely valuable for dynamic provisioning and cost–time analysis features. The value of these services depends on the identification and generation of critical algorithms and data-mining mechanisms utilizing these metrics. The authors of this book welcome any reports of progress in these areas, and other areas being discussed in this book.

COMMON DISTRIBUTED LOGGING

The distributed logging capability can be viewed as typical messaging applications where message producers generate log messages (e.g., informational, trace, error, or debug messages), and which may or may not be consumed by the interested message consumers over a period of time. The OGSA logging facility is an architecture model to separate the OGSA logging specific implementations to an intermediary or logging service.

These logging services or intermediaries should provide facilities for:

1. Decoupling. This helps to provide a clear separation of the roles of the log producers and log consumers. The producer has no previous knowledge of the message consumers, and how the message gets transformed.
2. Transformation and common representation. This facility provides plug-in transformation scripts to convert from one log format to another. Most notable among these transformation scripts is XSLT, which acts as an XML data transformation script. There is also a desirable approach to convert to a common data format based on a "common logging schema" representation suitable for canonical representation. This canonical schema can eliminate some transformation process and reduce the processing overheads.
3. Filtering and aggregation. Most of the logging may result in a huge amount of data and filtering of these data into certain buckets of desirable segments; this is a value-added feature. The OGSA logging service provides registration of such filtering criteria for each consumer, and aggregates the messages based on these criteria.
4. Configurable persistency. The durability of the logs is a major feature provided by the OGSA framework. We can enable this feature based on a per service and/or a per message basis (i.e., On Demand). For example, security logs and audits are kept intact for years to retrace some security vulnerability later on, should computer forensics become an issue.
5. Consumption patterns. Logging services should provide both synchronous (pull) and asynchronous (push) models of interaction of messages by the consumers. This service must provide out-of-band messaging facilities for critical messages and logs.
6. Secure logging. As we already know, many of these logs are critical, sensitive, and private; therefore, the need to store them and transport them in a secure fashion is an absolute requirement.

Figure 10.11 shows the OGSA logging service architecture and message flows. This facility utilizes the OGSI Notification framework for messaging semantics and includes consumer subscription for logs by providing filtering criteria and message delivery end points. The logs are delivered as messages based on specific notification topic changes and filtering criteria.

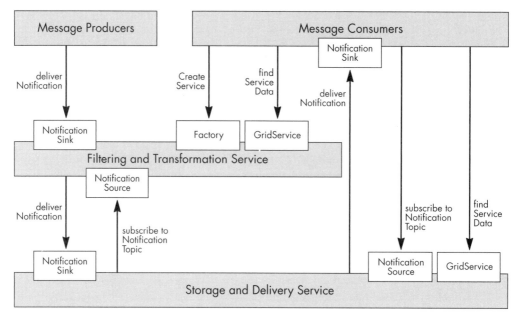

Figure 10.11
The OGSA logging service architecture model.

DISTRIBUTED DATA ACCESS AND REPLICATION

Distributed data forms a bottleneck for most of the grid systems. Earlier, we have discussed such grid applications (e.g., the EUROGRID project). This complexity of data access and management on a grid arises from the scale, dynamism, autonomy, and the geographical distribution of the data sources. These complexities should be made transparent to grid applications through a layer of grid data virtualization services. These services provide location transparency and easier data management techniques.

Data virtualization services, such as federated access to distributed data, dynamic discovery of data sources by its content, dynamic migration of data for workload balancing, and schema management, all help to provide transparencies (e.g., location, naming, distribution, ownership, etc.) to the data. These virtualization services need to address various types of data including flat files, relational, objects, and streaming data. In order to derive a common data management and interface solution to data access and integration, the OGSA initiative has started a working group titled the DAIS (Data Access and Integration Service) group. The DIAS group is responsible for data virtualization services and standard interfaces for data access and integration.

We will begin this discussion with OGSA platform requirements on data management, and then we will spend time reviewing the work done by the DAIS group on data access, integration interfaces, and the framework definition.

Some OGSA requirements on data management[9] are:

- Data access service. Exposes interfaces that help the clients to access the data in a uniform manner from heterogeneous data sources.
- Data replication. Allows local compute resources to have local data, and thereby improves the performance. Services that may be applied for data replica functions can include:
  - Group services for clustering and failover
  - Utility computing for dynamic provisioning
  - Policy services for QoS requirements
  - Metering and accounting services
  - Higher-level services such as workload management and disaster recovery services

The OGSA still needs to address these data replication requirements by providing common interfaces to replication services. The implementation has to provide an adapter that can move data in and out of the heterogeneous physical and logical environments, without any changes to the local data access systems.

- Data caching service. Utilized to improve data access performance.
- Metadata catalog and services. Allow us to search for a multitude of services, based upon the object metadata attributes.
- Schema transformation services. Allow for the conversion of schema from one form to another. An example of this transformation is the conversion of XML data using XSL transformation engines.
- Storage services. Storage activities are treated as resources and can be modeled as CMM services.

We have now provided discussions to better understand the required OGSA platform services. Let us now explore some of the initial work activities in this area.

Conceptual Model

The conceptual model captures the data management systems, the data resources they contain, and the data sets resulting from the data requests performed on these data resources.

Based upon the principle of keeping the existing data management systems and its interfaces intact, this model attempts to expose the underlying data model and native language/API of the resource manager.

There are two types of resources: resources that are "external" to the OGSI-complaint grid and their OGSI resource service logical counterparts.

Figure 10.12 represents both the external resources and its logical counter parts.

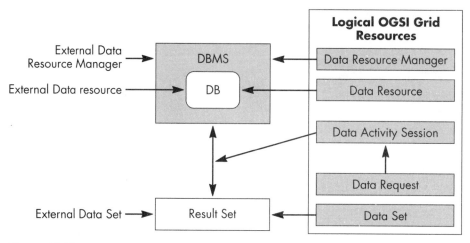

Figure 10.12
The external resources and Logical resources of a database management system.

Let us review this conceptual relationship model in the following details:

- External Data Resource Manager (EDRM) and the Data Resource manager (DRM). This represents a data management system, such as relational database management system, or a file system. The Data Resource Manager is a Grid service that represents the external data resource manager and it binds to an existing EDRM. This provides management operations, including start and stop. These management functionalities are managed by specific vendors, and hence, may be out of scope for DAIS. Figure 10.13 shows the relation between DRM and EDRM.

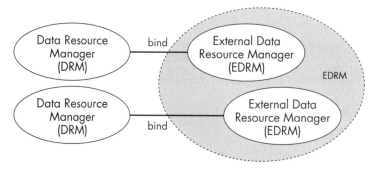

Figure 10.13
The conceptual model for the Data Resource Manager Grid service.

- External Data Resource (EDR) and Data Resource (DR). The external data resource is the data managed by the EDRM. This can be a database in a DBMS or a directory in a file system. The Data recourse is a Grid service that binds to EDR. Data resource is the contact point to the data and it exposes the metadata about the external data resource. It must provide the data management (access and update) and query capabilities. Figure 10.14 shows the relation between DR, EDR, and EDRM.

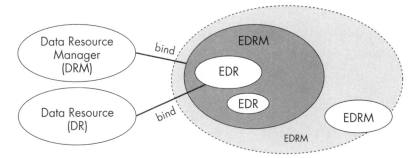

Figure 10.14
A logical data resource.

- External data set (EDS) and data set (DS). This is the logical data similar to a relational database view or file cache that is separate from the EDRM or EDR, however, it can be retrieved and stored in the EDR (see Figure 10.15). The data set forms a service wrapper for the EDS. These logical views exposed some challenging interfaces to manage the data.

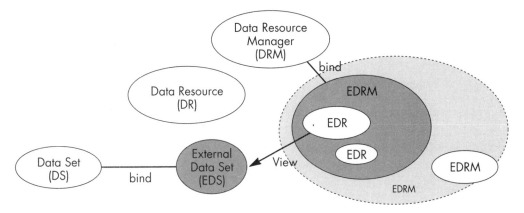

Figure 10.15
A logical data set.

In addition to the above external and logical models, the DAIS proposed some logical resources for the following topics:

- Data Activity Session. This is a logical data session for all data access operations. It must maintain and manage the context data operations. Figure 10.15 illustrates this activity session for a requester.

- Data Request. This is logical information regarding a request submitted by a requester to the data access session. There is currently no grid service to manage this activity. This request can be a query, data manipulation operations, or other such related activities.

Service Implementation

There have been some previous discussions regarding the GGF. These discussions are focusing on the service implementation modeling from the above grid services portTypes. There are two proposed models with their own advantages and disadvantages.

1. Each portType becomes a Grid service. The complexity surrounds the client-side utilization where it has to be concerned with a number of grid service instances (GSH and GSRs) in order to manage a database.
2. All portTypes are implemented in a single service implementation. This simple case provides an aggregated service view. The complexity lies with the service implementer to maintain state information on the client's discrete activities. However, the client has to manage only one GSH and its corresponding GSRs.

The DAIS portTypes are designed with the following principles in mind:

- OGSI complaint
- Extensible and pluggable with new storage systems and access mechanisms
- Easy to understand and use by the client
- This solution must satisfy Web service and grid service communities
- Easier integration with the existing data managers and resources

Based on the above design goals, the DIAS constructs the following logical portType hierarchy with a clear separation of the interface functionality (Figure 10.16).

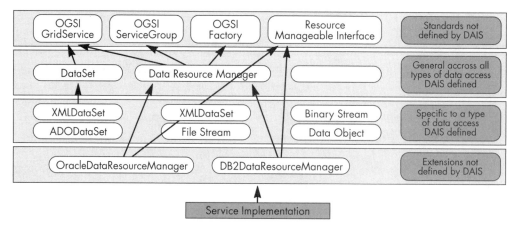

Figure 10.16
A logical portType functionality separation.

For more information on this topic, it is important to refer to the DAIS specifications for details.

Summary

The DIAS is a work-in-progress activity in the GGF. The specification has not yet matured, hence, we can expect a number of changes to this specification especially with the involvement of major database vendors. There are some reference implementations that exist today. The OGSA-DAI[10] project is one such major project that is concerned with the construction of a middleware to assist with access and integration of data from separate data sources, via the grid.

CONCLUSION

In this chapter, we discussed the core OGSA platform components that are identified as suitable candidates for implementation with any OGSA-based infrastructure. These provide value-added functionalities and enhance the common utility of the grid. We are acknowledging that the OGSA WG may identify other functional services and components over a period of time, and may standardize upon them, define behaviors, service interfaces, and information schema. This will occur and enrich the OGSA architecture model. As we have seen earlier, use cases are core for this evolutionary architectural transformation activity.

NOTES

1. For more information on CMM, please visit *http://forge.gridforum.org/projects/cmm-wg/*.

2. For more information, go to *http://www-106.ibm.com/developerworks/library/gr-servicegrid/*.

3. For more information on IETF and policy works, please visit *www.ietf.org*.

4. For details on DMTF and their policy works, visit *www.dmtf.org*.

5. For more information, go to *https://forge.gridforum.org/projects/ogsa-sec-wg/document/security _Architecture_for_Open_Grid_Services/en/2/Security_Architecture_for_Open_Grid_Services.doc*.

6. For more information, go to *http://www-106.ibm.com/developerworks/library/ws-secure/*.

7. For more information, go to *www.w3.org/Encryption/2001/*.

8. For more information, go to *www.w3.org/P3P*.

9. For more information, go to *https://forge.gridforum.org/projects/dais-wg/*.

10. For more details on OGSA-DAI, visit *www.ogsadai.org.uk*.

The Grid Computing Toolkits

In the realm of Grid Computing, there are many very innovative toolkits available to the Grid Computing community of developers and service providers. These toolkits are supported by some of the world's foremost participants in the Grid Computing disciplines.

This part of the book will unveil these toolkits, their application to industrial applications development, service provider delivery requirements, and the maintenance of Grid Computing environments. These toolkits address both the development of Grid applications as well as creating the necessary Grid Computing infrastructure for delivery of innovative services. Included in the presentation discussions is the development of applications and samples of how to accomplish this, Grid programming models, sample implementations, definitions of high-level services, and middleware solutions.

CHAPTER **11**

GLOBUS GT3
Toolkit:
Architecture

In a previous section, we were introduced to the Grid Computing concepts, the new open standard software architecture model (i.e., OGSA), and the new programming model for Grid Computing (i.e., OGSI). The GLOBUS software technology toolkit (Globus GT3) version 3[1] is the major reference implementation of the OGSI standard.

The Globus GT3 software is utilized by a number of worldwide technology initiatives, including utility-based computing, IBM's Business On Demand computing, virtualized resource sharing, and distributed job schedulers. These activities serve as proof of concept of open standard resource sharing and interoperability in Grid Computing. This software and its surrounding architectures are in the process of evolution, and we will therefore concentrate our discussions in this chapter to the recent (very stable) release of the Globus GT3 toolkit.

The Globus GT3 toolkit is the most widely utilized and explored infrastructure software for grid middleware development, worldwide, among grid practitioners. Hence, we explore this toolkit in depth. We introduce the Globus GT3 software architecture and the programming model using sample code listings.

We divide this discussion on GT3 into three subsequent chapters. First, we discuss the high-level architecture of this toolkit, and in the next chapter we cover the programming model and tools introduced by GT3. Finally, our discussion ends with an implementation sample of a grid service to explain the concepts we have learned in the previous chapters of this book. Also, we devote an entire chapter to discuss the high-level service defined by GT3.

Let us now begin to explore the GT3 software architecture.

GT3 Software Architecture Model

As shown in Figure 11.1, the GT3 architecture is a combination of:

- GT3 core
- Base services
- User-defined services

The GT3 core forms the basic building blocks for grid services. This core consists of:

- OGSI reference implementation. Provides OGSI-defined interfaces, messages, and grid behaviors. This implementation enables interoperability with the Web service engine and hosting platforms. Tools provided with this implementation infrastructure assists us with grid services creation.
- Security infrastructure. Provides the basic grid security, including message and transport level protection, end-to-end mutual authentication, and authorization. This security framework is working in conjunction with the WS-Security specifications.
- System-level services. Includes logging services, administrative services, handle resolver services, routing services, and other important complimenting services. These services are built on the top of the OGSI reference implementation and security implementation. They provide system-level services available to other OGSI services for better manageability and customization.

The higher-level base services are built on the top of the GT3 core. Some of the services provided by the GT3 base are information services, data management services, and job execution services. We are postponing this discussion until Chapter 14, which will focus on these topics. In Chapter 14, we also address each of these services available within the GT3 software bundle, the information model exposed by these services, and its usage patterns.

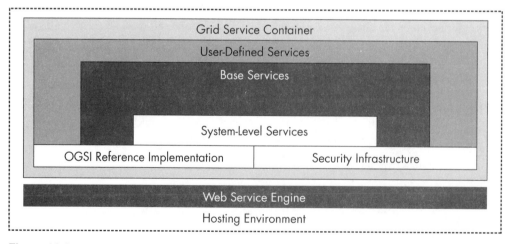

Figure 11.1
The Globus GT3 core architecture.

User-defined services are application-level services that are created to exploit the OGSI reference implementations and security infrastructure. These services may in turn work with other high-level services to provide an improved collective behavior related to resource management. Some such services include meta schedulers, resource allocation managers, and collaborative monitoring services.

This GT3 software introduces the notion of a grid service container, which forms an abstract notion of a runtime environment. This runtime environment provides capabilities for grid service persistence management, lifecycle management, and instance management. We call this container "abstract" because the real functionality implementation is likely to be using some existing hosting environment capabilities. For example, a service implemented as EJB may have a lifecycle managed by the J2EE EJB container. The current GT3 container is implemented on a J2SE/J2EE Web container. At the same time, we can create grid services EJBs by using the delegation service programming model defined by GT3. Note that the service lifecycle and management is still under the preview of the Web container.

Yet another important component requires our continued attention. This is the Web service engine, which is (again) responsible for managing the XML messages from a grid service client to the service. The functionality includes message decoding, unmarshalling, type mapping, and dispatching calls to the service methods. The layered architecture enables OGSI reference implementations to utilize any Web service engine of choice. Even though we can be selective in our choice of Web service execution engines, the current GT3 implementation is not entirely flexible. The current GT3 relies on the Apache Axis Web service engine for some of its programming models (i.e., MessageElement and type mapping) and message flows (i.e., grid handlers).

We can further explore the details of the implementation architecture model with the default software framework implemented in the Globus GT3 toolkit. We will begin our discussion with the server-side framework components.

Default Server-Side Framework

As shown in Figure 11.2, the major architecture components of the server-side framework are as follows:

1. Web service engine provided by Apache AXIS framework. The GT3 software uses the Apache AXIS framework to deal with normal Web service behaviors such as SOAP message processing, JAX-RPC handler processing, and Web services configuration.
2. Globus container framework. The GT3 software provides a container to manage the stateful Web service through a unique instance handle, instance repository, and lifecycle management that includes service activation/passivation and soft-state management.

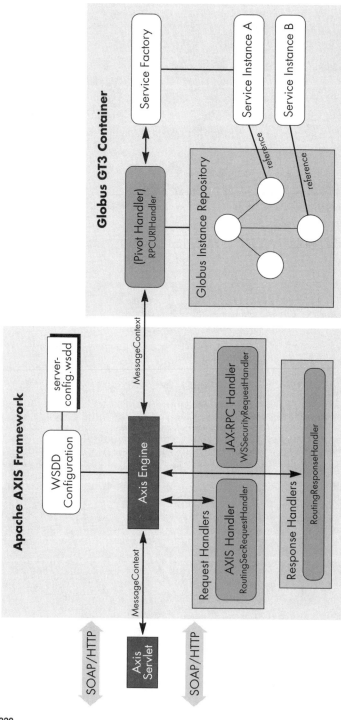

Figure 11.2
The current GT3 server-side reference implementation model.

Message Processing Details

As already mentioned, GT3 utilizes Apache AXIS as their Web service engine, which executes in a J2EE/J2SE Web container, and provides a SOAP message listener (i.e., the AXIS Servlet). It is responsible for SOAP request/response serialization and deserialization, JAX-RPC handler invocation, and grid service configuration. As shown in Figure 11.2, the GT3 container provides a "pivot" handler to the AXIS framework in order to pass the request messages to the Globus container.

The Globus GT3 container architecture is utilized to manage the stateful nature of Web services (readers must be aware that grid service instances are stateful Web services) and their lifecycle. Once a grid service instance is created by the service factory, a unique GSH is created for that instance by the framework. Note that the actual creation of a service depends on the service configuration properties, and the details are deferred to the programming model discussion in the next chapter. This instance is registered with the container repository. This container repository acts as a repository of all the stateful service instances. The other framework components and handlers contact the repository to invoke service methods, get/set service properties (e.g., instance GSH, GSR, etc.), activate/passivate service, resolve grid service handles to reference, and persist the service.

PIVOT HANDLERS

Pivot handlers are responsible for creating Web service instance and invoking operations on the service. There are different types of handlers available based on the style (document/rpc) of the SOAP message.

In GT3, we are using "wrapped"-style messaging, which is a special case of "document"-style messaging, where each parameter is bundled and treated separately. GT3 provides "RPCURIHandler" as a special case implementation of a "JavaProvider" of the AXIS framework. It handles wrapped messages and contacts the container repository, based on the service instance handle, to find the correct service and invoke the operations on it.

Based on the above discussion, now we are familiar with the high-level default framework implementation that comes with GT3. Let us now explore the GT3 architecture components in detail, using the above server-side implementation model.

Globus GT3 Architecture Details

This section introduces the Globus GT3 architecture discussion. This architecture is an open-ended reference framework, with specific implementations worthy of review.

Grid Service Container

The Globus container model is derived from the J2EE-managed container model, where the components are free from complex resource manageability and runtime infrastructure usage. These complex management processes include transaction, concurrency, connectivity, persistence, lifecycle, and security management. In such a managed environment, the container is responsible for managing and controlling these attributes. This helps to achieve a basic QoS requirement for the components. In addition, the programming model becomes less complex to implement.

The OGSI specification introduces and imposes a number of QoS requirements and behaviors on a grid service. The rendering of OGSI in a managed environment forces GT3 to reinvent a container model for grid services. In our previous discussions, we have explained these default implementation behaviors. The GT3 container is responsible for instance management, persistence, lifecycle management, and activation/deactivation of grid services. It also provides a repository for service instance identity and management.

In general, this container provides the following value-added features:

- Lightweight service introspection and discovery
- Dynamic deployment and soft-state management of stateful grid services
- Transport-independent, message-level security infrastructure supporting credential delegation, message signing, encryption, and authorization

OGSI Reference Implementation

The OGSI Reference implementation is a set of primitives implementing the standard OGSI interfaces, such as GridService, Factory, Notification (Source/Sink/Subscription), HandleResolver, and ServiceGroup (i.e., Entry/Registration). Among these, GT3 implementation provides the base implementation of GridService and Factory interfaces. This forms the basis of GT3 service implementation, container configuration, and the service invocation design pattern. These implementations can be extended to provide more behaviors. We will see the implementation and configuration details of these interfaces later in the next chapter.

GT3 provides implementations for all other interfaces defined by the OGSI. However, these implementations are dependent on the service requirements. In complex scenarios, these implementations can be replaced with more sophisticated services pertaining to the service requirements. For example, the simple point-to-point notification framework provided by GT3 may not always be sufficient, and should be replaced by asynchronous JMS-based message queues.

Security Infrastructure

GT3 supports transport-level and message-level security. Another notable feature provided by GT3 is a declarative security mechanism for authentication and authorization using the service deployment descriptors. This provides an extended plug-and-play security architecture using the JAAS framework.

Transport-Level Security

This is based on the GSI security mechanism, as it exists today in GT2. To communicate over this secure transport layer we need to use a different invocation scheme other than http; this is called *httpg*. We have to be aware that the current transport-level security may be depreciated in favor of the message-level security introduced through the WS-Security architecture.

Message-Level Security

As we have seen in the previous section regarding WS-Security, the message-level security is implemented at the SOAP message level. We can see that there are two message-level security mechanisms: GSI Secure Conversation and GSI XML Signature.

GSI Secure Conversation

Let us further explore a few points, as illustrated in Figure 11.3.

1. Initially the client establishes a security context with the service, utilizing a system-level service known as the "Secure Conversation Service." This security establishment is accomplished utilizing the Generic Security Services (GSS) API.
2. Once the security context is established, the client will use this context to sign on, verify, encrypt, and decrypt the request/response messages.
3. On subsequent calls, it passes the shared secret key along with the message.

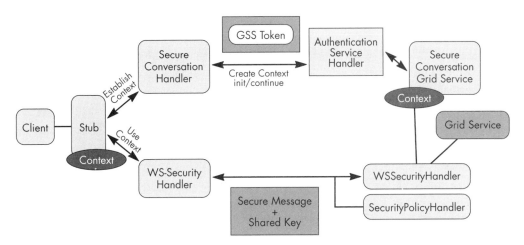

Figure 11.3
The establishment of a secure conversation.

GSI XML Signature

The GSI XML signature is a simple XML message encryption mechanism, where the message is encrypted using the X.509 certificate capability. This provides additional flexibility, as any intermediary can validate the certificates and, hence, the message.

We will discuss the details of the message, the transport-level security mechanisms, security programming, and the declarative security model for grid services in the next chapter.

Security Directions

The future security in GT3 will be aligned with the Global XML architecture standards on security. The WS-Security then becomes the default message-level security mechanism. The WS-Trust capability is used for security context creation, WS-SecureConversation for secure exchange of the aforementioned tokens. Figure 11.4 shows this architectural direction.

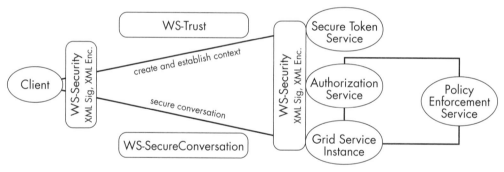

Figure 11.4
Emerging security standards and its implementation with a grid service.

The plug-and-play nature of GT3 security enables us to create the above architectural model, with our choice of service/security provider options. In addition, the future security mechanisms must provide facilities for supporting WS-Federation, for federating across virtual organizations and trust domains.

System-Level Services

Some of the system-level services are introduced to provide a framework to achieve the required QoS in a production environment. These services must provide logging, management, and administrate provisions for a grid environment. The functions can be used as standalone facilities, or they can be used in concurrence with each other. Some of the existing GT3 system-level services are:

- Logging service. This enables dynamic modifications of logging filters for the current runtime environment, or this can be persisted for subsequent executions. In addition, this service enables the grouping of log message producers to adjust the size of backlogs and to provide customizable message views.

- Management service. This service provides a facility to monitor the current status and the load of a service container. It also provides functionalities to activate and deactivate service instances.
- Admin service. This service provides administrative activities, including pinging the hosting environment and shutting down the container.

Hosting Environments

The current GT3 code is developed in Java and supports the following types of hosting environments:

1. Embedded utilities to be utilized with client and lightweight service deployments
2. Standalone containers for service hosting
3. Servlet-based environments, as we noted in Figure 11.2
4. EJB-based environments utilizing a delegation model to support existing EJB components, implemented as services

Load Balancing Features in GT3

Generally speaking, a grid service is created in the same hosting environment where its factory is located. This is fine in most cases; however, there may be cases when the service needs to be created in a different hosting environment than the local hosting scenario. The reason may be many, including load balancing, user account restrictions, and backend resource requirements. In such situations, the factory needs to create a service in a hosting environment other than the local one, and the service calls must then be routed to the hosting environment where the service is operating. The local host now acts as a virtual hosting environment, but the client is unaware of this. The client performs the normal operations as usual and the GT3 framework handles the routing. This routing information is embedded with the SOAP header.

Figure 11.5 illustrates such a virtual-hosting and load-balancing process. The most prominent example is the GT3 GRAM implementation. This environment provides a virtual-hosting environment for user account restrictions and load balancing.

In the next chapter, regarding programming discussions, we will further explore the details of this load-balancing feature provided by the GT3 framework.

Client-Side Framework

GT3 does not dictate an architectural framework for grid service clients. The default implementation comes with a number of tools supporting Apache AXIS and the corresponding Java code

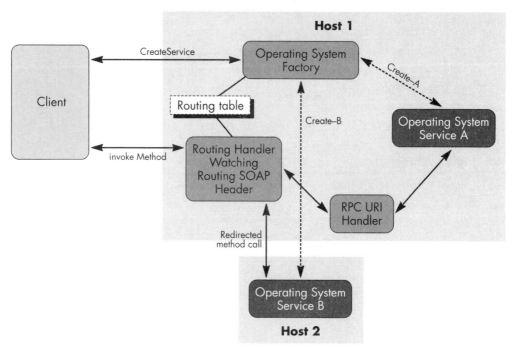

Figure 11.5
A virtual host and load balancing environment.

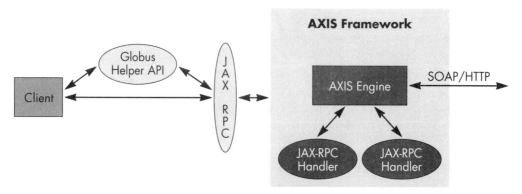

Figure 11.6
GT3 software framework, focusing on aspects of the client-side architecture components.

generation. The framework follows the JAX-RPC programming model. The AXIS framework provides the runtime JAX-RPC engine for client-side message processing and dispatching.

As shown in Figure 11.6 Globus GT3 uses the normal JAX-RPC client-side programming model and the AXIS client-side framework.

In addition to the normal JAX-RPC programming model, Globus provides a number of helper classes at the client side in order to hide the details of the OGSI client-side programming model. We will further address these details in the next chapter on the programming model.

Message Preprocessing Handlers

Handlers provide the mechanism for processing raw SOAP messages. This is mainly utilized for handling SOAP headers that are implemented to communicate security, correlation, and transactional semantics about a message exchange. The GT3 architecture utilizes the JAX-RPC handlers and the AXIS handlers to accomplish this SOAP message-processing functionality. These handlers are applicable at both client- and server-side implementations. We will see further details of this in the following chapter.

SUMMARY

The GT3 architecture is a layered architecture with the emphasis on separating the functionality at each layer. This flexibility enables high-level services to utilize the lower-layer services in a plug-and-play manner in order to facilitate simpler system designs. The provisioning for host environment independence and the provisioning to integrate into a Web service engine of choice makes this more attractive. Even though this is highly desirable, this level of extensibility is not yet available in Globus GT3, where the current Web service engine of choice is Apache Axis.

In the next chapter, we will see how this architecture can be converted into a flexible and extensible programming model. Later in the book, we will see some GT3-provided high-level services and their respective functionalities.

NOTE

1. Globus Toolkit can be found at *http://www-unix.globus.org/toolkit/download.html.*

GLOBUS GT3 Toolkit: Programming Model

INTRODUCTION

The GT3 software is providing OGSI functionalities, based on Web services and the Java programming model. The core software is written in Java and, hence, our discussion on the programming model will be based on that language. This programming model discussion includes the client/server-side programming models, tools available to help construct those programming models, and the deployment artifacts needed for the container. In the next chapter, we will design a sample grid service using a top-down approach, starting with WSDL, to validate the discussion points in this chapter.

SERVICE PROGRAMMING MODEL

The Service Programming model is based on the illustration in Figure 12.1, which shows the object system and the relationships as implemented by GT3. The core concepts we can infer from this model include grid service base and its implementation, grid service callback mechanisms, operation providers, factory and its callback concepts, and the service data. The next few sections explain the details on these concepts.

Grid Service Behavior Implementation

The OGSI-defined grid service behaviors are defined in the GridService interface, and is implemented by the default GT3-provided GridServiceBase interface. This GridServiceBase interface forms the basis of all grid services created by GT3. This base interface provides operations for OGSI-defined grid service behaviors, service instance–specific properties management, service data query and modifications, service data set management, and service facilities to add/delete operation providers.

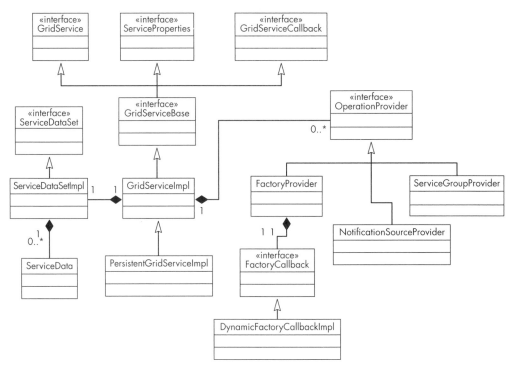

Figure 12.1
The Service Programming Model.

Figure 12.2 lists all the operations available with a GT3-created grid service. All these interface operations are not exposed to the client; only GridService interface operations are exposed through WSDL.

This framework utilizes the rest of the interfaces to control grid service behavior. This separation of responsibilities is controlled through a security authorization mechanism. In addition to these standard interfaces, the grid service may implement custom-exposed interfaces defined through WSDL. Another mechanism by which we can expose the service interfaces is through operation providers, and registering them with the service implementation. The next section provides the details on this topic.

As we have discussed in Figure 12.1, GT3 provides two default implementations of the Grid-ServiceBase interface. These are:

- GridServiceImpl. This implementation forms the base class for services that are transient. These services are created through the OGSI factory mechanism.
- PersistentServiceImpl. This forms the base class for all persistent services, which are created through configuration entries and always available in the container. These services are not created through the OGSI factory mechanism.

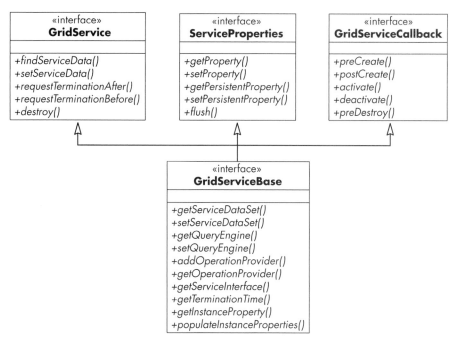

Figure 12.2
This illustration depicts the GT3 Grid Service exposed operations.

These base classes provide a number of functionalities, including service data management, operation provider management, and service instance lifecycle management. We are deferring the more detailed discussion on persistent and transient services to later sections of this book.

Based upon this discussion, there are two design patterns available for our service creation. These are:

> **1.** Service extending GridServiceImpl, or PersistentServiceImpl implementing our service exposed interface(s).

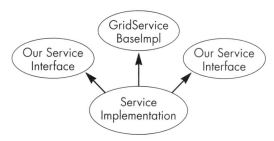

Figure 12.3
The grid service implementation pattern utilizing the service interface implementation.

2. Service extending GridServiceImpl or PersistentServiceImpl while using operation providers to implement our service interfaces (Figure 12.4).

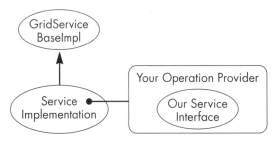

Figure 12.4
The Grid Service implementation pattern utilizing the operation provider.

Operation Providers

The above discussion addressed the base implementation classes (i.e., PersistentServiceImpl and GridServiceImpl) provided by GT3. These are useful for service developers to hide a number of complexities associated with the service creation. However, some have a number of extensibility problems with this approach, which are:

- Due to the unavailability of multiple inheritances in Java, service developers utilize the default interface hierarchy, as provided by the framework.
- Some of the behaviors implemented by the aforementioned classes are specific to the GT3 container, and hence porting the service implementation may not be possible.
- Dynamic configurations of service behaviors are not possible.

Related to resolving these problems, GT3 has introduced a dynamic delegation model for service operations. This is a flexible and dynamically customizable model, where these operation providers are integrated into the service configuration at deployment time. In addition to the above static deployment model, there are provisions available with GridServiceBase to dynamically add the operation providers during execution.

This flexibility allows one to program the business logic into these providers, and the grid service implementation will then delegate the service calls (as described in the WSDL) to these providers. Given this, we can change them, add new functionalities, and add new interfaces with new operations to expose more functional capabilities (i.e., provided these operations are listed in WSDL).

To assist grid service developers to handle some common design patterns, the default GT3 comes with three different types of operation providers: factory provider, ServiceGroup provider, and NotificationSource provider (respectively). Since these providers enable some of the important functionalities for any service's *Utility* value, we are providing a detailed discussion on these special types of providers later in this chapter.

Let us now examine some specific code segments behind an operation provider.

1. The following will create an "OperatingSystem" grid service that implements service behaviors, and then deploys this functionality to the GT3 container.

Listing 12.1 The operating system service implementation (most of the implementation is omitted for code clarity).

```
public class OperatingSystemImpl extends PersistentGridServiceImpl{
    public OperatingSystemImpl () {
        super("Operating system Service");
    }

    public void postPersistentCreate(GridContext context)
        throws GridServiceException {
    }
............................................
}
```

Listing 12.2 The operating system service deployment in a configuration file.

```
1. <service name="ogsa/cmm/OperatingSystemService" provider="Handler"
                     style="wrapped" use="literal">
2.    <parameter name="allowedMethods" value="*"/>
3.    <parameter name="className"
                 value="org.ogsa.core.cmm.OperatingSystemPortType"/>
4.    <parameter name="baseClassName" value=" org.ogsa.core.cmm
                 .OperatingSystemImpl "/>
5.    <parameter name="persistent" value="true"/>
6.    <parameter name="schemaPath" value="schema/core/cmm/
                 operatingsystem_service.wsdl"/>
7.    <parameter name="handlerClass"
                 value="org.globus.ogsa.handlers.RPCURIProvider"/>
8.    <parameter name="securityConfig" value="org/globus/ogsa/impl/
                 core/management/security-config.xml"/>
9. </service>
```

Listings 12.1 and 12.2 show how we are able to create a service and configure that service for the container. Here we are deploying the service into the default Apache AXIS Web service container using the Web Service Deployment Descriptor (WSDD). Once this service is deployed onto the container, the client should be able to start invoking methods on the service using the base OGSI GridService portType.

2. Later we decide that the above grid service needs to support OGSI Notification source behaviors so that interested clients can subscribe for service state change notifications.

If we find that the default NotificationSourceProvider function that is offered by GT3 is sufficient (see the discussion later on regarding this default provider), then we can establish that behavior just by changing the deployment configuration (next) from what was previously shown in Listing 12.2.

Listing 12.3   The operating system service deployment with a NotificationSourceProvider.

```
 1. <service name="ogsa/cmm/OperatingSystemService" provider="Handler"
 2.                 style="wrapped" use="literal">
 3.   <parameter name="allowedMethods" value="*"/>
 4.   <parameter name="className"
 5.   value="org.ogsa.core.cmm.OperatingSystemPortType"/>
 6.   <parameter name="baseClassName" value=" org.ogsa.core.cmm
                .OperatingSystemImpl "/>
 7.   <parameter name="persistent" value="true"/>
 8.   <parameter name="schemaPath"
 9.           value="schema/core/cmm/operatingsystem_service.wsdl"/>
10.   <parameter name="handlerClass"
                value="org.globus.ogsa.handlers.RPCURIProvider"/>
11.   <parameter name="securityConfig"
12.               value="org/globus/ogsa/impl/core/management/
                security-config.xml"/>
13.   <parameter name="operationProviders"
14.               value="org.globus.ogsa.impl.ogsi
                .NotificationSourceProvider"/>
15. </service>
```

Note these changes in the configuration information in Listing 12.3 on line 13. In addition to the normal grid service behaviors, the client can subscribe for notifications on the operating system service. This provides an amazing degree of flexibility for grid service developers.

Another way to add an operation provider is by using the "addOperationProvider" operation on the GridServiceBaseImpl class. This is performed in the service postCreate() or postPersistent-Create() calls, as shown in Listing 12.4.

Listing 12.4   The dynamically adding operation provider.

```
 1. public void postCreate(GridContext context){
 2. addOperationProvider(new NotificationSourceProvider ());
 3. }
```

3. After a while, the operating service provider now decides to use a new notification source provider with more complex functionalities. For example, the service developer decided to provide a JMS message queueing facility rather than the simple point-to-

point mechanism for notification. For this functionality, the service developer must create a new NotificationSource provider and register that with the container. Listing 12.5 shows a sample skeleton of the JMSNotificationSourceProvider.

Listing 12.5 The JMSNotificationSourceProvider implementation (the low-level details on the implementation are avoided for the sake of simplicity and clarity).

```
public class JMSNotificationSourceProvider implements
            OperationProvider, .......{

    private static final QName[] operations = new QName[] {new
        QName("http://www.gridforum.org/namespaces/2003/03/
                OGSI","subscribe")}

    public NotificationSourceProvider(){}

    public void subscribe(
                ExtensibilityType subscriptionExpression,
                LocatorType sink,
                ExtendedDateTimeType expirationTime,
                LocatorTypeHolder subscriptionInstanceLocator,
                TerminationTimeTypeHolder currentTerminationTime){
        //Our implementation goes here….
    }
.......................
}
```

In order for the service to use this new JMS Notification provider described in Listing 12.5, we need to change the class name in Line 13 of Listing 12.3 with the new operation provider class name. The framework will take care of the rest of the processing.

INTERNAL DETAILS OF OPERATION PROVIDER PROCESSING

One may be asking at this stage exactly how operation provider processing is happening inside the GT3 framework. Let us explore some basic information, as this will help us construct more robust services.

1. NotificationSource provider exposes the QNames of the operations it is exposing to the clients. These must match the WSDL-described operations name and their namespace. In Listing 12.5, we can see that the class contains a static QName list of the service operations (i.e., "subscribe" operation in the "OGSI" namespace) it is exposing. This operation matches the WSDL NotificationSource portType's "subscribe" operation. We can always add wildcard characters for QName parameters, namespace name, and operation name. For example,

in order to expose all public operations in a provider, create a QName with new QName("*"."*"). This is a flexible approach to expose all public operations in the provider. Note that for the standard interfaces defined by OGSI, it is required to provide the namespace qualifier that matches the OGSI operation namespace.

2. All notification providers expose the "getOperations()" method for retrieving the exposed operations (as described above).

3. For correct operation name lookup and invocation, all the exposed operations must follow the same signature, as described by the corresponding WSDL operation.

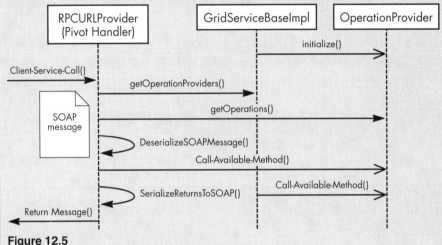

Figure 12.5
A sequence diagram for handling the operation providers.

4. The above sequence diagram (Figure 12.5) illustrates how the framework handles this operation provider, and then the corresponding invocation method.

Factory Callback Mechanism

The OGSI and GT3 provides standard mechanisms for the construction of grid services using a factory pattern. The factory extracts the grid service construction mechanisms as an abstraction. GT3 provided the "factory callback" mechanism, and enables the facilities for adding custom factories for additional services. These custom factories provide capabilities to create services in a remote hosting environment, and can then align with the native host/container-specific service creation patterns, for example, work with EJB Home to create an EJB service.

GT3 provides a default factory implementation through a factory provider, which delegates the service creations to the "default factory callback." This default factory callback is capable of creating services inside the same class loader where the factory is.

In Listing 12.6, we can see how to configure the deployment descriptor to add a factory provider and the GT3-provided default factory callback implementation.

Listing 12.6   The factory provider and the default factory callback.

```
 1.  <service name=" ogsa/cmm/OperatingSystemServicefactoryService"
     provider="Handler" style="wrapped">
 2.  ...........................................................
 3.  <parameter name="operationProviders"
     value="org.globus.ogsa.impl.ogsi.factoryProvider"/>
 4.    <parameter name="factoryCallback"
     value="org.globus.ogsa.impl.ogsi.DynamicfactoryCallbackImpl"/>
 5.  ...........................................................
 6.  </service>
```

The previous XML configuration fragment describes the factory operation provider and the callback implementation for the service.

Let us now implement a custom factory callback facility that is capable of connecting to an EJB Home to create an EJB service. Listing 12.7 explains how we can implement such a custom factory using the factory callback implementation.

Listing 12.7   The custom factory callback implementation.

```
 1.  public class EJBfactoryCallbackImpl implements factoryCallback {
 2.    private GridServiceBase base;
 3.
 4.    public void initialize(GridServiceBase base) throws
       GridServiceException{
 5.      this.base = base;
 6.    }
 7.    synchronized public GridServiceBase createServiceObject(
 8.      ExtensibilityType extensibility) throws GridServiceException {
 9.          ..............................
10.        Context initial = new InitialContext(env);
11.      //look up the home interface using jndi
12.      Object homeObj = initial.lookup(ejbLookupString);
13.      EJBHome home =
14.        (EJBHome) PortableRemoteObject.narrow(homeObj,
              EJBHome.class);
15.      // Create EJB object
16.          ..............................
17.      // Create Grid service object and assign with the EJB Object
18.    }
19.    <<other private methods>>
20.  }
```

Listing 12.8 The register and the new callback implementation, as shown in the configuration.

```
1. <service name=" ogsa/cmm/OperatingSystemServicefactoryService"
   provider="Handler" style="wrapped">
2. ...................................................................
3. <parameter name="operationProviders"
   value="org.globus.ogsa.impl.ogsi.factoryProvider"/>
4. <parameter name="factoryCallback" value="EJBfactoryCallbackImpl "/>
5. ...................................................................
6. </service>
```

Listings 12.7 and 12.8 describe how one can register the new factory callback implementation with a service.

One can now deploy the above service and all the calls to create the service (i.e., createService call on factory) and attain delegation to the EJBfactoryCallbackImpl's "createServiceObject" method. We can see more information on the internals of this factory pattern in the following discussion.

INTERNAL DETAILS OF FACTORY CALLBACK PROCESSING

The services can be configured to use an OGSI-provided factory mechanism by setting a factory operation provider for that service. On a service container startup, it reads the configuration and loads the necessary configurations to the Service container repository, and then activates the factory service based on the configuration property (i.e., 'activateOnStartup').

Following this activation, when a client attempts to create a service instance, the RPCURIHandler follows the pattern as depicted in the Figure 12.6.

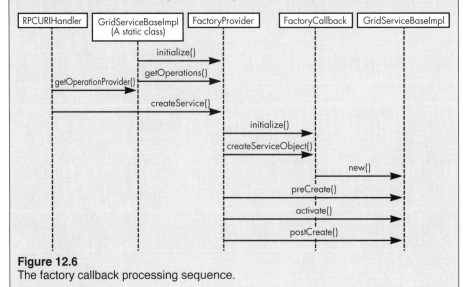

Figure 12.6
The factory callback processing sequence.

The next section discusses the GT3-provided grid service lifecycle model, where we will examine a grid service lifecycle, service state persistence mechanisms, and recovery capabilities.

Grid Service Lifecycle Callbacks and Lifecycle Management

Many of the distributed component models support efficient and scalable memory management through autonomic component activation and deactivation facilities. The GT3 container model is providing some basic scalability management functionalities. The following points describe these functionalities.

- Services getting activated only on the first utilization by the container, even if the services are statically deployed and persistent in nature.
- Container provides scalability mechanisms by deactivating unutilized services. Some of the most commonly deactivated services include notification subscriptions and service group entries. Normally speaking, these service instances are created in large numbers. GT3 utilizes algorithms for this deactivation process. These are referred to as:
  ○ TTL—Time to Live
  ○ LRU—Least Recently Used
  We are able to configure the TTL property in the configuration file. One notable thing about this deactivation is that the container still holds some metadata that is required to activate these services.
- Services are deactivated to a persistent storage in its entirety. GT3 provides a facility called "ServiceLoader," which we can use to achieve this kind of deactivation. This loader is also responsible for dynamically deploying and activating a service on its first activation.
- A provision for "lazy creation" enables a factory to return a unique handle for the service instance without any explicit deployment or activation of that service instance. The service deployment and activation happens later on, when the client tries to resolve the handle to a reference. For this, a lazy creation callback is involved.

All these scalability management functions are part of the container and transparent to the user of the container. Now we can take a closer inspection on these capabilities, and the programmatic/configuration requirements of a service to achieve these behaviors.

These services transition from activate to deactivate, and vice versa, and are enabled by the GridServiceCallback interface, as described in Listing 12.9.

Listing 12.9   The service lifecycle interface.

```
public interface GridServiceCallback  {
   public void preCreate(GridContext context) throws GridServiceException;
   public void postCreate(GridContext context) throws GridServiceException;
   public void activate(GridContext context) throws GridServiceException;
   public void deactivate(GridContext context) throws GridServiceException;
   public void preDestroy(GridContext context) throws GridServiceException;
}
```

All grid services implemented from GridServiceBase, in turn, implement this interface (as shown in Figure 12.2). The operation providers and factory callbacks should implement this interface to maintain fine-grain control on the underlying resource that they provide. Another very important interface associated with this service behavior is the ServiceLifeCycleMonitor, as shown in Listing 12.10. This is an *interceptor* to a grid service lifecycle state transition.

Listing 12.10 The service lifecycle interceptor.

```
public interface ServiceLifecycleMonitor {
  public void create(GridContext context) throws GridServiceException;
  public void preCall(GridContext context) throws GridServiceException;
  public void postCall(GridContext context) throws GridServiceException;
  public void destroy(GridContext context) throws GridServiceException;
}
```

For example, if there is a lifecycle monitor configured with a grid service, utilizing the "lifecycleMonitor" property, then the factory provider calls this interface operation "create" following the service instance creation. This factory provider only calls this operation after the service instance creation, and following the preCreate, postCreate, and activation calls on the created service.

The diagram in Figure 12.7 details the lifecycle interfaces and their interaction patterns. Let us now discuss the lifecycle management options available with a grid service in more detail.

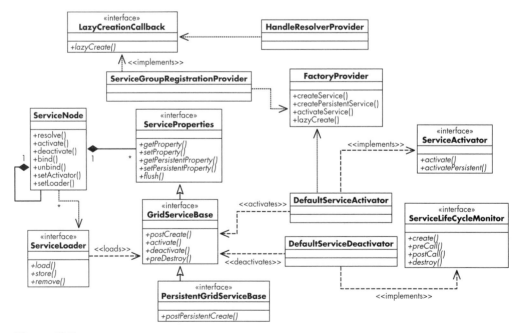

Figure 12.7
The service lifecycle interfaces and integration process.

Service Activation

Service activation is a key operation in any grid service. The following discussion provides treatment to the operations involved in this process.

Activate Utilizing the Lazy Creation Mechanism

As shown in Figure 12.7, the factory provider utilizes a method called lazyCreate(), which will create a GSH, and then returns that handle to the client without actually creating the real service instance.

An example of such a lazy creation is shown in Figure 12.7 where the ServiceGroupRegistration calls the factoryProvider "lazyCreate" operation to create the service entries. The lazy creation can be enabled by setting the "entryInstanceCreation" property to "true" in the configuration file. Later, when the client tries to utilize that service, the handle resolver provider calls the service's parent; this is because the specific service instance node is not in the repository. In this case, the handle provider calls the ServiceGroupRegistration service's "lazyCreate" method with the handle of the instance it wants to invoke. This service, in turn, creates the child service instance for that handle by calling createService in the factory.

Activation on Service Startup

Normally speaking, a service is activated on its first usage. This activation results in an activate call to the grid service lifecycle interface.

Service Deactivation

The default policy adopted by the framework is that activated services never get deactivated. The framework provides a default deactivation mechanism based upon the time to live (TTL) policy. This is easy to configure, as shown in Listing 12.11.

Listing 12.11 The default service deactivator configuration.

```
<service name=" ogsa/cmm/OperatingSystemServicefactoryService"
provider="Handler" style="wrapped">
<parameter name="className" value="=" org.ogsa.core.cmm.impl.
OperatingSystemImpl "/>
<parameter name="persistent" value="true"/>
.........................................
<parameter name="lifecycleMonitorClass"
value="org.globus.ogsa.repository.DefaultServiceDeactivator"/>

<!-- idleTTL before deactivation in milliseconds-->
<parameter name="instanceDeactivation" value="10000"/>

</service>
```

This deactivator is configured with a factory, as shown in Listing 12.11. This helps to monitor all the service instances created by a factory. The functionality of this deactivator is to integrate into the described ServiceLifeCycleMonitor interface calls, and update the service usage timestamp. This current usage time is utilized by a Timer task, already executing, based on a Java Timer event. This is to validate the time to live parameter of a service, and calls the deactivate method on the service if the TTL time expires. This may not, however, be sufficient for more complex scenarios. There are provisions available to integrate deactivators with a service factory, or instance, using the "lifecycleMonitorClass" configuration option.

Service State Data Persistence Mechanisms

This discussion addresses the state of the data, the persistence of the data, and the operations that affect this process.

Service Loader

Most of the services require state data to be persistent, such that it can be recovered from the subsequent startups, as required. For this reason, the framework provides a service persistence mechanism through a ServiceLoader interface, as shown in Listing12.12. This allows a service to store and load the service related state into a persistent storage area.

Listing 12.12   The serviceLoader interface.

```
public interface ServiceLoader {
    public boolean load(String id) throws ServiceLoaderException;
    public void store(String id) throws ServiceLoaderException;
    public void remove(String id) throws ServiceLoaderException;
}
```

The framework provides default SimpleFileLoader implementation that can be used with any service. This is a primitive mechanism, and can be extended with backend database storage for maintaining all the configuration data and state data.

In addition to the above framework mechanism, GT3 provides a default mechanism of storing the configuration information for a transient service in the deployment configuration file, utilizing the "ServiceDeployment" framework component. In these situations, we can observe that the service instance specific configuration information is written to the WSDD configuration file.

GT3-Provided Service Types

Let us examine the types of services available with the GT3 framework, its configuration properties, and its creation semantics. There are two types of services: transient services and persistent services.

Transient Services

These kinds of services are created by the OGSI factory and deployed at runtime to the deployment descriptor. These services are extensions of the GridServiceImpl base class, supplying a factory provider and a callback implementation class in the configuration.

Persistent Services

A persistent service is deployed when it is added to the deployment descriptor through some type of out-of-band mechanism. These services usually extend the PersistentGridServiceImpl GT3 class. These services usually do not have a factory or provider.

Grid Service Lifecycle Model

In addition to the above service lifecycle, there are two kinds of lifecycle models associated with the state data recovery on service restart: persistent and transient.

Persistent

For the lifecycle to be recoverable, all persistent services need to have a configuration property in their configuration file with 'lifecycle="persistent"'.

```
<parameter name="instanceLifecycle" value="persistent"/>
```

The framework creates deployment information for these service instances and will be stored in the deployment configuration file. This deployment information is removed from the configuration file upon service destruction and deactivation using a ServiceLoader, as shown above.

Transient

This is the default behavior and no information is persistent in the deployment descriptor.

To conclude, Table 12.1 shows the GT3-provided service lifecycle properties, their options, and their default values.

Table 12.1 The Default State Management Support in GT3

Service Property	Options
Service Type	Persistent (default), Transient
Lifecycle Model	Persistent, Transient (default)
Activation	Startup, Lazy (default)
Deactivation	None (default), TTL/LRU

GT3-Supported Programming Model for Service Data Management

The service data forms the globally exposed state of a service. We have already discussed the details and importance of service data during our discussion on the OGSI. Let us now see how GT3 is implementing this core OGSI feature.

In GT3, there is a concept called service data set (ServiceDataSet class), which holds all the service data for a service. Figure 12.8 shows this relationship model. Every grid service instance has a service data set that holds a collection of service data wrapper objects. This service data set is responsible for sending notification of any service data changes, with the changed service data wrapper element, to the interested listeners. A service data wrapper (ServiceData class) is holding the service data values, or uses a callback mechanism often referred to as service data "pull," to get the value from other registered data providers. These callbacks must then implement the ServiceDataValueCallback interface, and must be registered with the service data wrapper class.

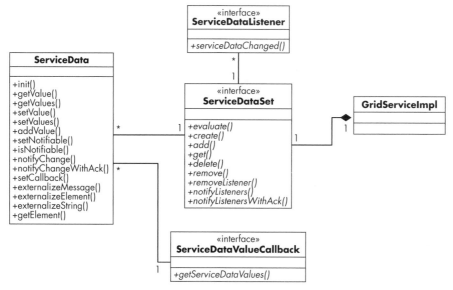

Figure 12.8
The service data classes and relationships.

There are three ways by which we can create and add service data to a service data set:

1. **Predefined service data elements in GWSDL.** Normally speaking, on the service startup, all the service data is loaded into the service data set. There are APIs in service data set (create/add/remove) to dynamically add service data, provided that they are conforming to their descriptions in WSDL (service data descriptions).

We will explore this process in detail in the following discussion.

Service data elements are defined in the WSDL. Every standard OGSI-defined interface already contains some SDE definitions. Listing 12.13 shows the OGSI GridService portType GWSDL with SD elements defined.

Listing 12.13   OGSI-defined GridService portType with service data elements and static values.

```
<!-- Grid Service Port Type -->
<gwsdl:portType name="GridService">
  <operation name="findServiceData">
.............................................
</operation>
.............................................
<sd:serviceData name="interface"
                type="xsd:QName"
                minOccurs="1"
                maxOccurs="unbounded"
                mutability="constant"
                modifiable="false"
                nillable="false"/>

<sd:serviceData name="gridServiceHandle "
                type="ogsi:HandleType "
                minOccurs="0"
                maxOccurs="unbounded"
                mutability="extendable"
                modifiable="false"
                nillable="false"/>


.............................................
  <sd:staticServiceDataValues>
    <ogsi:findServiceDataExtensibility
        inputElement="ogsi:queryByServiceDataNames"/>
    <ogsi:setServiceDataExtensibility
        inputElement="ogsi:setByServiceDataNames"/>
    <ogsi:setServiceDataExtensibility
        inputElement="ogsi:deleteByServiceDataNames"/>
  </sd:staticServiceDataValues>
</gwsdl:portType>
```

Upon service startup, these already defined service data elements are created and added to the service data set during the GridServiceBase's postCreate() call. See the sample algorithm code in Listing 12.14, which is taken from the GridServiceBaseImpl class to illustrate this process.

Listing 12.14   Service data wrapper objects creation from GWSDL SDE definition elements.

```
I.  private void addServiceData() throws GridServiceException {
2.      // All Service Data elements are defined in WSDL GSR
3.      Get the GSR (WSDL) for the current service
4.      Get all the 'GWSDL' portTypes in the GSR (not the WSDL portTypes)
5.      For each GWSDL portType (portTypes qualified with GWSDL namespace)
6.          // Create SD wrapper classes using SDE definition in GWSDL
7.          Get the service data elements defined in that portType
8.          For each service data element
9.              Get the Service data name and its namespace
10.             Create a service Data Wrapper class with the above attributes
11.             Add wrapper to the Service Data Set
12.
13.         // Now get the default static values defined in GWSDL
14.         Get the Static Service Data values in the GWSDL portType
15.         For each Static Service Data
16.             Get each static service data value
17.             Add the all service data values to the Service Data Wrapper
                class provided their name and namespace matches
18. }
```

The above postCreate() mechanism in the GridServiceBaseImpl class sets up the service data set with the appropriate service data wrappers, and their associated predefined (static) values.

Later, if there is a need to update some service data value that already has a wrapper in the service data set, Listing 12.15 explains how to do this.

Listing 12.15   Creating and adding service data values.

```
1. Get the Service Data Wrapper class from the service data set using the
   QName of the service data element as defined in WSDL
       for example:
       To get the predefined (already created from GWSDL) "Handle" Service
       Data element, use the code below.

       ServiceData handleServiceDataElement =
       this.serviceDataSet.create("gridServiceHandle");

2. Now create the value for that service data element. This element must
   be of the ServiceDataElement type. These types are defined in the XSD
   and the framework must have already created corresponding Java types
   (using tools WSDL2JAVA).
```

Listing 12.15 Creating and adding service data values. (Continued)

```
Here "gridserviceHandle" is of the type "HandleType" and hence can create
and add the value to the ServiceDataElement wrapper class:
      HandleType handle = new HandleType(handle)
      handleServiceDataElement.setValue(handle);

3. Update the service data set with Service Data Wrapper and the new value
      for example:
      this.serviceDataSet.add(handleServiceDataElement);
```

      2. Dynamic service data elements and values. So far, we have been discussing the service data elements, which are statically defined in the WSDL. There may be cases when a grid service needs to create the service data elements and add them dynamically to the service data set.

Creating Dynamic Service Data Elements

The code in Listing 12.16 shows how to construct a dynamic service data element for a service. Normally speaking, this is done on a postCreate call to make the service data available to the clients upon service startup.

Listing 12.16 Creating and adding dynamic service data elements.

```
// Create Service Data Element
serviceData = this.getServiceDataSet().create("MyServiceData");
// Set the value of the SDE to a MyServiceDataType instance
MyServiceDataType sd = new MyServiceDataType ();
serviceData.setValue(sd);
// Set initial values of MyServiceData
ad.setName("test");
// Add SDE to Service Data Set
this.getServiceDataSet().add(serviceData);
```

As shown in Listing 12.16, these are the steps we must follow to create an SDE and add it to the service data set:

- Create a new SDE by calling the create method of the service instance's service data set with a unique name or QName. This SDE is initially *empty* and has no value. In our example, the name of the SDE will be MyServiceData with an empty namespace.
- Set a value for the SDE. The value of the SDE of type MyServiceDataType.
- Set the initial values of MyServiceDataType.
- Add the SDE to the service data set.

The client must be aware of this SDE and SDE type to work with the above example. It can find out the available SDEs through service introspection using the "findServiceData" operation on the grid service with "serviceDataName." This operation should list all the available SDEs in the service.

Service Data from Service Annotation

We can now turn our attention to the third mechanism of creating service data using Java service documentation and associated tools, or *doclets*. This process includes a service annotation, running tools to create the service data callback classes and corresponding service data element WSDL, and finally registering these callbacks with the service data wrapper upon service startup. Let us go through each step:

- Annotate Java service implementation with service data element information

Listing 12.17   A service Java file decorated with Service data element definition.

```
/**
 * The current value of the lifecycle.
 * @ogsa:service-data
 *      name = "currentLifecycleValue"
 *      minOccurs = "1"
 *      maxOccurs = "1"
 *      mutability = "mutable"
 */
public string getValue() throws RemoteException {
    return currentLifecycleValue;
}
```

Listing 12.17 illustrates two concepts: how to define the service data element using the service annotation and how we can define the callback for service data values.

The above callback method gets registered with the service data wrapper class upon service instance startup. This method is invoked each time someone tries to access the service data element "currentLifecycleValue."

- Run tools to create the corresponding service data wrapper class and service data element definition.

Once we are done with the above annotation on the service, then we can run the "javadoc" command with a GT3-provided "ServiceDataDoclet" callback class on this service file. This extracts all the service data and creates a ServiceDataAnnotation class that corresponds to the above definition, and stores it in a disk file with an extension of "-sdAnnotation."

Once we have created the above file, we can export the service data element definitions to the WSDL using the *"GenerateSDD"* tool.

- Register the callbacks with the service implementation.

The registration of the ServiceDataAnnotation classes as callbacks are done during service initialization using the calls found in Listing 12.18.

Listing 12.18   Service data annotation callback setup process.

```
// lifecycle callbacks
public void postCreate(GridContext context) throws GridServiceException {
    ServiceDataAnnotation.setupServiceData(this, serviceData);
}
```

This results in the ServiceDataAnnotation class loading the already created "-sdAnnotation" file, setting up the callback with the service data wrappers, and adding the service data element with the service data set.

IMPORTANT INFORMATION ON SERVICE DATA ELEMENT TYPES AND THEIR VALUES

Each service data element has a type associated with it, which can be used to define an XML schema type of the SD value. This is shown below in the SDE definition.

```
<sd:serviceData name="gridServiceHandle " type="ogsi:HandleType "
                minOccurs="0"
                maxOccurs="unbounded"
                mutability="extendable"
                modifiable="false"
                nillable="false"/>
```

The above example shows a "type" attribute associated with the service data element.

Normally speaking, upon running the tools (WSDL2Java) a corresponding Java type gets generated from the above XSD type. We can use this type directly in our program to create new SDE values. The example below shows the type generated by running WSDL2Java.

```
package org.gridforum.ogsi;
public class HandleType
                implements Java.io.Serializable,
                org.apache.axis.encoding.SimpleType {

    private org.apache.axis.types.URI value;

    public HandleType() {    }
    // Simple Types must have a String constructor

    public HandleType(org.apache.axis.types.URI value) {
        this.value = value;
    }
```

```
      public org.apache.axis.types.URI getValue() {
         return value;
      }
      public void setValue(org.apache.axis.types.URI value) {
         this.value = value;
      }

   // type mapping and serialization / de serialization information
   }
```

These generated classes contain necessary type-mapping and serialization/deserialization information to convert the types from XML messages to native language (Java) types, and vice versa.

Service Data Query Support in GT3

Query on service data is the most complex and powerful capability provided by the OGSI specification. Based on OGSI, every grid service exposes a "findServiceData" operation which allows the client to query the service for the service data. The default query supported by the framework is based on the service data name ("queryByServiceDataName"). However, we know that the specification provides an extensible query capability by allowing service to provide different query mechanisms. Some of the notable queries we can think of are Query by XPath, XQuery, and SQL. GT3 supports a plug-and-play query framework to support these requirements to an agreeable level. It provides facilities for extensible query engine support.

A service provides support to add a query execution engine of our choice. This query engine provides capabilities for adding any number of query expression evaluators. Some of the expression evaluators supported in GT3 are:

1. ServiceDataNameEvaluator
2. ServiceDataNameSetEvaluator
3. ServiceDataNameDeleteEvaluator
4. ServiceDataXPathEvaluator

We can see the Query Framework object model in Figure12.9.

Let us go through these available evaluators found in GT3. We will explore the details on the query execution feature in the next section.

ServiceDataNameEvaluator. This is a simple evaluator that enables the client to call the service to get service data values, using the service data element names. The client invokes a "findServiceData" operation to start the query execution process.

ServiceDataNameSetEvaluator. This evaluator enables the client to call the service to set service data values for service data elements identified by their QName. The addition of elements to

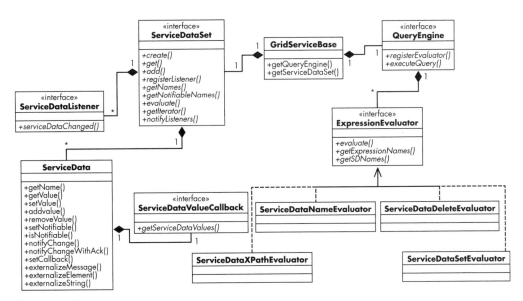

Figure 12.9
Service query framework.

a service data value depends on the other constraints, including minOccurs, maxOccurs and mutability. The client invokes a "setServiceData" operation to start this query execution process.

ServiceDataNameDeleteEvaluator. This evaluator enables the client to call the service to delete service data elements identified by their QName. The client invokes a "setServiceData" operation to start the query evaluation process.

ServiceDataXPathEvaluator. This is a complex evaluator to enable the client to call the service to evaluate an XPath expression on service data elements. The client invokes a "findService-Data" operation to start the query evaluation process. We will explore the details below.

Another notable feature is the ability to register the engine and evaluators at different levels. Normally speaking, these objects are registered at the service level, but we can also register them at the global factory level. This enables the service to use an engine of choice at runtime.

Service Data Retrieval and Transformation Support

The Service Data framework provides a number of mechanisms to enable query support. This includes mechanisms to transform service data values to:

- XML document where we can apply the XPath
- XML string
- Apache AXIS MessageElement Object arrays

Internal Query Processing Information

Every service instance has a query engine and each query engine has a number of query evaluators. A service-specific query engine may contain a parent engine to delegate expressions that it
cannot handle. The global query engines are normally initialized at the factory level (global
query engines). The local engines are set at the service instance level. The normal processing
sequence of a query engine is in Figure 12.10.

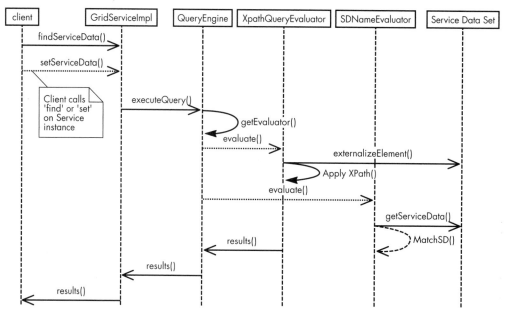

Figure 12.10
Normal processing sequence of a query engine in GT3.

Custom Query Engines and Evaluators

We can write our own query engine by inheriting from QueryEngine interface. This query engine
can be registered as part of the service instance, or can become a global engine. As shown in the
configuration in Listing 12.19, we can set the default evaluators available for the container.

Listing 12.19 Query engine and evaluator configurations.

```
<parameter name="queryEngine" value="com.ph.test.myQueryEngineImpl"/>
<parameter name="queryEvaluators"
  value="org.globus.ogsa.impl.core.service.ServiceDataNameEvaluator
         org.globus.ogsa.impl.core.service.ServiceDataXPathEvaluator
          org.globus.ogsa.impl.core.service.ServiceDataNameDeleteEvaluator
           org.globus.ogsa.impl.core.service.ServiceDataNameSetEvaluator"/>
```

As shown in Figure 12.10, on the "findServiceData" call, our engine will be called to execute the query with the current service data set of the service instance and the query expression. One thing to notice is that the real query execution functionality is occurring at the evaluators registered with the engine. It is possible to register a global query engine with our local query engine, such that we can delegate the calls to that engine for the expressions we have not designed. This is a flexible and hierarchical approach. For example, it helps us write global query engines with more general query handling mechanisms (QueryServiceDataByName or XPath), while our service can implement more specific evaluators for the service.

Another interesting aspect of OGSI and GT3 is the capability to discover the queries supported by a service using the "findServiceData" operation with the input expression "findServiceDataExtensibility."

XPath Query Support in GT3

Let us examine how the XPath query is supported by the GT3 framework.

We can perform an XPath query by issuing a "findServiceData" operation on the service instance and passing a ServiceDataXPathQueryExpressionType object as the parameter.

The structure of this expression type is shown in Listing 12.20.

Listing 12.20   XPath expression type.

```
<complexType name="ServiceDataXPathQueryExpressionType">
    <sequence>
        <element name="name" type="QName"/>
        <element name="XPath" type="string"/>
        <element name="namespaces" type="string" minOccurs="0"
                     maxOccurs="unbounded"/>
    </sequence>
</complexType>
```

Since XPath queries are going to be the flexible approach for service data query, we need a detailed discussion on its capabilities and usage model. These elements in Listing 12.20 are:

- The name element denotes the name of the service data element to which we are applying the query. This can be a wildcard, which specifies applying the XPath on the service data elements that match. This may result in an array of result elements for the XPath query.
- The XPath parameter represents the real XPath expression for the service data element identified by the name parameter.
- Finally, a set of namespace arrays that require special attention. This namespace array is used to convey the namespace of the nodes of the service data element in the XPath query. If namespace mappings are not provided, the default behavior is to use the current

context node, the SDE root element, to resolve the namespaces. However, this may not be sufficient when searching for child nodes, which contain namespace attributes that are not present in the root node. One must be careful to provide all possible namespaces of interest that are likely to be encountered when traversing the SDE. There are some XPath APIs, including local-name() and namspace-uri(), to overcome this problem but may not be sufficient for all cases.

Let us now review some sample XPath queries. For example, the code in Listing 12.21 explains how we can do this in GT3. This code shows how to write an XPath to test whether the service supports XPath queries.

Listing 12.21   A sample XPath expression.

```
xmlns:gsdl=http://www.gridforum.org/namespaces/2002/10/gridServices
//gsdl:queryExpressionType[.='gsdl:queryByServiceDataXPath'
```

We will see in the next chapter some runtime sample codes that detail the service data usage and the application of query on the service data.

Service Data Change Notification

The most important part of a distributed system is the capability to send asynchronous messages to the interested parties on some topic of interest. The OGSI specification provides a standard mechanism to send asynchronous messages on state changes. This provision is handled through a set of OGSI-provided interfaces, NotificationSource, NotificationSubscription, and NotificationSink, respectively. We have already discussed the behaviors exhibited by these interfaces in the last section. Now we will focus our discussion on the GT3 implementation aspects of these interfaces.

There are two important aspects to this notification: make service available for notification and enable service data to send notification messages on its state change.

Let us now discuss these concepts in greater detail.

Make Service Available for Notification

A service can expose to its clients, for Notification purposes, by implementing the NotificationSource interface. We have already discussed the operation provider concepts, which allow a service to expose some of the core operations through an external mechanism, rather than implementing this by itself. GT3 provides a default NotificationSource provider, which enables us to do that. See Listing 12.3, which shows how we can expose our operating system service with the NotificationSource interface. The client can now subscribe for notifications on service data changes. The default implementation supports subscription of the type "subscribeByServiceDataNames" subscription. The other possible subscriptions may include "subscribeByXPath."

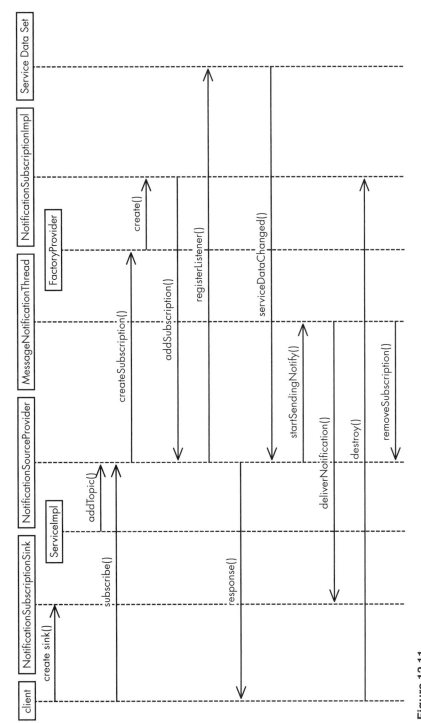

Figure 12.11
The GT3-provided service notification process.

Another notable feature is that this framework is a topic-based messaging framework. By default, when the client subscribes for notification on a service data change, a topic will be created for the service data name. This topic will be evaluated before sending a change notification to the client.

We can now extend the above topic-based concept to other areas of notifications, such as enabling a service to send a notification on some topic of interest other than the service data name. For example, our operating system service wants to send a notification on a call to its method "reboot." We can do that easily by letting the service instance register a new topic called "Reboot" with the notification provider. This is, normally speaking, on our service preCreate() method. The service instance can then send a notification message during the reboot operation. This is illustrated in Listing 12.22.

Listing 12.22   Service sending notifications.

```
public class OperatingSystemImpl extends GridServiceImpl {
  NotificationProvider provider = null;
  public void postCreate(GridContext context) throws GridServiceException {
    try {
      super.postCreate(context);
      this.provider = (NotificationProvider) getProperty(ServiceProperties
                     .NOTIFICATION_SOURCE);

      // create a Topic and add that to the provider
      this.provider.addTopic("RebootNotificationMessage",new
                    QName("http://com.ph.sample/cmm/OperatingSystem",
                    "RebootNotifDataType"));
    } catch (Exception e) {
      throw new GridServiceException(e);
    }
  }

  public void reboot() throws RemoteException {
    // do reboot and inform our listeners
    try {
      this.provider.notify(
        " RebootNotificationMessage", new RebootNotifDataType ("The
                    system rebooted") );
    } catch (Exception e) {
    }
  }
  ..........................
}
```

Enable Service Data to Send Notification on State Change

The service data set is associated with a service instance, and it provides mechanisms to register listeners to receive notifications on service data changes. Regarding a service data change, the service data wrapper sends a change notification message to the service data set, and it will then evaluate the change and send the message to the interested parties.

As shown in the above sequence diagram, the listener can evaluate the change with the topic created during subscription. If the change is valid for the constraints expressed in the topic, then a separate thread is created to deliver the change message.

The process we have just described and shown is a simple notification mechanism on service data change. We can envision and program this to complex situations, including service stage changes, dynamic notification topics, and so forth.

Another value-added enhancement may be the support for a broker, and how it can reside between the grid service clients and the service instance, as shown in Figure 12.12. This enables a more flexible model with different transport bindings and notification mechanisms (e.g., pub-sub/topic, and so forth).

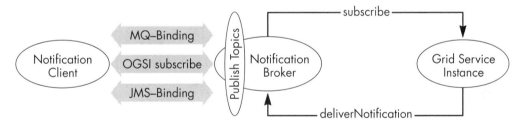

Figure 12.12
The notification broker.

Client Programming Model

We discussed in the architecture chapter that the OGSI, and in turn the GT3, do not dictate any specific programming models for the client. The client is based on the JAX-RPC programming model. By default, it provides Apache AXIS client-side framework, tools, and runtime. GT3 provides a set of helper classes to deal with the concepts surrounding GSHs, its resolution to GSR, and GSR introspection without client involvement. GT3, in fact, provides a number of tools to deal with these extensions and add grid service behaviors to the normal JAX-RPC stubs. We will discuss the details on these tools later in this chapter.

Figure 12.13 shows the extension to the JAX-RPC programming model through the service locator construct.

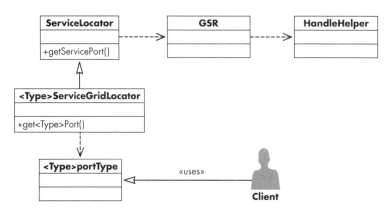

Figure 12.13
Grid service client helper class and usage.

The basic client-side invocation pattern is:

- A client accesses the GSH to a service from a registry, or some other out-of-band mechanisms.
- The client passes this handle to the service grid locator, that in turn talks to the handle resolution service to dereference the GSH to a service GSR. The resolution process constructs and associates the instance address with the necessary stub. The proxy, so generated, exposes the JAX-RPC style interface to the service.
- The client calls service methods on that proxy using the normal JAX-RPC invocation model.

Let us now spend some time understanding aspects of the client-side programming models provided by JAX-RPC. We can always write GT3 clients that can support the entire JAX-RPC programming model invocations.

Based on JAX-RPC specifications, there are three different models for invoking a service endpoint from a client, as shown in Figure 12.14.

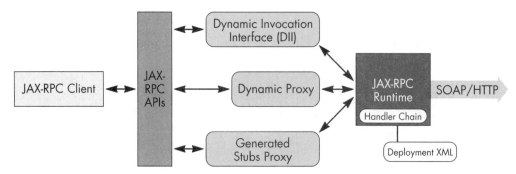

Figure 12.14
JAX-RPC client-side programming models.

These client-side programming models are independent of any specific service implementation or endpoint model, however, provide well-defined interfaces for the users. We will explore the details of each in the following discussion.

Stub-Based Model (Static Stubs)

These static stub classes are created either from the WSDL or from a service endpoint interface. A generated stub class is required to implement both Javax.xml.rpc.stub and the service endpoint interface. This stub interface provides APIs to configure stubs by setting properties such as endpoint address, typemapping, session, user name, password, and so on.

Dynamic Proxies

In contrast to the static stubs discussed above, the client at runtime creates these dynamic proxy stubs using the Javax.xml.rpc.Service interface. The client has *a priori* knowledge of the WSDL and the service it is going to invoke. It uses the Servicefactory classes to create the service and get the proxy.

DII (Dynamic Invocation Interface)

This software pattern eliminates the need for clients to know in advance a service's exact name, operations, and parameters. A DII client can discover this information at runtime using a service broker that can look up the service description (WSDL).

GT3 Tools

Transformation Tools

We know from our earlier discussion that grid services are stateful Web services and are hosted in a Web service hosting environment. For example, GT3 is deployed to the Apache AXIS Web service container environment. This necessitates the need to convert some of the grid-specific extensions to Web service operateable entities. Most notable of this transformation is the transformation of multiple interface inheritance in OGSI grid service to a single interface Web service model. This requires tooling to do the transformation from OGSI-defined GWSDL to WSDL 1.1.

GWSDL2WSDL. This is an interesting tool that requires a detailed discussion. In the previous section, we have discussed the GWSDL namespace and how OGSI supported the open portType extensions and portType inheritance model using the GWSDL portType. OGSI allows multiple portType inheritance and open content model for portTypes. This flexibility is not available with WSDL 1.1 and hence developers can use the new GWSDL namespace and GWSDL portType provided by OGSI specification to create this multiple inheritance and portType extensibility model. Once WSDL 1.2 becomes standard, frameworks and tools will support this feature. However, in order to support the current WSDL1.1 tools and framework, OGSI GWSDL portTypes are con-

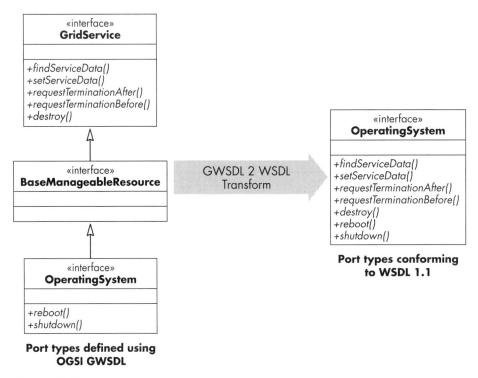

Figure 12.15
Transformation of OGSI GWSDL to WSDL 1.1 using the GWSDL2WSDL tool.

verted to the WSDL 1.1 based single portType model. This tool is used to transform GWSDL port-Type definitions to the corresponding WSDL 1.1 definition.

Figure 12.15 illustrates how a GWSDL with the "OperatingSystem" portType has an inheritance hierarchy is converted to a WSDL 1.1 "OperatingSystem" portType model single interface using the GWSDL2JAVA tool.

As developers and senior technical leaders, we should be aware of the important aspects about this conversion:

1. A new WSDL port type is constructed containing the same operations as the GWSDL port type, as well as all operations from the extended port types.
2. All operations messages are qualified with the namespace definitions as defined origi-nally and hence no operation overloading is allowed.
3. The name of the new WSDL portType is the same as the name of the old GWSDL port-Type.
4. The newly generated WSDL keeps the old GWSDL portType as a WSDL extensibility element, but does not contain any operations—only service data.

Service and Client-Side artifacts

In order to avoid client-side and server-side developers from dealing with the complexity marshalling and demarshalling of parameter types, creation of artifacts to deal with the Web service messaging (SOAP) and support to the programming models (JAX-RPC) tools are required. These tools are used to create stubs/proxies, language artifacts, type-mapping, deployment information, and helper classes. Below are some of the commonly used GT3 tools.

- **GenerateBinding**. A WSDL file can be divided into an abstract portType representation, and a valid binding representation. Normally speaking, clients do not need to be concerned with the valid binding generation. GT3 provides this tool to generate the necessary binding information for a given portType.

The default values used by this tool are "http" for transport binding protocol, "document" for SOAP message style, and "literal" for message encoding. This flexibility helps the clients concentrate on the design of the portType definitions and then use this tool to generate the necessary bindings.

Sample usage:

```
GenerateBinding <filename>.wsdl, where the input file contains the portType
declaration.
```

This will generate <filename>_service.wsdl and <filename>_binding.wsdl, respectively.

- **GSDL2Java**. This is a special case implementation of the WSDL2Java tool provided by AXIS, which is used by the clients to generate the stubs, bindings, service interfaces, server-side service implementation skeletons, and client locator classes. We can use this tool against a WSDL file, which contains the <wsdl:service> element declaration to achieve a top-down design model.

Sample usage:

```
GSDL2Java service.wsdl
```

- **ServiceDataDoclet**. This is running *javadoc* on the Java service implementation code with GT3-provided "doclet" callback class "org.globus.ogsa.utils.ServiceDataDoclet." This results in the creation of ServiceDataAnnotation class for each service data element defined in the service file. Finally, all these generated ServiceDataAnnotation classes will be dumped into a file with <className>"-sdAnnotation."

Usage:

```
Javadoc <org.globus.ogsa.utils.ServiceDataDoclet> <service implementation
Java file>
```

- **GenerateSDD**. This utility tool reads the above generated service class file with SD annotations and collects all the service data elements in the file stored as

ServiceDataAnnotation list and then adds those service data elements to the specified WSDL.

Sample usage:

```
GenerateSDD <wsdl definition file> <class name with service data annotations>
```

GT3 Configuration

GT3 uses AXIS WSDD to configure

- the services and its parameters
- JAX-RPC and AXIS handlers and the parameters needed for the handlers
- Request and response flow with the handlers
- Global parameters for AXIS engine and the GT3 container

Listing 12.23 shows such a deployment configuration file with one service in it. We will use this listing for our discussion of the server-side deployment configuration.

Listing 12.23   A sample server-config.wsdd.

```
<deployment ....>
<globalConfiguration>
    <parameter name="adminPassword" value="admin"/>
    <parameter name="sendMultiRefs" value="true"/>
           ...........................................
    <requestFlow>
        <handler type="URLMapper"/>
        <handler type="PersistentServiceHandler"/>
           ...........................................
    <requestFlow>

    <responseFlow>
        <handler type="RoutingResponseHandler"/>
           ...........................................
    </responseFlow>
</globalConfiguration>
<transport name="http">
    <requestFlow>
        <handler type="URLMapper"/>
    <requestFlow>
    <responseFlow>
           ...........................................
    </responseFlow>
</transport>

<service name="ogsa/cmm/OperatingSystemService" provider="Handler"
            style="wrapped" use="literal">
```

Listing 12.23 A sample server-config.wsdd. (Continued)

```
    <!- service factory name- ->
    <parameter name="name" value="Operating system Provider factory"/>

    <!- service instance specific information - ->
    <parameter name="instance-name" value=" Operating system Service"/>
    <parameter name="instance-schemaPath" value=
                    "schema/core/cmm/operatingsystem_service.wsdl"/>
    <parameter name="instance-className" value=
                    "org.ogsa.core.cmm.OperatingSystemPortType"/>
    <parameter name="instance-baseClassName" value=
                    "org.ogsa.core.cmm.impl.OperatingSystemImpl "/>
    <parameter name="instance-operationProviders" value=
                    "org.ogsa.core.cmm.impl.OperatingSystemProvider"/>

    <!- service factory specific information - ->
    <parameter name="schemaPath" value="schema/ogsi/
                    ogsi_notification_factory_service.wsdl"/>
    <parameter name="baseClassName"
            value="org.globus.ogsa.impl.ogsi.PersistentGridServiceImpl"/>
    <parameter name="handlerClass"
            value="org.globus.ogsa.handlers.RPCURIProvider"/>
    <parameter name="className"
            value="org.gridforum.ogsi.Notificationfactory"/>
    <parameter name="allowedMethods" value="*"/>

    <parameter name="factoryCallback"
            value="org.globus.ogsa.impl.ogsi.DynamicfactoryCallbackImpl"/>
    <parameter name="operationProviders"
            value="org.globus.ogsa.impl.ogsi.factoryProvider
            org.globus.ogsa.impl.ogsi.NotificationSourceProvider"/>

    <!-This service is a Grid service - ->
    <parameter name="persistent" value="true"/>
    <parameter name="allowedMethods" value="*"/>
  </service>
  </deployment>
```

We will examine the service-specific configuration requirements. Upon careful examination of Listing 12.23, we can see that the service has a unique service name (remotely accessible name of the service) using a "wrapped" message style and the provider is a handler. This enables the AXIS machine to dispatch the calls to the GT3-provided container and instantiate the service inside the GT3 container.

Let us now see the specific parameters utilized for the grid service. Note that we may find an Axis Web service along with grid services in a container. We can easily identify grid services if they have a parameter "persistent" with a value of "true." We must be aware of this important distinction. Table 12.2 lists all the parameters of interest for grid services. To help us understand better, note that the parameters starting with instance are specific to the service instance while others may be for a factory or other providers.

Table 12.2 Deployment and Configuration Parameters

Parameter	Description
className	This class specifies a class or an interface that has public methods corresponding to all operations in the WSDL. This interface/class must expose all the operations exposed by the service and providers.
persistent	If this attribute value is true, it represents a GRID service. Otherwise, a normal Web service using Apache Axis.
baseClassName	The name of the class that implements the service. If this is the same as the className parameter, this is optional.
operationproviders	The list of classes to be loaded along with the service. Note that order indicates the initialization order.
handlerClass	This handler specifies the dispatcher to use at the server side. AXIS engine dispatches the call to this dispatcher (pivot handler).
schemaPath	The WSDL of the service identified by className.
factoryCallback	The factory callback class used to create a service.
instance-name	This identifies the name of the service instance to be created.
instance-schemaPath	This indicates the service instance WSDL.
instance-className	This indicates the service instance class name.
instance-baseClassName	This indicates the service instance base class name.
instance-Operationproviders	Lists the service instance–specific operation providers.

In addition to the above configuration parameters, there are other service-specific and global configurations, such as static type-mapping, query engine/evaluator, lifecycle, and container-specific configurations, which act upon host name, port name, and mapping.

GT3-Provided Default Implementation Classes

GT3 provides a number of built-in classes to provide some default functionality, which helps the service and client developer to hide the complexity of a grid service programming model. We have already covered most of these classes in the earlier sections. In Table 12.3, we list some of these classes for quick reference.

Table 12.3 GT3-Provided Default Implementation Classes

Class Name	Description	Used By (Service/Client) Developer
`GridServiceBaseImpl,` `PersistentGridServiceImpl`	Provides the basic grid service behaviors and lifecycle management functionalities. Grid service can be implemented by deriving from these classes.	Service
`factoryProvider,` `DynamicfactoryCallbackImpl,` `DynamicfactoryLifecycleCallbackImpl`	This factory provider is an operation provider and these classes together provide a service instance creation framework.	Service
`HandleResolverProvider`	Default handle resolution service operation provider. By default it supports http and https protocols.	Service
`NotificationSourceProvider,` `NotificationSubscriptionImpl`	These classes together provide the support for a service notification framework. This framework enables a topic whereby a service can support different topics. By default all service supports notification on "service data name."	Service
`<portTypeName>ServiceGridLocator`	A client-side helper class that provides the JAX-RPC programming model but hides the details of grid execution workflow including handle resolution, GSR validation, and stub address management through GSR location address. In addition, supports the normal Web service calls.	Client

We will see the utilization of these default classes in the next chapter.

Significance of Message Handlers in GT3

Message handlers provide additional message-handling facilities to the Web/grid service endpoints (both client and server) as extensions to the basic service implementation logic. As we have seen in the architecture section, these handlers can manage encryption and decryption, logging and auditing, and so on. By now we are already familiar with this powerful feature and its use with GT3.

There are two types of handlers supported in AXIS, JAX-RPC handlers and the default AXIS handlers. The JAX-RPC handlers are based on the JAX-RPC specification whereas the AXIS handlers are native to AXIS framework. On runtime, AXIS wraps these JAX-RPC handlers using an AXIS standard handler (JAXRPCHandler). Being the core implementation part of the system, we can spend some time analyzing these handlers and their usage patterns.

JAX-RPC Handlers

The current JAX-RPC runtime system defines only SOAP message handlers. The JAX-RPC runtime system can flexibly define other handlers and is free from any processing model of the messages.

The JAX-RPC Handlers API defines three basic methods, along with two lifecycle methods, as shown in Listing 12.24.

Listing 12.24   *JAX-RPC handler methods.*

```
package Javax.xml.rpc.handler;
public class Handler{
        handleRequest(MessageContext context);
        handleResponse(MessageContext context);
        handleFaults(MessageContext context);

        init(HandlerInfo info);
        destroy();
        // return the headers processed by this handler
        QName[] getHeaders();
}
```

The handler invocation pattern is shown in Figure 12.16. A handler should be implemented as a stateless instance. By providing the initialization interface (Handler.init [HandlerInfo info]), the runtime system can pass the required context information to the handler. This will help a handler obtain access to container-specific value-added features, including authentication mechanisms, transaction processing, logging framework, and so on.

A handler chain represents an ordered list of handlers. This grouping helps to define policies that we want to associate with the handler invocation model. Examples of such policies include order of invocation, style of invocation (for example, one-way call invokes only handleRequest(); no handleResponse()), and so on.

This association can be configured to the handler through the Handler.init() method passing a HandlerInfo object. The handler chain continues processing the handlers only if the current processing handler returns "true." Listing 12.25 shows a sample implementation of a handler that can access a SOAP message header.

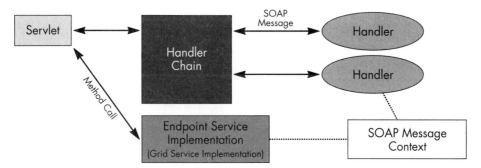

Figure 12.16
Service and handler invocation model.

Listing 12.25   Sample handler implementation.

```
Public class WSSecurityHandler extends GenericHandler{
    Public Boolean handleRequest(MessageContext ctx){
        try{
            SOAPMessageContext mc = (SOAPMessageContext)ctx;
            SOAPMessage msg = mc.getMessage();
            SOAPPart sp = msg.getSOAPPart();
            SOAPEnvelop se = sp.getEnvelop();
            SOAPHeader header= se.getHeader();

            // Now we can process the header
            Document doc = WSSecurityRequestEngine.getEngine().
                              processSecurityHeader(se, ctx);
            if (security validation is fine )
                    return true;
                    //continue processing
            else{
                    //Return false results in chaining to stop
                    return false;
            }
        }catch(Exception ex){
        }
    }
    .....................
}
```

As shown in Listing 12.25, this is a simple handler implementation to validate WS-Security headers. The GenericHandler is a JAX-RPC-provided default "Handler" implementation class. It is recommended to use JAX-RPC handlers wherever possible for interoperability purposes. These are J2EE/J2SE standard based and, hence, can be ported to any environment.

AXIS Handlers

Before JSR 101, the AXIS decided to establish a standard for SOAP message processing, resulting in the generation of widely accepted AXIS handlers. This is different from JAX-RPC handlers. The most commonly used interface method is the "invoke." See Listing 12.26.

Listing 12.26   Handler methods.

```
package org.apache.axis ;
public class Handler{
    public void invoke(MessageContext msgContext) throws AxisFault ;
    public void onFault(MessageContext msgContext);
    public boolean canHandleBlock(QName qname);
    public void init();
......................
}
```

As shown in the code in Listing 12.26, the JAX-RPC handlers API defines three basic methods, along with two lifecycle methods.

The code in Listing 12.27 explains a sample implementation of a handler that can access a SOAP message header.

Listing 12.27   Sample AXIS handler implementation.

```
public class HandleResolverHandler extends BasicHandler {

    public void invoke(MessageContext messageContext) throws AxisFault {
        try {
            String target = (String) messageContext.getTargetService();
        ................................

        }catch (Exception e) {
            throw AxisFault.makeFault(e);
        }
    }
    public void onFault(){
    // to do a fault processing
    }
}
```

We have already noticed that one of the main differences between the AXIS handler and the JAX-RPC handler is the return value. In JAX-RPC a value of true or false indicates the continuation of the execution process. A value of "false" will stop the handler chain execution process. In the case of AXIS handler an exception must be thrown to stop the processing. All the handlers that previously processed this specific message get a chance to do some fault processing using an "onFault" operation. This feature is not mandated in the JAX-RPC handlers.

GT3 Security Implementation and Programming Model

In the previous architecture section, we did mention the available security mechanism in GT3, which are transport-level GSI security and message-level security. We also mentioned that the transport level security would be depreciated in the coming Globus toolkit releases in favor of message-level security. The GT3 message-level security is based on WS-Security and associated standards (WS-SecureConversation, WS-Trust, and so forth). Our discussion would concentrate around the message-level security part of the GT3. This discussion includes the details on security architecture, the programming aspects, and deployment/configuration requirements.

The message-level security is based on WS-Security, XML Encryption, and XML Signature standards. We did cover these topics earlier in the book when we talked about Web services and global XML architecture. The GT3 framework provides two different message-level authentication mechanisms:

- GSI Secure Conversation. In this protocol, at first, a secure context is established between the client and the service. On the subsequent calls to the service this context is used to sign/verify/encrypt/decrypt the messages. Figure 12.17 illustrates a high-level view of this secure conversation.

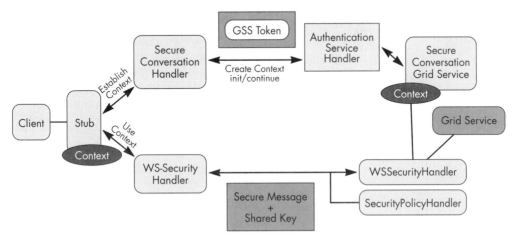

Figure 12.17
GSI secure conversation.

- GSI XML Signature. This process is simple, where a message is signed with a given set of credentials.

GT3 Security Handlers

In GT3 the security is handled by using a number of AXIS and JAX-RPC handlers. Figure 12.17 shows the message flow and the available handlers (some of them). The figure depicts a secure conversation establishment between the client and server. This needs an exchange of tokens to establish a context. Once the context is established, that context token is used to secure the message. GT3 provides services to establish the token, and revalidate the token in case of expiry. We will discuss internal details on the secure context establishment process later in this section.

Now, let us do a quick overview on some of the most commonly used handlers to secure the message exchange in GT3 using Table 12.4.

Table 12.4 Common Server-Side Handlers

GT3 Security Handlers	Request/ Response	Description
AuthenticationServiceHandler	Request	Responsible for mapping incoming GSI Secure Conversation requests to authentication service.
WSSecurityHandler	Request/ Response	Responsible for processing WS-Security Header elements in a SOAP message. These messages are delegated to a WS-SecurityEngine for XML signature handling and XML encryption/decryption.
SecurityPolicyHandler	Request	This handler in turn loads and executes two other handlers, AuthHandler and RunAsHandler. AuthHandler is responsible for checking whether the invocation of a method on a service is allowed or not. If the service is available, it needs to be activated to get the method-level security info. RunAsHandler is used to set the subject for invocation of the method. This enables service of a method to specify the identity required to run. These identities are Caller, System, or Service level.
AuthorizationHandler	Request	The above handlers set the subject for method invocation. This handler is trying to authorize the subject based on the service authorization needs. Service specifies this through configuration (we will discuss details later). This can be none, self, or gridmap.
X509SignHandler	Response	If signature is requested for the response message, this handler is used. This handler uses a JAAS lookup to get the credential of the call originator. This originator may be different from the thread-level subject. Used with GSI XML signature.
GSSHandler	Response	In a GSI secure conversation, the return message is protected either by XML signature or XML encryption.

The handlers described in Table 12.4 are the most commonly used handlers. One thing we must pay close attention to is the processing sequence of these handlers. So we must be careful of their order in the configuration file. Another important aspect we must be aware of is the type of handler. There are two types of handlers available, JAX-RPC and AXIS. The difference is mainly on the signature and parameters processing. Listing 12.28 describes the handler flow.

Listing 12.28   Security handler configuration in the service side.

```
<globalConfiguration>
<parameter name="authenticationService" value="gsi/AuthenticationService"/>
<requestFlow>
.......................
<handler type=
"Java:org.globus.ogsa.impl.security.authentication.service
                                          .AuthenticationServiceHandler"/>
<handler type="Java:org.globus.ogsa.handlers.RoutingSecRequestHandler"/>

<handler type="Java:org.globus.ogsa.utils.JAXRPCHandler">
        <parameter name="className"
        value="org.globus.ogsa.impl.security.authentication.wssec
        .WSSecurityHandler"/>
</handler>

<handler type="Java:org.globus.ogsa.impl.security.authentication
                                          .SecurityPolicyHandler"/>
<handler type="Java:org.globus.ogsa.impl.security.authorization
                                          .AuthorizationHandler"/>
<handler type="Java:org.globus.ogsa.impl.security.authentication
                                          .CredentialRefreshHandler"/>
    ..............................
</requestFlow>

<responseFlow>
..............................
<handler type="Java:org.globus.ogsa.utils.JAXRPCHandler">
  <parameter name="className"
    value="org.globus.ogsa.impl.security.authentication.X509SignHandler"/>
</handler>
<handler type="Java:org.globus.ogsa.utils.JAXRPCHandler">
  <parameter name="className"
    value="org.globus.ogsa.impl.security.authentication.GSSHandler"/>
</handler>
</responseFlow>
</globalConfiguration>
```

Listing 12.28 Security handler configuration in the service side. (Continued)

```
<service name="gsi/AuthenticationService" provider="Handler"
                                    style="wrapped" use="literal">
<parameter name="baseClassName"
value="org.globus.ogsa.impl.security.authentication.service
                                    .AuthenticationServiceImpl"/>
.................................
</service>
```

Secure Authentication Service

This grid service (AuthenticationService) is used to establish a security context. This service is configured in the configuration section, as shown in Listing 12.28.

If the authentication service handler is present in the request handler chain, and the service call is targeted toward a secure authentication (i.e., the target endpoint ends with "/authService"), then the calls will be directed to this "AuthenticationService" for creating or refreshing the secure context.

This "AuthenticationServiceImpl" class is responsible for secure context establishment and implements "continueTokenExchange" and "initTokenExchange" methods. We will see the internal implementation of this call later in the section.

Configuring Service-Specific Secure Authentication and Authorization Information

A service can specify its authentication and authorization requirements through an external configuration file. A service informs the framework about this configuration file through its configuration property in the WSDD file. This is shown in Listing 12.29. The sample specifies a "self" authorization process and provides an XML file for security configuration.

Listing 12.29 Configuring a service with security information.

```
<service name="ogsa/cmm/OperatingSystemService" provider="Handler"
style="wrapped">
    .................................
  <parameter name="securityConfig" value=" ogsa/cmm/impl/security-
      config.xml"/>
  <parameter name="authorization" value="self"/>
    .................................
</service>
```

We can now explore the details of the security configurations, as specified through the security-config.xml file. A sample configuration discussing a secure service is in Listing 12.30.

Listing 12.30 GT3 security mapping file.

```
<securityConfig xmlns="http://www.globus.org">
 <method name="cmm:reboot"
         xmlns:cmm="http://ogsa.org/cmm/operatingsystem">
   <run-as>
     <caller-identity/>
   </run-as>
   <auth-method>
    <gsi/>
   </auth-method>
 </method>

 <!-- defaults -->
 <auth-method>
  <none/>
 </auth-method>

</securityConfig>
```

The authorization information in the configuration file enables a service to specify method-level authorization and code execution policy (run-as identity). For example, this enables the operating system service to specify the reboot operation to run under the caller's identity and use a GSI authorization mechanism. This provides fine-grained control over method execution. In addition, it enables a service to specify the authentication mode of choice from the list of "none," "gsi," and "self."

We can now move on to the commonly defined client-side security handlers listed in Table 12.5.

Table 12.5 Client-Side Security Handlers

GT3 Security Handlers	Request/ Response	Description
X509SignHandler	Request	If signature is requested for the request message, this handler is used. This is used with GSI XML signature.
SecContextHandler	Request	This is the core security handler responsible for establishing the security context. Once the context is established, it will be associated with the stub.
GSSHandler	Request	In a GSI secure conversation, the request message is protected either by XML signature or XML encryption using the context established using SecContextHandler.
WSSecurityClientHandler	Response	Responsible for handling the response from the service either with GSI XML signature or secure conversation messages.

The handlers, as shown in Table 12.5, are the most commonly used for the client-side security enabling mechanisms. The processing sequence of these handlers is very important. So, we must be careful of their order in the configuration file. Listing 12.31 shows the usage.

Listing 12.31   Client-side security configuration.

```
<globalConfiguration>
<requestFlow>
        ............................................
  <handler type="Java:org.globus.ogsa.utils.JAXRPCHandler">
    <parameter name="className"
              value="org.globus.ogsa.impl.security.authentication
                    .X509SignHandler"/>
  </handler>
  <handler type="Java:org.globus.ogsa.utils.JAXRPCHandler">
    <parameter name="className"
              value="org.globus.ogsa.impl.security.authentication
                    .SecContextHandler"/>
    <parameter name="authService" value="auto"/>
  </handler>
  <handler type="Java:org.globus.ogsa.utils.JAXRPCHandler">
    <parameter name="className"
              value="org.globus.ogsa.impl.security.authentication
                    .GSSHandler"/>
  </handler>
</requestFlow>

<responseFlow>
        ....................................
    <handler type="Java:org.globus.ogsa.utils.JAXRPCHandler">
      <parameter name="className"
              value="org.globus.ogsa.impl.security.authentication.wssec
                    .WSSecurityClientHandler"/>
    </handler>
  </responseFlow>
</globalConfiguration>
```

Client-Side Programming Model to Enable Security

The following GSI properties can be set on the client stub to control the authentication/authorization process:

- The credential to use
  It is used to pass a specific set of credentials for authentication. User can specify a credential of type *"org.ietf.jgss.GSSCredential"* instance. By default, if not specified, the default user proxy credential is used.

- Authorization mechanism to use

  It is used to set authorization type to perform. There are different authorizations available: SelfAuthorization, HostAuthorization, BasicSubjectAuthorization and so on. By default, if not specified, host authorization is performed.

- GSI delegation mode

  This delegation mode can be one of:

  o GSIConstants.GSI_MODE_NO_DELEG—performs no delegation (default)

  o GSIConstants.GSI_MODE_LIMITED_DELEG—performs limited delegation

  o GSIConstants.GSI_MODE_FULL_DELEG—performs full delegation

  o These constants are used for GSI Secure Conversation or transport security only. It is used to set GSI delegation mode.

Here is a sample client-side code snippet that illustrates the usage pattern of these properties:

```
OGSIServiceGridLocator factoryService = new OGSIServiceGridLocator();
  factory factory = factoryService.getfactoryPort(new HandleType(handle));

  // enable GSI Secure Conversation message level security
  ((Stub)factory)._setProperty(Constants.GSI_SEC_CONV, Constants.SIGNATURE);
  // enable limited delegation
  ((Stub)factory)._setProperty(GSIConstants.GSI_MODE,GSIConstants.GSI_MODE
    _LIMITED_DELEG);
  // set client authorization to none
  ((Stub)factory)._setProperty(Constants.AUTHORIZATION,
NoAuthorization.getInstance());
```

The handlers described in Table 12.5 will kick off the security enabling process. It provides message level security through message signatures and encryption without user involvement.

Internal Security Design Workflow Details

Secure Context Establishment

GT3 provides a plug-and-play mechanism for secure context establishment process. It defines Secure Authentication service, which implements SecureContextEstablishmentPortType. This service is a stateless Grid service, which in turn talks to other security managers to get hold of a secure token for that service.

In the client-side, a secure context is established for each instance of the stub the client is using to communicate with the service. These stubs in turn use "SecContextHandler" handler (defined in client-config.wsdd) to create and hold the context information. Since the context is established for the user associated with the current thread, it is illegal to use the same stubs from other thread. This context is negotiated each time there is a change in the GSI mode. The allowable modes include:

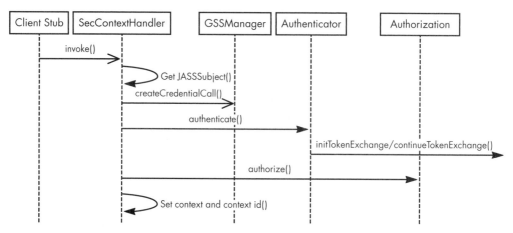

Figure 12.18
Client-side secure conversation establishment.

- Full delegation
- Limited delegation
- No delegation

This secure context is established by communicating to the Secure Authentication Service deployed in the server. For this the client has to get the current JAAS subject and credential. For GSI, the client contacts the GSS Manager to get the context by calling manager.createCredentialCall(...) using the subject and context. Then the client calls the authentication service's "initTokenExchange" or "continueTokenExchange" method depending on whether the call is first time or not.

This operation is a normal SOAP call through an SSL. The authentication service returns a context ID and a binary token. The client runs this authentication process till they get the context. Once the client gets the context, it is attached with the current stub.

WS-Security Handling

The above secure negotiation creates a secure token and the WS-Security handler uses this token to sign the message and encrypt the message. This token is passed along with the SOAP message header. Work is going on to define a standard security profile for this GSI token exchange through WS-Security header.

Service Message Exchange Logging

Based upon our experiences, we find that the most valuable information we need to collect during message interaction between a client and a service is the real messages exchanged between them. This is valuable during development of services. The current default GT3 configuration enables SOAP message exchange over HTTP. This message helps us understand the target service, the operations to be invoked, and the message exchanged. We can do a number of debugging and compatibility tests with these messages. For example, if we can collect a SOAP message from a client to a service, we can do a WS-I basic profile validation on the collected message to check for compatibility with other implementers. In fact, WS-I basic profile tools are working in a similar fashion, as we can see in the TCPMon case below.

There are three mechanisms we can do to enable this message capture:

1. Using GT3-provided MessageHandler in both client and service side. This is the simplest process by putting a global handler on the client and server side. Listing 12.32 below shows how we can perform this in our server-config.wsdd and client-config.wsdd files.

Here is how we account for that in server-config.wsdd:

Listing 12.32 MessagingLoggingHandler configuration.

```
<requestFlow>
    <handler type="Java:org.globus.ogsa.handlers.MessageLoggingHandler"/>
    ......................
</requestFlow>

<responseFlow>
    <handler type="Java:org.globus.ogsa.handlers.MessageLoggingHandler"/>
    ......................
</responseFlow>
```

Note that the message displayed by this handler is dependent on their position in the configuration handler list. This is because some handler may modify the message. Since handlers are using Apache common logging mechanisms for message logging, we must configure that to display the messages correctly.

Listing 12.33 shows a sample message displayed by the above setting.

Listing 12.33 A sample SOAP message.

```
[7/22/03 13:40:50:649 EDT]  f9f2b20 MessageLoggin I
org.globus.ogsa.handlers.MessageLoggingHandler  SOAPEnvelope:
<soapenv:Envelope xmlns:soapenv="http://schemas.xmlsoap.org/soap/envelope/"
xmlns:xsd="http://www.w3.org/2001/XMLSchema" xmlns:xsi="http://www.w3.org/
2001/XMLSchema-instance">
 <soapenv:Body>
  <createService xmlns="http://www.gridforum.org/namespaces/2003/03/OGSI">
   <terminationTime ns1:before="infinity" ns1:after="infinity"
xmlns:ns1="http://www.gridforum.org/namespaces/2003/03/OGSI"/>
   <creationParameters xsi:nil="true"/>
```

Listing 12.33   A sample SOAP message. (Continued)

```
  </createService>
 </soapenv:Body>
</soapenv:Envelope>
```

2. Using the TCPMon utility with some configuration changes. Using the TCPMon utility, we can relay all the messages through a TCP port. Start the tcpmon using

```
Java org.apache.axis.utils.tcpmon [listenPort targetHost targetPort]
```

This will help us display most of the messages flowing through the wire. For complex situations we may need to do more work on the server configuration to get all the messages. This is because the server is modifying the dynamic soap address for the GSR using the information available with it. This is normal in the case of handle resolution. In such situations the client's call using the above soap address may not be directed to the tcpmon's port unless we change some configurations in the server. This includes changing "httpPort" and "schemaRoot" properties. In some cases (distributed machines) we may need to change the server host name too. Listing 12.34 indicates how to change the default port number to be displayed in the GSR soap address (and instance of elements).

Listing 12.34   A sample configuration for setting internal service port numbers.

```
<globalConfiguration>
    <!-- to change the port number -->
    <parameter name="httpPort" value="8080"/>

    <!-- to change the WSDL retrieval schema root  -->
    <parameter name="schemaRoot" value="http://localhost:8080/ogsa/"/>
    ...........................................
</globalConfiguration>
```

3. Using the Apache AXIS logging feature. This enables us to configure the select Apache AXIS classes for message logging. The properties (ogsilogging.properties) needed to set are shown in Listing 12.35.

Listing 12.35   Configuring message log for Apache AXIS messages.

```
org.apache.client.Call=console,debug
  org.apache.axis.transport.http.HTTPSender=console,debug
```

Other Important Elements in GT3

Before we conclude our discussion on the programming model aspects of GT3 grid service, there are some concepts needing special discussion. These concepts include:

- Message encoding
- Type-mapping and serialization support

Let's examine these concepts in more detail.

Message Style and Encoding

We know that there are two SOAP message styles, *document* and *rpc,* which define how a SOAP message body is formatted. In addition, there are two modes to encode an operation's parameters, *literal* and *encoded.*

SOAP Message Encoding

- Message encoding. This encoding is based on SOAP graph encoding, as described in the SOAP specification.
- Literal encoding. This SOAP encoding is using XML schema for message description.

SOAP Message Style

RPC. This is based on "rpc"-style message formatting where operation name and signatures are defined correctly in XML and embedded in the SOAP body. The process is complicated, as each body element must map to the parameter of the operation.

Document. In this case, the operation name maps to a document, and the SOAP body contains that document with the operation name as the first element. In most of the implementations (AXIS and .NET) this encoding is actually resulting in "wrapped"-style messaging. In AXIS, we can see this configuration for each service in the server-config.wsdd and the generated SOAP stubs.

To conclude, readers must note that the WS-I organization is encouraging the use of document/literal messaging and deprecating the other encoding formats. As we can see, GT3 also encourages the use of the document/literal approach. The bottom line is, unless we have strong reasons in favor of other kinds of encoding, we should use the document/literal approach.

Type-Mapping and Serialization

The type mapping and serialization/deserialization process involves

- Creating native language types from XML schema elements. The AXIS-provided WSDL2Java can convert the XSD types defined in the WSDLs to its corresponding Java types.
- Mapping the XML messages fragments to native language type created in the previous process and vice versa. This mapping process needs the conversion guidelines to be defined by the client-side stub or the service container. The client-side process is simple based on the fact that these types are created and registered with the stubs. The framework can handle this conversion on runtime during SOAP message parsing. There

we may need to register this type-mapping information with the configuration files. Listing 12.36 shows how we can register type-mapping information statically in a container. There are dynamic AXIS APIs available to set the type-mapping on runtime.

Listing 12.36 A sample type-mapping configuration.

```
<typeMapping
      xmlns:ns="http://www.gridforum.org/namespaces/2003/03/OGSI"
      qname="ns:handleSet"
      type="Java:org.gridforum.ogsi.LocatorType"
      serializer="org.apache.axis.encoding.ser.BeanSerializerfactory"
      deserializer="org.apache.axis.encoding.ser.BeanDeserializerfactory"
      encodingStyle="" />
```

GT3 handles XML types using generic XML Infoset type for the cases where these type-mappings are not available.

- Deserializing the native language types to XML fragments.

SUMMARY

In this chapter, we have covered much of the programming model information related to the Globus GT3 software. This discussion was aimed at providing an introduction into the basic components present in the framework, how they are working together, the GT3-provided helper classes, and some basic information on the inner working details of these components. In the next chapter, we will develop a sample application using this programming model.

GLOBUS GT3 Toolkit: A Sample Implementation

I n this chapter, we explore a sample Globus GT3 implementation. This sample will introduce the concepts we have discussed in the previous two chapters, in terms of a Grid Computing implementation. In order to better understand this, familiarity with the basic concepts of Web services is a must. This includes understanding the concepts of the basic structure of SOAP messages, the JAX-RPC programming model,[1] and Apache AXIS runtime.[2]

This sample discussion will discuss most of the programming aspects of grid services, which we can also find in the Globus GT3 toolkit. Should one desire to implement this sample as we are describing it, we are assuming that GT3 is correctly installed on the development machine (e.g., http://localhost:9080)[3] as a Web application with a root name of "ogsa." Before we begin working, we have to ensure that GT3 samples are properly working in the machine. This is because we are not including any service deployment and installation information in this chapter. Our intension is to introduce the concepts of GT3, from the point of view of the service developers and clients.

This is a sample that is intended to be simple in nature. The sample is that of a search engine implemented as multiple grid services. Figure 13.1 shows this sample.

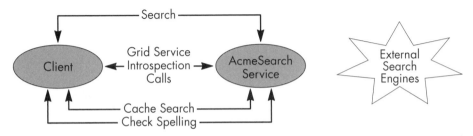

Figure 13.1
The Acme Search Engine service utilized as the sample in this chapter.

It is important to understand that, although simple, this is a real functional sample; however, this sample is very primitive for purposes of understanding. This is, however, a powerful and extensible sample service implementation to explain the programming details on GT3. One may want to think about extending this sample to a real search engine, or delegate this to an existing search engine.

The UML diagram in Figure 13.2 shows the interface hierarchy of this service implementation.

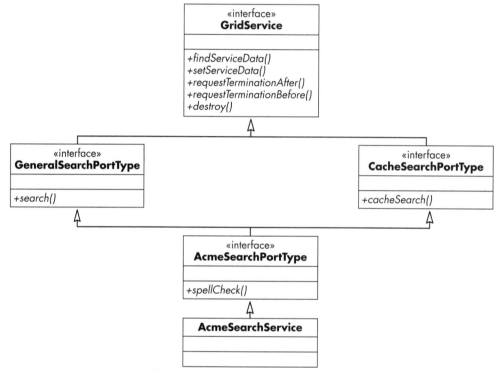

Figure 13.2
UML diagram showing the Acme portTypes and service implementation.

This sample will be developed in a step-by-step fashion by adding functionalities one by one. The approach taken is a top-down approach, where we will start with a GWSDL description of the service to be implemented.

ACME SEARCH SERVICE IMPLEMENTATION IN A TOP-DOWN APPROACH

Base Service Implementation

This discussion surrounds the base implementation.

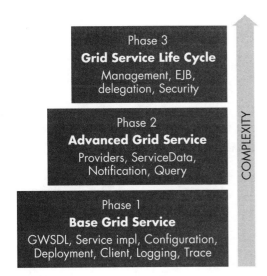

Figure 13.3
Recommended development process.

GWSDL Creation

In a top-down development effort, we must start with a GWSDL, and the necessary artifacts that the service should expose to the external world. These artifacts include service interfaces and their hierarchy, public operations, messages exchanged between a client and service, and the exposed public state data information. This information is coded (i.e., except for public state data, which we will add later) in the GWSDL description shown in Listings 13.1, 13.2, and 13.3.

Listing 13.1 describes the complete GeneralSearchPortType.gwsdl.

Listing 13.1 The complete GeneralSearchPortType.gwsdl.

```
<?xml version="1.0" encoding="UTF-8"?>
<definitions name="GeneralSearch"
            targetNamespace="http://org.ph.gridbook.sample/base/general"
            xmlns:general="http://org.ph.gridbook.sample/base/general"
            xmlns="http://schemas.xmlsoap.org/wsdl/"
            xmlns:ogsi="http://www.gridforum.org/namespaces/2003/03/OGSI"
            xmlns:gwsdl="http://www.gridforum.org/namespaces/2003/03/
                        gridWSDLExtensions"
            xmlns:xsd="http://www.w3.org/2001/XMLSchema">
<!--
The below WSDL fragment imports ogsi.gwsdl, which is part of the core GT3
distribution and defines the OGSI-defined service portTypes.
 -->
<import location="../../ogsi/ogsi.gwsdl" namespace="http://
www.gridforum.org/namespaces/2003/03/OGSI"/>
```

Listing 13.1   The complete GeneralSearchPortType.gwsdl. (Cont.)

```
<types>
  <xsd:schema targetNamespace="http://org.ph.gridbook.sample/base/general"
              xmlns:general="http://org.ph.gridbook.sample/base/general"
              xmlns:xsd="http://www.w3.org/2001/XMLSchema"
    attributeFormDefault="qualified" elementFormDefault="qualified">
    <xsd:complexType name="SearchType">
      <xsd:sequence>
        <xsd:element name="phrase" type="xsd:string"/>
</xsd:sequence>
    </xsd:complexType>
    <xsd:complexType name="SearchResponseType">
      <xsd:sequence>
<xsd:element name="URL" type="xsd:string"/>
        <xsd:element name="summary" type="xsd:string"/>
            <xsd:element name="cached" type="xsd:boolean"/>
      </xsd:sequence>
    </xsd:complexType>
    <xsd:element name="search">
<xsd:complexType>
      <xsd:sequence>
        <xsd:element name="searchInput" type="general:SearchType"/>
      </xsd:sequence>
    </xsd:complexType>
    </xsd:element>
    <xsd:element name="searchResponse">
<xsd:complexType>
      <xsd:sequence>
        <xsd:element name="searchResult"
type="general:SearchResponseType"/>
      </xsd:sequence>
    </xsd:complexType>
    </xsd:element>
</xsd:schema>
</types>
<message name="SearchInputMessage">
  <part name="parameters" element="general:search"/>
</message>
<message name="SearchOutputMessage">
  <part name="parameters" element="general:searchResponse"/>
</message>
<gwsdl:portType name="GeneralSearchPortType" extends="ogsi:GridService">
  <operation name="search">
    <input message="general:SearchInputMessage"/>
```

Listing 13.1   The complete GeneralSearchPortType.gwsdl. (Cont.)

```
        <output message="general:SearchOutputMessage"/>
  </operation>
</gwsdl:portType>
</definitions>
```

Listing 13.2 describes the complete CacheSearchPortType GWSDL.

Listing 13.2   The complete CacheSearchPortType GWSDL.

```
<?xml version="1.0" encoding="UTF-8"?>
<definitions name="GeneralSearch"
             targetNamespace="http://org.ph.gridbook.sample/base/cache"
             xmlns:cache="http://org.ph.gridbook.sample/base/cache"
             xmlns="http://schemas.xmlsoap.org/wsdl/"
             xmlns:ogsi="http://www.gridforum.org/namespaces/2003/03/OGSI"
             xmlns:gwsdl="http://www.gridforum.org/namespaces/2003/03/
                          gridWSDLExtensions"
             xmlns:xsd="http://www.w3.org/2001/XMLSchema">
<!--
The below wsdl fragment imports ogsi.gwsdl, which is part of the core GT3
distribution and defines the OGSI-defined service portTypes.
 - ->
<import location="../../ogsi/ogsi.gwsdl" namespace="http://
www.gridforum.org/namespaces/2003/03/OGSI"/>

<types>
  <xsd:schema targetNamespace="http://org.ph.gridbook.sample/base/cache"
             xmlns:general="http://org.ph.gridbook.sample/base/cache"
             xmlns:xsd="http://www.w3.org/2001/XMLSchema"
attributeFormDefault="qualified" elementFormDefault="qualified">
    <xsd:complexType name="CacheSearchMessageType">
      <xsd:sequence>
        <xsd:element name="cacheSearch" type="xsd:boolean"/>
        <xsd:element name="phrase" type="xsd:string"/>
      </xsd:sequence>
    </xsd:complexType>

    <xsd:complexType name="CacheSearchMessageResponseType">
      <xsd:sequence>
        <xsd:element name="URL" type="xsd:string"/>
        <xsd:element name="summary" type="xsd:string"/>
        <xsd:element name="cached" type="xsd:boolean"/>
</xsd:sequence>
    </xsd:complexType>
  <xsd:element name="cacheSearch">
```

Listing 13.2   The complete CacheSearchPortType GWSDL. (Cont.)

```
<xsd:complexType>
      <xsd:sequence>
        <xsd:element name="cacheSearchInput"
type="cache:CacheSearchMessageType"/>
      </xsd:sequence>
    </xsd:complexType>
   </xsd:element>
   <xsd:element name="cacheSearchResponse">
<xsd:complexType>
      <xsd:sequence>
        <xsd:element name="cacheSearchResult"
type="cache:CacheSearchMessageResponseType"/>
      </xsd:sequence>
    </xsd:complexType>
    </xsd:element>
</xsd:schema>
</types>

<message name="CacheSearchInputMessage">
  <part name="parameters" element="cache:cacheSearch"/>
</message>
<message name="CacheSearchOutputMessage">
  <part name="parameters" element="cache:cacheSearchResponse"/>
</message>

<gwsdl:portType name="CacheSearchPortType" extends="ogsi:GridService">
  <operation name="cacheSearch">
    <input message="cache:CacheSearchInputMessage"/>
    <output message="cache:CacheSearchOutputMessage"/>
  </operation>
</gwsdl:portType>
</definitions>
```

Listing 13.3 describes the complete AcmeSearchPortType GWSDL.

Listing 13.3   The complete AcmeSearchPortType GWSDL.

```
<?xml version="1.0" encoding="UTF-8"?>
<definitions name="AcmeSearch" targetNamespace="http://
org.ph.gridbook.sample/base/acme"
   xmlns:acme="http://org.ph.gridbook.sample/base/acme"
          xmlns:general="http://org.ph.gridbook.sample/base/general"
          xmlns:cache="http://org.ph.gridbook.sample/base/cache"
          xmlns="http://schemas.xmlsoap.org/wsdl/"
          xmlns:ogsi="http://www.gridforum.org/namespaces/2003/03/OGSI"
```

Listing 13.3   The complete AcmeSearchPortType GWSDL. (Cont.)

```
            xmlns:gwsdl="http://www.gridforum.org/namespaces/2003/03/
                        gridWSDLExtensions"
            xmlns:xsd="http://www.w3.org/2001/XMLSchema">
<!--
The below code imports ogsi.gwsdl and other gwsdl's defined earlier
 -->
<import location="../../ogsi/ogsi.gwsdl" namespace="http://
www.gridforum.org/namespaces/2003/03/OGSI"/>
<import location="../../gridbook/base/general_search_port_type.gwsdl"
namespace="http://org.ph.gridbook.sample/base/general"/>
<import location="../../gridbook/base/cache_search_port_type.gwsdl"
namespace="http://org.ph.gridbook.sample/base/cache"/>

<types>
  <xsd:schema targetNamespace="http://org.ph.gridbook.sample/base/acme"
            xmlns:acme="http://org.ph.gridbook.sample/base/acme"
            xmlns:xsd=http://www.w3.org/2001/XMLSchema
attributeFormDefault="qualified" elementFormDefault="qualified">

    <xsd:complexType name="SpellCheckMessageType">
<xsd:sequence>
        <xsd:element name="word" type="xsd:string"/>
      </xsd:sequence>
    </xsd:complexType>


    <xsd:complexType name="SpellCheckMessageResponseType">
      <xsd:sequence>
        <xsd:element name="word" type="xsd:string"/>
        <xsd:element name="correct" type="xsd:boolean"/>
        <xsd:element name="correctedWord" type="xsd:string"/>
      </xsd:sequence>
    </xsd:complexType>
  <xsd:element name="spellCheck">
<xsd:complexType>
      <xsd:sequence>
        <xsd:element name="spellCheckInput"
type="acme:SpellCheckMessageType"/>
      </xsd:sequence>
    </xsd:complexType>
  </xsd:element>
  <xsd:element name="spellCheckResponse">
 <xsd:complexType>
<xsd:sequence>
<xsd:element name="spellCheckResult"
type="acme:SpellCheckMessageResponseType"/>
```

Listing 13.3   The complete AcmeSearchPortType GWSDL. (Cont.)

```
        </xsd:sequence>
      </xsd:complexType>
      </xsd:element>
  </xsd:schema>
  </types>
  <message name="SpellCheckInputMessage">
    <part name="parameters" element="acme:spellCheck"/>
  </message>
  <message name="SpellCheckOutputMessage">
    <part name="parameters" element="acme:spellCheckResponse"/>
  </message>
  <gwsdl:portType name="AcmeSearchPortType"
  extends="ogsi:GridService general:GeneralSearchPortType
  cache:CacheSearchPortType">
    <operation name="spellCheck">
      <input message="acme:SpellCheckInputMessage"/>
      <output message="acme:SpellCheckOutputMessage"/>
    </operation>
  </gwsdl:portType>
  </definitions>
```

The design of WSDL is a complex process. Therefore, care needs to be taken and we must follow some design patterns for creating interoperable, standards-based, and error-free GWSDL/WSDL. What follows are some of the important design decisions we take into account when we create the above service description language. These considerations are:

- While creating grid services for OGSI, it is recommended to use GWSDL/OGSI namespaces for declaring and use OGSI-related concepts including service data, open and extendable portTypes, and common data types.
- We must import the OGSI behaviors from the GT3-provided "ogsi.gwsdl" declaration file.
- We need to create only "portType" declarations (as shown in the above listings) in the GWSDL files: There is no need to create a service and the binding declarations. The GT3 tools (GWSDL2WSDL and GenerateBinding) generate the necessary WSDLs for services, bindings, and portTypes from the GWSDL portType definition. The default binding support is SOAP/HTTP with "document/literal" encoding.
- Utilize the "document-literal" approach when designing WSDL for interoperability among implementations. Since there are some anomalies with the AXIS tools, one must embellish the appropriate design patterns in order to get the "best" generated code. This code generates SOAP messages that are interoperable, and could be validated with WS-I basic profile tools.[4]
- The "targetNamespace" declaration must be done with care and this value is used to create the default package structure. We will see later how we can override this default tool generation feature.

- XSD types must be defined with the XSD schema attribute of "elementFormDefault" and "attributeFormDefault" to get qualified with the appropriate namespace declarations.

RECOMMENDED WSDL CODING PATTERN FOR DOCUMENT/ LITERAL MESSAGES

As shown in Listing 13.3, the <wsdl:message> must contain <wsdl:parameters> referring to XML elements with the same name as the <wsdl:operation> name. These XML elements in turn may contain xsd:ComplexType/SimpleType types to hold the real message type. This is analogous to sending message documents with the name of the operation within a SOAP body as the first element.

For example, Listing 13.4 is the SOAP message generated for the "search" operation based on the above WSDL schema. The *highlights* indicate that we are sending an XML document based on its schema definition.

Listing 13.4   A sample SOAP message for document/literal WSDL definition.

```
<soapenv:Envelope xmlns:soapenv="http://schemas.xmlsoap.org/soap/envelope/"

                  xmlns:xsd="http://www.w3.org/2001/XMLSchema"
                  xmlns:xsi="http://www.w3.org/2001/XMLSchema-instance">
<soapenv:Body>
       <search xmlns="http://org.ph.gridbook.sample/base/general">
               <searchInput>
                       <phrase>IBM Grid computing</phrase>
               </searchInput>
       </search>
</soapenv:Body>
</soapenv:Envelope>
```

Generating WSDL from GWSDL

We have now completed our service portType definition in GWSDLs, and it's time to focus on creating the real WSDL.

This is a transformation process from GWSDL to WSDL and is done using the GWSDL2WSDL tool, which we have discussed in the last chapter. Listing 13.5 shows the generated WSDL file with the generated WSDL portType declaration.

Listing 13.5 addresses the WSDL file generated from the GWSDL transformation operation.

Listing 13.5   WSDL file generated from the GWSDL transformation.

```
<?xml version="1.0" encoding="UTF-8"?>
<definitions name="AcmeSearch" targetNamespace="http://
org.ph.gridbook.sample/base/acme" xmlns="http://schemas.xmlsoap.org/wsdl/"
xmlns:acme="http://org.ph.gridbook.sample/base/acme" xmlns:cache="http://
org.ph.gridbook.sample/base/cache" xmlns:general="http://
org.ph.gridbook.sample/base/general" xmlns:gwsdl="http://
www.gridforum.org/namespaces/2003/03/gridWSDLExtensions"
xmlns:ogsi="http://www.gridforum.org/namespaces/2003/03/OGSI"
xmlns:xsd="http://www.w3.org/2001/XMLSchema">

<import location="../../ogsi/ogsi.gwsdl" namespace="http://
www.gridforum.org/namespaces/2003/03/OGSI"/>
<import location="../../gridbook/base/general_search_port_type.gwsdl"
namespace="http://org.ph.gridbook.sample/base/general"/>
<import location="../../gridbook/base/cache_search_port_type.gwsdl"
namespace="http://org.ph.gridbook.sample/base/cache"/>


<types>
  <!—omitted for clarity ; Same as what we have defined in the
AcmeSearchPortType - ->
</types>

<message name="SpellCheckInputMessage">
  <part element="acme:spellCheck" name="parameters"/>
</message>
<message name="SpellCheckOutputMessage">
  <part element="acme:spellCheckResponse" name="parameters"/>
</message>

<portType name="AcmeSearchPortType">

<operation name="spellCheck">
   <input message="ns0:SpellCheckInputMessage" xmlns:ns0="http://
org.ph.gridbook.sample/base/acme"/>
   <output message="ns1:SpellCheckOutputMessage" xmlns:ns1="http://
org.ph.gridbook.sample/base/acme"/>
  </operation>

<operation name="search">
   <input message="ns31:SearchInputMessage" xmlns:ns31="http://
org.ph.gridbook.sample/base/general"/>
   <output message="ns32:SearchOutputMessage" xmlns:ns32="http://
org.ph.gridbook.sample/base/general"/>
  </operation>
```

Listing 13.5 WSDL file generated from the GWSDL transformation. (Cont.)

```
<operation name="cacheSearch">
    <input message="ns62:CacheSearchInputMessage" xmlns:ns62="http://
org.ph.gridbook.sample/base/cache"/>
    <output message="ns63:CacheSearchOutputMessage" xmlns:ns63="http://
org.ph.gridbook.sample/base/cache"/>
  </operation>


<operation name="setServiceData">
    <input message="ns70:SetServiceDataInputMessage" xmlns:ns70="http://
www.gridforum.org/namespaces/2003/03/OGSI"/>
    <output message="ns71:SetServiceDataOutputMessage" xmlns:ns71="http://
www.gridforum.org/namespaces/2003/03/OGSI"/>
    <fault message="ns72:ExtensibilityNotSupportedFaultMessage"
name="ExtensibilityNotSupportedFault" xmlns:ns72="http://
www.gridforum.org/namespaces/2003/03/OGSI"/>
  <!--Other faults are omitted for clarity ; -->
  </operation>


<operation name="destroy">
    <input message="ns89:DestroyInputMessage" xmlns:ns89="http://
www.gridforum.org/namespaces/2003/03/OGSI"/>
    <output message="ns90:DestroyOutputMessage" xmlns:ns90="http://
www.gridforum.org/namespaces/2003/03/OGSI"/>
  <!--Other faults are omitted for clarity ; -->
  </operation>
<operation name="requestTerminationAfter">
    <input message="ns81:RequestTerminationAfterInputMessage"
xmlns:ns81="http://www.gridforum.org/namespaces/2003/03/OGSI"/>
    <output message="ns82:RequestTerminationAfterOutputMessage"
xmlns:ns82="http://www.gridforum.org/namespaces/2003/03/OGSI"/>
</operation>


<operation name="requestTerminationBefore">
    <input message="ns85:RequestTerminationBeforeInputMessage"
xmlns:ns85="http://www.gridforum.org/namespaces/2003/03/OGSI"/>
    <output message="ns86:RequestTerminationBeforeOutputMessage"
xmlns:ns86="http://www.gridforum.org/namespaces/2003/03/OGSI"/>
  <!--Other faults are omitted for clarity ; - -->
  </operation>


<operation name="findServiceData">
    <input message="ns64:FindServiceDataInputMessage" xmlns:ns64="http://
www.gridforum.org/namespaces/2003/03/OGSI"/>
    <output message="ns65:FindServiceDataOutputMessage" xmlns:ns65="http:/
/www.gridforum.org/namespaces/2003/03/OGSI"/>
  <!--Other faults are omitted for clarity ; - -->
```

Listing 13.5   WSDL file generated from the GWSDL transformation. (Cont.)

```
  </operation>

</portType>

<gwsdl:portType
extends="ogsi:GridService general:GeneralSearchPortType
cache:CacheSearchPortType" name="AcmeSearchPortType">

</gwsdl:portType>

</definitions>
```

In Listing 13.5, we note that a new <wsdl:AcmeSearchPortType> was created with all the operations of the portTypes that we have extended in the GWSDL. This process is explained in the UML diagram below in Figure 13.4.

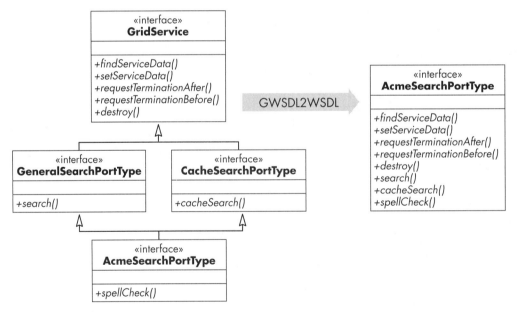

Figure 13.4
The GWSDL to WSDL transformation process.

One item to note regarding this process is that the generated WSDL is still keeping the GWSDL portType information for backward transformation purposes, and to help at runtime with the GT3 tools.

Generating Other WSDL Files

Once we have completed the above process, the next step in the process is to create the necessary WSDL files for service and binding. These files are created from the WSDL portType created in the above step. GT3 provides a helper class to assist us in this step. We are using the "Generate-Binding" tool to create default binding and service implementation.

TOOLS USED IN THE ABOVE TWO STEPS ARE:

1. GWSDL2WSDL

Usage: Java GWSDL2WSDL

        acme_search_port_type.gwsdl

        acme_search_port_type.wsdl

2. GenerateBinding

Usage: Java GenerateBinding

        acme_search_port_type.wsdl

        acme_search_service.wsdl

We now have all of the WSDLs we require for our service. In our sample, the generated files are:

1. acme_search_bindings.wsdl
2. acme_search_port_type.wsdl
3. acme_search_port_type.xsd
4. acme_search_service.wsdl

Generating Stubs, Helper Classes

So far we have been working with XML, WSDL, and XSD schema. Let us now begin to generate the native language implementation artifacts from the WSDL files. We need to make sure that the default implementation is using the correct name for the Java package, because the default code generation process generates the source information in a package, constructed from the targetNamespace of the WSDLs. The sidebar below illustrates how we can override the targetNamespace to a meaningful package name of our choice, should we need to do this.

> ### OVERRIDING THE DEFAULT PACKAGE CREATION PROCESS IN THE APACHE AXIS WSDL2JAVA TOOL
>
> In WSDL2JAVA , there are three options to map the namespace to some user-defined package name:
>
>   -N, --NStoPkg <argument>=<value>
>
>   Mapping of namespace to package
>
>   -f, --fileNStoPkg <argument>
>
>   File of NStoPkg mappings (default NStoPkg.properties)
>
>   -p, --package <argument>
>
>   Override all namespace to package mappings, use this package name instead
>
> Here, we are using the default NStoPkg.properties file. The new package definitions are:
>
>   http\://org.ph.gridbook.sample/base/acme=org.ph.gridbook.base
>
>   http\://org.ph.gridbook.sample/base/acme/bindings=org.ph.gridbook.base.bindings
>
>   http\://org.ph.gridbook.sample/base/acme/service=org.ph.gridbook.base.service

Once we have decided on the package names, the next step is the process of generating the Java sources for stubs, endpoint interface, helpers, and types. GT3 comes with a number of tools to help us accomplish this. We have already discussed the details on these tools in the last chapter. Readers can see how these tools are used for this sample.

```
GWSDL2Java
Usage : GWSDL2Java  acme_search_service.wsdl
```

This results in a number of Java classes. We will see some of the important Java classes that are generated, and we will then spend some time analyzing these Java files. These files form the base implementation artifacts for the grid services at both the client and the server side. So, familiarity with these Java classes is a must for proper service and client-side development.

AcmeSearchPortType

This is the service endpoint interface generated from the WSDL portType definition. Service developers extend their service implementations from these service endpoint interfaces. This class is generated in accordance with the JAX-RPC specification, in the service endpoint interface definition. Listing 13.6 shows the interface generated for our sample.

Listing 13.6   The Acme Search interface.

```
package org.ph.gridbook.base;

public interface AcmeSearchPortType extends org.gridforum.ogsi.GridService
{

    // Most of the Exceptions are not shown for code clarity............
    public org.gridforum.ogsi.ExtensibilityType
findServiceData(org.gridforum.ogsi.ExtensibilityType queryExpression)
throws java.rmi.RemoteException, .................................;

    public org.ph.gridbook.base.SearchResponseType
search(org.ph.gridbook.base.SearchType searchInput) throws
java.rmi.RemoteException;

    public void destroy() throws java.rmi.RemoteException,.........;

    public org.ph.gridbook.base.CacheSearchMessageResponseType
cacheSearch(org.ph.gridbook.base.CacheSearchMessageType cacheSearchInput)
throws java.rmi.RemoteException;

    public org.ph.gridbook.base.SpellCheckMessageResponseType
spellCheck(org.ph.gridbook.base.SpellCheckMessageType spellCheckInput)
throws java.rmi.RemoteException;

// some methods are not shown for code readability..................
}
```

We should not try to code this "by hand." We must use the tools because the code generation is dependent on a number of WSDL constructs. This includes encoding (SOAP encoding/literal), style (rpc/document), and the operation parameter direction (in/out or inout). We could see JAX-RPC holder classes getting generated for the <wsdl:inout> operation parameter type.

Another helpful feature of using the tools is the creation of the corresponding Java types for the message parameters, and for the XSD elements defined in the WSDL. For example, a SearchType Java class is generated for the XSD complex type "SearchType" defined in the earlier WSDL listing. These objects are XML-serializable Java classes, and the framework can marshal/demarshal them into SOAP message body elements. Now let's move on to the other valuable construct, "AcmeSearchService," an implementation of javax.xml.rpc.Service.

AcmeSearchService

The JAX-RPC client at runtime creates "dynamic proxy" stubs using the javax.xml.rpc.Service interface. The client has *a priori* knowledge of the WSDL, the service it is going to invoke, and the service ports defined. It uses the "ServiceFactory" classes to create the service and get the proxy. In the last chapter, we have discussed this JAX-RPC service implementation class and its programming model. Listing 13.7 shows the service class for Acme Search Service.

Listing 13.7   The JAX-RPC service implementation class.

```
public interface AcmeSearchService extends javax.xml.rpc.Service {
    public java.lang.String getAcmeSearchPortAddress();
    public org.ph.gridbook.base.AcmeSearchPortType getAcmeSearchPort()
throws javax.xml.rpc.ServiceException;
    public org.ph.gridbook.base.AcmeSearchPortType
getAcmeSearchPort(java.net.URL portAddress) throws
javax.xml.rpc.ServiceException;
}
```

AcmeSearchServiceGridLocator

This locator class is the most important GT3 specific helper class. This class is generated to help the grid service client by hiding the complexity of grid service message exchange patterns including GSH to GSR conversion, GSR validation, handle extraction from GSR, and so on. Listing 13.8 shows the grid locator class for the Acme Search Service. By careful observation on the class definition described in Listing 13.8, we could see that there are three public operations with different signatures available to the client.

It enables the client to pass the following information:

- A handle (GSH) for a service instance
- A locator of a service instance. This locator is normally returned on a service creation (Factory.createService).
- A normal URL for the service instance.

As listed above, the utilization of this client helper class is based on the service instance availability information. In the last chapter, we discussed the internals of these operations. We will see the value of this helper class, and its utilization model, when we start working with our client code.

Listing 13.8   AcmeSearchServiceGridLocator, which is a grid service specific helper class.

```
public class AcmeSearchServiceGridLocator extends
org.globus.ogsa.impl.core.service.ServiceLocator
implements org.globus.ogsa.GridLocator {
    public org.ph.gridbook.base.AcmeSearchPortType getAcmeSearchPort
(org.gridforum.ogsi.HandleType handle)  throws org.gridforum.ogsi.FaultType,
org.globus.ogsa.GridServiceException {

setStubClass(org.ph.gridbook.base.bindings.AcmeSearchSOAPBindingStub.class);
        return (org.ph.gridbook.base.AcmeSearchPortType)
getServicePort(handle);
    }
```

Listing 13.8   AcmeSearchServiceGridLocator, which is a grid service specific helper class.

```
    public org.ph.gridbook.base.AcmeSearchPortType getAcmeSearchPort
(org.gridforum.ogsi.LocatorType locator) throws
org.gridforum.ogsi.FaultType,
org.globus.ogsa.GridServiceException {


setStubClass(org.ph.gridbook.base.bindings.AcmeSearchSOAPBindingStub.class);
        return (org.ph.gridbook.base.AcmeSearchPortType)
getServicePort(locator);
    }
    public org.ph.gridbook.base.AcmeSearchPortType
getAcmeSearchPort(java.net.URL url)
throws  org.globus.ogsa.GridServiceException {


setStubClass(org.ph.gridbook.base.bindings.AcmeSearchSOAPBindingStub.class);
        return (org.ph.gridbook.base.AcmeSearchPortType)
getServicePort(url);
    }
}
```

AcmeSearchServiceLocator

This is also a service locator helper class located at the client side. This is mainly utilized for Web service clients. This locator class (Listing 13.9) is different from the previously discussed locator class. We can see the difference by a careful examination of the name of the locator. The GT3 grid service specific locator has a name, <portType>GridServiceLocator, whereas the normal Web service locator has a name of <portType>ServiceLocator.

Listing 13.9   The Web service locator class.

```
public class AcmeSearchServiceLocator extends org.apache.axis.client.Service
implements
org.ph.gridbook.base.service.AcmeSearchService {
    // Use to get a proxy class for AcmeSearchPort
    private final java.lang.String AcmeSearchPort_address = "http://
localhost:8080/ogsa/services/";

    public java.lang.String getAcmeSearchPortAddress() {
        return AcmeSearchPort_address;
    }
    public org.ph.gridbook.base.AcmeSearchPortType getAcmeSearchPort()
throws javax.xml.rpc.ServiceException {
    }
...........................
}
```

This previous class implements AcmeSearchService to expose the JAX-RPC dynamic proxy behaviors.

AcmeSearchSOAPBindingStub

This is a core client-side static stub, which contains all the information about the service, and implements the service endpoint interface for compatibility verifications. The code in Listing 13.10 illustrates these concepts. This stub connects to the Apache SOAP client "Call" object to create a SOAP message for the corresponding method invocation. This stub contains the entire type-mapping and serialization information to map Java types in the operation signatures to the corresponding SOAP body elements, and vice versa.

Listing 13.10   The client-side static SOAP binding stub.

```
public class AcmeSearchSOAPBindingStub extends org.apache.axis.client.Stub
implements
org.ph.gridbook.base.AcmeSearchPortType {
    private java.util.Vector cachedSerClasses = new java.util.Vector()
    public AcmeSearchSOAPBindingStub() throws org.apache.axis.AxisFault {
        this(null);
    }

    public AcmeSearchSOAPBindingStub(java.net.URL endpointURL,
javax.xml.rpc.Service service)
throws org.apache.axis.AxisFault {
        this(service);
        super.cachedEndpoint = endpointURL;
    }
    public AcmeSearchSOAPBindingStub(javax.xml.rpc.Service service) throws
org.apache.axis.AxisFault{
. . . . . . . . . . . . . . . . . . . . . .
    }
    public org.gridforum.ogsi.ExtensibilityType
setServiceData(org.gridforum.ogsi.ExtensibilityType
updateExpression) throws java.rmi.RemoteException,
org.gridforum.ogsi.MutabilityViolationFaultType, ..............{
    }
    public org.ph.gridbook.base.SearchResponseType
search(org.ph.gridbook.base.SearchType searchInput)
throws java.rmi.RemoteException {
// Implementation calls the Apace Axis call object
    }
    // A number of operations are not shown
. . . . . . . . . . . . . . . . . . . . . .
}
```

Since we have completed the code generation process, it is time to move on to the real service creation constructs. Utilizing these tools to continue to generate code, we will now be able to write a service skeleton implementation quickly.

Implementing Search Grid Service

We will now begin with a simple server-side implementation to explain the basic service constructs. We will move on to the complex features later in this chapter.

Listing 13.11 illustrates how we are implementing this basic service. "AcmeSearchServiceImpl" implements AcmeSearchPortType, the endpoint service interface. It also implements the Globus-provided GridServiceImpl class, which provides the default implementations for the grid service behaviors, service data set, and service properties. We already covered the details on this helper implementation class in the previous chapter.

Listing 13.11   The Acme Search Service implementation.

```
package org.ph.gridbook.impl.base;

import org.globus.ogsa.impl.ogsi.GridServiceImpl;
import org.globus.ogsa.GridContext;
import org.globus.ogsa.GridServiceException;
import org.globus.ogsa.ServiceProperties;
import org.apache.axis.MessageContext;
import java.rmi.RemoteException;

import org.ph.gridbook.base.AcmeSearchPortType;
import org.ph.gridbook.base.*;

public class AcmeSearchServiceImpl extends GridServiceImpl implements
AcmeSearchPortType {
    public AcmeSearchServiceImpl () {
        super("Simple Search Service");
    }
    public AcmeSearchServiceImpl(String name) {
        super(name);
    }
    public void postCreate(GridContext context) throws
GridServiceException {
        super.postCreate(context);
    }
    public SearchResponseType search(SearchType searchInput)
throws java.rmi.RemoteException{
// Ignore the input
// create the output object
SearchResponseType response = new SearchResponseType();
```

Listing 13.11   The Acme Search Service implementation. (Cont.)

```
response.setURL("www.ibm.com");
response.setSummary("IBM");
response.setCached(true);
return response;
    }
    public CacheSearchMessageResponseType
cacheSearch(CacheSearchMessageType cacheSearchInput)
throws java.rmi.RemoteException{
    return null;
    }
    public SpellCheckMessageResponseType spellCheck(SpellCheckMessageType
spellCheckInput)
throws java.rmi.RemoteException{
    return null;
    }

}
```

This is a fully functional grid service implementation for the Acme search engine. The only functional method here is the search method, which accepts the search request and returns the search responses. We will see the SOAP message flows, the instance creation process, and other details in the client-side code described in the next section. Prior to this, let us explore the configuration of this service for the deployment of the service to the AXIS container.

Grid Service Configuration

As of now, the GT3 supports the Apache AXIS as their Web service engine. Due to this fact, we have to utilize the AXIS service configuration and deployment process. AXIS uses the WSDD to configure service for an AXIS engine. For our sample service, see the configuration listed in Listing 13.12.

Listing 13.12   The Acme Search Service deployment configuration.

```
 1. <service name="ph/acme/AcmeSearchService" provider="Handler"
    style="wrapped">
 2. <parameter name="name" value="Acme Search Service Factory"/>
 3. <parameter name="instance-name" value="Acme Search service Instance"/>
 4. <parameter name="instance-schemaPath" value="schema/gridbook/base/
    acme_search_service.wsdl"/>
 5. <parameter name="instance-baseClassName"
    value="org.ph.gridbook.impl.base.AcmeSearchServiceImpl"/>
 6. <!-- Start common parameters -->
 7. <parameter name="allowedMethods" value="*"/>
 8. <parameter name="persistent" value="true"/>
```

Listing 13.12 The Acme Search Service deployment configuration. (Cont.)

```
 9. <parameter name="className" value="org.gridforum.ogsi.Factory"/>
10. <parameter name="baseClassName"
    value="org.globus.ogsa.impl.ogsi.PersistentGridServiceImpl"/>
11. <parameter name="schemaPath" value="schema/ogsi/
    ogsi_factory_service.wsdl"/>
12. <parameter name="handlerClass"
    value="org.globus.ogsa.handlers.RPCURIProvider"/>
13. <parameter name="factoryCallback"
    value="org.globus.ogsa.impl.ogsi.DynamicFactoryCallbackImpl"/>
14. <parameter name="operationProviders"
    value="org.globus.ogsa.impl.ogsi.FactoryProvider"/>
15. </service>
```

We have previously discussed these configuration properties. The Acme Search Service specific parameters are seen in lines 2–5, which lists the name, instance name, WSDL schema path, and service implementation class. The rest are default configurations with the GT3-provided default factory provider (FactoryProvider), a callback (DynamicFactoryCallbackImpl) to create the service, and the pivot handler (RPCURIProvider). Another important point is the use of a "wrapped" style and using a "handler" provider.

Once we have the service and the configuration ready, we can deploy them into the service container by updating the class path and extending the existing server-config.wsdd with the above configuration fragment. And, from this point forward, when the container starts up, the Acme Search Service will be available for the client to use.

> **NOTE**
>
> Normally, we will use the deployment files "client-config.wsdd" and "server-config.wsdd," respectively, for client and server Web service configuration. These default names and locations can be overridden by providing a Java system property variable with axis.ServerConfigFile and axis.ClientConfigFile. For example, to use the configuration file "my-server-config.wsdd," one should provide the Java system property, –Daxis.ServerConfigFile=my-server-config.wsdd.

Simple Client Implementation

Let us list the client-side requirements, first, and then start coding for those requirements.

1. Create an Acme Search Service using the OGSI-defined factory pattern.
2. Call the "search" operation on the service using the locator returned from the above step.
3. After some time we need to call the service again. Now use a service handle we got during the first step.

4. Now get some grid service specific properties or service data.

5. Finally, we are now done with the service, by calling an explicit destroy on the service.

This process is shown in Figure 13.5.

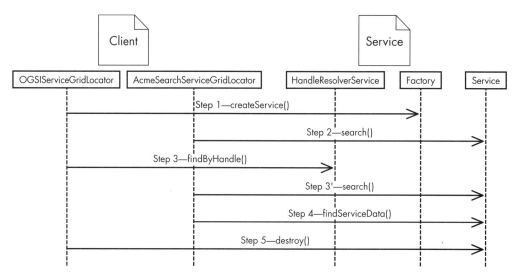

Figure 13.5
The client-side interaction UML.

We will discuss each of these steps in detail, with the annotated code in Listing 13.13. We must pay close attention to the comments and the sequence of the process.

Listing 13.13   The Acme Search Service simple client.

```
package org.ph.gridbook.impl.base.client;

import org.globus.ogsa.wsdl.GSR;
import org.gridforum.ogsi.*;
import org.globus.ogsa.utils.*;

import java.net.URL;
import javax.xml.namespace.QName;

import org.ph.gridbook.base.service.AcmeSearchServiceGridLocator;
import org.ph.gridbook.base.AcmeSearchPortType  ;
import org.ph.gridbook.base.*;

public class AcmeSearchClient1 {
    public static void main(String[] args) {
try{
```

Listing 13.13 The Acme Search Service simple client. (Cont.)

```
// Get command-line arguments
URL GSH = new URL("http://localhost:9080/ogsa/ph/acme/AcmeSearchService");

// Get the GT3 provided Grid locator helper for OGSI service
OGSIServiceGridLocator gridLocator = new OGSIServiceGridLocator();

// Get the factory using the URL to the factory
Factory factory = gridLocator.getFactoryPort(GSH);
GridServiceFactory acmeSearchFactory = new GridServiceFactory(factory);

// Create a new AcmeService instance using the Grid service factory
interface
// Get a locator pointing to the Acme Search service
LocatorType locator = acmeSearchFactory.createService();
// Done creating an Acme Grid service instance

//Now we got an Acme search service instance, ready to invoke search on it
// Get the GT3 created Grid locator helper
AcmeSearchServiceGridLocator acmeSearchLocator =    new
AcmeSearchServiceGridLocator();
AcmeSearchPortType   searchService =
acmeSearchLocator.getAcmeSearchPort(locator);

// Call remote method 'search'
SearchResponseType response = searchService.search(null);
System.out.println("Search response url = " + response.getURL());
System.out.println("Search response summary = " + response.getSummary());


// Now we are running a handle resolution to the service before making a
service call
// Get the GSR from the locator created returned by the factory
GSR reference = GSR.newInstance(locator);

// Get the handle from the reference using GSR helper class
String location = reference.getHandle().toString();
HandleType handle = new HandleType(location);

// We got a handle to the instance now. Let us run a handle resolution
process before service call
searchService = acmeSearchLocator.getAcmeSearchPort(handle);
// The above call will go through a Handle resolution process
// Finally will return a service reference

//Now we can call remote method 'search'
```

Listing 13.13   The Acme Search Service simple client. (Cont.)

```
response = searchService.search(null);

// Produces the results
System.out.println("Search response url = " + response.getURL());
System.out.println("Search response summary = " + response.getSummary());

// Now we can explore some Grid service specific calls
//1. Based on OGSI spec, every Grid service has "serviceDataNames" service
data element
// Get the above service data value from our acme search grid service.

// Names of Service Data offered by this Grid Service
extensibility =

searchService.findServiceData(QueryHelper.getNamesQuery("serviceDataName")
);
serviceData = AnyHelper.getAsServiceDataValues(extensibility);
Object[] serviceDataNames = AnyHelper.getAsObject(serviceData);
for(int i=0; i<serviceDataNames.length; i++){
QName serviceDataName = (QName) serviceDataNames[i];
System.out.println("service data name: " + serviceDataName);
}
// interfaces
// Names of interfaces exposed by this Grid Service
extensibility =
searchService.findServiceData(QueryHelper.getNamesQuery("interface"));
serviceData = AnyHelper.getAsServiceDataValues(extensibility);
Object[] interfaces = AnyHelper.getAsObject(serviceData);
for(int i=0; i<interfaces.length; i++){
 QName iface = (QName) interfaces[i];
 System.out.println("interface name: " + iface);
 }
// Finally get a reference to the GridService PortType and destroy the
instance
GridService gridService = gridLocator.getGridServicePort(locator);
gridService.destroy();
      }catch(Exception e){
e.printStackTrace();
    }
   }
}
```

1. Create an Acme Search Service. The client uses the normal GT3-provided "OGSIServiceGridLocator" class to get hold of the factory stub and calls create service on that stub using the well-known Acme Search Service factory URL. To better understand, we will show the SOAP messages flowing through the wire. This will give us a clear understanding of the process. Listing 13.14 shows the SOAP message generated for the "createService" operation on the factory. The target address URL we used to connect to the factory is http://localhost:9080/ogsa/ph/acme/AcmeSearchService."

Listing 13.14 The SOAP request message for the Factory createService operation.

```
<soapenv:Envelope xmlns:soapenv="http://schemas.xmlsoap.org/soap/envelope/
" xmlns:xsd="http://www.w3.org/2001/XMLSchema" xmlns:xsi="http://
www.w3.org/2001/XMLSchema-instance">
 <soapenv:Body>
  <createService xmlns="http://www.gridforum.org/namespaces/2003/03/OGSI">
   <terminationTime ns1:before="infinity" ns1:after="infinity"
xmlns:ns1="http://www.gridforum.org/namespaces/2003/03/OGSI"/>
   <creationParameters xsi:nil="true"/>
  </createService>
 </soapenv:Body>
</soapenv:Envelope>
```

Listing 13.15 describes the response from the server after the creation of the Acme Search Service using the default GT3 factory provider. This listing illustrates the encoded WDL reference information of the Acme Search Service (acme_search_service.wsdl). The GSR helper class can convert the WSDL reference to the corresponding "WSDLReferenceType" class and can retrieve the handle to the service instance.

Listing 13.15 The SOAP response message for the Factory createService operation.

```
<soapenv:Body>
  <createServiceResponse xmlns="http://www.gridforum.org/namespaces/2003/
03/OGSI">
    <locator>
     <reference xsi:type="ns1:WSDLReferenceType"
xmlns:ns1="http://www.gridforum.org/namespaces/2003/03/OGSI">
<definitions name="AcmeSearch"
targetNamespace=http://org.ph.gridbook.sample/base/acme/service
xmlns="http://schemas.xmlsoap.org/wsdl/"
xmlns:acmesearchbinding="http://org.ph.gridbook.sample/base/acme/bindings"
xmlns:soap="http://schemas.xmlsoap.org/wsdl/soap/">
<import
location="http://localhost:9080/ogsa/schema/gridbook/base/
acme_search_bindings.wsdl"
namespace="http://org.ph.gridbook.sample/base/acme/bindings"/>
```

Listing 13.15   The SOAP response message for the Factory createService operation. (Cont.)

```
<service name="AcmeSearchService" xmlns:gsdl="http://ogsa.globus.org/">
<gsdl:instanceOf
handle="http://9.56.37.43:9080/ogsa/services/ph/acme/AcmeSearchService
/hash-262089504-1058895681694" xmlns=""/>
<gsdl:instanceOf handle="http://9.56.37.43:9080/ogsa/services/instance"
xmlns=""/>
<port binding="acmesearchbinding:AcmeSearchSOAPBinding"
name="AcmeSearchPort">
<soap:address
location="http://9.56.37.43:9080/ogsa/services/ph/acme/AcmeSearchService/
hash-
262089504-1058895681694"/>
</port>
</service>
</definitions>
</reference>
    </locator>
    <ns2:currentTerminationTime xsi:type="ns2:TerminationTimeType"
ns2:before="infinity"
ns2:timestamp="2003-07-22T17:41:22.405Z" ns2:after="infinity"
xmlns:ns2="http://www.gridforum.org/namespaces/2003/03/OGSI"/>
    <extensibilityOutput xsi:nil="true"/>
  </createServiceResponse>
 </soapenv:Body>
</soapenv:Envelope>
```

Paying close attention to Listing 13.15, we can observe that:

- The factory creates the handle of the service instance.
- The SOAP address location is updated with the new instance address and the necessary instance information.
- The current termination time element is related to the service instance–created time, and with a termination time of infinity.

Once the client can establish a relationship with this reference, it can always go back to the service until the explicit termination of the service by client/container, or the soft state service expiration occurs.

   2. Call the "search" operation on the service using the locator returned from the above step. We have seen earlier that the <portType>GridServiceLocator class can be called with three types of parameters, LocatorType, HandleType, and URL, respectively. We will invoke the "search" operation on the server using the LocatorType class returned from the above "createService" call. Listing 13.16 shows how it is done.

Listing 13.16 The client invoking the "search" operation on the service.

```
AcmeSearchServiceGridLocator acmeSearchLocator =    new
AcmeSearchServiceGridLocator();
AcmeSearchPortType  searchService =
acmeSearchLocator.getAcmeSearchPort(locator);
SearchType searchRequest = new SearchType();
searchRequest.setPhrase("IBM Grid computing");
SearchResponseType response = searchService.search(searchRequest);
```

Note that the target address utilized is http://localhost:9080/ogsa/ph/acme/AcmeSearchService/ hash-262089504-1058895681694. This address points to a specific instance of the search service created by the client. The above grid service call resulted in the SOAP message in Listing 13.17.

Listing 13.17 The SOAP message trace on the "search" method call to the Acme Search Service.

```
<soapenv:Envelope xmlns:soapenv="http://schemas.xmlsoap.org/soap/envelope/
" xmlns:xsd="http://www.w3.org/2001/XMLSchema" xmlns:xsi="http://
www.w3.org/2001/XMLSchema-instance">
 <soapenv:Body>
  <search xmlns="http://org.ph.gridbook.sample/base/general">
   <searchInput>
    <phrase>IBM Grid computing</phrase>
   </searchInput>
  </search>
 </soapenv:Body>
</soapenv:Envelope>
```

The results are retrieved from the SearchResponseType object. Listing 13.18 below describes the SOAP return message for the above call.

Listing 13.18 The SOAP message trace on the "search" method call return from the Acme Search Service.

```
<soapenv:Envelope xmlns:soapenv="http://schemas.xmlsoap.org/soap/envelope/
" xmlns:xsd="http://www.w3.org/2001/XMLSchema" xmlns:xsi="http://
www.w3.org/2001/XMLSchema-instance">
 <soapenv:Body>
  <searchResponse xmlns="http://org.ph.gridbook.sample/base/general">
   <searchResult xsi:type="ns1:SearchResponseType"
xmlns:ns1="http://org.ph.gridbook.sample/base/general">
    <URL>www.ibm.com</URL>
    <summary>IBM</summary>
    <cached>true</cached>
   </searchResult>
  </searchResponse>
 </soapenv:Body>
</soapenv:Envelope>
```

At this stage, we are done creating an acme search grid service instance, and we have invoked a "search" call on that instance using the service locator returned from the createService operation. Now, assume that we are holding the service instance for a long period of time. By now, the service GSR may have changed but the GSH holds validity. In this kind of situation, we may need to go back to the container to do a handle resolution process before we start accessing the service. This should happen without the client's involvement. Now, let us see how we can do this in a real-world scenario.

> **3.** After some time we need to call the service again. This time around, we will use a service handle that we received during the first step.

The client can still use the normal "AcmeSearchServiceGridLocator" class, however, the only difference is the use of a different operation signature. This time we will use the HandleType parameter. This example code is described in Listing 13.19.

Listing 13.19   Getting a handle from the locator and calling service.

```
GSR reference = GSR.newInstance(locator);
// Get the handle from the reference using GSR helper class
String location = reference.getHandle().toString();
HandleType handle = new HandleType(location);
// We got a handle to the instance now. Let us run a handle resolution
process before service call
searchService = acmeSearchLocator.getAcmeSearchPort(handle);
```

The above operation results in a call to the container's handle revolver service to perform a handle to the reference resolution (GSH to GSR resolution) for that specific handle. This is happening in an autonomic sense. This handle resolution SOAP request, and the response message, is shown in Listings 13.20 and 13.21.

Listing 13.20   The invoking handle resolution service with the handle to resolve to a service instance reference.

```
<soapenv:Envelope xmlns:soapenv="http://schemas.xmlsoap.org/soap/envelope/
" xmlns:xsd="http://www.w3.org/2001/XMLSchema" xmlns:xsi="http://
www.w3.org/2001/XMLSchema-instance">
 <soapenv:Body>
  <findByHandle xmlns="http://www.gridforum.org/namespaces/2003/03/OGSI">
   <handleSet>
    <handle>http://9.56.37.43:9080/ogsa/services/ph/acme/
AcmeSearchService/hash-262089504-1058895681694</handle>
   </handleSet>
   <gsrExclusionSet/>
  </findByHandle>
 </soapenv:Body>
</soapenv:Envelope>
```

Listing 13.21 A handle resolution result from the handle resolution service, with a GSR (WSDL reference).

```
<soapenv:Envelope xmlns:soapenv="http://schemas.xmlsoap.org/soap/envelope/
"
xmlns:xsd="http://www.w3.org/2001/XMLSchema"
xmlns:xsi="http://www.w3.org/2001/XMLSchema-instance">
 <soapenv:Body>
  <findByHandleResponse xmlns="http://www.gridforum.org/namespaces/2003/
03/OGSI">
   <locator>
    <reference xsi:type="ns1:WSDLReferenceType" xmlns:ns1="http://
www.gridforum.org/namespaces/2003/03/OGSI">
<definitions name="AcmeSearch" targetNamespace="http://
org.ph.gridbook.sample/base/acme/service"
<!—deleted for clarity - ->
<service name="AcmeSearchService" xmlns:gsdl="http://ogsa.globus.org/">
<!—deleted for clarity - ->
<port binding="acmesearchbinding:AcmeSearchSOAPBinding"
name="AcmeSearchPort">
<soap:address
location="http://9.56.37.43:9080/ogsa/services/ph/acme/AcmeSearchService/
hash-262089504-1058895681694"/>
</port>
</service>
</definitions>
</reference>
   </locator>
  </findByHandleResponse>
 </soapenv:Body>
</soapenv:Envelope>
```

Now we are finished with this handle resolution, and the stubs are updated with the new location information. The client can begin using these stubs and start invoking operations on the service.

We have previously discussed the grid service client-side invocation models and the corresponding SOAP messages generated for each process. This information provides us with valuable information, including message interoperability, validation facility information, and derived information about the client service interaction. We can now move on to our next step of working with grid service behaviors.

    4. Get some grid service–specific properties or service data. By now, readers are familiar with the OGSI-provided grid service behaviors, and can assert that the AcmeSearchService is a grid service based upon our server-side implementation and configuration options. Now we will spend time analyzing the grid service exposed state data and the operations provided to access these service behaviors.

First, let us explore the state data exposed by the grid service. We can use the OGSI-provided intro-spection API, "findServiceData," to get the list of exposed service data elements. We can do this by asking the grid service to send back the list of QName of service data elements kept in the "service-DataName" SDE's service data values. This operation is invoked as shown in Listing 13.22.

Listing 13.22   Calling findServiceData operation on a service.

```
extensibility =
searchService.findServiceData(QueryHelper.getNamesQuery("serviceDataName")
);
serviceData = AnyHelper.getAsServiceDataValues(extensibility);
Object[] serviceDataNames = AnyHelper.getAsObject(serviceData);
for(int i=0; i<serviceDataNames.length; i++){
QName serviceDataName = (QName) serviceDataNames[i];
System.out.println("serviceDataName: " + serviceDataName);
}
```

The above routine results in the output message in Listing 13.23.

Listing 13.23   Results of find service data operation on a service.

```
Service data name: findServiceDataExtensibility
Service data name: terminationTime
Service data name: factoryLocator
Service data name: serviceDataName
Service data name: gridServiceReference
Service data name: setServiceDataExtensibility
Service data name: gridServiceHandle
Service data name: interface
```

This lists all the OGSI-defined service data elements. Later on we will see how we will add our own service-specific service data elements, including dynamic and static SDEs.

> ## DETAILS OF findSERVICEDATA OPERATION INPUT EXTENSIBILITY ELEMENT
>
> The findServiceData input extensibility element is constructed using a query type "queryByServiceDataNames" query. This query type definition is simple, as shown below:
>
> ```
> <element name="queryByServiceDataNames" type="ogsi:QNamesType"/>
> <complexType name="QNamesType">
>     <sequence>
>         <element name="name" type="QName" minOccurs="0"
>             maxOccurs="unbounded"/>
> ```

```
        </sequence>
    </complexType>
```

The wire representation is shown below:

```
<soapenv:Envelope
        xmlns:soapenv="http://schemas.xmlsoap.org/soap/envelope/"
        xmlns:xsd="http://www.w3.org/2001/XMLSchema"
        xmlns:xsi="http://www.w3.org/2001/XMLSchema-instance">
  <soapenv:Body>
        <findServiceData    xmlns="http://www.gridforum.org/namespaces/
2003/03/OGSI">
        <queryExpression>
        <queryByServiceDataNames xsi:type="ns1:QNamesType"
        xmlns:ns1="http://www.gridforum.org/namespaces/2003/03/OGSI">
        <name>serviceDataName</name>
            </queryByServiceDataNames>
        </queryExpression>
        </findServiceData>
  </soapenv:Body>
</soapenv:Envelope>
```

GT3-supported QueryHelper provides helper functionalities such as this one to convert QName to a query expression with queryByServiceDataNames as inner XML elements.

We will see later on how we can extend the findServiceData to accept XPath queries.

As shown in Listing 13.24, now we can go back to the service and ask each of the above listed service data elements for its value using the same "findServiceData" operation and "queryByServiceDataNames" expression.

Listing 13.24 Find service data operations on a service to get the interfaces implemented by the service.

```
extensibility =
searchService.findServiceData(QueryHelper.getNamesQuery("interface"));
serviceData = AnyHelper.getAsServiceDataValues(extensibility);
Object[] interfaces = AnyHelper.getAsObject(serviceData);
for(int i=0; i<interfaces.length; i++){
QName iface = (QName) interfaces[i];
System.out.println("interface: " + iface);
}
```

The above client-side implementation code accesses the "interfaces" SDEs values defined for our service. The results are shown in Listing 13.25.

Listing 13.25   Results of the find service data operations to get the interfaces implemented by the service.

```
interface name:  {http://org.ph.gridbook.sample/base/
acme}AcmeSearchPortType
interface name:  {http://org.ph.gridbook.sample/base/
cache}CacheSearchPortType
interface name:  GridService
interface name:  {http://org.ph.gridbook.sample/base/
general}GeneralSearchPortType
```

Listing 13.25 illustrates a runtime behavior of a grid service whereby we can infer the interfaces exposed by the services.

So far our discussion was centered on the grid service's default public exposed state. We will see more complex behaviors later in this chapter when we cover advanced topics on service data and notification.

> **5.** Finally, we are now done with the service. We can remove the service instance by calling an explicit destroy on the service instance.

A client can control the service lifecycle using soft state mechanisms or by explicitly calling the Gridservice "destroy" operation on the service. Listing 13.26 illustrates the use of the explicit "destroy" operation by the client.

Listing 13.26   Calling explicit destruction on the grid service instance.

```
GridService gridService = gridLocator.getGridServicePort(locator);
gridService.destroy();
```

The success of the above routine depends on various factors including the service policies applicable to the client and the service hosting environment properties.

We can enable a soft state destruction by using the termination time of the createService call parameter or by explicitly modifying the modifiable service data element "terminationTime." In such cases the GT3 container will take the responsibility to destroy the service after the termination time expiration. The destruction semantic is depending on container implementation logic with the only assertion that, once destructed, the clients cannot access the service instance anymore using the same GSH.

By now we have been introduced to the basic service implementation, configuration, and grid service behaviors. Now we can move on to more complex service implementation concepts.

We must note that enabling the logging and tracing information helps us understand the message flow between the client and the service. In the previous chapter on the programming model, we have covered the details on the various options to enable this feature.

Advanced Grid Service

In this section we will go through some advanced concepts around grid services. These include the use of operation providers to implement service port types, different types of service data, its creation and usage patterns, and notification mechanisms. We will start with service data concepts.

Advanced Service Data Concepts

These are publicly available states of a service. There are two types of service data elements, static and dynamic.

The static service data elements are declared in the GWSDL and added to the service instance service data set upon service instance startup. The framework does this by reading the GWSDL descriptions of the service. These service data elements will be available in the data set of the instance throughout the lifetime of the service. However, their values and availability are depending on the configuration of these elements, including mutability attributes and lifetime attributes. In our example, we are going to create two service data element declarations, one in the CacheSearchPortType and the other in the GeneralSearchPortType. Listings 13.27 and 13.28 are extensions to the portType declarations we have created earlier in this chapter.

Listing 13.27   Extended GeneralSearchPortType portType with service data elements.

```
<definitions name="GeneralSearch"
.................................................
<types>
  <xsd:schema
.................................................
<xsd:complexType name="SearchProviderType">
      <xsd:sequence>
        <xsd:element name="name" type="xsd:string"/>
        <xsd:element name="url" type="xsd:string"/>
      </xsd:sequence>
  </xsd:complexType>

</xsd:schema>
</types>
.................................................
<gwsdl:portType name="GeneralSearchPortType" extends="ogsi:GridService">
  <operation name="search">
      .................................................
  </operation>

<sd:serviceData name="searchProvider"
                type="general:SearchProviderType"
                minOccurs="1"
                maxOccurs="unbounded"
```

Listing 13.27   Extended GeneralSearchPortType portType with service data elements. (Cont.)

```
                        mutability="static"
                        modifiable="false"
                        nillable="false"/>

<sd:staticServiceDataValues>
        <general:searchProvider>
                        <name>Google</name>
                        <url>www.google.com</url>
        </general:searchProvider>
        <general:searchProvider>
                        <name>MSN</name>
                        <url>www.msn.com</url>
        </general:searchProvider>
  </sd:staticServiceDataValues>


</gwsdl:portType>
</definitions>
```

By careful observations we can see that this publicly exposed state "searchProvider" is a static service data element and needs to be initialized in the WSDL using staticServiceDataValues, as shown in Listing 13.27.

Listing 13.28   Extended CacheSearchPortType portType with service data elements.

```
<?xml version="1.0" encoding="UTF-8"?>
<definitions name="GeneralSearch"
.....................................

<types>
  <xsd:schema
      .....................................
    <xsd:complexType name="searchCacheSizeType">
      <xsd:sequence>
        <xsd:element name="newSize" type="xsd:int"/>
</xsd:sequence>
    </xsd:complexType>

</xsd:schema>

</types>
.....................................
<gwsdl:portType name="CacheSearchPortType" extends="ogsi:GridService">
  <operation name="cacheSearch">
      .....................................
```

Listing 13.28   Extended CacheSearchPortType portType with service data elements. (Cont.)

```
    </operation>

    <sd:serviceData name="searchCacheSize"
                    type="cache:searchCacheSizeType"
                    minOccurs="1"
                    maxOccurs="unbounded"
                    mutability="mutable"
                    modifiable="true"
                    nillable="false"/>

  </gwsdl:portType>

</definitions>
```

As shown in Listing 13.28, the publicly exposed state "`searchCacheSize`" is a mutable service data element. This enables the service clients to modify (modifiable='true') this service data value using the "setServiceData" operation.

One thing to notice is the type of SDE and their corresponding XML schema type. The SDE values are initialized using those types. As we have noticed earlier, these types are converted to their corresponding Java types by the tool WSDL2Java. The above XSD types in the example generate "`SearchCacheSizeType`", "`SearchProviderType`" classes.

By default, these service data elements are loaded to the Acme Search Service instance's service data set upon service initialization. We must be aware that the AcmeSearchPortType extends the above portTypes and thereby has all these SDEs with it. One thing to notice is that these service data elements defined by the super types can be overridden by the derived types. Refer back to our discussions in the OGSI chapter for more details on these capabilities.

On the assumption that we have deployed this service to the container, let us move to the client side to start working with these service data constructs.

Now, if running the client code shown in Listing 13.22, it must display two more additional service data elements in addition to the standard GridService defined ones. We can ask the service for the specific values of the static service data element "`searchProvider`" using the findServiceData method shown in Listing 13.29.

Listing 13.29   Calling find service data to get the statically configured search providers.

```
// Get the service data values for SDE "searchProvider"
extensibility =
searchService.findServiceData(QueryHelper.getNamesQuery("searchProvider"))
;
// Get the base the service data value type
serviceData = AnyHelper.getAsServiceDataValues(extensibility);
```

Listing 13.29   Calling find service data to get the statically configured search providers. (Cont.)

```
// Convert the elements to the know type SearchProviderType
Object[] providerValues =
AnyHelper.getAsObject(serviceData,SearchProviderType.class);

// display the search provider information
for(int i=0; i<providerValues.length; i++){
SearchProviderType searchProvider = (SearchProviderType)
providerValues[i];
System.out.println("searchProvider name: " + searchProvider.getName());
}
```

The routine in Listing 13.29 should display the information in Listing 13.30, which are configured as static service data element values.

Listing 13.30   Results on calling the find service data operation.

```
searchProvider name: Google
searchProvider name: MSN
```

One of the service data elements (searchCacheSize) we have added to the WSDL is changeable by the client. We have mentioned earlier that for this to be successful we need to set service data element attribute "modifiable" with a value of "true." This enables the client to invoke a setServiceData operation on this service data element with a new value for the "SearchCacheSize-Type" object. The code in Listing 13.31 illustrates this process.

Listing 13.31   Set service data operation on a service data element.

```
SearchCacheSizeType newCacheValue = new SearchCacheSizeType();
// set a new cache
newCacheValue.setNewSize(34);

org.apache.axis.message.MessageElement elem =
(org.apache.axis.message.MessageElement)AnyHelper.toAny(newCacheValue);
org.apache.axis.message.MessageElement setWrapper = new
org.apache.axis.message.MessageElement();
setWrapper.setQName(org.globus.ogsa.GridConstants.SET_BY_NAME);
setWrapper.addChild(elem);

ExtensibilityType any = new ExtensibilityType();
any.set_any(new org.apache.axis.message.MessageElement[] { setWrapper });

// calls the setServiceData operation to update the service data
searchService.setServiceData(any);
```

To further illustrate this, let us examine the SOAP message in Listing 13.32 for the above update message.

Listing 13.32 SOAP request message for set service data.

```
<soapenv:Envelope xmlns:soapenv="http://schemas.xmlsoap.org/soap/envelope/
" xmlns:xsd="http://www.w3.org/2001/XMLSchema" xmlns:xsi="http://
www.w3.org/2001/XMLSchema-instance">
 <soapenv:Body>
  <setServiceData xmlns="http://www.gridforum.org/namespaces/2003/03/
OGSI">
   <updateExpression>
    <setByServiceDataNames>
     <ns2:value xsi:type="ns1:searchCacheSizeType" xmlns:ns1="http://
org.ph.gridbook.sample/servicedata/cache" xmlns:ns2="http://
ogsa.globus.org/">
       <ns1:newSize>34</ns1:newSize>
     </ns2:value>
    </setByServiceDataNames>
   </updateExpression>
  </setServiceData>
 </soapenv:Body>
</soapenv:Envelope>
```

So far we have been dealing with the static service data elements declared as part of GWSDL. Now let's turn our attention to some dynamic service data elements created by the service.

The dynamic service data elements can be created at any time and can be added to the service data set. This is done with the help of an instance-specific service data set object. The routine in Listing 13.33 illustrates how our Acme Search Service instantiates a dynamic service data object and adds that to the service data set.

Listing 13.33 Creating dynamic service data element.

```
//Create Service Data Element
ServiceData serviceDataElement =
this.getServiceDataSet().create("MyServiceData");
// Create a service data value and set that value
// Can be complex objects or simple. What is shown here is a simple java
'string'
serviceDataElement.setValue("my simple service data element");
//Add SDE to Service Data Set
this.getServiceDataSet().add(serviceDataElement);
// now onwards available for client discovery
```

Once this dynamic service data is added to the service data set, the client can query for them and can work with them (Listing 13.34).

Listing 13.34   Accessing the dynamic service data element.

```
extensibility =
searchService.findServiceData(QueryHelper.getNamesQuery("MyServiceData"));

serviceData = AnyHelper.getAsServiceDataValues(extensibility);
Object[] mySDValue = AnyHelper.getAsObject(serviceData);
for(int i=0; i<mySDValue.length; i++){
String myValue = (String) mySDValue[i];
System.out.println("Dynamic sd value : " + myValue);
}
```

The clients can do dynamic service introspection on the service to find the available SDEs (static and dynamic) at any point in time. The problem with dynamic service data elements is the unavailability of the semantics of the service state data to the clients. This may get complicated on the processing of these dynamic service data unless the client knows or there is an a priori agreement on the semantics and type of this data.

Operation Providers

The concept of operation providers helps the server-side developers to separate the application logic external to the service implementation code. We have discussed the value-added features provided by this framework. Now we will see how we can come up with an extendable and manageable application design for our service. We decided that all our business logic should be external to the service implementation so that they can grow as the service gets matured.

For example, our caching search service is very primitive at this stage. However, later we may come up with more complex and valuable implementations for the same without disrupting the existing service implementation. We can plug in the new provider through the service configuration options. This provides a highly flexible approach.

We are going to implement the GeneralSearchPortType and CacheSearchPortType interfaces in different providers. We will create two providers, GeneralSearchProvider and CacheSearchProvider.

Our service implementation looks similar to the UML diagram shown in Figure 13.6.

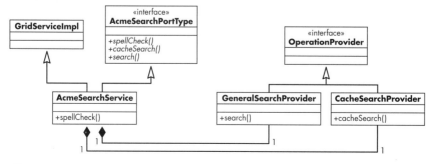

Figure 13.6
Acme service implementation using OperationProvider.

Let us now take a look into the code of one provider, CacheSearchProvider in Listing 13.35.

Listing 13.35 Operation provider implementation.

```
public class GeneralSearchProvider implements OperationProvider {
    public static QName[] operations =
        new QName[] {
            new QName(http://org.ph.gridbook.sample/base/general, "search"
        };
    public QName[] getOperations() {
        return operations;
    }

    public void initialize(GridServiceBase base) throws
GridServiceException {
    }

    public GeneralSearchProvider () {
    }

    public SearchResponseType search(SearchType searchInput)
                                    throws java.rmi.RemoteException{
        SearchResponseType response = new SearchResponseType();
        response.setURL("www.ibm.com");
        response.setSummary("IBM");
        response.setCached(true);
        return response;
    }
}
```

Listing 13.35 illustrates how we can separate our portType implementation out of the service code and move that to an operation provider. On careful examination, we can see that the public operations we are exposing are listed in the QName list. These operations correspond to their WSDL counterparts. These are exposed through the getOperations() method. Our service implementation only implements the spellCheck method. Since our AcmeSearchPortType lists all the abstract interfaces, we need to add these additional operations to our service code as templates to satisfy our compilers. The client code remains the same. However, we need to add the above provider to the configurations list, as shown in Listing 13.36.

Listing 13.36 Configuring operation provider with the service configuration.

```
<service name="ph/acme/operationprovider/AcmeSearchService"
provider="Handler" style="wrapped">
.........................
<parameter name=" instance-operationProviders"
    value="org.ph.gridbook.impl.operationprovider.CacheSearchProvider
        org.ph.gridbook.impl.operationprovider.GeneralSearchProvider "/>
</service>
```

We are now done with the service configuration and our client can start invoking operations on our service using the same client code shown earlier.

Providing Asynchronous Behaviors through Notification

The notification mechanism defined by OGSI is very flexible. It provides a flexible subscription mechanism by allowing different types of subscription expressions as specified by the service. All service is required to provide the "subscribeByServiceDataName" expression. This enables clients to register for notification on service data element value changes. The Globus GT3 framework supports this default behavior. In addition, it can be extensible to support a topic-based subscription, which is a derivative model from the above, "subscribeByServiceDataName" type of subscription. In the previous chapter, we have covered the details on the GT3 architectural and programming support for notifications. Now it's code time; we will discuss the topics we have covered in the last chapter with some sample code. We will extend our AcmeSearchService as a notification provider. These samples will illustrate:

1. Subscribing for service data change using service data name element
2. Subscribing for some interesting topics exposed by the AcmeSearchService.

Let us explore the details.

Subscribing for Service Data Change Using Service Data Name Element

Figure 13.7 illustrates the basic concept. Clients can subscribe for service data value change through subscription by providing the interested service data element name.

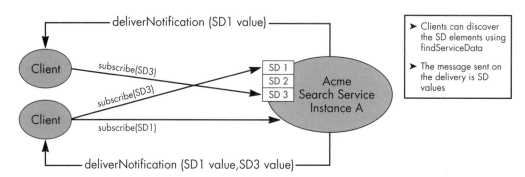

Figure 13.7
Notification based on service data change.

First and foremost, the change we have to make is to let the service implement the Notification Source portType as defined by OGSI. We can do this by changing the GWSDL portType definition of our service. Listing 13.37 shows how we will change the AcmeSearchPortType in the gwsdl.

Listing 13.37 Acme service extending notification source portType.

```
<?xml version="1.0" encoding="UTF-8"?>
<definitions name="AcmeSearch" targetNamespace="http://
org.ph.gridbook.sample/base/acme"
.............................">
.......................................
<gwsdl:portType name="AcmeSearchPortType"
extends="ogsi:GridService ogsi:NotificationSource
general:GeneralSearchPortType
cache:CacheSearchPortType">
  <operation name="spellCheck">
    <input message="acme:SpellCheckInputMessage"/>
    <output message="acme:SpellCheckOutputMessage"/>
  </operation>
</gwsdl:portType>
</definitions>
```

As shown in Listing 13.37, we have extended our portType from ogsi:NotificationSource interface. While running the tools (GWSDL2WSDL, GenerateBinding, and then GWSDL2Java), we will be able to generate the necessary stubs and portTypes that can handle the notification subscription process.

In the previous chapter, we described these listed tools and their utilization model. The generated AcmeSearchPortType interface contains a "subscribe" operation, in addition to the other operations we saw earlier. This interface is in Listing 13.38.

Listing 13.38 Endpoint interface for Acme Search Service with notification operations.

```
package org.ph.gridbook.notification;

public interface AcmeSearchPortType extends org.gridforum.ogsi.GridService
{

    // Most of the Exceptions are not shown for code clarity.............
    public org.gridforum.ogsi.ExtensibilityType
findServiceData(org.gridforum.ogsi.ExtensibilityType queryExpression)
throws java.rmi.RemoteException, ...................;

    public void subscribe(org.gridforum.ogsi.ExtensibilityType
subscriptionExpression, org.gridforum.ogsi.LocatorType sink,
org.gridforum.ogsi.ExtendedDateTimeType expirationTime,
org.gridforum.ogsi.holders.LocatorTypeHolder subscriptionInstanceLocator,
org.gridforum.ogsi.holders.TerminationTimeTypeHolder
currentTerminationTime) throws java.rmi.RemoteException,....;
.......................................
    public void destroy() throws java.rmi.RemoteException,.............;
```

Listing 13.38   Endpoint interface for Acme Search Service with notification operations. (Cont.)

```
    public org.ph.gridbook.notification.SpellCheckMessageResponseType
spellCheck(org.ph.gridbook. notification.SpellCheckMessageType
spellCheckInput) throws java.rmi.RemoteException;

// some methods are not shown for code readability................
}
```

The GT3 framework comes with a number of framework components to deal with the service data change notification. The default NotificationSourceProvider class provides most of the required functionality, so we need to configure our service to use the default notification source provider. Listing 13.39 shows how to add this new instance operation provider to our configuration.

Listing 13.39   Service configuration with notification source provider.

```
<service name="ph/acme/operationprovider/AcmeSearchService"
provider="Handler" style="wrapped">
..............................
<parameter name=" instance-operationProviders"
        value="org.ph.gridbook.impl.operationprovider.CacheSearchProvider
            org.ph.gridbook.impl.operationprovider.GeneralSearchProvider
            org.globus.ogsa.impl.ogsi.NotificationSourceProvider"/>
</service>
```

At the client side we need to provide two implementation artifacts:

- Create a sink listener to receive notification. A sink should implement the OGSI NotificationSink interface and expose the "deliverNotification" operation. This sink is a grid service with a unique handle (GSH) and the client sends this handle to the service during subscription in order to receive notification callbacks. This process is simpler if our client is a grid service. However, since our current client is a Java application, we need a container to support this at the client side to create the sink service, and to listen for the message delivery. For this to occur, we will make use of the lightweight client container included with GT3.

The routine in Listing 13.40 explains how we are initializing this container and listening on a port. We can always configure some of the properties, including the port, protocol, and hostname of this client-side container through the client-server-config.wsdd file.

Listing 13.40   Configuring the client sink container.

```
// Create a sink manager, which provides a lightweight container capability
NotificationSinkManager notifManager =
NotificationSinkManager.getManager();
```

Listing 13.40 Configuring the client sink container. (Cont.)

```
// Start listening on a port
notifManager.startListening(NotificationSinkManager.MAIN_THREAD);

// Need to create a sink callback object, which implements the
NotificationSinkCallback interface
NotificationSinkCallback client = new myNotificationSinkCallbackImpl();
```

- Create a subscription with the service. The subscription process is simple, provided we are using the notification manager as shown above. The only requirement is to add a delivery message listener of type NotificationSinkCallback and add that listener to the manager along with the service data element name (identified using name or QName) for which we are listening for changes. This listener implements a "deliverNotification" operation, which will be called on notifications from the service. The routine in Listing 13.41 shows how we will be enabling the callback and sending a subscribe call to the source service.

Listing 13.41 Subscribing for service data change notifications.

```
// Subscribe for service data notification by passing the service data
name, handle of the service instance whose SD changes we are watching, and
the notification sink callback method
String sink  =  notifManager.addListener("MyServiceData", null, handle,
client);
```

Next, we will implement the notification receiver to receive change notification messages from the service instance (Listing 13.42).

Listing 13.42 Receiving messages from the service.

```
Class myNotificationSinkCallbackImpl implements NotificationSinkCallback  {
    public void deliverNotification (ExtensibilityType any) throws
    RemoteException{
        ServiceDataValuesType serviceData =
        AnyHelper.getAsServiceDataValues(any);
        Object[] mySDValue = AnyHelper.getAsObject(serviceData);
        for(int i=0; i<mySDValue.length; i++){
            String myValue = (String) mySDValue[i];
            System.out.println("Received a notification from service
                            with value: " + myValue);
        }
    }
}
```

It is important to understand whenever there is a change in the service data element (identified by "MyServiceData"), a notification message will be sent to the client. As shown in Listing 13.43, we can force this notification push from our service code using a "notifyChange()" message.

Listing 13.43   Service code to push an SD notification change to the client.

```
/* We saw earlier that this is a dynamic service data element and it is
already defined and created for the service. Now get the SDE and change
its value */
ServiceData serviceDataElement= getServiceDataSet().get("MyServiceData");
serviceDataElement.setValue("A changed service data value…");
// Notify the service data element change
serviceDataElement.notifyChange();
```

Paying close attention to the above implementation logic, we can infer that the above process is static in nature, based upon the service data and its type. We can extend this model to a more generalized solution for asynchronous messages, where the topics can be broader than the service data elements, and the data can be of any type.

Subscribing for Some Interesting Topics Exposed by the AcmeSearchService

Figure 13.8 explains a dynamic notification process using the concept of "topics." A service can expose some topics, to which it feels relevant for the clients to subscribe. These topics can be created dynamically upon service startup. These topics are added to the provider. The provider currently exposes these dynamic topics in the service data element set. The routine in Listing 13.44 explains how we can do this. There is no configuration change needed for the service.

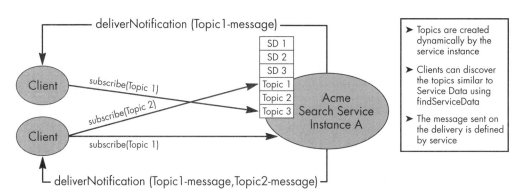

Figure 13.8
Dynamic topic-based subscription.

Listing 13.44   Creating dynamic topics and adding to the provider.

```
NotificationProvider provider =(NotificationProvider) getProperty(
ServiceProperties.NOTIFICATION_SOURCE);
```

Listing 13.44   Creating dynamic topics and adding to the provider. (Cont.)

```
// adding a topic of interest with the notification provider with a
namespace and message type
provider.addTopic("ServiceDestroyNotification", new QName("http://
org.ph.gridbook.sample/notification/acme",
"xsd:string")
```

The clients can now discover this topic through the "findServiceData" operation and can register for that dynamic topic (Listing 13.45).

Listing 13.45   Finding the dynamic topics adding to the provider.

```
extensibility =
searchService.findServiceData(QueryHelper.getNamesQuery("serviceDataName")
);
serviceData = AnyHelper.getAsServiceDataValues(extensibility);
Object[] serviceDataNames = AnyHelper.getAsObject(serviceData);
for(int i=0; i<serviceDataNames.length; i++){
QName serviceDataName = (QName) serviceDataNames[i];
System.out.println("serviceDataName: " + serviceDataName);
}
```

The above call should list {http://org.ph.gridbook.sample/notification/acme: ServiceDestroyNotification} as one of the service data elements. This is the exposed "topic" and the clients can register their interest in this topic using the routine shown in Listing 13.46.

Listing 13.46   Adding a listener on the dynamic topics.

```
QName sdname = new QName("http://org.ph.gridbook.sample/notification/
acme",
" ServiceDestroyNotification ");
String sink  =  notifManager.addListener(sdname, null, handle, client);
```

On running the code in Listing 13.46, the client is ready to receive notification from the service instance when it is trying to destroy the service.

Let us now see how the service is sending the change notifications related to the above topic. The routine in Listing 13.47 shows how we can do this.

Listing 13.47   Sending a notification.

```
provider.notify("ServiceDestroyNotification","I am destroying...");
```

One thing we didn't mention is regarding the lifecycle of the subscription. On a subscription message from the client, the grid service instance creates a NotificationSubscription object with the necessary subscription information, including the subscription lifetime. This is a grid service instance and a GSH is passed back to the client. The client can control the lifecycle of a subscription through soft state management mechanisms. Once the client feels that the subscription is no longer needed, it can call the normal grid service "destroy" operation on the subscription object to get the subscription removed.

The above-described notification mechanisms can be further extended to support more complex mechanisms including the subscription criteria for filtering, message batching, and the use of a more reliable message exchange model.

EJB Delegation

As shown in Figure 13.9, GT3 provides a delegation model to support the business logic implemented in the EJB.

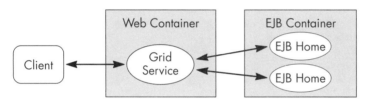

Figure 13.9
Delegation-based grid services.

The default factory can be configured to have an EJB callback implementation provided with GT3, which provides support to connect to EJB home and create an EJB remote object of choice. The configuration for the JNDI name for the home lookup is configured as a service configuration parameter. The service developers are required to derive their service implementations from the abstract EJBServiceImpl class to provide a constructor that can accept the EJB Home and EJB Remote objects.

The UML diagram (logical) in Figure 13.10 shows a delegation model.

The internal implementation of the callback object is simple. Based on the type of EJB, it either creates the EJB or tries to find the EJB. This is done by introspection on the metadata provided by the EJB home object (through the call home.getEJBMetaData()). This introspection provides information such as the type (stateless, stateful, or entity) of EJB. Based on these metadata information it either creates the bean or tries to find the bean using the primary key. After the retrieval of the home and remote objects, the callback creates the grid service instance and initializes the service with the EJB home and remote objects.

Now let us see how our Acme service's cache can be implemented in an EJB entity bean. We won't talk about the EJB implementation. Our assumption is that we have already created an

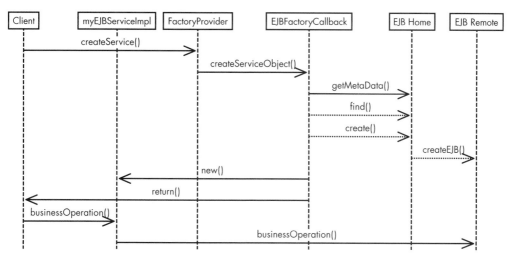

Figure 13.10
EJB delegation model.

entity EJB bean object, and its corresponding Home object, and both are deployed to the J2EE container. The home is identified through the JNDI name "ph/cache/EjbCache."

Let us now create our Acme Search grid service, and the delegate calls to the "cacheSearch" for the corresponding EJB remote operation. Listing 13.48 shows how we can do this.

Listing 13.48   Grid service implemented with EJB delegation mechanism.

```
public class myEJBServiceImpl extends EJBServiceImpl implements
AcmeSearchPortType {
    public myEJBServiceImpl( String name, EJBHome _home, EJBObject
_remote) {
        super(name, _home, _remote);
    }
    public CacheSearchMessageResponseType
cacheSearch(CacheSearchMessageType cacheSearchInput) throws
java.rmi.RemoteException{
// extract the search input data
// convert to EJB acceptable serializable objects
// call method on the remote object
    getRemote().cacheSearch();
// get the results and convert that to CacheSearchMessageResponseType
// send back the result
return new CacheSearchMessageResponseType ();
    }
.................................
}
```

The deployment of the service with the EJB home JNDI name is in the configuration fragment in Listing 13.49.

Listing 13.49　Grid service and delegation EJB home JNDI configuration.

```
<service name="ph/acme/ejb/AcmeSearchService" provider="Handler"
style="wrapped">
.................................
<parameter name="ejbLookupString" value=" ph/cache/EjbCache"/>

<parameter name="factoryCallback"
value="org.globus.ogsa.impl.core.factory.EJBFactoryCallback"/>
<parameter name="operationProviders"
value="org.globus.ogsa.impl.ogsi.FactoryProvider"/>
.................................
</service>
```

We can now call the service and start using the business methods. The calls to cacheSearch will be delegated to the corresponding EJB instance. The default operation removes the session EJBs on the service destroy, but it will not touch the entities. If we need to, we can override this feature by implementing the destroy method.

The EJB callback implementation, as we observed in this section, is sufficient for the simple delegation model we have discussed. Note that we can always plug in our own callback implementations for more sophisticated functionalities.

CONCLUSION

We have been discussing the GT3 toolkit, providing a reference implementation of OGSI and explaining the core concepts of a grid service and its behaviors through some rather simple examples. The main idea of this discussion was to introduce the toolkit core components and capabilities. This GT3 framework provides a rich enough environment to support a number of complex service creation scenarios. As we have noted, the Globus GT3 high-level services, such as index services, information services, and GRAM are all built upon this core GT3 framework.

In the next chapter, we will see more details on these high-level grid services.

NOTES

1. For more information, go to *www.jcp.org/aboutJava/communityprocess/final/jsr101/index.html.*

2. For more information, go to *http://ws.apache.org/axis/index.html.*

3. GT3 is a Web application and when we install it will function like this. This is the default URL to the Web application.

4. For more information, go to *www.ws-i.org/schemas/conformanceClaim/ProfileConformance-1.0-WGD.pdf*

GLOBUS GT3 Toolkit: High-Level Services

INTRODUCTION

G rid technologies enable large-scale sharing of resources within a group of individuals and/ or institutions. There are three complex areas in the grid environment that requires our attention: resource discovery/monitoring, resource allocation, and data management. This chapter will address these key areas.

RESOURCE DISCOVERY AND MONITORING

The complex grid environment, with a number of dynamic behaviors and complex geographical distribution, introduces a number of challenges, including discovery, optimization, classification, aggregation, and monitoring of sharable resources.

These resources can be broadly classified as computational data resources. In order to reduce this complexity from the end user of the grid system, a number of information services are generated with fundamental capabilities of resource discovery, classification, and monitoring. Once the clients are able to discover and monitor these resources, these resources will help clients to plan the resource utilization, and can then adapt clients to the application behavior. These types of services are generally classified as information services.

RESOURCE ALLOCATION

Allocation of resources in a grid environment is complex. It requires the knowledge of user requirements, resource capabilities, and other economic criteria (e.g., price and time metrics). The more precise the allocation process, the more efficient the resource utilization is, and ultimately the user satisfaction. There are provisions available today to accomplish advance resource reservations in order to provide On Demand, dynamic resource provisioning.

DATA MANAGEMENT

Many of the grid systems that exist today are data intensive and must be capable of transporting very large amounts of data, both static and in real time. The ability to access and manage data is another important area in computational and data grids. This involves moving data between grid resources, and/or allowing resource access to the data, On Demand. These kinds of data movement activities are very common in job schedulers.

Figure 14.1 shows the logical layers in grid architecture. The base services and the data services together provide most of the basic facilities we have previously discussed. These are required for high-level grid applications and services, including job managers, schedulers, resources, and provisioning agents. These high-level services and applications utilize these base services for resource discovery, classification, resource allocation, resource usage planning, monitoring, and scheduling.

It is recommended that one implement a middleware tool to provide some of these base services. Globus Toolkit (GT3) provides a number of these high-level services. These high-level services are utilizing the core GT3 framework as the fundamental set of building blocks. In GT3, there are information services, resource allocation services, and data services available to the developer. We will discuss each of these component details in the coming pages.

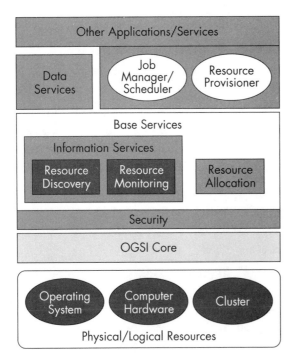

Figure 14.1
This illustration depicts a logical view of the levels of grid services.

INFORMATION SERVICES

In the context of GT3, information services have to fulfill the following requirements:

- A basis for configuration and adaptation in heterogeneous environments
- Uniform and flexible access to static and dynamic information
- Scalable and efficient access to data
- Access to multiple information sources
- Decentralized maintenance capabilities

Our discussion will be focused on GT3, the latest toolkit based on the OGSI. In the GT3 base, the information services consist of a broad framework that includes any part of GT3. This framework can generate important capabilities, such as register, index, aggregate, subscribe, monitor, query, and/or display service data. The core concepts of information services in GT3 are centered on how to create, update, and query service data; this forms the public state of a service/resource.

GT3 provides a set of information services built utilizing a service data component model. Utilizing the GT3 core programming features, which we have discussed in the last two chapters, develops this component model. The development of a component model helps service developers to deal with the complexity of software management in relatively small manageable software modules. The GT3-offered component model is based upon Java.

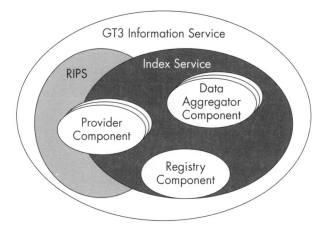

Figure 14.2
The GT3 components and information services.

Figure 14.2 shows the major information services available with the GT3 base, and the components utilized by these services. The details related to this discussion on this component model and services are as follows:

1. The GT3 framework provides a component model that can be utilized to create and deliver information services.

2. The GT3 framework provides high-level applications and services, built upon the above component model.

Component Model for Information Services

These components provide a standard means

- to create the service data from other grid services and external applications.
- to aggregate the service data values and categorize them in a form required by the application.
- to provide the storage location(s) to register and store grid service handles. These registered grid services provide service data either through a provider "pull" or through notification on the service data change.

Generally speaking, there are three types of components available: service data provider components, service data aggregation components, and registry components.

Let us now further explore each of these components, their functionalities, and their programming models.

Service Data Provider Components

These providers enable a standard mechanism for dynamic service data generation from external programs. The GT3 core provides a set of providers, which provides some common set of functionalities. We will cover the usage of these providers later in this chapter when we introduce the index services. We can extend these providers, or add on new providers.

The service data provider interfaces are designed to support the execution in either synchronous (pull) or asynchronous (push) modes. Different provider interfaces are available and selected based on their functionalities.

These provider interfaces are:

SimpleDataProvider. This is a synchronous provider that is capable of producing output in XML format in a Java OutputStream.

Listing 14.1   The simpleDataProvider interface.

```
public interface SimpleDataProvider {
    ...............................................................
    /* Triggers the execution of the provider in order to update the
    provider's internal state, but does not perform any output.*/

    void update(String args) throws Exception;
```

Listing 14.1   The simpleDataProvider interface. (Continued)

```
    /* Triggers the provider to serialize its current internal state to
    the specified OutputStream */

    void output(java.io.OutputStream outStream) throws Exception;

    /*Triggers the execution of the provider in order to update the
    provider's internal state, sending the output to the specified
    OutputStream. */

    void run(String args, java.io.OutputStream outStream) throws Exception;
}
```

Listing 14.1 shows the important operations allowed on a simpleDataProvider.

DOMDataProvider. Similar to the above SimpleDataProvider, this object, shown in Listing 14.2, is also a synchronous provider that can generate XML output in a w3c.dom.Document XML format.

Listing 14.2   The DOMDataProvider interface.

```
public interface DOMDataProvider extends SimpleDataProvider{
    public org.w3c.dom.Document outputDocument() throws Exception;
}
```

This is an extension to the SimpleDataProvider, and provides an additional method to output the internal state of the provider as a DOM Document.

AsyncDataProvider. Shown in Listing 14.3, this is an asynchronous provider that can support the above two data formats (i.e., XML data in OutputStream object, and XML document in w3c.dom.document format).

Listing 14.3   The AsyncDataProvider.

```
public interface AsyncDataProvider extends SimpleDataProvider{
    /* Triggers the asynchronous execution of the provider, sending the
    output to the specified callback object. It will execute the callback
    name on the callback object. Context is defined by the calling thread.
    */

    void run(String args, String callbackName,
    ServiceDataProviderDocumentCallback callback, Object context) throws
    Exception;

    /* Signals the provider to shut down, cease data callbacks, and free
    any associated resources */

    void terminate() throws Exception;
```

Listing 14.3 The AsyncDataProvider. (Continued)

```
    /* Retrieve the current state */
    int getState();
}
```

This provider enables an asynchronous call to a specified object. The following section describes some of the internal details on this provider implementation.

INTERNAL DETAILS ON PROVIDER EXECUTION

There is a provider manager (ServiceDataProviderManager) that is responsible for scheduling and managing the provider execution. This provider manager is a GT3 operation provider with two exposed methods, "enumProvider" and "executePro-vider." These operations are exposed in the WSDL portType definition for the provider manager. The provider manager, in turn, delegates the execution to the provider of choice. These available providers are listed in a configuration file.

For example, to register the provider called HostScriptProvider, add the following entry in the configuration file:

```
<provider class="org.globus.ogsa.impl.base.providers.servicedata.impl
.HostScriptProvider"/>
```

The list below describes a simple ServiceDataProviderManager implementation:

```
public class ServiceDataProviderManager implements
                                ServiceDataProviderExecutionPortType,
                                ServiceProviderExecutionCallback,
                                ServiceDataProviderDocumentCallback,
                                OperationProvider{
...................................
    public ServiceDataProviderEnumType[] enumProvider(boolean
                                rescanConfig){
    }
    public void executeProvider(ServiceDataProviderExecutionType
                                newServiceData, Object callback){
    }
    ...............................................
}
```

Normally speaking, the provider manager will convert the provider output to an XML message in a ServiceDataElement, and then add that to the service's Service-DataSet. Registering a custom callback (ServiceDataProviderExecutionCallback) with provider manager, and accessing the results from the provider, can override the preestablished functionality. This operation is simple to establish, as one can pass the callback object along with the "executeProvider" operation. The callback object

> must be of the type ServiceDataProviderDocumentCallback, it must provide an oper-
> ation name, and the expected parameters. The provider manager will perform run-
> time introspection on the object method, and invoke the method with the expected
> parameters.
>
> The following describes how one can perform this operation:
>
> ```
> Public class myCallbackObject implements ServiceDataProviderDocumentCallback{
>     public String getdefaultCallbackMethodName(){
>         return  "myMethod";
>     }
>     public class[] getCallbackParamSig(String methodName){
>         return new class[] ={Class.forName("org.w3c.dom.Document")};
>     }
>     public boolean myMethod(org.w3.dom.Document){
>         // the results of the provider execution comes here
>         // we can do whatever we want
>     }
> }
> ```
>
> To pass the above callback object call, execute the following:
>
> ```
> executeProvider(service data provider execution type, new
> myCallbackObject());
> ```
>
> This is a very powerful feature by which grid developers can override the provider
> manager's default internal logic without having the provider manager source code.

As we have just discussed, a provider manager can maintain two unique types of operations,
"enumProviders" and "executeProvider." The "executeProvider" operation expects to receive a
parameter of complex type, defined in WSDL, with the anticipated information, such as provider
name, provider implementation class, provider argument, and service data name. This is relevant
information for the provider for three reasons, which are instructions regarding service data type,
refresh frequency, and whether to execute in synchronous or asynchronous fashion. We will later
see how this powerful feature is utilized in the index service implementation.

Service Data Aggregation Components

This discussion will explore another very interesting aspect of service data management, where
we will begin to better understand the aggregation component. Service data coming from various
providers can be aggregated in different ways, and then indexed to provide for improved efficiencies related to query processing.

This aggregator component is similar to server-side notification *sink*.[1] In addition to listening for
notification of a service data change, this operation provides a mechanism to copy the incoming
notification data as local service data elements. This component is implemented as an operation

provider with the exposed operations "addSubscription," "removeSubscription," and "deliverNotification." Listing 14.4 shows an example of this implementation, with the extended interfaces.

Listing 14.4   The serviceData aggregation operation.

```
public class ServiceDataAggregatorImpl implements ServiceDataAggregatorPortType,
                        OperationProvider,
                        NotificationSinkCallback{
.................................
public String addSubscription(AggregatorSubscriptionType type){
}
public void removeSubscription(String subscriptionID){
}
public void deliverNotification(ExtensibilityType message){
}
```

Registry Components

Registry components are sets of available grid services that are maintained in a registry. This
provides a soft state registration mechanism to periodically update service availability. This registry is implemented using the OGSI ServiceGroup mechanisms.

A Sample Provider Creation

Here are the steps for constructing a sample provider that can read system configurations, and
send these as an XML document to the provider manager.

  1. Write a sample executable that can run and read system properties from the current
     runtime and dump the results to the output stream as a DOM document (here we are
     using System.out).

Listing 14.5   A sample executable reading the system information and emitting a DOM document.

```
public class SystemInformationCollector{
    public static void main(String args[]) {
        try {
            SystemInformationCollector sysInfoCollector = new
SystemInformationCollector();
// pass the default arguments and System.out as parameters
sysInfoCollector.run(argstr,System.out);
        }
        catch(Exception e) {
            e.printStackTrace();
        }
    }
    public void run(String args, java.io.OutputStream outStream) throws
Exception{
```

Listing 14.5 A sample executable reading the system information and emitting a DOM document.

```
    Document doc = getSystemInfo();
 // Write the DOM document to the provided output stream
        outStream.write(doc.toString());
    }

    protected Document getSystemInfo() throws Exception{
        Runtime runtime = Runtime.getRuntime();
        // sample system information
        long totalMem = runtime.totalMemory();
        long freeMem = runtime.freeMemory();
        long usedMem = totalMem - freeMem;

Document dom = doc = org.apache.axis.utils.XMLUtils.newDocument();
// initialize the DOM document with the above system information

return dom;
    }
}
```

2. Write a sample provider, following the programming model that is discussed earlier, that can start the above executable we have created in step 1 and read the output from the output stream.

Listing 14.6 A sample DOMDataProvider emitting org.w3c.dom.Document.

```
public class SimpleExecutionProvider implements DOMDataProvider{
    protected Document resultDoc = null;
    protected Process process = null;
    protected String errorString = "";

    /** Creates a new instance of SimpleExecutionProvider */
    public SimpleExecutionProvider () {
    }

    /**
     * Triggers the execution of the provider in order to update the
provider's
     * internal state, sending the output to the specified OutputStream
     */
    public org.w3c.dom.Document run(String args) throws Exception{
        Document doc = null;
        /****
Execute the information provider application with the necessary arguments
as we defined earlier
        **/
```

Listing 14.6   A sample DOMDataProvider emitting org.w3c.dom.Document. (Continued)

```
        this.exec(args);

        // read the output stream of the above created process
        try{
if (this.process != null) {
// assuming the results are written in XML format as specified in the
earlier listing
            doc =
org.apache.axis.utils.XMLUtils.newDocument(this.process.getInputStream());
}
        }catch (Exception e){
         throw e;
         }finally{
// check for the exit state
int exit = 0;
            try {
                exit = this.process.exitValue();
                }catch (IllegalThreadStateException itse) {
        // if the process is running wait for that process to end.
exit = this.process.waitFor();
            }
        }
        return doc;
    }

    // execute the above defined sample system information application
    private void exec(String args) throws Exception{
        // run the sample
Runtime runtime = Runtime.getRuntime();
        try {
            this.process = runtime.exec(args);
        }
        catch (Exception e) {
            this.errorString = "Provider Execution error: " + e.getMessage
();
            throw new Exception(this.errorString);
        }
    }
}
```

Listing 14.5 and 14.6 demonstrate how to construct a sample provider and how to manage the data.

Conclusion

Thus far, we have been discussing the component model introduced by GT3 for information services. In addition, we provided treatment to the programming model, and the interfaces associated with the core components. GT3 provides a set of standard components to support some of the built-in information services that comes with the toolkit. You can always create new components and add them to the high-level services through simple configuration options.

Having discussed the component model in detail, now it is time to explore some of the GT3 high-level services that are integrated with the GT3 Toolkit. These information services are providing a wide variety of value-added features, and have remained in the Globus toolkit from its inception.

This discussion covers the details of the information services, including their value, usage, and implementation aspects. Exploring the designs of these services help us to better understand the component model we have previously discussed. Some of the high-level services we will be reviewing include index services, resource information provider (RIP), and container/virtual organization registry.

INDEX SERVICES

One of the most important high-level services delivered with the GT3 information services is the index services capability. This service is responsible for managing static and dynamic state data for grid services. Figure 14.3 shows the index service high-level overview. As shown is the illustration, the important components in the index service core are:

- Service data providers
- Data aggregators
- Grid service registries

The GT3-provided index service has the capability of constructing an interface for connecting external service data provider programs to grid service instances. These providers enable a standard mechanism for dynamic service data generation from external programs. The GT3 core provides a set of sample providers via the SimpleSystemInformation and HostScriptProvider objects.

These providers are:

- *SimpleSystemInformation.* These are native system probes. This enumerates the following data: CPU count, memory statistics, OS type, and logical disk volumes.
- *HostScriptProvider.* These are Linux-specific shell scripts that monitor system-specific host data.

One can always extend these providers or add on new custom providers, depending on the requirements. It is important to note that these providers are configured using the "index-service-config.xml" file.

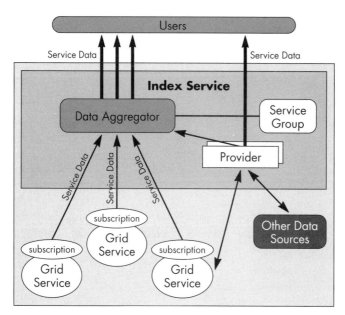

Figure 14.3
An overview of the GT3 Index Service.

These providers are simple Java applications that are rendering their results of execution to the Java output stream. In the above two cases, the output stream is mapped to Java System.out. In our previous discussions, we reviewed a sample implementation of a provider. One can always add their own provider and register them in a configuration file.

A generic framework for aggregating data from other services involves service data originating from various providers (and other services) that can be aggregated and indexed to provide efficient query processing. This index service utilizes the standard OGSI notification mechanisms for subscription, notification, and updating of the service data.

A Registry of grid services is a set of available grid services that is maintained in the registry. The registry allows a soft state registration mechanism for services to periodically update the overall services availability.

A dynamic data generating and indexing node is another valuable feature of the index service. The index service combines ServiceDataProviderExecution components with ServiceDataAggregator and ServiceGroup components to create a dynamic data generating and indexing node. This capability can be utilized to create hierarchical index services.

Index Service Information Model

The base information data model used by the index service is XML. The service data is an XML construct and both client and service know how to deal with this data model. The index service information model provides the exposure of the service data to the clients and aggregation of service data from heterogeneous grid services.

As we know, every grid service has service data associated with it and the purpose of index services is to provide an interface to access, aggregate, generate, and query this data. The OGSI-defined GridService interface exposed by all grid services provide a unique way to access and update the service data. These operations are "findServiceData" and "setServiceData."

The constructs that are of importance for index service are:

- Factory, the creator of a grid service.
- GSH, the unique instance identifier. These GSHs should be converted to GSR before use.
- GSR, the reference to a grid service with information that includes portTypes exposed by a service, and how the client can communicate with a service.

A service data query mechanism enables a service to be queried for the service data information. We have already explained in earlier chapters that this is one of the strong areas in the grid service specification and GT3. These queries can be of different types based on the service and the service container capabilities. The types of queries supported by GT3 include query by service data name and query by XPath.

Registries are used as a common repository for grid services. These registries allow soft state registration of grid services. The most important aspect of index service is the ability to get notified on service data changes anywhere in the grid system. The OGSI-defined notification mechanism provides this powerful feature. This provides a dynamic resource state and the availability of the updates.

Functional Aspects of Index Service

A primary function of index service is to provide an interface to a query on an aggregated view of service data collected from other services. The findServiceData operation of the GridService interface is utilized to exploit this query. The index service engine becomes registered as notification sink to other grid services. These notification-enabled grid services establish the subscriptions for notifications on topics of interest that are related to service data.

A notification is sent to the sink on state changes. This is illustrated in Figure 14.3. These asynchronously sent notification messages (i.e., XML messages) are used to monitor the status of the resource, and the current service state information. This notification process can be considered as a *push* mechanism.

The other facility provided by GT3 is the *provider* concept, where the service data gets pulled from the resource utilizing the service data providers. Globus GT3 has a plug-and-play provider mechanism that enables index services to dynamically *pull* the service data from other services.

We can find some integrated clients with GT3 index services, which are service data browsers and a command-line tool called "ogsi-find-service-data." These tools are used to get the service data from a service and display the data for the user. The input for the query can be simple, based on a service data name query, or may be a complex XPath expression.

Index Service Configuration Model

There can be any number of index services in a service container. The configuration of each of them is available in the server-congif.wsdd file.

Listing 14.7   The ServiceData aggregation.

```
<service name="base/index/IndexService" provider="Handler" style="wrapped">
   <parameter name="name" value="Index Service"/>
   <parameter name="schemaPath"
             value="schema/base/index/index_service.wsdl"/>
   <parameter name="className"
             value="org.globus.ogsa.base.index.IndexService"/>
   <parameter name="baseClassName"
             value="org.globus.ogsa.impl.base.index.IndexServiceImpl"/>
.....................................
   <parameter name="serviceConfig"
             value="index-service-config.xml"/>
</service>
```

The Index service deployment shown in Listing 14.7 is similar to other grid services with one notable exception: there is a configuration parameter indicating the index service configuration file. This index-service-config.xml file warrants some further discussion.

The functions of the index service configuration file are as follows:

- Specifies the service data provider to be enabled for each of the services referencing this configuration file.
- Specifies which of the enabled providers are to be executed at startup and/or when the configuration file is read. It contains the necessary parameters relevant to the provider's execution.
- Specifies notification and subscription of service data to other service instances, which allows for aggregation of service data from multiple services.

A sample configuration is described in Listing 14.8.

Listing 14.8 The service data aggregation.

```
<serviceConfiguration ...>
    <installedProviders>
    <providerEntry class="org.globus.ogsa.impl.base.providers.servicedata
                            .impl.SimpleSystemInformationProvider"/>

    <providerEntry class="org.globus.ogsa.impl.base.providers.servicedata
            .impl.HostScriptProvider" handler="com.test.myCallBackObject"/>
    </installedProviders>

    <executedProviders>
        <provider-exec:ServiceDataProviderExecution>

        <provider-exec:serviceDataProviderName>SystemInformation
        </provider-exec:serviceDataProviderName>

        <provider-exec:serviceDataProviderImpl>
            org.globus.ogsa.impl.base.providers.servicedata.impl
                            .SimpleSystemInformation
        </provider-exec:serviceDataProviderImpl>
        <provider-exec:serviceDataProviderArgs></provider-
                            exec:serviceDataProviderArgs>
            <provider-exec:serviceDataName
                xmlns:mds="http://glue.base.ogsa.globus.org/ce/1.1">
            mds:Host
        </provider-exec:serviceDataName>
            <provider-exec:refreshFrequency>
            60
        </provider-exec:refreshFrequency>
            <provider-exec:async>
            true
        </provider-exec:async>
        </provider-exec:ServiceDataProviderExecution>
    </executedProviders>

<aggregatedSubscriptions>
    <aggregator:AggregatorSubscription>
    <aggregator:serviceDataName xmlns:ce="http://glue.base.ogsa.globus
            .org/ce/1.1">
    ce:Cluster
    </aggregator:serviceDataName>
        <ogsi:source>
        http://127.0.0.1:8080/ogsa/services/base/gram/
                    MasterForkManagedJobFactoryService
        </ogsi:source>
    <aggregator:lifetime>
```

Listing 14.8   The service data aggregation. (Continued)

```
    1200
    </aggregator:lifetime>
    </aggregator:AggregatorSubscription>
 </aggregatedSubscriptions>
 </serviceConfiguration>
```

Listing 14.8 illustrates some of the important configuration information for an index service provider. There are three sections in this configuration file.

1. **Installed providers**. These are the available providers in the container. These may be GT3-provided or custom Java providers. These providers must implement either of the DOMDataProvider, SimpleDataProvider, or AsyncDataProvider interface. In Listing 14.8, we have two providers installed, SimpleSystemInformationProvider and HostScriptProvider. There is only one required parameter for each provider entry, a "class" attribute that informs the implementation class name of the provider. There can be an optional "handler" attribute indicating a user-provided custom callback object for post-processing of the data. This handler must implement the ServiceDataProviderDocumentCallback interface.

2. **Executed providers**. These providers are executed, producing one or more service data results. This configuration allows one to pass parameters to this execution behavior. The service data name parameter indicates the name of the new service data to create. If this parameter is not present, the service data name will be created from the tag name of the root element of the XML document produced by the execution. The "refresh" property indicates how often the provider should execute.

3. **Aggregated subscriptions**. These subscriptions specify the grid services to be indexed by the index service. Here, we are specifying the GSH of the grid service from which we are receiving notifications, and the service data name for which we are subscribing. These subscriptions are controlled by the lifetime attributes.

Monitoring and Discovery

The MDS in GT3 is merged with the core GT3 (i.e., service data and notification model), and the higher-level index service (i.e., the collective layers functionalities). One must be aware of this fundamental change. This way, there will not be a specific MDS component in GT3. However, at the same time GT3 provides all the facilities available with MDS (version 2) through the previously described core and index services.

Summary

The above index service architecture provides a data aggregation (push and pull mechanisms) from external services and data sources, service collection management, while providing an information model based on service data aggregation XML schema. These are valuable sources of information for applications built upon Globus GT3 high-level services. The sources can exploit these indexing behaviors of the data collected from various services/resources for purposes of creating meaningful models, such as resource utilization, availability, performance, and cost matrices.

RESOURCE INFORMATION PROVIDER SERVICE

The resource information provider service (RIPS) is a part of the GRAM. This service utilizes service data providers to execute system-level information-gathering scripts and tools. When used in conjunction with GRAM, it's purpose is to monitor *forked* processes, scheduled queues, and host system statistics.

Figure 14.4 shows the major components utilized by the RIPS operation. The interested parties can register for subscriptions, based on service data of interest. The illustration also shows how the GRAM master hosting environment is using data aggregator components to collect aggregated service data.

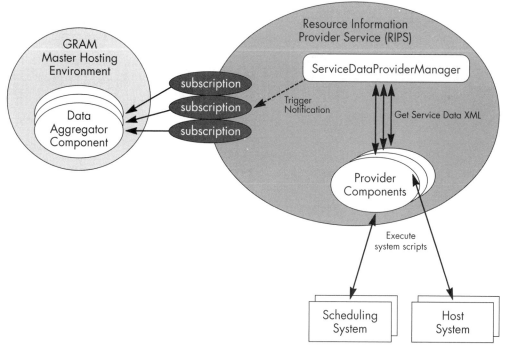

Figure 14.4
The resource information provider service operation.

Internal Operations of RIPS

Listing 14.9   The RIPS implementation prototype.

```
public class RIPSImpl extends PersistentGridServiceImpl implements
                                ServiceDataProviderDocumentCallback {
  // this is the callback method name
  public String getDefaultCallbackMethodName() {
    return "jobDataHandler";
  }
  public Class[] getCallbackParamSig(String methodName)    {
      Class[] paramSig = { Class.forName("org.w3c.dom.Document"),
                  Class.forName("java.lang.Object"),
                  Class.forName("java.lang.Integer")};
      return paramSig;
  }
  public void postPersistentCreate(GridContext context) throws
      GridServiceException{
        // do initialization
  }

  public ServiceDataProviderEnumType[] enumProviders(boolean rescanConfig)
    throws RemoteException  {
      // these calls are delegated to the ServiceDataProviderManager,
        which we have seen earlier
  }
  public void executeProvider(ServiceDataProviderExecutionType newServiceData)
    throws RemoteException  {
      // these calls are delegated to the ServiceDataProviderManager
  }
  public void subscribe(ExtensibilityType subscriptionExpression,
            LocatorType sink,
            ExtendedDateTimeType expirationTime,
            LocatorTypeHolder subscriptionInstanceLocator,
            TerminationTimeTypeHolder currentTerminationTime) {
  /*Any subscribers can subscribe to the dynamic service data generated
    by this service through this method. Initially, there may not be any
    service data available and hence dummy service data will be created
    for the service data name specified by subscribe. This dummy SD will
    be deleted if no value is coming from the provider for a specific
    period of time
  */
  }
  public boolean jobDataHandler(org.w3c.dom.Document doc,
                  Object context,
                  Integer providerState{
```

Listing 14.9 The RIPS implementation prototype. (Continued)

```
/*This is the callback function that is doing the real job of splitting
   the XML document into service data elements and updating the service
   data set of this service */
}
```

Listing 14.9 describes the main operations provided by the RIPS component. Some of the points of interest related to the RIPS topic are as follows:

- The providers are polled at specified intervals. There are two ways we can control the poll time's values:
  1. These values can be configured through the external configuration file, and then this value is applicable to all instances of the provider.
  2. Another possibility is to configure this poll time value by the client on the call to "executeProvider." This new timer value will be applicable to the specific provider instance.
- RIPS perform special processing utilizing its custom "jobDataHandler" function by separating out the specific child "Job" elements from the logical result document. This creates individual SDEs by assigning the appropriate TTL metadata to the new entries, and updating the TTL data on the existing SDEs.
- RIPS execute a separate thread called a *sweeper*, which periodically traverses the service's internal SDE list and invalidates any entries that have not received updates to the specified timestamp metadata.

Summary

In general, RIPS provides service data aggregation mechanisms and management of data utilizing the service provider components included with the GT3. Any interested service can register for notification on the service data of choice. This is a flexible architecture when integrated with other high-level services such as resource managers.

RESOURCE MANAGEMENT SERVICES

Grid resource management involves the coordination of a number of components, including resource registries, factories, discovery, monitoring, allocation, and data access. The Globus toolkit includes a set of components to help users have a standard set of interfaces for the coordination of the above activities.

The main functionalities of these components (called GRAM) are job submission and resource management. Figure 14.5 shows the architectural components of the GRAM. Even though this architecture appears complex, in practice it is an aggregation and collective functionality of a set of well-defined components. Another advantage of this architecture is that the client is free from these architecture complexities.

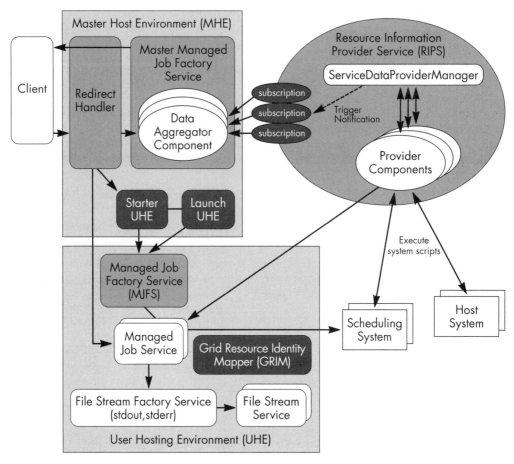

Figure 14.5
The architecture of GRAM.

THE MAJOR COMPONENTS OF THE GRAM ARCHITECTURE

Master Host Environment and User Host Environment

This concept enables the separation of functionalities and provides an improved abstraction on the functions supported by each environment. The master host is responsible for providing information on aggregated resource state/status, and to manage its user hosts start and launch services. This is the direct point of contact for the client. The user host environment (UHE) provides specific abstraction capabilities and securities to execute a job. All the jobs are executed in the UHE.

Master Managed Job Factory Service

This factory is always available and responsible for receiving the client request on aggregated resource queries and subscriptions. This factory manages the aggregated service data through aggregation providers for resource status, and notifications from resources.

Virtual Host Redirect Handler

This is the core component responsible for redirecting all of the calls to the UHE. These calls include creation of the job and invoking job operations on the created job service.

Starter UHE/Launch UHE

On a client request to execute a job, the virtual hosting engine directs the calls to the starter. This Java class is responsible for security mapping, user validation, and for ensuring that the job is executing so that the virtual host can redirect the calls to the executing job service. If the user host is not up and running, then it uses the help of the Launch UHE Java class to start that host under the user's credentials.

Managed Job Factory Service/Managed Job Service

The MJF service exposes a CreateService method, which accepts an RSL-specified job. The MJF then creates a managed job instance for the user. It acts as a local scheduler, monitoring its status and sending notifications. In addition to this, the MJS will start two file streaming factory services; one for the job's stdout, and the other for the job's stderr.

File Stream Factory Service/File Stream Service

These are helpful services to manage the data needed for the job execution. The factory service creates two file stream services: stdout and stderr. Each of these services has two service data results: the URL for the stream destination, and a flag to indicate the activity.

Grid Resource Identity Mapper (GRIM)

The GRIM service is executing in the UHE to create a user host certificate. The user host certificate is utilized for mutual authentication between the MJS service and the client.

Resource Information Provider Service (RIPS)

A specialized notification service providing data about a scheduling system, file system, host, etc.

Two Aspects to the GRAM Architecture

1. *Job submission.* A user starts the job scheduling with the creation of a managed job service. This process involves multiple steps.

   - The client knows about the master host environment and the master managed factory service. It sends a request to create a job to the master factory service in the MHE.
   - The Virtual Hosting Redirect handler manages this request with the help of the starter/launch Java classes; it then creates and/or connects to the user hosting system. One

must be aware that these processes are created under user credentials. Once the UHS is available, the Redirect handler transfers the Create Job request to the managed job factory service in UHS.

  ° The Managed Job Factory creates a managed job service instance for the user with the necessary job description parameter encoded in the Resource Specification Language. Also, it creates the necessary file streaming classes to handle the data for the job.

  ° From this stage forward, the client is able to talk to the managed job created in the user hosting environment. All the calls are then redirected to the correct job instance.

2. *Resource management.* A client knows about the master host environment and the master managed factory service. This process involves multiple steps.

  ° The master factory provides an aggregated view of the state of the job and other resource information. The master factory gathers this information using the RIP service.

  ° The client can now find and register for notification on the aggregated service state from the master factory.

  ° The client can now locate the state information from the job service instance.

Resource Specification Language

The power of GRAM is associated with its capabilities to describe a job. The Resource Specification Language (RSL) is an XML standard for describing a job. The RSL includes XML standard elements for specifying executables, directory, arguments, and data files.

The RSL is created by the client, and passed to the managed job service (MJS) where it is then converted to the local scheduler-specific language. The current standard language is RSL2. Listing 14.10 describes this RSL example.

Listing 14.10   An RSL example.

```
<rsl:rsl
<!---insert GRAM RSL Namespace --->
  <gram:job>
      <gram:executable>
          <rsl:pathElement path="/bin/ls"/>
      </gram:executable>
      <gram:directory>
          <rsl:pathElement path="/user/jjp"/>
      </gram:directory>
      <gram:arguments>
          <gram:argument>-l</gram:argument>
          <gram:argument>-a</gram:argument>
      </gram:arguments>
  </gram:job>
</rsl:rsl>
```

Summary

GRAM provides a set of standard interfaces and components to collectively manage a job task, and to provide resource information including job status and resource configuration. This information can then be utilized for resource allocation of a specific Job.

We can build high-level meta-job schedulers, and resource brokers/managers on the top of this layer, while using the resource information provided by this layer. The other aspect of using this standardized middle layer is that we can also build lower-layer local jobs and resource management functions, without affecting the high-level schedulers and monitors. This layer provides an abstraction from high-level manageability to lower-layer manageability functionalities. One notable aspect of the GRAM is the absence of accounting and billing features.

DATA MANAGEMENT SERVICES

The data management services provide standard means for helping to manage the Grid Computing environment.

Grid File Transfer Protocol (GridFTP)

GridFTP is a standard extension to the normal FTP (File Transfer Protocol) that works with the Grid Computing data requirements. This is a high-performance, secure, reliable, data transfer protocol that is optimized for high bandwidth across wide area networks. This is a standard that provides GSI security, parallel transfer capabilities, and channel reusability.

Reliable File Transfer (RFT)

The reliable file transfer service (RFT) is an OGSA-based service that provides interfaces for controlling and monitoring third-party file transfers using the GridFTP servers. The client controlling the transfer is hosted inside of a grid service so that it can then be managed using the soft state model, and queried using the service data interfaces available to all grid services.

Replica Location Service (RLS)

The replica location service (RLS) maintains and provides access to mapping information from logical names regarding data items to target names. These target names may represent physical locations of data items, or an entry in the RLS may map to another level of logical naming for the data item.

Summary

We summarize the data management services discussion by simply addressing their usability, which enables:

- Computational grids to manage a job by allowing the data required for the processing of the job to be transferred in a secure, reliable manner.
- Data grids to utilize these management features providing scalable and secure access and integration facilities for data storage.

Conclusion

These introductions on the high-level services help us to better understand the basic functionalities provided by them in the context of the Globus GT3 framework. The main utility value of GT3 lies with these high-level services; it provides a framework for the creation of a computational grid.

The basic requirements for computational grids address scalable job management and resource monitoring aspects. GT3 provides these capabilities through GRAM, index services, service data constructs, and a common language definition for job descriptions. We can now better understand that there are a number of applications and services required in order to start using GRAM, and the resource management features of GT3.

Major accomplishments in this area include Condor-G and Nimrod-G. Practitioners in the grid community are expecting these meta-schedulers and resource managers to continue evolving toward utilization of the GT3-provided index services, GRAM, and the exposed XML-based information model. A common agreement on RSL, or a similar common language for job description, will further strengthen these high-level applications.

Note

1. The term "*sink*" is a term defined in the OGSI, which is defined as a client-side class that is listening for notification messages by implementing the OGSI NotificationSink portType and thereby exposing deliverNotification operation.

OGSI.NET
Middleware
Solutions

We have discussed throughout this book many of the architectural benefits provided by OGSA to Web services and grid services communities. Likewise, we have discussed throughout this book the benefits the OGSI specifications provide as a common set of XML messages and definitions using WSDL for interoperable grid service implementations. In the previous chapters, we also learned about the major infrastructure developments for hosting an OGSI-based grid services implementation. Those developments were centered on Java and J2SE/J2EE.

In this chapter, we will see other reference implementations of OGSI in Microsoft .NET, another prominent hosting platform. The main value additions of these implementations are to validate the interoperability between services hosted by different environments, and to influence the OGSI communities on interoperable message definitions and standardizations. This will provide a means for a wide range of acceptability advancements for the OGSI standard.

There are a number of reference implementations of OGSI in .NET, which are available today. The most prominent reference implementations are: OGSI.NET by the University of Virginia[1] and MS.NETGrid by National eScience Center (NeSC).[2]

Both of the above implementations are available for distribution. We will explore the architecture, programming model, and a sample implementation on these platforms.

In this final chapter of the book, we will concentrate on the OGSI.NET toolkit framework implementation.

OGSI.NET FRAMEWORK IMPLEMENTATION

The OGSI, as we have already noted, provides a rich and robust infrastructure for the implementation of Grid Computing environments. This section addresses the .NET solutions, in conjunction with the OGSI.

Architecture Overview

The concept of the .NET framework is centered on the service instance requirements for the management between the client invocations, and using the Internet Information Server (IIS) to dispatch the client request to the actual instance. Although .NET provides a rich set of Web services capabilities, the evidence of these two basic requirements for a grid service being apparent is somewhat less than remarkable. To satisfy these requirements, the OGSI.NET team must construct the architecture to maintain the service instances between the client invocations, and the ability to then dispatch the requests to the correct service instances.

The architecture suggests the introduction of a concept of grid service wrappers and a dispatcher. These are .NET AppDomains, self-contained entities that can execute objects in its own memory space. This concept provides a number of advantages including scope the code execution, fault isolation, and security isolation. The grid service wrappers (GSW) are OGSI grid service instances that are created in its own AppDomain. The dispatcher is the pivot AppDomain that contains references to the grid service wrapper objects in another AppDomain and executes methods upon it.

This concept of creating grid services using wrappers with AppDomain isolation provides security, memory, and code isolation. Any problem (fault or exceptions) with the specific service may not affect other services in the same container. Yet another important functionality of these wrappers is that they are self-contained with the necessary serializer, deserializers, and portType implementations required for the service operation dispatch.

Another important architectural decision is the extension of the request dispatching functionalities of the IIS. A client request is filtered by the OGSI.NET ISAPI (Internet Server API) filter. This filter intercepts the client requests, then rewrites the request and dispatches this request to the HttpHandler provided by the OGSI.NET framework. This Http handler routes the messages to the OGSI.NET container process. This process, in turn, handles this raw message in one of its threads. The Dispatcher AppDomain takes over the raw request message in the thread and this dispatcher routes the messages to the GridServiceWrapper class for further processing. This dispatching is done based on the instance URL.

The above request processing is illustrated in Figure 15.1.

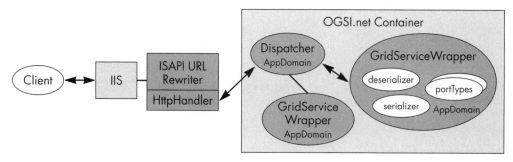

Figure 15.1
The OGSI.NET architecture and request flow.

Let us now spend some time analyzing the internal functionalities of the GridServiceWrapper. This wrapper is running in its own AppDomain. It maintains a list of portTypes implemented by the service and contains the necessary information to serialize and deserialize the SOAP messages coming from the client.

The framework also provides capabilities to plug in message handlers for SOAP message header processing. The standard SOAP-based headers (for example, WS-Security) are processed using the Web service Enhancement (WSE) handlers.[3] Once the message is deserialized and the operation is identified from the raw SOAP message, a runtime reflection is executed on the service to invoke the operation. The responses from the method invocations are serialized and sent back to the client.

The discussion topics below on the architectural components helps us to better address an improved programming model.

Dispatcher

The main function of the Dispatcher AppDomain is to route the request from the client to the appropriate service instance and return the results to the client without any processing. It keeps a list of URIs to the service instance for proper instance dispatching. This architecture helps to isolate the security and other runtime problems to an isolation level of service instance AppDomain.

Grid Service Wrapper

This is a wrapper executing in its own AppDomain and providing functionalities, such as:

- Pluggable, service-specific message handlers to process messages prior to dispatching to the service instance
- Mechanism to specify portTypes similar to OperationProviders in GT3
- Pluggable implementations for system-defined portTypes
- Built-in support of extended standard-based SOAP headers using WSE

The wrapper is initialized with the necessary assemblies needed for the service as specified by the service class. This includes portType implementations, serializers, deserializers, and message handlers.

One important thing to notice is that the complete processing of the message is accomplished on the thread provided by the container. So if the service needs to create more threads it must create the .NET-provided *soft threads* in the AppDomain using the .NET-provided System.Threading.Thread class.

Factory

Factories are service instances that can create other service instances and wrappers in different AppDomains. They implement OGSI Factory portType with createService operation. These service instance wrappers are remote referable objects of the type *MarshalByRefObject* and stored in the Dispatcher AppDomain. The Dispatcher stores these objects in a table with service instance handle (GSH) as the key.

Message Handlers

OGSI.NET provides two message handlers, one for SOAP messages and the other for .NET "remoting" message formats. We will see how we can configure these handles later in the configuration section. These message handlers will deserialize the request message and identify the operation to invoke and create the needed parameters from SOAP body. On the completion of the call, the client serializes the message to byte stream and returns the binary stream back to client. The current runtime uses the Microsoft WSE pipeline mechanism to process the standard defined SOAP headers such as WS-Security and WS-Addressing. For application specific headers we must provide custom handlers.

Security

The message-level security is handled using WS-Security and the WSE extensions for WS-Security. One thing to notice is that this is handled in the service instance wrapper domain. The concept of wrapping service instance in an AppDomain provides security, memory protection, and other .NET protections including code access, assembly access, and so forth.

Persistence

The framework provides a soft state service destruction pattern as defined by OSGI specification. This enables a service client to define a lifecycle time for a service instance. There is a garbage collector thread running with the dispatcher AppDomain, which is responsible for this service destruction on timeouts.

Programming Model

Now let us discuss the programming model constructs provided with this framework. One noticeable feature of this framework is its alignment with the .NET programming model for Web services. The use of "attributes" in service class is one such interesting aspect of the programming model.

Attribute-Based Programming

One of the most attractive and powerful features in .NET is the attribute-based programming. This feature is used to annotate the classes, methods, and code blocks with metadata. This language feature is extensively used in .NET to support Web services. OGSI.NET uses this facility to define some commonly defined attributes for grid services to help the service developer form the inner details of the implementations.

OGSIPortTypeAttribute

This tells the GSW that the service implements a particular portType.

NotificationSourcePortType

This service implements a NotificationSourcePortType functionality as defined by the OGSI OGSIOperationOverrideAttribute. This enables a service author to override some of the port-Type methods using OGSIPortTypeAttribute, OGSISoapHeaderAttribute, and OGSIRemoting-HeaderAttribute. These attributes provide additional header information to these operations.

This is a replacement for the .NET SoapHeaderAttribute, which provides no type information, as shown below:

```
[OGSISoapHeader("invocationID", "http://ogsa.globus.org/", typeof(InvocationID))]
```

versus

```
[SoapHeader("invocationID")]
```

Listing 15.1 illustrates the use of attributes in a service class.

Listing 15.1   A sample attribute-based programming for OGSI.

```
[OGSIPortType(typeof(GridServicePortType))]
[OGSIPortType(typeof(NotificationSourcePortType))]
public class AcmeService : GridServiceSkeleton{
}
```

Listing 15.1 specifies that Acme Service is implementing the GridServicePortType and Notifica-tionSourcePortType.

Configuration

Let us now move on to the configuration of a service. We can best explain the configuration process through Listing 15.2.

Listing 15.2   The grid service configuration.

```
<service name="ph/acme/AcmeSearchFactoryService">
<parameter name="schemaPath" value="schema/core/factory
               factory_service.wsdl"/>

<parameter name="class" value="ph.acme.Factory.AcmeSearchFactoryService,
                          ph_acme.dll"/>

<parameter name="messageHandlers"
            value="UVa.Grid.SoapMessageHandlerLib.SoapMessageHandler,
```

Listing 15.2 The grid service configuration. (Continued)

```
                        SoapMessageHandlerLib.dll;
                        UVa.Grid.SoapMessageHandlerLib.RemotingMessageHandler,
                        SoapMessageHandlerLib.dll"/>


<parameter name="createSchemaPath" value="schema/gridbook/base/
                        acme_search_service.wsdl"/>
<parameter name="createClass" value="ph.acme.basic.impl.AcmeSearchService,
                        ph_acme.dll"/>


<parameter
    name="createMessageHandlers"
        value="UVa.Grid.SoapMessageHandlerLib.SoapMessageHandler,
                SoapMessageHandlerLib.dll;
                UVa.Grid.SoapMessageHandlerLib.RemotingMessageHandler,
                SoapMessageHandlerLib.dll"/>
</service>
```

Upon careful examination of the above grid service configuration, we could infer that:

- Every service factory has a unique name and uses the OGSI-defined factory _service.wsdl.
- The real implementation factory class is defined using the "class" parameter, which accepts the class name and the assembly name.
- A list of handlers for the service factory is specified in the "messageHandlers" property.
- The service must provide its wsdl and class name using createSchemaPath and createClass parameters, respectively.
- A list of handlers for the service instance is specified in the "createMessageHandlers" property.

SUMMARY

This reference implementation successfully illustrates the OGSI implementation in .NET platforms. There are a number of issues that still need to be addressed at this time, including security, scalability, and interoperability between GT3 and OGSI.NET. Most of these are platform dependent and will become mature with .NET. Adopting WSE for most of the standard SOAP header processing will alleviate the system architecture from a number of these complexities.

We are assuming that adapting a document/literal approach can solve most of the interoperability issues with regard to the message exchange topic. This reference implementation will indeed be a beneficial addition for Grid Computing applications using .NET as their core platform.

NOTES

1. For more information, go to *www.cs.virginia.edu/~gsw2c/ogsi.net.html*

2. For more information, go to *www.epcc.ed.ac.uk/~ogsanet/*

3. For more information, go to *http://msdn.microsoft.com/webservices/*

Glossary

Apache AXIS

An implementation of the Simple Object Access Protocol (SOAP) specification. It defines a core technology framework to build SOAP message enveloping and transport of messages.

Autonomic Computing

A computing environment with the ability to manage itself and dynamically adapt to change in accordance with business policies and objectives. Self-managing environments can perform such activities based on situations they observe or sense in the IT environment rather than requiring IT professionals to initiate the task. These environments are self-configuring, self-healing, self-optimizing, and self-protecting.

Business On Demand

An enterprise whose business processes—integrated end-to-end across the company and with key partners, suppliers, and customers—can respond with flexibility and speed to any customer demand, market opportunity, or external threat.

Business Web

Collections of businesses that dynamically come together on the Internet in unique ways to sell new products and services, build new channels, and create new business models.

Common Information Model (CIM)

Describes management information and offers a framework for managing the system elements across distributed systems.

Common Management Model (CMM)

Defines a set of common management functions for managing the resource in a grid. CMM is an abstract representation of real IT resources such as disk, file systems, operating systems, network ports, and IP addresses. CMM defines a set of common management interfaces by which these manageable resources are exposed to external management applications for the purpose of managing these resources.

Computational Grid

An infrastructure framework that provides dependable, consistent, pervasive, and inexpensive access to high-end computational capabilities including compute power, hardware, and software.

Data Grid

Deals with all aspects of grid data including data location, transfer, access, management, and security.

Distributed Computing

A method of computing in which very large problems are divided into small tasks that are distributed across a computer network for simultaneous processing. Individual results are then brought together to form the total solution.

e-Business

(1) An organization that connects its core business systems to key constituencies using intranets, extranets, and the Web; (2) The process of building and enhancing business relationships through the thoughtful use of network-based technologies; (3) The leveraging of Internet technologies to transact and interact with customers, suppliers, partners, and employees in order to achieve and sustain competitive advantage.

e-Business Infrastructure

The products and services one needs to build or run e-business applications. It is made up of the hardware, software, connectivity, and services needed to plan, build, and maintain a highly scalable, secure, adaptable, reliable, available, and manageable environment to support multiple applications to meet the e-business needs of organizations with both traditional and Web-based models. "Applications" or "solutions" themselves are specifically excluded from the e-business infrastructure definition since they utilize the infrastructure but are not part of it. Five elements are included in an e-business infrastructure: Web application servers, directory and security servers, edge servers, data and transaction servers, and storage systems.

Evolution of the Internet

Initially, the Internet provided a means for networking individuals and enabling electronic communication. Then the Internet became a source for sharing information on a global scale as the World Wide Web evolved. In the next decade, IBM views the Internet as the computing platform enabling dynamic e-business.

Generic Security Service Application Program Interface (GSS API)

Defined in IETF RFC-1508. GSS-API provides a way for applications to protect data that is sent to peer applications. This might be from a client on one machine to a server on another. The current Globus Grid toolkit uses GSS API for security programming.

Global XML Architecture

Builds on current XML Web services baseline specifications of SOAP, WSDL, and UDDI. This architecture is a design-based principle of creating modular, integrateable, general-purpose, and open standard architecture solutions for Web services.

Grid Computing

A kind of distributed computing over a network (public or private) based on the principle of virtualization of computing and data resources such as processing, network bandwidth, and storage capacity to provide seamless access to vast IT capabilities. At its core, grid computing is based on an open set of standards (e.g., OGSA) and protocols that enable communication across heterogeneous, geographically dispersed environments.

Grid Job Scheduler

Responsible for the management of jobs such as allocating resources needed for a specific job, partitioning jobs to schedule parallel execution, data management, and service-level management.

Grid Resource Allocation Manager (GRAM)

A Globus-provided resource manager. GRAM provides a set of standard interfaces and components to collectively manage a job task and to provide resource information including job status and resource configuration. This information can be used for resource allocation for a specific job.

Grid Resource Brokers

Provides matchmaking services between service requester and service provider. This matchmaking enables the selection of best available resources from the service provider for the execution of a specific task.

Grid Security Infrastructure (GSI)

Based on public key encryption, X.509 certificates, and the Secure Sockets Layer (SSL) communication protocol. Extensions to these standards have been added for single sign-on and delegation. The Globus toolkit uses GSI for enabling secure authentication and communication for participants in the grid.

GWSDL

Description language for grid services modeled after WSDL, trying to overcome some of WSDL 1.1's drawbacks on inheritance and open content extensibilities.

Index Service

A Globus-provided high-level service responsible for managing static and dynamic state data for grids.

Model-Driven Architecture

A platform-independent modeling architecture for building interoperable solutions buildup on standards such as Universal Modeling Language (UML) and Meta-Object Facility (MOF). This is the core architecture for future computing and driven by the Open Management Group.

.NET Framework

A framework and tool set to develop Common Language Runtime (CLR) solutions and XML Web services.

On Demand Operating Environment

The new computing architecture initiative from IBM designed to help companies realize the benefits of Business On Demand. The On Demand operating environment exhibits the four essential characteristics: it is integrated, open, virtualized, and autonomic.

On Demand Operating Infrastructure

Defines a set of core components and solutions to meet the On Demand operation environment characteristics.

Ontology

Used to describe collections of information like concepts and relationships that can exist between resources and objects. This taxonomy defines classes of objects and relations among them.

Open Grid Service Architecture (OGSA)

Open standards architecture for next-generation grid services to enable the creation, maintenance, and integration of grid services maintained by virtual organizations.

Open Grid Service Infrastructure (OGSI)

A core component of the OGSA, which provides a uniform way to describe grid services and defines a common pattern of behavior for all grid services. In short, this architecture defines grid service behaviors, service description mechanisms, and protocol binding information by using Web services as the technology enabler.

Peer-to-Peer Computing

The sharing of computer resources and services by direct exchange between systems. These resources and services include the exchange of information, processing cycles, cache storage, and disk storage for files. Peer-to-peer computing takes advantage of existing desktop computing power and networking connectivity, allowing economical clients to leverage their collective power to benefit the entire enterprise.

Resource Description Framework Language (RDF)

A standard for the notation of structured information, recommended by the W3 Consortium for meta-data interoperability across different resource description communities.

Resource Specification Language (RSL)

A Globus Grid Toolkit–defined XML standard for describing a job.

Semantic Web

The next-generation Web in which information is given well-defined meaning and computers and people are better enabled to work in cooperation. This enables the data on the Web to be defined and linked together for computing agents for automatic decision making.

Service-Level Agreements (SLA)

An agreement between a service provider and service requester to provide certain quality of service guarantees.

Service-Oriented Architecture (SOA)

The architecture to define loosely coupled and interoperable services/applications and to define a process for integrating these interoperable components. In SOA, the software system is decomposed into a collection of network-connected components/services and applications are composed dynamically from the deployed and available components in the network.

Simple Object Access Protocol (SOAP)

Provides the definition of the XML-based information, which can be used for exchanging structured and typed information between peers in a decentralized, distributed environment. This includes message packaging and message exchanges scenarios.

Software Architecture

An abstraction of the runtime elements of a software system during some phase of its operation. A system may be composed of many levels of abstraction and many phases of operation, each with its own software architecture. [Fielding]

Universal Description, Discovery, and Integration of Web Services (UDDI)

The building block that will enable business to quickly, easily, and dynamically find businesses and transact with each other. This is based on open standard UDDI specifications that provide seamless interoperability and integration capabilities. There are many directory services, both Internet/intranet, based on UDDI, which can be treated as global registries for Web services.

Universal Modeling Language

Modeling is the process of designing software applications. UML provides a standard and industry-driven methodology for software modeling. This modeling language is defined by the Open Management Group and is not limited to software and can also form the basis for designing non-software systems.

Utility Computing

The network delivery of information technology and business process services by utility computing providers.

Virtual Organizations

Coordinated resource sharing and problem solving in dynamic, multi-institutional organizations. Sharing is with direct access to computers, software, data, and other resources by a range of collaborative problem-solving and resource-brokering strategies. The sharing is controlled with resource providers and consumers defining what is shared, who is allowed to share, and the conditions under which sharing occurs. The set of individuals and/or institutions defined by the sharing rules form the virtual organization.

Web Services

A software system identified by a URI, whose public interfaces and bindings are defined and described using XML. Its definition can be discovered by other software systems. These systems may then interact with the Web service in a manner prescribed by its definition, using XML-based messages conveyed by Internet protocols.

Web Services Architecture (WSA)

Provides a common definition for Web services. This is a standard initiative from W3C. WSA is trying to define and relate the necessary technologies (XML, SOAP, and WSDL) to construct interoperable Web services. It will define how to construct interoperable messages, message exchange patterns, enveloping mechanisms, and a definition mechanism for interoperable services. In addition, WSA will define the manageability, security, and correlation aspects of Web services.

Web Service Description Language (WSDL)

An XML language for describing Web services. This language provides a model and XML format. WSDL provides facilities for service developers to separate abstract definitions of the service (interface, message, and schema definitions) from concrete definitions (service, port, and binding definitions).

Websphere Application Server (WAS)

A J2EE/J2SE-built application server framework from IBM. It provides reliable, high-volume transactions for customers. It forms the basis for the IBM On Demand infrastructure framework with built-in support for Web services and OGSA-based grid services.

References

De Roure, D., Baker, M. A., Jennings, N. R., & Shadbolt, N. R., *The Evolution of Grid.* Available at *http://semanticgrid.org/documents/evolution/evolution.pdf*

Fellenstein, C. *Business On Demand: Technology and Strategy Perspectives.* 2003.

Fielding, Roy Thomas, Architectural Styles and the Design of Network-based Software Architectures. Available at *www.ics.uci.edu/-fielding/pubs/dissertation/rop.htm.*

Foster, I. *What is the Grid? A Three Point Checklist.* Available at *http://www-fp.mcs.anl.gov/~foster/Articles/WhatIsTheGrid.pdf*

Foster, I., & Iamnitichi, A. *On Death, Taxes, and the Convergence of Peer-to-Peer and Grid Computing.* Available at *http://people.cs.chicago.edu/~anda/papers/foster_grid_vs_p2p.pdf*

Foster, I., & Kesselman, C. *Computational Grids.* Morgan Kaufmann, 1998.

Foster, I., Kesselman, C., Nick, J. M., & Tuecke, S. *The Physiology of the Grid—An Open Grid Service Architecture for Distributed Systems Integration.* Available at *www.globus.org/research/papers/ogsa.pdf*

Foster, I., Kesselman, C., & Tuecke, S. *Anatomy of a Grid.* Available at *www.globus.org/research/papers/anatomy.pdf*

Kendall, S. C., Waldo, J., Wollrath, A., & Wyant, G. *Note on Distributed Computing.* Available at *http://research.sun.com/techrep/1994/smli_tr-94-29.pdf*

Index